THE WOLVES
OF ISLAM

Also by Paul J. Murphy, Ph.D.

Brezhnev: Soviet Politician
The Soviet Air Forces
Naval Power in Soviet Policy

THE WOLVES OF ISLAM

RUSSIA AND THE FACES OF CHECHEN TERROR

PAUL J. MURPHY, Ph.D.

POTOMAC BOOKS, INC.
WASHINGTON, D.C.

First paperback edition published 2006
Copyright © 2004 by Paul J. Murphy

Library of Congress Cataloging-in-Publication Data

Murphy, Paul J.
  The wolves of Islam : Russia and the faces of Chechen terror / Paul J. Murphy.
  p.cm.
  Includes index.
  ISBN 1-57488-830-7 (alk. paper)
  1. Terrorism—Russia (Federation)—Chechnëíìa.   2. Basayev, Shamil, 1965-
3. Chechnëíìa (Russia)—History—Civil War, 1994—Atrocities.   4. Chechnëíìa
(Russia)—History—Autonomy and independence movements.   5. National
liberation movements—Russia (Federation)—Chechnëíìa.   I. Title.
  HV6433.R9M87   2004
  947.086—dc22   2004019949

ISBN 1-57488-831-5 (paperback)
Printed in Canada.

Potomac Books, Inc.
22841 Quicksilver Drive
Dulles, Virginia 20166

First Edition

10 9 8 7 6 5 4 3 2 1

To "Yulia," thrice a survivor.
She is safer now.

Contents

Sources, Methods, and Acknowledgments xi

Prologue 1

I Shamil Basayev: Russia's Osama bin Laden 7

   The Beginning 7

   Two Grenades for Yeltsin 9

   In the Footsteps of Imam Shamil 11

   Establishing Terrorist Credentials 12

   Drinking Georgian Blood 14

   Jihad Training in Afghanistan 16

   Doing Dudayev's Dirty Work and the First Chechen War 17

   The First Suicide Mission to Moscow 20

   Enter Arab Fighters and a Dirty Bomb 24

   The "Grozny Offensive" 27

   A Terrorist Turns Reluctant Politician 28

II "The Black Arab" and the Wahhabi Factor 32

   Embodying the Islamic Warrior Persona 32

   Khattab's Real Combat Movies 33

   Slaying Armed Russian Infidels—A Religious Calling 35

   Suspect in the Red Cross Murders 38

   Khattab's Terrorist Schools 39

   The Closed City and Wahhabi Subversion 40

   The Little Wahhabi Republic 44

III Two Presidents and Two Armies 47

   Raduyev, "The Lone Wolf" Terrorist 47

   Wolves Have Come to You! 49

Rising from the Dead   53
The Thorn in Maskhadov's Side   56
Shootout at Teatralnaya Square   59
The Jamaat Military Alliance and the
Berezovsky Hostage Deals   62
What Raduyev's Islamic Manifesto Had to Say   65

IV The Godfather of Kidnapping and the
    Ideologist of Apocalypse   67
People for Sale   67
Mutiny in Gudermes   73
The Akhmadov Brothers   75
Beheadings and Betrayal   77
The Many Faces of Movladi Udugov   79
Udugov's Respectable Day Job   82
The Great Chechnya Ideologist   85
Another Maskhadov Betrayal   87

V   Holy Wars in Dagestan and Bombs in Moscow   90
The "Brothers" Basayev   90
The Holy Mission   91
Ganging Up on Maskhadov   94
Establishing the New Imamate   97
Khattab's Bombs in Moscow   103

VI The Wars that Shamil Started   108
A War to Establish Islamic Rule Everywhere   108
Wolves Are Trapped   110
Planning How to Fight the Jihad   112
Basayev's "Bee Sting" Guerrilla Tactics   115
Targeting Civilians in the Terror War   117
Basayev's Second Suicide Battalion   122
Did Basayev Really Sink the Kursk?   125
Assassination Terror   126
Udugov's Information Wars   128
The Maskhadov-Udugov Internet Wars   131

VII	The Chechen Money Tree	134
	The Chechen Mafia Branches	135
	Oil Theft, Narcotics, and Counterfeiting	135
	Embezzlement and the Sale of Nuclear Materials	137
	The Captives-for-Sale and Berezovsky Branches	139
	Pakistan and the "Noble Cause of the Chechen Muslims"	140
	Saudi and Jordanian Branches	141
	Chechnya's Turkish Commissars	144
	Azeri Traditional Routes	147
	The Shevardnadze Trail	148
	International Islamic Branches and Other Assistance	149
	Internet, Personal Appeals, and Video Sales	152
	The Osama and Afghan Branches	153

VIII	Hunting Down Terrorist Wolves	156
	Sinking the "Titanic"	156
	The Trial and Sentencing of Raduyev	159
	Dancing with Wolves	161
	Khattab's Lethal Letter	163
	Death of the Messenger and Terror Retribution	166
	Is Basayev Dead or Alive?	168

IX	Nord Ost	169
	A Leaderless Jihad	169
	The Summer of Radicalization	172
	Military Offensives and Planning Terror	175
	The Dubrovka Siege	179
	Terrorists Killed at Dubrovka: The Official List (With Items Found on Body)	192

X	The Third War	197
	A New Terror War	197
	Recognizing Terror as the Greatest Threat to National Security	202
	Who Are the Real Masters of Chechnya?	204
	What's Ahead—Are Wolves Thinking Globally Too?	211

Epilogue   **221**

Basayev's Terror "Whirlwind"—
5 July 2003–5 June 2004   221

"Black Widows" Hunt at a Rock Concert—5 July 2003   221

Death Stalks Moscow's Main Street—9–10 July 2003   224

Bombs, Bombs, and More Bombs—17–24 July 2003   229

Suicide Inferno at Mozdok's Military Hospital—
1 August 2003   229

Terror Prevented and Named—8 August 2003   230

Bus Stop and Train Terror in Southern Russia—
25 August, 3 September, and 1–5 December 2003   230

A Joint Suicide Operation in Magas—
15 September 2003   231

A Black Widow Hunts Near the Kremlin—
9 December 2003   232

Beheading, Hostage Taking, and Death of
the Angel—15–31 December 2003   233

Tunnel Terror in Moscow—6 February 2004   234

"A Small but Important Victory":
The Assassination of President Kadyrov—9 May 2004   236

24 August 2004 Postscript   241

Appendix: Chronology of Terror, 1991–June 2004   **242**

Index   **269**

About the Author   **281**

SOURCES, METHODS, AND ACKNOWLEDGMENTS

I have relied on both public and personal information for this book. There is a wealth of public information, Russian and Chechen, in the Russian language realm. Movladi Udugov, the Wolves' propagandist, and his kavkaz.org and KavkazCenter Web sites are prolific with information. Russian government and news agency sites like infocentre.ru, mid.ru, chechnya.genstab.ru, gazeta.ru and many others publish vast amounts of information too. Just look in *Kommersant Daily* or any other Russian newspaper and you will also find articles on Chechnya and the war on terrorism, lists of those killed in the latest terror act, and terrorist profiles. Television is also replete with video footage of terror attacks filmed by Wolves themselves, as well as FSB footage of hostage rescue operations, arms and explosives caches found, and counterterrorism operations.

The quality of public information varies. Sometimes, it is downright ridiculous, such as the Wolves' claim that the "military industrial mafia" or the Moussad were responsible for the 11 September 2001 terror attacks on America. Both Russia and Wolves routinely exaggerate each other's war casualty figures too and undercount their own, and of course misinformation and disinformation have to be carefully filtered out. Good Russian language competency and solid analytical experience are essential to understanding the nuances of the information being studied, to know what makes sense, what fits, and what doesn't.

I have relied heavily on quotes from many of the star characters in this book. Most quotes are taken from video or audio tapes sent to Russian television stations or "interviews" and "e-mailed messages" published on Udugov's Web site or one of the English-language Islamic sites like azzam. com or IslamicAwakening. These Azzam sites provided useful biographical information on Khattab and other Arab fighters and terrorists in this book.

xii   *Wolves of Islam*

The human factor is, of course, a critical resource for a book of this kind. My book would not have been possible without the thoughtful and valuable contributions made by countless people over the course of nine years of working, living, and travelling in Russia. It is not necessary, or even desirable, to mention people by name here, but they include former Chechen, Georgian, and Russian students of mine, business colleagues and associates, university professors and political analysts, journalists and politicians, Russian diplomats, State Duma deputies, and many others.

Each person had something unique to say and was generous in sharing his or her knowledge or perspective. Some were very opinionated. Others were surprisingly objective. But all were fascinating, and each and every person was worth getting to know, if only briefly. Some people told me personal stories of tragedy, abduction, crime, and corruption. Others contributed firsthand knowledge of a particular event, while still others offered suggestions or kindly consented to read pieces of the manuscript and correct my factual errors. I am especially grateful to those who gave me good advice for my own personal safety and to others for their help and sympathy when things went terribly wrong.

I would also like to express my gratitude to Congressman Jim Saxton, chairman of the House Armed Services Committee's Terrorism, Unconventional Threats and Capabilities Subcommittee, for asking me to work on issues related to counterterrorism cooperation between the United States and Russia in 2002.

I am also grateful to former senior Indian government officials who provided information on Basayev's training in Pakistan and his links with Islamic organizations there.

Finally, I would like to say thanks to Professor Edward Rozek, a great scholar, mentor, advisor, teacher, and friend for over thirty-five years.

PROLOGUE

THE SETTING

When I mention to friends that I'm doing a book about terror and Chechnya, they almost always comment: "Oh, you're writing about Russian atrocities!" In the West, Chechnya is synonymous with Russian military brutality. But I wrote this book to tell a different story.

In telling this story, I would like the reader to know that the ordinary Chechen is neither a proponent of war nor terror, but their victim—a casualty of fear, suspicion, revenge, and Islamic extremists who have imposed their ideological will on them and led them into war with Russia. Chechens are a proud people who want to work and live in peace. They respect their ancestral land, prize freedom, and have strong blood and family ties. They are a good people and it is not my intention here to portray them otherwise.

For the reader who doesn't know, Chechnya is an oil rich land of roughly six thousand square miles situated on the northern slopes of the Greater Caucasus and in the adjoining Chechen plain and the Terek-Kuma lowlands of southern Russia. It had a prewar (1994) population of a little over one million. Once a part of the former Soviet Union, Chechnya's centuries old history is one of ethnic pride, independence, and fierce resistance to outside authority. In his book, *Gulag Archipelago,* Alexandr Solzhenitsyn described the Chechen people as never yielding to obedience, always proud, and respecting only insurgents.

Chechens have a particularly bloody history of relations with Russia; notable are the nearly half century of holy wars against Tsarist Russia in the nineteenth century and Stalin's 1944 deportations, which Chechens see as an attempt to eliminate them as a nation. Once upon a time, no respectable Chechen girl would marry a Chechen man unless he had killed at least one Russian soldier in battle.

1

In 1991, the former Soviet Air Forces General and rebel Chechen President Dzokhar Dudayev unilaterally declared Chechnya independent from the Russian Soviet Federated Socialist Republics (RSFSR). Chechen military forces, powerful warlords with their private armies and hired foreign Islamic mercenaries, criminals, and terrorists—and ordinary Chechens too—have fought multiple wars with Russia ever since.

Chechnya won the first war (1994–1996) with Russia. The second war began in August 1999, when Chechen warlord and terrorist Shamil Basayev, accompanied by his heavily armed "international peacekeeping brigade" made up of Chechens, Arabs, Turks, and other foreigners, crossed into Dagestan (Russia's sovereign territory) to forcibly carve out a new Taliban-like Islamic state. Basayev and his Saudi-born military commander, Khattab, vowed to create "a pure Islamic land wiped clean of kafir" (infidels) and "non-Islamic civilians." Khattab described this new state as a place where "Russians, Christians, and Jews" would be excluded; an idyllic "Allah's land" that would ultimately stretch from the Caspian to the Black Sea and serve as a springboard for a "new world Islamic order."

This physical act of war, accompanied by official declarations of holy war (jihad) against both Dagestan and Russia—and the subsequent terrorist bombings of apartment buildings in Moscow and in other Russian cities—started the 1999 apocalyptic war with Russia that has left Chechnya in physical ruin, between eight and ten thousand Russian soldiers and policemen dead, and a Chechen population displaced and decimated by half.

THE CAST OF CHARACTERS

At a little past 9 p.m. on Wednesday, 23 October 2002, no fewer than nineteen young men and twenty-two men bounded from their vehicles and sprinted through the front doors of the sprawling Theater Center at Dubrovka in Moscow, Russia. Once inside, they hurriedly took their designated places for the dramatic finale of the evening.

But these were not starring actresses and actors in the second act of the family hit musical *Nord Ost*, which was entertaining a sellout crowd of 711 spectators inside. They were Chechen Islamic terrorists, suicide hostage takers, who had come to Moscow to die and take their captive prey with them. Four years earlier, on 3 October 1998, the body of Akmal Saidov, a Russian government official, was found near a checkpoint on the Chechen-Ingush border. Pinned to his coat was a bloody note signed "the Wolves of Islam."

The Chechen terrorists at Dubrovka and the killers of Saidov were not ordinary Chechens but Islamic extremists, "Allah's warriors," whose proclaimed strategic objective is the creation of a radical Islamic state in

southern Russia. The wolf is the proud national symbol of their Chechen homeland.

Wolves are small in number, but their terror victims count into the thousands. At least 164 men, women, children, and terrorists died at Dubrovka. During their first war with Russia, Wolves took more than three thousand hostages in two Russian hospitals. Many innocent people died.

Their multiple apartment building bombings in Moscow and other cities of Russia in September 1999 killed more than three hundred people, moving then Russian President Boris Yeltsin to proclaim, "Chechen terrorist wolves have declared war on us." The deadly bombs that Wolves have put on buses, trams, and in busy markets, train, and subway stations have killed hundreds more.

Other Wolves and Chechen criminals have kidnapped men, women, and children—Russians and Westerners—for ransom or sale into human slavery, cutting off their victims' fingers and hands, or worse, executing them or selling the severed heads of captives to Osama bin Laden for millions of dollars.

More Wolves slaughtered International Red Cross workers in their sleep and mutilated or decapitated hundreds of captured Russian soldiers, spies, collaborators, and suspected traitors. The carnage is filmed and posted on the Internet, the human heads paraded before television audiences or driven onto stakes in public places to warn others.

Pack leader Shamil Basayev has sent boys, teenage girls, grown women, and men to their deaths in suicide bombings, killing hundreds of people. Nearly nine years ago, Basayev carried out the first-ever act of nuclear terrorism, and, in June 2003, said that he would use an intercontinental missile on Russia if he could get his hands on one. In March 2004, he announced that he might even employ chemical weapons against Russia and soon attack Russia abroad.

The starring character in this story is the now one-legged Shamil Basayev, the 1991 hijacker of a Russian airliner and "Hero of Budennovsk" who single-handedly forced Russia to the negotiating table by holding a Russian hospital hostage in 1995. Basayev is the most famous, ferocious, and, so far, invincible fighter in contemporary Chechen history. A Che Guevara–like figure who now lives in forests, caves, and dugouts, he is a living legend in a land that thrives on myths of wolves, warriors, and great battles. He is also Russia's most wanted terrorist who leads terrorist structures that are ideologically aligned with and helped by Osama bin Laden and linked to al Qaeda, structures that both the United States and the United Nations put on their terrorist lists in 2003.

Costarring is "The Black Arab," Khattab, the "one handed" professional Saudi-born Wahhabi religious warrior who Basayev brought to Chechnya in February 1995. This medieval-like Islamic extremist who fought against the Soviets in Afghanistan; promoted the Taliban brand of Wahhabism in Chechnya; armed and conspired with radical Wahhabis in Dagestan to revolt against their government and Russia; trained fighters and international terrorists in his special camps; and procured Osama bin Laden money to establish the new Islamic imamate—not to mention mutilated and beheaded his prisoners of war and filmed and posted this on the Internet—was the Russian Army's worst nightmare until Russian secret services assassinated him with a poison letter in March 2002.

The rabid red-headed "Lone Wolf" terrorist, Chechen warlord and not-so-common criminal Salman Raduyev, is the third principal character. Russia's President Vladimir Putin once described him as "the most odious of all." When he was alive, Raduyev, an in-law of President Dzokhar Dudayev, took more hostages than probably anybody in modern history. He was defiant of all authority; stole teachers' salaries; blew up train stations, buses, and trolleys; threatened to attack Russian nuclear facilities; refused to ever end his personal war with Russia; and, after taking an assassin's bullet through the eye, later rose from the "dead" and then lost his mind.

The barbaric Arbi Barayev (nicknamed "The Wahhabi" for his religious fanaticism), his nephew, Movsar Suleimenov, and their close associates, the Akhmadov brothers, play feature roles too. Arbi Barayev was far more psychotic and maniacal than either Khattab or Raduyev. He was the godfather of the multimillion dollar kidnapping and "people for sale" business and the warlord who beheaded three Britons and a New Zealander in 1998 for an alleged $30 million from Osama bin Laden. Barayev's nephew, Movsar Suleimenov, also a converted Wahhabi, participated in his uncle's people business, changed his last name to Barayev, and took command of his uncle's "Special Purposes Islamic Brigade" when Arbi Barayev was killed by Russian forces. Movsar was recruited by Shamil Basayev to lead the Dubrovka theater siege.

A key role is also played by Chechnya's Foreign Minister Movladi Udugov, the organizer and intellectual ideologist and propagandist dubbed "Chechnya's Goebbels" by Russia, the same Udugov who threatened kamikaze airplane attacks against the Kremlin in 1996. A year later, he founded the "Islamic Nations" movement and became the chief ideologist of that movement's drive to unite Chechnya and Dagestan into a single Islamic state. These activities led Udugov into opposition to the president of Chechnya who ultimately charged him with "large scale ideological sabotage of the Chechen state" and treason.

Finally, there is the ex–Soviet Army Colonel and President of the Chechen Republic of Ichkeria (as Chechnya was renamed) Aslan Maskhadov, the beleaguered and tragic political figure legitimately elected president in 1997 by 64.8 percent of the popular vote. He was opposed to Khattab's brand of religious fanaticism and expansion of Chechnya to include Dagestan. His single goal was Chechen independence. Yet Maskhadov bears as much responsibility as anybody for the anarchism, the social and economic decay of Chechnya in the interwar years (1997 to 1999) because of his inability as president to control the actions of Basayev, Khattab, Raduyev, Barayev, and others; his unwillingness to follow through on his threats of punishment for "field commanders" who broke the law; and his indecisiveness and determination to avoid a civil war with his former war comrades.

THE STORY

This book is about these tragic events and the principal cast of characters who individually and collectively (and for their own personal, ideological, religious, and criminal reasons) led post-Soviet Chechnya down the road to chaos, political anarchy, economic ruin, and, ultimately, war and physical destruction. Incomprehensible terror is at the core of this story. Described on these pages are some of the most horrific acts of terror against humanity imaginable, terror that in a decade has left behind a casualty count that no Western country would ever tolerate; neither has Russia. Of course, not all of the terror in Russia originates in Chechnya, but most of it does. The graphic descriptions of terror, acts of torture, and human cruelty in this book will disturb the reader.

This story is also about corruption, greed, money, and terror financing. It has all the ingredients and colorful characters of a good novel—powerful warlords; revolution and a struggle for independence; ethnic hatred; the mafia; Islamic extremism; perpetual jihad; international terrorism; a barbaric disregard for human life; a clash of civilizations; and yes, even Osama bin Laden and al Qaeda. This grim tale would be amusingly entertaining if it weren't so tragically true.

The story is worth telling. Some observers argue that the second Chechen war and today's terror in Russia could have been avoided if the Kremlin had only recognized Chechnya's independence after the first war ended in 1996. I contend that such recognition would not have prevented a new war because the president of Chechnya was unable to control Chechen criminal gangs and because many of the star characters in this book were already conspiring to take Russian territory in Dagestan by force to carve out their new Islamic state in the North Caucasus. Russia's recognition of Chechen independence in 1997 would not have stopped that process, only hastened it.

Other observers say that Russia's brutality in Chechnya is to blame for the rise of Islamic extremism in the North Caucasus and for the terror in Russia. I do not agree. However, Russia's brutal conduct of war and human rights violations in Chechnya have served to further alienate many Chechens, radicalize youth who have known nothing else but war for nearly all their lives, and drive some ordinary Chechens into the ranks of the extremists. It is also true that corruption and the willingness of some Russian police and military personnel to take bribes and sell arms and explosives to anyone willing to pay the hard cash not only exacerbates the war in Chechnya but actually facilitates the terror in Russia.

This book portrays a grotesque and bizarre world of crime, religious extremism, war, and terror in Russia.

I

SHAMIL BASAYEV: RUSSIA'S OSAMA BIN LADEN

> I warned that we would fight in Russia, and there are a lot more targets. We have radioactive elements and biological weapons that Russia left us. We could put a biological weapon in Yekaterinburg and let the people who live there all get sick. It would only require one person to put Uranium in Moscow. One of our people would die, but a whole city would die with him.
>
> Shamil Basayev, *Lidove Noviny*, July 1995

THE BEGINNING

Every Chechen knows the tale of how the "Hero of Budennovsk" seized a Russian hospital in 1995 and forced the Kremlin to negotiate a cease-fire in its war with Chechnya. Basayev's bold hijacking of a Russian airliner in 1991 and his famous "Grozny Offensive" five years later in which he defied all odds to beat superior Russian forces in Chechnya's capital also contribute to the Chechen living legend of Shamil Basayev. But what Chechen President Aslan Maskhadov once said about Basayev is the most telling: "The Chechen people respect the president, but they love Basayev."

Indeed, Shamil Basayev, who now goes by the Islamic nom de guerre of Abdullah Shamil Abu-Idris, is the most famous, ferocious, and, so far, invincible fighter in contemporary Chechen history. In a decade of wars, he has been wounded eight times and suffered seven brain concussions. For many Chechens, he is a national hero. He is also Russia's most hunted terrorist, rising from being simply a leader of an "illegal armed formation" fourteen years ago to becoming Russia's greatest national security threat with a \$5 million price tag on his head. How did Basayev become all these things in such a short time?

Shamil Salmanovich Basayev comes from a traditional Chechen family and a social structure where tribal and clan ties, loyalties, and solidarity largely dictate behavior and elders collectively make the decisions. He was born on 14 January 1965 in the village of Dyshne-Vedeno located in the mountainous Vedensky district of what was then the Chechen-Ingush Autonomous Soviet Socialist Republic, a historically defiant and rebellious part of the Russian Soviet Federated Socialist Republics of the Soviet Union. Generations of Basayev's family had lived there except for a time when Joseph Stalin forcibly deported his grandfather and a half million other Chechen and Ingush people to Central Asia in 1944 as collective punishment for fascist collaboration. Many of the "punished people" were massacred or died in the deportations and exile, which Chechens consider an attempt to eliminate them as a nation.

Some people who knew Basayev in his youth remember him as being very smart and ambitious, with a quiet, calm, deliberate, and calculating manner. He is also strong willed, very unconventional in his approach to problem solving, and a vehement Chechen nationalist—all characteristics typical of a people Alexandr Solzhenitsyn described in *Gulag Archipelago*.

Chechens like to compare their national character to that of the Chechen wolf, long ago chosen as the republic's national symbol because it will attack a stronger foe, using its daring, adroitness, and courage to compensate for its smaller size and lack of strength. Basayev is proud to be compared to the wolf.

Although brazen, defiant, and proud of his martial culture, he is also someone with lots of personal charisma and an active sense of humor, and a great storyteller—all qualities that helped make him a favorite with foreign journalists in the 1994–1996 war with Russia. They are also characteristics that make him a hit with women.

When Basayev finished high school, he was drafted into the Soviet Air Forces and served his mandatory two years putting out fires as a firefighter. After military service, Basayev aspired to argue jurisprudence in the Russian courtroom. Three times he took the entrance exam to the prestigious legal faculty at Moscow State University and three times he failed. Basayev says that he wasn't admitted because he is Chechen.

Basayev worked at a government-run state farm in the Aksaisky-Volgogradsky oblast of the Soviet Union until he went to Moscow in 1986. His relatives persuaded him to enroll in the Institute of Land Tenure Engineers in Moscow the following year.

Basayev was a great soccer player at the Institute. He didn't do well in his studies, though, and, in 1988, was expelled. But instead of going home where he would not have found work, Basayev stayed in Moscow and became (in his own words) "a Moscow-based businessman" dealing in computers. He stayed just long enough to get himself into debt and left Moscow in a hurry. After a brief visit home, he went to Istanbul, Turkey, and studied at the Islamic Institute there until the tumultuous events in Moscow of August 1991.

TWO GRENADES FOR YELTSIN

In the summer of 1991, old guard communist coup plotters in Moscow dispatched Soviet tanks and armored personnel carriers (APCs) to the central part of the city and blocked off the capital's main street. General Secretary of the Communist Party of the Soviet Union Mikhail Gorbachev was put under house arrest, but the newly elected Russian Soviet Federated Socialist Republics president, Boris Yeltsin, got through the blockades and, at 1 p.m. on 20 August, climbed on top of a friendly tank at the White House parliament building and appealed to Muscovites to support democracy. People swarmed to the White House and built a barricade to defend the building against attack. One reporter described the scene this way: "The action around the parliament building is reminiscent of an anthill. The defenders have automatic weapons and bottles of homemade incendiary liquid, boxes of which are standing right here."

Basayev, who had returned to Moscow by now, armed himself and answered Yeltsin's call. He bought two hand grenades from a mafia friend, put them in a shopping bag, and ran to defend Yeltsin. "I knew that if the Communists won it would be the death of independence [for Chechnya]," he told the Russian newspaper *Moskovskaya Pravda* in January 1996.

Fighting at the White House started just after midnight when a column of military vehicles approached the barricades. Several people attempting to block the vehicles were killed. The crowd then swarmed the column and set one APC on fire. After that, the other tanks and APCs retreated and the coup was over.

Anti-communist Chechens loved President Yeltsin. Dzokhar Dudayev, the Chechen-born former Soviet Air Forces general who had returned home earlier in the year to lead the National Congress of the Chechen People, vehemently condemned the coup plotters, called on all Chechens in Moscow to support Yeltsin, organized demonstrations and a general strike in Chechnya to protest the coup attempt, and again called for the dissolution of the local communist party structure that supported the coup. After all, Yeltsin had been telling the Soviet republics on his visits to grab as much sovereignty as they could swallow. Everyone was certain that he stood for freedom and national self-determination. At last, the North

Caucasus would get to determine its own future. The psychosis of "rebirth" infected everyone.

The events of August 1991 had a profound effect on Basayev. He again left for home, arriving in Grozny in the midst of Dudayev's Chechen Revolution, which had been sparked by the events in Moscow. Basayev had never seen so many people on the streets of the city before—they were demonstrating and waving green Islamic flags and shouting anti-communist—and anti-Russian—slogans in daily demonstrations. There were also armed men everywhere. Some belonged to the few-days-old National Guards headed by Beslan Gantemirov, the armed wing of the National Congress of the Chechen People, which seized the communist-run television center on 22 August. Others were gangs of armed men who just came to Grozny looking for a fight.

Basayev rounded up friends and relatives too, as well as volunteers from Benoi, Vedeno, Dyshne-Vedeno, Bamut, and other mountain villages, and formed his own armed gang called Vedeno. Its purpose was to protect the premises in Grozny where the National Congress of the Chechen People and another organization, the Assembly of Caucasus Mountain Peoples, regularly met.

Basayev quickly became swept up in events that were now moving at near light speed. Dudayev was plotting to remove the republic's communist party boss, Chechen Doku Zavgayev, who had lost President Yeltsin's backing because of his support of the Moscow attempted coup. The Chechen-Ingush Supreme Soviet was still sitting, but only until early September when a Dudayev mob burst into the House of Political Education building, beat up forty deputies, threw the head of the city Soviet through the window, killing him, and dragged Zavgayev out into the street, where they beat him up too and made him resign.

But it was Dudayev's armed seizure of the new multiple-story KGB building on 5 October 1991 that triggered Russian Vice President Alexandr Rutskoi to fly to Grozny, take one look around, and declare, "This is not democracy, it's banditry."

Basayev participated in the raid, which took place on a weekend when the building was practically empty. When the angry crowd pounded on the entrance door, a Russian guard inside attempted to reason with its leaders, but a second guard, a Chechen, shot him dead and then opened the door. Basayev and others ransacked the building and stole uniforms, armaments, and everything else that could be carted away. What wasn't taken was smashed and shot up. The mob then urinated on the walls and left human excrement everywhere. Basayev says that he personally led a similar attack on the headquarters of the Russian Main Intelligence Directorate of the General Staff (GRU-military intelligence) in Grozny.

These and other armed uprisings, shootings, murders, carjackings, hostage taking, armed robberies, and random hate killings of local Russian residents prompted Moscow to demand that Grozny disarm Basayev's Vedeno gang along with the multitude of other "illegal armed formations" that were popping up like mushrooms.

IN THE FOOTSTEPS OF IMAM SHAMIL

Like little Chechen boys, every Chechen fighter has his military heroes—Basayev's are Che Guevara and Chechnya's nineteenth-century hero Imam Shamil.

Basayev kept a big poster of Che Guevara in his room at the Land Tenure Engineers Institute, where he read and heard about the exploits of the famous Latin American revolutionary from Cuban students studying there. What Basayev would remember about Che Guevara later in his own political struggle was not the revolutionary's Marxist politics, but the strength, zeal, self-sacrifice, and methods with which the Latin American guerrilla leader fought.

Like Che, Basayev would become a guerrilla warrior, national hero, and politician. He would display suicidal courage and extraordinary military skills; opt for extremist solutions; quit his government post to pursue his political ideals; lead guerrillas into foreign regions to inspire local revolt; become a potent symbol of rebellion and political idealism; and thrive on harsh living conditions.

Basayev sees himself as a Chechen Che Guevara carrying on the work of the most famous Chechen national hero of all, Imam Shamil, who between 1830 and 1859 led the mountain people of the North Caucasus in a bloody holy war against the Tsarist Russian empire. Imam Shamil also created the first unified state (imamate) in the history of the Caucasus.

There is a long lineage of guerrilla fighters in Basayev's family, and he proudly carries on that tradition. His great-grandfather fought against the Bolsheviks. Basayev is very proud of the fact that he is a direct descendant of one of Imam Shamil's deputies. Once, when asked by Prague's *Lidove Noviny* if he felt like a modern-day Imam Shamil, Basayev modestly replied, "My name is Shamil. . . . I am a different Shamil. Nevertheless, I was given his name and I honor his memory."

This statement is key to understanding Basayev's political vision. Ever since returning to Chechnya in 1991, Basayev has been fighting to do one thing and one thing only: reestablish the imamate for which his family ancestors fought. Only Basayev's imamate would include today's Russian republics of Dagestan, Ingushetia, North Ossetia, and Karachaevo-Cherkessia, and would ultimately stretch from the Black Sea to the Caspian Sea.

The idea of again uniting the North Caucasus powerfully arose in July 1989, when ethnic differences erupted between Georgians and Abkhazians. Only a government state of emergency avoided large-scale bloodshed in Abkhazia, the once beautiful citrus Black Sea coast region strategically located in the former Soviet republic of Georgia. Those who sought unification of the North Caucasus organized three unification "congresses" in the three years that followed the 1989 disturbances. The third congress of the Assembly of Caucasus Mountain Peoples met in Sukhumi, Abkhazia's capital, on 1–2 November 1991, and formed the Confederation of Caucasus Mountain Peoples.

The November 1991 congress formed a parliament, an arbitration tribunal, a defense committee, and declared that a combined fighting force to be called the Troops of the Confederation of Caucasus Peoples made up of military units drawn from each of the member republics would be organized. At that congress, Basayev pledged to build the Chechen military contingent of the Confederation troops.

The Confederation had the full backing of Dzokhar Dudayev, who was convinced that a Chechnya free of Russia would provide a solid foundation for a unified mountaineer republic. He told the third Confederation congress, "The union of all Caucasian nations on an equal basis is the only possible way for the future. As we [Chechens] hold a central geographic, strategic, and economic position in the Caucasus and have the necessary human potential, we must be the initiators of this future union."

Basayev has never forgotten these words; they have driven his every tactical decision since 1991. If Imam Shamil is the key to understanding Basayev's political vision for the North Caucasus, then Dudayev's statement is the key to understanding Basayev's tactics to achieve his dream of a new imamate; his sometimes odd decisions; the acts of terror he commits; the alliances he has formed with Arab extremists and the likes of Salman Raduyev; his crossover to Wahhabi religious extremism; and his 1999 military actions in Dagestan to seize Russian territory for this new Islamic imamate. Chechens would be the initiators of this future union.

ESTABLISHING TERRORIST CREDENTIALS

Why Basayev threw his name into the ring as a candidate for the presidential election that Dudayev called on 27 October 1991 is unclear because he was never a serious contender. Dudayev probably urged him to run to make the election look more democratic. Basayev never seriously campaigned.

There were also three other candidates, but Dudayev won with 90 percent of the vote in an election that was in violation of the RSFSR's constitution. Dudayev took office on 2 November 1991, one month before the USSR was dissolved. That same day, the Congress of Peoples Deputies of the RSFSR declared the election illegal.

President Dudayev's first act was to unilaterally declare Chechnya independent from the RSFSR. But President Yeltsin immediately ruled this act of secession illegal, appointed a pro-Moscow Chechen government, and, on 8 November, imposed a one-month state of emergency on Chechnya. He also ordered Dudayev's arrest. Yeltsin flew in several hundred Interior Ministry troops to enforce the state of emergency, but Dudayev's National Guards surrounded them when they landed at Khankala airbase. Contravening the president of the RSFSR, Gorbachev ordered Russian troops not to fight. They subsequently surrendered, and Dudayev bused them back to Russia.

Basayev decided to act on his own to force his one-time hero, Yeltsin, to lift the state of emergency on Chechnya. He chose a radical course of action—one that would forever brand Shamil Basayev a terrorist.

On 9 November 1991, Basayev and two friends, Said-Ali Satuyev and Lom-Ali Chachayev, went to the Russian town of Mineralnye Vody, boarded a Russian TU-154 plane with 178 passengers, and hijacked the airliner to Turkey. Basayev threatened to blow up the aircraft if the Kremlin did not lift the state of emergency. The plane landed safely in Ankara, the hijacking received a lot of international media attention, and Basayev negotiated safe passage for himself and his accomplices back to Chechnya in exchange for the release of some Chechens held in Russian prisons. Within a few hours, the aircraft with Basayev and his men, the crew, and the passengers left Ankara and flew to Grozny where the passengers were released.

Nine months later, a Chechen hijacked another TU-154 and demanded that it be flown to Turkey. While the plane was refuelling at Moscow's Vnukovo Airport, police stormed the aircraft and killed the hijacker.

Basayev's hijacking was a nice present for Dudayev's presidential inauguration. President Dudayev gave Basayev a hero's welcome, commissioning him a colonel and giving him a regimental command in the new Chechen Presidential Guards. Two days later, Yeltsin's state of emergency was lifted—not because of Basayev's hijacking, but because the Russian Supreme Soviet had voted to reverse Yeltsin's state of emergency decree.

President Dudayev soon dispatched Basayev to Azerbaijan to assist the Muslim Azerbaijani national army in fighting the Russian-backed Christian Armenian forces over the Nagorno-Karabakh region. In exchange for Chechnya's help, Basayev would get to keep the "trophies of war" (the weapons and ammunition that he captured from Armenian forces) to take back to Chechnya. But within a few months the deal went sour and, as Basayev recalls, "I led my own mujahideen out of Azerbaijan."

Back home, Dudayev was further arming. Basayev and his men helped Dudayev confiscate goods from military warehouses or took armaments from Russian troops leaving their bases. There are numerous stories about Russian generals selling their country's military arsenal in Chechnya to President Dudayev, including a nuclear-tipped air-to-surface missile. Two more nuclear warheads were reportedly found in a burned-out missile silo in Bamut, Chechnya, but no one has been able to prove they ever existed. Chechnya was quickly arming, evident by the abundance of weapons and ammunition being sold and traded in markets all over Grozny.

DRINKING GEORGIAN BLOOD

The July 1992 decision of the Abkhaz parliament to restore the 1925 constitution of independent Abkhazia so infuriated the leadership of Georgia that it launched a land and air attack on Abkhazia on 14 August 1992, beginning a bloody war that would claim twenty thousand lives.

The Confederation of Caucasus Mountain Peoples Parliament in Grozny immediately voted to send Confederation troops to fight for Abkhazia's independence from Georgia. Yusuf Soslambekov, head of the Confederation parliament, personally dispatched Basayev.

Georgia's President Shevardnadze says that the Kremlin sent buses to Grozny to take Basayev, Ruslan Gelayev (another influential Chechen figure), and others to Abkhazia. But Basayev and twenty to thirty of his Vedeno fighters left Chechnya on their own by car caravan. However, they did commandeer a Russian bus (with passengers) in Pyatigorsk, Russia, when the Russian police attempted to detain these "soldiers of fortune." Basayev took the bus into the Karachaevo-Cherkessia Republic, where he freed the passengers after the police received orders from a higher authority to abandon the chase so Basayev and his men could go on to Abkhazia.

Basayev arrived in Abkhazia with his small "peacekeeping force" just after Georgian troops occupied all major cities. Ironically, for most of the next year Basayev would fight alongside Russians sent by President Yeltsin to support Abkhazia against Georgia. Russian military intelligence turned a blind eye to the 1991 terrorist arrest warrant against Basayev to train him and his detachment in Abkhazia, and the Russians even helped direct Basayev's combat operations. Long after the war, Basayev praised the professionalism and courage of his Russian trainers in Abkhazia—praise that led some of his enemies in Grozny, even President Maskhadov, to later call him a "longtime GRU agent."

In August 1992, the separatist Abkhaz leadership made Basayev Abkhaz deputy minister of defense in charge of the Gagry front. By November of that year, Basayev had routed Georgian troops from the city of Gagra, once a subtropical health resort on the Black Sea. But stories about Basayev's cruelty and the atrocities committed by his men soon began to circulate.

Georgians say that Basayev's Wolves drank Georgian blood by the glassful. That could be fact or fiction. But it is documented fact that the veins of captured Georgian soldiers were cut open and the victims made to drink their own blood as a toast to the victors.

This, however, was not the worst atrocity attributed to Basayev and his men. One hundred Georgian soldiers were herded into the central stadium in Gagra where they were beheaded and their heads used as footballs in a soccer match. Georgia has charged Basayev with these war crimes.

Basayev's Abkhaz battalion also used a form of torture and execution called the "Chechen tongue." A hole is made in the throat and the tongue is pulled down through the hole, thereby gagging the victim to death.

In the summer of 1993, the Abkhazian parliament approved a cease-fire that called for the withdrawal of all forces from Sukhumi. However, Georgia repeatedly violated the agreement. On 19 September 1993, Basayev, Abkhaz insurgents, and other Confederation units launched a major offensive, catching Georgian troops unprepared and undermanned. Chechen and Abkhaz forces retook Sukhumi in a ten-day battle that left the capitol in ruins and corpses littering the streets. The battle focused on the parliament building. It was taken and torched, and all prisoners were executed.

Abkhazia then launched a campaign of ethnic cleansing that prompted an exodus of two hundred thousand Georgian refugees. Georgia says that Basayev participated. He was still in Abkhazia in October 1993. Anatol Lieven recalls in his book *Chechnya: Tombstone of Russian Power* that he met the twenty-eight-year-old Basayev in Abkhazia in October 1993, "grinning cheerfully as he [Basayev] was sitting on the pavement in the temporary Abkhaz capital of Gudauta with other leaders of the volunteers from the Confederation of Mountain Peoples." Basayev jokingly congratulated him for not running into Chechen mujahideen when Lieven had been reporting on the war with the Georgian side.

Basayev built his Abkhaz Battalion into a well-disciplined and battle-hardened fighting force that attracted volunteers by the dozens. He lost fifty-six fighters in Abkhazia, but, by the time he returned to Chechnya in February 1994, he had in those who survived the most experienced and combat-ready force of any of President Dudayev's armed men. He also had a personally loyal unit of Chechen fighters that would stay with him until they were killed off, one by one, in subsequent wars with Russia.

History professor-turned-fighter Ruslan Gelayev also built a credible fighting force in Abkhazia that became known as the Gelayev Spetnaz (special forces). He would prove his mettle in the first war with Russia and go on to build a loyal group of fighters nine hundred strong, his spetnaz group even becoming the heroes of a popular Chechen song.

The fifth congress of the Confederation of Caucasus Mountain Peoples in February 1993 made Basayev commander of the Confederation troops.

Besides fighting in Abkhazia, Basayev fell in love and married an Abkhazian girl. Some information says that she was from the city of Gudauta and that her name was Angela. Basayev took her back to Chechnya in 1993. Other information says he married a seventeen-year-old girl from the Gudautsky district and they had a son together. His Abkhazian wife and children were killed in Russian bombings in 1995. He married again in 2002.

JIHAD TRAINING IN AFGHANISTAN

By 1994, Grozny had established good communication channels with the Pakistani government, particularly with the Pakistani Inter-Service-intelligence (ISI). It was through these channels that Basayev and twenty of his best men went to train in the Amir Muawia training camp in Afghanistan—the same camp that was struck by U.S. cruise missiles in August 1998 in an attempt to kill Osama bin Laden. After Muawia, Basayev's group would receive advanced training in the Markaz-i-Dawar camp in Pakistan. The ISI made all the arrangements, but Basayev recalls, "I had to pay for the training myself. I sold my weapon and I borrowed some money from my friends and went to Afghanistan." He told the Russian newspaper *Nezavisimaya Gazeta* in April 1996 that he still owed $3,500 for the trip.

In late March or early April, the twenty-nine-year-old Basayev arrived in Pakistan where he met high-ranking Pakistani officials, including the minister of intelligence and head of the ISI branch in charge of supporting Islamic causes. Through them, he was introduced to the leadership of two organizations dedicated to the forceful revival of Islam—the Harkat-ul-Ansar (HUA), later designated a terrorist organization by the United States, and Tablighi Jamaat (TJ), led by the former director-general of the ISI, retired Lieutenant General Javed Nasir. The HUA was originally formed to recruit volunteers to fight the Soviets in Afghanistan and drew many of its recruits from the TJ.

Basayev and his Chechen entourage became members of the secretive TJ organization, which had offices in Bosnia, Central Asia, France, the United States, Russia, and elsewhere. An article in the February 1998 issue of *Newsline*, a Pakistani monthly magazine, quoted TJ workers as saying that the organization had many members in the Chechen cabinet, including the first deputy prime minister of Chechnya (Basayev).

The training of Basayev and his men went well until they got sick handling chemical weapons. Because of that, Basayev cut short his stay in Pakistan and returned home in July 1994.

DOING DUDAYEV'S DIRTY WORK AND THE FIRST CHECHEN WAR

During the lull in the fighting in Abkhazia in the summer of 1993, Basayev returned home briefly to help the besieged President Dudayev. By then, Dudayev had made enemies of just about every political ally he ever had, especially Gantemirov. Open rallies were being staged daily at Grozny's Teatralnaya Square to protest Dudayev's string of undemocratic actions, like dissolving the parliament and the constitutional court. Dudayev tolerated the opposition to his regime until it announced a national referendum on his presidential rule. In the days running up to the referendum, tension mounted and Dudayev's supporters and opposition demonstrators frequently clashed, resulting in the deaths of several people, including one of Dudayev's relatives.

On 4 June, the Chechen president struck back with Basayev and some of his armed men doing the dirty work. They stormed the town hall building in which Gantemirov and his electoral commission were working. Then they dispersed opposition demonstrators on Teatralnaya Square. At least thirty people were killed.

By the late spring of 1994, the opposition consisted of a strange collection of intellectuals, ex-communists, gangsters, Dudayev's former bodyguard, longtime enemies, and former allies. All had the common goal of toppling Dudayev. Moscow secretly financed and armed the opposition's organization, the Provisional Council of United Opposition.

Basayev had only just returned from Pakistan when he and his Abkhaz Battalion engaged elements of the armed opposition in Grozny. The opposition struck again in August 1994, falsely declaring that they had seized the reigns of power in Grozny. Russia put intense pressure on Basayev to defect—in exchange for the safety of his family—but he refused to abandon Dudayev. On the contrary, Basayev and his Abkhaz Battalion became Dudayev's staunchest defenders. More opposition attacks came the following month and in October, but the incompetence of those leading the opposition forces made it easy to beat them.

Basayev played a key role in defending Grozny in November when Russian-backed opposition forces attacked the city. Russian tank crews signed mercenary contracts to support the opposition in an all-out attack on Grozny. Seventeen Russian tanks moved up from Urus-Martan under the command of Gantemirov while another thirty came in from the direction of Tolstoy-Yurt. They penetrated the center of the city, but then Basayev's battalion and Dudayev's National Guards ambushed them with rocket-propelled grenades. The attack was thwarted and twenty-one Russian soldiers were taken prisoner and put on public display to prove Russian military involvement in the attempted coup. After this, Dudayev handpicked his personal bodyguards from the ranks of the Abkhaz Battalion.

On 11 December 1994, Russia launched its military operation to "disarm illegal armed formations" and "restore constitutional order" in Chechnya. Troop strength on the Russian side initially numbered 23,800. On the Chechen side, there was "one battalion of Basayev's and the spetnaz regiment of Gelayev's which numbered about five hundred fighters. There was also a regiment of new Chechen recruits, but there were few of them," according to then acting Chechen Vice President Zelimkhan Yandarbiyev. Chechnya also had twenty to twenty-five Soviet tanks, thirty APCs, an artillery unit of eighty men, and a police and national security force of about three hundred.

These forces and mobilized civilians totaling about five thousand fighters formed the core of Grozny's defense directed by former Soviet Army artillery Colonel and Chechen Chief of Staff Aslan Maskhadov from the basement of the Presidential Palace, the former building of the CPSU's "obkom" headquarters. The actual strength of the Chechen side is unknown. Russian General Gennady Troshev says there were ten thousand "well-armed fighters." Other Russian sources say that Basayev alone had two thousand fighters under his command.

Yandarbiyev recalls that when the Russian tank assault on Grozny began, Maskhadov (who had returned to Chechnya in 1991 from his Soviet military post and was quickly snapped up by Dudayev because of his expertise in military leadership) ordered Basayev and Gelayev to pull up to the center, to the Presidential Palace. Basayev came up from the south, from Chernorechye.

The hardened Abkhaz Battalion floated between districts of the city to meet the fight wherever they were needed. They engaged Russia's 131st Independent Motorized Infantry Brigade in a battle for Grozny's railroad station. Russian tanks penetrated without resistance to the railroad station square. Some crews crawled out of the hatches and began looking around. Others jumped off and went into the train station. The Russian commander reported that all was calm. That's when Chechen forces opened fire with Mukha grenade launchers, Shmel flamethrowers, and RPG-7s (rocket-propelled grenade launchers) armed with a modified warhead that could blow the turret off an armored tank in one hit. Chechen forces destroyed just about the entire brigade, including twenty tanks and 102 APCs. As many as one thousand Russian soldiers died. On 29 December, Basayev scored a second victory at Khankala, driving Russian forces from the airbase.

In his book *ya byl na etoi voine (Grozny 1995) (I Was in That War (Grozny 1995))*, Vyacheslav Mironov tells about the Chechen atrocities in the early days of the war, including the nailing of a Russian soldier to a rooftop cross and the mutilation of his body. "A dead soldier's body was up there just like Jesus," he writes, "his own penis cut off and stuffed in his mouth."

A version of this scene is portrayed in the 1997 Russian film *chistilishche (Purgatory)*. After a Russian soldier loses both his legs in an attack on his tank, Chechen fighters drag him out alive and throw him onto a large wooden cross. His wrists and hands are nailed to the cross with large U-shaped spikes driven in by a gun butt. He is then propped up in a second-story window in clear view of Russian soldiers below. With life seeping from his body, a faint smile creeps across his face as he sees his comrades begin a counterassault on the Chechen position.

Many Russian soldiers had little guilt about executing Chechen prisoners of war after seeing things like this.

In late December, Russia bombarded Grozny. Then on 17 and 18 January, Russian SU-25 aircraft bombed the Presidential Palace, killing many fighters. Maskhadov abandoned the Presidential Palace on 18 January. Dudayev had long since moved his headquarters to Shali, south of Grozny. On 7 February, Basayev and his fighters as well as Gelayev and his spetnaz also left the city and headed for the mountains. The fighting and Russian bombardment left Grozny in ruins. Already, twenty-seven thousand people had died.

With such overwhelming Russian military superiority, it was clear that Chechnya would have to fight a guerrilla war. Ichkeria would need help in building its guerrilla war fighting capability, so Basayev sent for the twenty-five-year-old Arab veteran of the Afghan-Soviet war that he had met earlier in Azerbaijan. He brought Saudi-born Khattab and his team of Afghan veterans to Chechnya as "consultants" to teach Chechens how to fight using the same guerrilla tactics that proved so successful against Soviet forces in Afghanistan in the 1980s. Basayev later recalled, "We have benefited from studying the Afghan Jihad, particularly from Commanders Khattab, Yaqub al-Ghamibi and his deputy Abu Waleed al-Ghamibi, Abu Jafar al-Yemeni, Hakim al-Madani, and Abu Bakr Aqeedah." All except Abu Waleed have been killed.

Although Russia expected early Chechen capitulation in the war, it didn't materialize. It took Russia until early June 1995 to bring the last serious stronghold of resistance, the village of Shatoi, under control. In the meantime, small, highly mobile armed groups trained by Khattab and fellow Arab fighters began to fight from mountain enclaves and engaged in a guerrilla war in the south and southeast of Chechnya.

THE FIRST SUICIDE MISSION TO MOSCOW

The Chechen leadership was desperate in the summer of 1995. Earlier, Dudayev and Basayev had threatened to take the war to the heart of Russia, Dudayev saying that he would make Russian cities "disaster zones." Now, Basayev decided to personally do it.

Basayev says the decision to go into Russia was made for two reasons: First, "We could no longer fight [the Russians] normally. They were shelling our villages. They were destroying our houses with six-ton bombs." Second, "We needed to show the people in Russia that this war is very close to them too; we wanted them to see what blood looks like, and how it is when people are dying. We wanted them to understand it, to wake up."

On 3 June 1995, two of those six-ton bombs had hit Basayev's uncle's house, killing eleven members of his family. Six children aged five months to twelve years, four women, and Basayev's uncle died. Basayev's sister, Zinaida, also died in the attack. So did Basayev's wife and child. Another twelve relatives were injured. Alla Dudayeva, Dzokhar Dudayev's wife, who is still alive and lives in Baku, recalls that her house was right next to Basayev's and nothing was left of either house when Russian bombs hit them. Basayev vowed after these events to kill every Russian pilot he captured—and he has.

In the summer of 1995, Basayev came up with a crazy plan to go all the way to Moscow and "either die or stop the war." He recalls, "We wanted to get to Moscow, to the Kremlin." But the Russians say that Moscow was not his objective at all—it was Budennovsk, a Russian city of about one hundred thousand people located 137 miles northwest of Grozny. They say that Basayev sent men ahead and the Chechen mafia in Budennovsk prepared everything well in advance for him. Whatever the destination, President Dudayev and Chief of Staff Aslan Maskhadov later denied that they knew about the suicide mission, Dudayev condemning the raid as discrediting the "national liberation struggle of the Chechen people."

Basayev meticulously planned everything, keeping the final destination secret from almost everybody. He would conceal 142 of his best fighters (Chechens and Arabs) in three large Russian KamAZ trucks that would enter Russia under the pretext of transporting "spoils of war" back to Russia. Two men disguised as Russian police sergeants would occupy a dummy police car to escort the trucks. Basayev shaved off their beards, cut the hair on top of their heads, and dressed them in Russian police uniforms to make them look the part. Basayev himself sat in the cab of the first truck. The budget for the whole operation was $25,000; most of it ($15,000) was spent on buying the trucks and the car. He paid out another $8,000 to $9,000 in bribes at the border and to police along the road in Russia.

"Operation Jihad" began on 14 June. Basayev bribed Russian border guards to ignore the cargo in his trucks and crossed the border into the Stavropol district of Russia. But on the southern outskirts of Budennovsk, a policeman spotted the unusual convoy and reported back to police headquarters in the city. He was joined by other policemen who were ordered to stop the convoy. They did so and were told that the trucks were carrying the bodies of dead Russian soldiers back home for burial. However, Basayev refused to show them the bodies. The convoy was escorted back to police headquarters in Budennovsk. It arrived around noontime.

At the police station, Basayev's men bolted from the trucks, killed all the policemen in sight, and shot up police headquarters. They then fanned out across town.

Basayev raised the green Chechen flag over Budennovsk's city hall. Elsewhere, Wolves engaged police reinforcements in street battles, catching pedestrians and civilian vehicles in the crossfire. Forty-one townspeople were killed. A squad of Basayev's men also secured the town's hospital to treat twelve wounded fighters (eight had already been killed). The former monastery with its high walls would provide the best defensive fortification in town, so Basayev headed for the hospital, gathering up hundreds of hostages on the way, marching them in a column to their destination while his captives provided a human shield.

With the hostages inside the hospital, Basayev sealed the entrances and exits with explosives. It was the biggest hostage taking (more than sixteen hundred victims) in modern history—at least until his rival, Salman Raduyev, did the same thing in Dagestan five months later. Thus began a sixteen-day ordeal that left 143 hostages dead and 415 people wounded, made a Chechen national hero out of Basayev, and compelled Russia to agree to a cease-fire in Chechnya.

From the beginning, Basayev methodically controlled everything. His demands to Russia were bold but simple: cease combat operations in Chechnya; withdrawal Russian troops; and enter into negotiations with President Dudayev.

Basayev demanded a press conference on the second day of the siege, which materialized only after he executed five hostages. At that media event, Basayev repeated his demands and talked about how his plan to go to Moscow went wrong:

We are an intelligence-diversion battalion. We are not going to seize Budennovsk; we had another goal. We wanted to go to Moscow, to go there for a little while and watch Russians bombing Moscow. Our operation failed because of the greediness of the local police officers. We just didn't have enough money to pay them off. That's why they started picking on us and escorted us back to GUVD [police headquarters] . . . in Budennovsk . . . I only had $100 left in my pocket when we got to Budennovsk so we had to change our plans. We therefore decided to take as many hostages as possible.

Basayev said that neither Dudayev nor Maskhadov had sent him and warned, "We don't care when we die. What is important is how [we die]."

Dudayev denied that he had ordered Basayev to "initiate terrorist actions in Russia" because "such actions might discredit the Chechen people's struggle for freedom." It was suggested by some that "a group of the president's desperate comrades" carried out the act on their own. The same story was told about Raduyev's raid on Kizlyar, Dagestan, a few months later and even Movsar Barayev's siege of the Dubrovka theater in October 2002.

Shamil Basayev rejected all Russian counteroffers to settle the siege, including huge amounts of money. The Orel-Avia Company provided an airliner and the Russian Air Forces guaranteed its safe passage if Basayev would just leave Russia. His older brother, Colonel Shirvani Basayev, was even picked up by a Russian helicopter and brought to Budennovsk to help negotiate, but Shamil Basayev said that he would shoot his brother if he showed up at the hospital. When Shirvani arrived and told Shamil that he had been ordered by Maskhadov to come and talk to him, he was let in. He stayed about an hour and then came out with the bad news—Shamil would not budge.

As one Russian politician put it, "All carrot dangling was useless." No one—not his brother, not Chechen crime bosses related to Basayev, not Islamic mufti elders, not the leader of the radical Russian LDPR Party, Vladimir Zhironovsky—could sway him.

Basayev personally executed six Russian pilots found among the hostages. He threatened to kill more hostages and made human shields of the hospital patients and pregnant women from the maternity ward by standing them in the windows.

Basayev claims that the Russians told him they had rounded up two thousand local Chechens and would begin executing them if he didn't surrender. But as far as he was concerned, the Russians could shoot all Chechens living in Russia in front of his eyes and he would "not even flinch." In his opinion, they were all traitors anyway because real Chechens must live in Chechnya and fight.

Basayev repeated his demands for two more days. On the fourth day, the Russian minister of defense decided it was time to undertake a "special operation" to rescue the hostages. Yevgenny Loginov, a Russian Duma deputy, said that just before the assault, fifty-four bodies were brought out of the hospital, all shot through the head.

At dawn and again at 2 p.m. on Saturday, 17 June, Russian forces stormed the building. They took the first floor, but more than one hundred hostages were killed in the assault. There were another forty-three armed casualties on both sides, but Basayev moved to the third floor and in the end held the building. A hundred or more hostages, the wounded, women, and children, were released.

On the fifth day of the crisis, Russia conceded not only to negotiate with Basayev, but to do it publicly, live on television. I remember watching the Russian prime minister, Viktor Chernomirdin, pleading with Basayev by telephone not to harm the hostages. Chernomirdin agreed to all of Basayev's demands, including safe passage for Basayev and his battalion back to Chechnya, for the simultaneous release of the hostages. "Moscow is on its knees," the newspaper *Argumenty i Fakty* wrote.

The escape from Budennovsk was no less strange than the televised telephone negotiations. Basayev took 139 volunteer hostages (nine Russian Duma deputies, sixteen journalists who had come to cover the story, and 114 local male residents) back with him to Chechnya in a convoy of six buses and a refrigerated truck for the bodies of his men.

The convoy, shadowed by Mi-24 armed helicopters, left Budennovsk on 19 June in the late afternoon. The Russian authorities changed the route several times, the convoy ending up in the suburbs of Stavropol, Russia, overnight, then crossing into Khasavyurt, Dagestan, the next morning, and staying there almost the entire day before finally entering Chechnya late in the evening. Once Basayev reached the village of Zondak, he freed the hostages as promised and buried his dead.

Basayev had won. He had succeeded in his mission to stop the war and negotiate the start of peace talks. Basayev got a jubilant hero's welcome and a hero's medal when he arrived home.

"You can think what you want of the event [Budennovsk], but for the Chechen people this was a heroic act which put the lives of those who tried to stop the war at extreme risk. . . . We consider this an act of heroism; it [Budennovsk] was a valuable prize and we admire and have deep respect for those who died to save our people," Movladi Udugov, Chechnya's propagandist, later told Svoboda Radio.

Chechnya's new national hero vowed that if Russia failed to follow through on its end of the bargain he would use weapons of mass destruction on Moscow. He told Russian leaders that he had radioactive substances and containers with deadly bacteria at his disposal, and he would blow them up on the streets of Moscow if necessary. This was no idle threat.

Only a few of Basayev's Budennovsk fighters have been caught and prosecuted; all are Chechen, including one woman, Raisa Dundayeva. Most of the participants have died in subsequent fighting with Russia. Askhab Mutalibov was apprehended in Chechnya in 2002 and went on trial in March 2003. Another terrorist, Ise Mafusayev, was caught in October 2003.

At the end of July 1995, Russia and Chechnya signed a peace agreement providing for Russian troop withdrawal and the disarming of Chechen fighters. But sporadic clashes continued anyway, and, in October, in Grozny, somebody tried to assassinate MVD Lieutenant General Anatoly Romanov, the Russian peace negotiator, in a bomb attack. They didn't kill him, but they did leave him in a coma. Russia consequently suspended participation in post-Budennovsk negotiations with Dudayev, who in turn suspended the military accord with Russia.

ENTER ARAB FIGHTERS AND A DIRTY BOMB

Basayev introduced two new elements into the war with Russia: foreign fighters and nuclear terrorism.

Khattab and his men trained fighters for Chechen field commanders. But the brand new Islamic Regiment made up of thirty-nine fighters of various nationalities as well as a few TJ members that Basayev had personally invited to Chechnya—and led by Khattab—also struck for the first time in October 1995. The attack took place in Basayev's home district and killed twenty-five to thirty Russian soldiers. Basayev made no attempt to keep secret the fact that foreign Islamic fighters were responsible for the ambush of the Russian convoy. On the contrary, the attack was filmed and shown on television in Chechnya and Afghanistan. Basayev wanted Russia to know that Chechnya had international Islamic allies who were to be feared.

Dudayev had already warned Russia about this but exaggerated the threat so much that it had not been taken seriously. In an *Izvestiya* interview in December 1994, he claimed, "In every village and every district, independent Islamic battalions have been organized. Islamists have poured in from all corners of the earth—instructors and fighters. And when our Chief of Staff [Maskhadov] instructs them to take up a defensive position in this or that sector, they reply, 'We are God's soldiers now, not yours. We will exact revenge and go further, and you and your democracy can go play with the Russians.'"

A month after Khattab's attack, Basayev decided to remind the Kremlin about his promise to use nuclear terrorism to stop the war. He told Gennady Zhavorokov, a journalist with *Obshchaya Gazeta*, that he had a nuclear bomb that he was prepared to set it off in Moscow. "But the information was absolutely impossible to verify, so I didn't publish it," Zhavorokov recalls.

In October 1995, Russian Interior Minister General Anatoly Kulikov warned that Basayev might have taken radioactive isotopes from the Budennovsk hospital back to Chechnya. But it's more likely that Basayev got them closer to home.

There is a big radioactive waste dump in Chechnya called Radon. It was established in 1965 to handle industrial and medical waste for all of the North Caucasus and is located northeast of the village of Tolstoy-Yurt. At one time, Radon contained 906 cubic meters of cobalt-60, beryllium, radium-226, cesium-137, thorium, and other radioactive waste. Since the beginning of the 1994 war, the site has been left largely unguarded. In 1996, a Russian government commission found that nearly half of the material there had been stolen. The culprits were either underpaid Russian soldiers who wanted to sell what they took on the black market, other looters, or terrorists.

Wherever he got it, Basayev stole a large canister of cesium-137—a powdered or pellet-shaped highly radioactive isotope that emits lethal gamma radiation material—to show that he could easily make a dirty bomb and detonate it in Moscow. Basayev smuggled the cesium into Moscow and hid it in busy Izmailovsky Park in November 1995. He then publicly threatened to turn the city into a radioactive eternal desert. He did not detonate the cesium. Nevertheless, the first act of nuclear terrorism in history that was broadcast live by Russia's NTV created fear of contamination and radiation sickness in the area around Izmailovsky Park.

President Yeltsin conceded in February 1996 that maybe he had made a mistake about the war in Chechnya. He halted military action and offered to open peace talks again. Yet another agreement was struck to withdraw Russian troops, but on 7 March Basayev's fighters forcibly took back Grozny for three days. Fifteen hundred fighters, many of whom had earlier slipped into Grozny and still others dressed as Russian policemen who came in on the morning train from Gudermes, stormed the city. They took control of most of Grozny, not with the objective of holding it, but to humiliate Russian forces and prove that neither Russia nor the pro-Moscow Chechen government was truly in control of the city as was being proclaimed. After three days, they ran low on ammunition and left.

The Russian news service RIA Novosti reported that a few days earlier Basayev and his men had surrounded the village of Bamut and then set out to take the military airport at Khankala on the outskirts of Grozny with the objective of capturing Pavel Grachev, the Russian minister of defense, who had just arrived.

In April, Chechnya punished Russian troops with another special Arab attack. This time, Khattab's target was a withdrawing Russian convoy near the town of Yaryshmardy. The attack was brutal. Khattab said that he killed two hundred Russian soldiers (Russia says seventy), including twenty-six senior officers in the ambush. He was filmed cutting off the heads of Russian soldiers and holding his "trophies" up for the world to see. Victories like this inspired Islamic organizations in Ethiopia, Somalia, and Sudan to send fighters to Chechnya in 1996 and convinced Russia to take Dudayev's earlier warning about foreign Islamic mujahideen seriously.

Was it the devastating ambush at Yaryshmardy that prompted the Russian missile strike on the person of President Dudayev on 21 April 1996? Honing in on the signal from Dudayev's satellite phone, a Russian reconnaissance aircraft relayed Dudayev's location in Gheki-Chu, Chechnya, to a Russian ground-attack aircraft equipped with laser and television guided missiles. A photo of Dudayev taken from the warhead moments before it struck was published in the 18 May 1996 issue of the Russian newspaper *Argumenty i Fakty.*

Ordinary Chechens could not believe that President Dudayev had died this way or that he was even dead. There was no body and no grave, just a big hole in the ground. Some people speculated that he had gone into hiding; others believed that there had been a "palace coup."

Basayev publicly swore on the Koran that Dudayev had been killed by a Russian missile. He interrupted Chechen television broadcasts to announce the president's death and proclaim a three-day mourning period. In accordance with Ichkeria's constitution, playwright, nationalist, and acting Vice President Zelimkhan Yandarbiyev would become acting president. He was no warrior and had little real authority, but in a show of solidarity and constitutional continuity, Basayev and the other field commanders rallied behind Yandarbiyev, who officially became acting president on 24 April.

At the end of April, Chechen field commanders "elected" Basayev "commander" of the Chechen armed forces in place of Maskhadov. The following month brought another truce with Russia and round three of negotiations, but Basayev did not participate because Yeltsin objected. This cease-fire agreement lowered the intensity of fighting for a while, but, immediately after Yeltsin's presidential election victory, the Russian Army unleashed a fresh offensive. At the end of June 1996, Russian forces began another partial withdrawal, but fighting continued in some regions and peace negotiations stalled again. The next month, Russian forces began a new assault on villages suspected of harboring Chechen guerrillas.

THE "GROZNY OFFENSIVE"

Basayev spent June in Abkhazia resting up. The following month, he began to work on something big. On Tuesday, 6 August, it became clear what it was. The famous "Grozny Offensive" took place that day.

Basayev's combined forces (he says eleven thousand fighters but Russian estimates are much lower), including Khattab's foreign fighters and Gelayev's spetnaz forces, stormed the large Russian military garrison in Grozny in a three-pronged attack. Within hours, they took the city's key districts, seized the Russian posts and base, and advanced on the government compound in the center. Then Basayev lured several thousand Russian troops into Grozny's center, encircled them, and bombarded the trapped soldiers with grenades, mortars, and automatic weapons fire.

The smell of battle lingered in the air for days as the corpses of teenage Russian soldiers cluttered the streets. The few major buildings that had been renovated between 1995 and 1996—the Ministry of the Interior, the main government building, and the police station—were all again gutted.

Basayev took a bullet to the leg in fighting for the police station. When it was all over, he claimed his men had killed two thousand soldiers in the battle for the city while only thirty-four mujahideen gave their lives. But the Russian command said it lost only three hundred soldiers. Russian casualties were in reality somewhere in between Basayev's estimate and the official Russian count, and Chechen losses were certainly more than thirty-four. Three Russian aircraft were also shot down. "Two of them I shot down personally," Basayev says.

The ferocity of Basayev's men on that day astonished Russia. Indeed, Alekhandr Lebed, the retired Air Forces general whom Yeltsin appointed to negotiate a settlement of the war, publicly acknowledged the military discipline and courage of Basayev's fighters.

"I am glad that Lebed thinks highly of our skills," Basayev commented to a journalist in Grozny, but as for the Russian soldiers, "They refuse even to come out of their bases and fight. That is the only reason Russia is even talking about a cease-fire. Even they won't let thousands of soldiers die of hunger.

"As for us," Basayev jokingly added, "we will not go hungry because we can always eat the Russian soldiers if we have to."

When asked if he thought that General Lebed could finally bring the war to an end, Basayev replied, "I don't believe in the words of any Russian. I believe it was Winston Churchill who said an agreement with Russia isn't worth the paper it was written on. So agreements mean little to me."

The first war officially ended with the cease-fire agreement signed at Khasavyurt, Dagestan, on 31 August 1996. The official death count for Russian troops in the first war was fifty-five hundred, but some say that as many as fourteen thousand died. Those troops remaining in Chechnya were to be withdrawn, and the political status of Chechnya was to be decided in negotiations by 31 December 2001. On 23 November 1996, President Yeltsin ordered the last Russian troops withdrawn from Chechnya.

A TERRORIST TURNS RELUCTANT POLITICIAN

In 1995, Basayev told the Russian newspaper *Komsomolskaya Pravda* that he had no intention of running for political office in any future election in Chechnya because he did not consider himself a politician. "What kind of politician am I?" he asked.

Yet Basayev did have some good ideas about how a democratic election should be run. He said that any citizen of the republic has the right to participate in elections irrespective of his views or status, but, he cautioned, conditions must be created for voters to express their will without coercion. One of those conditions was that Russian troops must withdraw and Chechen detachments must lay down their arms. A second condition was that the election itself be monitored by the United Nations and the Organization for Security and Cooperation in Europe (OSCE). The main thing, he said, is that the "men of war must not interfere."

A year later, Basayev had a change of heart about running for political office. In early December 1996, as required by Chechen election law, the thirty-one-year-old Basayev resigned as commander of the Chechen armed forces to seek the presidency. This time, he had a good shot at getting elected. The Hero of Budennovsk was well known, and his military prowess was legendary even outside Chechnya—the Ukrainian Academy of Military Sciences had invited him to deliver a series of lectures on guerrilla warfare, but he declined. Basayev easily collected the ten thousand signatures needed to enter the race.

The campaigning got started on 27 December. Basayev faced sixteen opponents. Acting President Zelimkhan Yandarbiyev—who four days before the election officially changed the name of Grozny to Dzokhar Ghala (Dzokhar City) in hopes of garnering some extra votes from Dudayev supporters—was one; the forty-five-year-old prime minister and head of the coalition government, Aslan Maskhadov, was another; and deputy prime minister and renowned propagandist Movladi Udugov was a third. They were the most serious contenders.

The fact that Yandarbiyev was acting president didn't give him any advantage. He called a special meeting at his house to get the top five candidates to rally around "one candidate" (himself), but Maskhadov and the others rejected the idea.

All the campaigns turned out to be disappointingly dull and very much alike. Basayev appeared on television and talked about building a peaceful way of life, about creating an Islamic state and promoting Islam as the ultimate guarantor of the poor. The war hero promised that under his Islamic presidency, each man would get a privatization voucher worth $10,000. Basayev would also build a children's Disneyland-style park in the center of Grozny.

Basayev pledged law and order and a redistribution of national wealth too. He campaigned on a platform of a Chechnya independent from the Russian Federation, but in doing so tried to appeal to the radical vote. This contrasted to Aslan Maskhadov, who was politically moderate and low-key in his election campaign.

Maskhadov became the target of Basayev's negative campaign speeches, which accused him of being too willing to talk to Russia and someone who would risk Chechnya's independence if elected. By comparison, Basayev called many of his other rivals criminals. Maskhadov countered by accusing Basayev of conducting a slanderous and dirty campaign.

Basayev hammered away at the theme of independence. Chechnya had been independent since 1991, and, for him, it wasn't a negotiable topic with Russia. But surprisingly, Basayev said that in other areas—in the economic, social, and even military spheres—he would be willing to work with Moscow: "It is beneficial for both Russia and Chechnya to have a common economic and energy sphere, a unified monetary system, and a unified defense system."

Basayev summed up the two themes of his campaign in a way that everyone in Chechnya easily understood: "We want to live in the same house [apartment building] as the Russians [i.e., share a common economy, defense, etc.], but we want our own apartment [as opposed to living in a communal apartment in which families have their own rooms but have to share a kitchen and a bath, i.e., be subjugated to the Russian Federation]." We need our "political freedom" too, he told voters. His words echoed an earlier Dudayev, who argued that Chechnya should not be part of the RSFSR but an equal republic within the Soviet Union and later the Commonwealth of Independent States that was formed following the dissolution of the USSR in December 1991.

Although Movladi Udugov, the propaganda expert, had the best campaign slogans, on election day, it really boiled down to a race between Maskhadov and Basayev. A half million votes were cast in the 1997 election. The Organization for Security and Cooperation in Europe (OSCE) monitored the polls with observers. Except for a few minor glitches, foreign observers all agreed: the elections were free and fair. When the ballots were counted on 28 January 1997, 64.8 percent of the votes went to Aslan Maskhadov. Basayev came in second with 23.5 percent.

Reacting to Maskhadov's win, Basayev told reporters that he would neither oppose nor support Maskhadov as president and that any support would depend on the president's future policies. Basayev flat-out said, though, that he could not work with Maskhadov's aides, whom he described as crooks.

At his election victory news conference, President-elect Maskhadov pledged to work with his former allies. He implored Basayev to "come and be my comrade again" and, on 30 January, asked Basayev to join him as "first deputy prime minister."

What could Maskhadov have been thinking? Maybe the new president wanted to blur the image that the Kremlin had of him as being eager to negotiate. That same month, Maskhadov complained about this very perception to *Argumenty i Fakty*. Maskhadov probably also hoped that Basayev's appointment would demonstrate to Moscow that the situation in Chechnya was really under his control. Maybe Maskhadov also hoped that Basayev's appointment would help eliminate the radical opposition to the peace process like that coming from field commander Salman Raduyev.

Basayev's appointment put Moscow in a predicament. The Kremlin ultimately came to terms with the fact that Basayev had taken an impressive percentage of the Chechen vote, but he was still a terrorist. Russia's negotiators did not want to sit across the table from him. The assassination attempt on Basayev in the Oktyabrsky district of Grozny in March may have been an operation by Russian special services to resolve the Kremlin's dilemma. On the other hand, the secretary of the Kremlin's Security Council suggested that maybe Basayev could be granted amnesty along with many others who had fought Russian forces during the war. But in April, Basayev was told by the Russian prosecutor-general that the amnesty granted to others did not apply to him.

The new Chechen president asked Basayev to submit a list of his cabinet choices. When Maskhadov finally announced the new cabinet, it was clear that a lot of seats had gone to prominent war veteran field commanders who, together with Basayev, formed a powerful bloc. It didn't surprise anyone that just a day after the announcement, Maskhadov rejected all the Russian draft peace treaty agreements and declared that the negotiations with Russia had reached a deadlock.

Basayev never let up on criticism of the Kremlin. Sounding like Raduyev, in February 1997, he said that the war with Russia will continue until Russia formally recognizes Chechen independence. He promised Maskhadov too that if the president did anything on his own to jeopardize Chechnya's independence, he would go into opposition. As each day passed, Basayev sounded more and more like Salman Raduyev.

In the meantime, Basayev's men were redeployed to his home district with about three hundred of them staying in Grozny. Basayev officially set up a special unit with a mission to assist governmental structures in maintaining law and order. On the contrary, they fought with them more than they helped. His units were armed with five APCs, six tanks, two self-propelled artillery systems, and several combat vehicles.

That summer, Basayev took a leave of absence for health reasons—he suffers from sugar diabetes. He resumed his government responsibilities only in the fall, and, in November 1997, tackled the hard issues of being a politician with noticeable discomfort.

Basayev said he was determined to pull Chechnya up out of its economic bankruptcy and help the needy. In a cabinet meeting with his ministers, he demanded that the chairman of the National Bank and the head of the Tax Inspectorate come clean about which government ministries and government departments were not paying into the Chechen National Bank. He threatened to fire the men in charge if they did not cooperate. Basayev calculated that if all government ministries and departments remit the 50 percent of their intake to the National Bank each month as required by law, then 150 billion rubles could be collected every month instead of the meager twenty billion being collected.

Basayev's proposed "extraordinary measures" to solve pressing social issues and establish "social justice" were interesting. He wanted to impose a 2 percent property tax on the well off, starting with himself and the cabinet. He assessed his own personal wealth at $600,000—which included personal property worth $300,000, a house costing $200,000, and a few imported cars at $100,000. He didn't say anything, though, about the oil refinery that he operated in Benoi and the $2 million that he made from it that year.

Basayev's unusual tax proposal never got very far, though. Other matters, namely the idea of reuniting Chechnya and Dagestan, began to occupy his mind and his time. That idea soon became an obsession.

▌▌

"THE BLACK ARAB" AND THE WAHHABI FACTOR

> When I saw [on television] groups of Chechens wearing head-bands with "La ilaha illalah..." ["There is no god but Allah and Muhammad is His messenger"] written on them, and shouting takbeers ["Allahu Akbar"], I decided that there was a jihad [holy war] going on in Chechnya and I must go there.
>
> Khattab, 1999

For years, Russia has loudly proclaimed that fanatical Arab foreigners with ties to extremist Islamic organizations, Afghanistan, and even Osama bin Laden are responsible for horrific acts of terror in Chechnya and Russia. One of those accused was Khattab, the Arab Islamic warrior whom Basayev brought to Chechnya in February 1995 to help fight Russia.

Little is known about Khattab in the West, but the Russians knew him well because they fought him for fourteen years in many different countries. In fact, this one-handed Arab who took no prisoners, liked to behead and display his prize, cut off noses and ears, took the scalps, and bullet riddled the bodies of dead soldiers was the Russian Army's worst nightmare until Russian secret services killed him in March 2002. By that time, he had already taken the lives of thousands of Soviet and Russian Army soldiers and used hexogen bombs to mercilessly kill sleeping Russian civilians in the name of his and Basayev's holy war.

EMBODYING THE ISLAMIC WARRIOR PERSONA

Samir bin Salekh al-Suweilem—alias al-Khattab, Ibn-ul-Khattab, Amir Khattab, one-handed Akhmed, The Black Arab, field commander Khattab, and the Lion of Chechnya—was born into a large, wealthy, and educated family in Avar, a northern border city in Saudi Arabia in 1969. Khattab claimed that his mother was from the Caucasus.

Khattab was no lion in appearance. He was slightly built and had a round face with a large nose and flaring nostrils, mustache, wide black beard, and a swarthy complexion. He had long wavy hair down to his chest and was missing two fingers and parts of fingers from his right hand. He walked with a limp.

Khattab was very religious. Like Osama bin Laden, Khattab was a radical Muslim and a warrior of the Afghan brand of Wahhabism, an extreme ideology-orthodoxy based on the fundamentalist Sunni Islamic movement founded by Abd al-Wahhab in eighteenth-century Arabia.

Strict Wahhabis advocate a literal interpretation of the Koran, which forbids all practices not sanctioned by the Koran and views those who do not practice their form of Islam as infidels. They reject secular authority and institutions, as well as the veneration of saints and holy places.

Wahhabis also practice a stringent form of Shariah law (a legal code of Islam based on the Koran). Under Shariah, those who steal from a fellow Muslim (the first time) will have their right hand cut off. A left foot is taken for stealing a second time. Death by stoning awaits those who commit adultery. A victim of bodily injury has the right to "punishment in kind" against the perpetrator of the crime. Capital punishment for murder is beheading, beating with stones, or execution in the same manner that the assailant killed his victim. Russian television audiences in 1998 got to witness Shariah law at work in Chechnya when relatives of a murdered husband publicly executed the man's unfaithful wife (who had stabbed him with a butcher knife) and her lover before a television camera.

KHATTAB'S REAL COMBAT MOVIES

Khattab had a distinct trademark. He filmed his bloody military operations in Russia and then put them on the Internet at azzam.com and elsewhere.

Until November 2001, you could buy your own personal copy of a Khattab video on CD-Rom from Azzam Publications for $20.00. The videos, called *Chechnya from the Ashes* and *Russian Hell in the Year 2000,* show live footage of Chechen suicide truck bombings of Russian military barracks in the Chechen towns of Argun and Gudermes in July 2000. The films also have combat footage of other mujahideen operations, ambushes, and remote-controlled mine bombings of Russian military vehicles in 2000.

A third clip shows the bodies of nine OMON (Russian special forces police) personnel after Khattab executed them because Russia refused to hand over Colonel Yuri Budanov for raping and murdering Elza (Kheda) Kungayeva, an eighteen-year-old Chechen girl. On 6 March 2000, Colonel Budanov took the girl from her home in the village of Tangi-Chu, Chechnya, back to his camp. There, Colonel Budanov cut her dress off, raped, and then killed her. Khattab claimed Budanov drove a tank over her, but photographs of her body do not show that. The Russian prosecutor says she was strangled. Still standing in his underwear, Budanov summoned his soldiers to dispose of her body in the woods.

Basayev says that Khattab was correct in executing the OMON soldiers because it was done "within the bounds of Islamic Shariah [law] after they were sentenced to death according to the best interests of the jihad." Another eight were beheaded "so that the Budanov case would get brought to the Russian court and Budanov would be arrested."

According to the Azzam Internet advertisement, the video containing the execution of the OMON troops was produced by the Islamic Army of the Caucasus, and "any enquiries regarding the content of this CD should be directed to Field Commander Basayev, Field Commander Khattab, or their spokesman Movladi Udugov."

Khattab filmed his bloodiest operations for a number of reasons. He often said it was to counter Russian propaganda that distorts reporting on casualties. "Allah orders us to fight the disbelievers as they fight us. They fight us with media and propaganda, so we should also fight them with our media," he said.

However, the videos also served a greater purpose: to attract donations and financing from outside Chechnya with sales or by showing potential Islamic financiers what they are buying for their money. Khattab was the best fund raiser of all the field commanders.

Another reason Khattab filmed his military operations was to immortalize himself. He carefully cultivated his own personality cult, fueled by his own self-promotion; by the stories his supporters outside Chechnya told about his bravery and threshold for pain as a teenage fighter in Afghanistan; and by his own ruthlessness, daring, and genuine success against Russian forces.

Part of this legend arises from one popular story about a teenage Khattab with long hair and a beard who arrived at the mujahideen training camp near Jalalabad, Pakistan, in 1987. "Immediately, he went to the commander of the training camp and started pleading with him to let him go to the front line." Khattab soon became "known for his refusal to duck from oncoming fire and his refusal to show pain after an injury." Once, shot in the stomach by an armor-piercing bullet, he pretended that it was nothing serious and refused to go to the field hospital. Instead, he walked into the room where fighters had gathered and sat down. "Khattab was unusually quiet, so the brothers sensed that something must be wrong, even though he did not even flinch once nor show any signs of pain. We asked him if he had been hurt; he replied that on the front, he had received a light injury but it was nothing serious. We saw that his clothes were soaked in blood and he was bleeding heavily. We then called for a vehicle and rushed him to the nearest field hospital, during which he was complaining all the time that the injury was light and nothing serious."

Later on, Khattab lost two fingers from his right hand while throwing a homemade grenade. Fellow mujahideen tried to persuade him to go for medical attention, "but Khattab refused, insisting that putting some honey on the wound and bandaging it will do the job." After that, he always wore a specially fitted black leather glove on this hand.

SLAYING ARMED RUSSIAN INFIDELS— A RELIGIOUS CALLING

When asked by a reporter why he went to Chechnya in 1995, Khattab replied, "When I saw [on Afghan television] groups of Chechens wearing headbands with 'La ilaha illalah . . .' ["There is no god but Allah and Muhammad is His messenger"] written on them, and shouting takbeers ["Allahu Akbar"], I decided that there was a jihad going on in Chechnya and I must go there."

By 1995, Khattab had already been at war with the Russians for eight years in three countries. In 1987, he had been given the choice to study at a school in the United States. He followed the call of the jihad to Afghanistan instead. He first trained at a training camp in Pakistan run by Sheikh and Doctor Abdullah Azzam, the spiritual guide of Osama bin Laden and head of the Azzam organization until his assassination in 1989. At Azzam's camp, Khattab received military, physical, and religious training. He then went to fight the Soviets and the pro-Soviet regime in Kabul.

Over the next six years, Khattab fought in the Afghan jihad until victory over the pro-Soviet Kabul regime. He also fought alongside Osama bin Laden in northern Afghanistan.

In 1992, hundreds of mujahideen belonging to the "Afghan Alumni" were left without a war to fight. The Israeli International Policy Institute for Counter-Terrorism divides the Alumni into four groups. Some became leaders of radical Islamic organizations in their own countries. Others became founders of new terrorist organizations like Osama bin Laden's al Qaeda. Still others set up their own independent terrorist cells. A fourth group became leaders and participants in the struggle of Islamic populations in places like Azerbaijan, Bosnia, Chechnya, Kashmir, Kosovo, and Tajikistan. Khattab belongs to this group.

The government of Azerbaijan appealed to Afghanistan in 1992 to send seasoned Afghan Alumni fighters to help the Muslim Azeri forces fight the Christian Armenians for control of the Nagorno-Karabakh region. The Afghans sent one thousand fighters. Khattab went too. It was in Azerbaijan that he first met Shamil Basayev.

Next, Khattab moved to Tajikistan. Before 1994, the Russian government probably had never heard of Khattab. But he got their attention in the spring of that year. Commanding a group of seven Arabs as part of an Afghan-Tajik opposition detachment of twenty men, he brutally attacked Russian Outpost Number Twelve of the Panj Border Guard unit. Khattab's group completely destroyed the outpost and killed all the Russian border guards.

When Tajik opposition forces agreed to open peace negotiations with the Russians, Khattab personally objected and was asked to leave Tajikistan. He returned to Afghanistan but didn't stay long. Chechnya presented the twenty-five-year-old Islamic warrior with new opportunities to fight the Russian "infidels." Khattab and his team of eight loyal Arab veteran mujahideen arrived in Chechnya as paid "consultants" in February 1995.

Khattab immediately went to work training green Chechen recruits in guerrilla warfare. The Arabs that he brought with him formed his core of instructors. He trained fighters for the Chechen field commanders, and his graduates joined elite special operations units run by Basayev, Salman Raduyev, Arbi Barayev, and others.

Khattab wanted to fight too, so he sent for more Afghan Alumni from Pakistan, Bosnia, and elsewhere and built his own elite Islamist assault/saboteur unit with newly arriving Alumni, TJ fighters that Basayev invited, and some of his best Wahhabi Dagestani training camp graduates. This unit became known as the Islamic Regiment. Commanded by Khattab—the "amir [commander] of the foreign mujahideen in Chechnya"—the ethnically mixed Islamic Regiment scored several devastating attacks against Russian military forces, earning Khattab the nickname "Lion of Chechnya."

The Islamic Regiment struck in October 1995 in the first military operation carried out by Islamic foreign fighters in Chechnya. The battlefield was a mountainous road passing through Basayev's home Vedensky district and the town of Kharachoi. The operation's specific objective was to demonstrate the fighting capabilities of Arab and other foreign mujahideen in the war. The strength of the enemy numbered one hundred soldiers, one battle tank, three armored fighting vehicles, one truck, and an assortment of weapons including RPGs and machine guns.

From four o'clock in the evening until just before midnight, Khattab and thirty-nine of his fighters armed with their personal weapons and one

82 mm Hound Russian mortar, two AT-3 Fagot wire-guided missiles, three PK machine guns, and five rocket-propelled grenade launchers attacked. The tank and all three vehicles were destroyed. Forty-seven Russian soldiers were killed.

Khattab didn't have a video camera so he photographed everything. Until September 2001, a picture of the proud commander of the Islamic Regiment standing beside the burned-out Russian tank could be seen on the Azzam Web home page.

Khattab picked a bigger target for his next strike, which was from a mountain pass near the town of Yaryshmardy in April 1996. The prize was a Russian convoy of fifty trucks, APCs, fuel tankers, and a T-80 mine-clearing tank that was passing through a canyon on its way out of Chechnya. The engagement was swift. The convoy was destroyed. By Khattab's count more than two hundred Russian soldiers died, including twenty-six senior officers. Russia suspended its troop withdrawal as a result.

The Yaryshmardy operation was videotaped, broadcast over television, and widely celebrated all over Chechnya. It was even used as a recruiting film in Afghanistan. The video, once sold in the market in Grozny, shows Khattab holding up the severed heads of dead Russian soldiers and shouting "Allah Akbar!"

Decapitating the enemy dead or alive was not unique to Khattab. Arab and Chechen mujahideen commonly do it. Aukai Collins, an American mujahideen who fought in the first war in Chechnya, writes about one of these grotesque executions in his book *My Jihad*: "He [the Chechen fighter] pulled the [Russian] soldier's head back by his filthy hair and ran the knife back and forth over his neck in a ghastly sawing motion. Bright red blood squirted out as the . . . throat was severed. . . . A noise came from his throat as his last breath escaped through his gaping neck. Then the Chechen simply let the soldier's head flop onto the ground. It was tilted so far back now that it was almost completely severed."

In April, when Basayev became commander of the armed forces of the Chechen Republic of Ichkeria, he took Khattab and his foreign mujahideen under his direct command. They helped plan and execute the biggest assault ever against Russian forces, which came on the eve of President-elect Yeltin's inauguration. On Tuesday, 6 August 1996, Khattab's regiment and other fighters personally led by Basayev stormed the large Russian military garrison in Grozny. The Grozny Offensive ended the first war in Chechnya.

For his part in the offensive, Khattab was declared a national hero of Chechnya and awarded two of the highest military awards of the Republic of Ichkeria: the Order of Nations Honor and the Brave Warrior medal. He was also promoted to the rank of general.

SUSPECT IN THE RED CROSS MURDERS

After Khattab pinned on his general's star, he paid a visit to the newly opened International Committee of the Red Cross (ICRC) hospital in Novye-Atagi. Nazhmudin Takhigov, head of administration at Novye-Atagi, in sworn legal testimony, tells what happened next: "Khattab arrived in the village and demanded that the Red Cross symbols be taken down. He warned that if his orders were not carried out, he would destroy the entire hospital. Three days later he came back again with the same demands, but this time he made hospital workers paint over the crosses on the fence and remove the Red Cross flag from the water tower."

A couple of months later, tragedy befell the hospital. In the early morning hours on 17 December 1996, a group of eight men dressed in black ski masks and camouflage fatigues and carrying weapons with silencers burst into the rooms of sleeping staff workers at the hospital and shot six men and women in the head at close range. Those murdered were from New Zealand, Spain, Norway, Canada, and the Netherlands.

In opening its criminal case, the Chechen prosecutor's office immediately turned up Khattab as the prime suspect. Nazhmudin Takhigov gave sworn testimony to the prosecutor general and so did others. The official ICRC chronology of events states that Khattab and a group of his mujahideen fighters entered the compound on 17 September 1996, fifteen days after the hospital had opened, and demanded that the ICRC's symbols be removed from the hospital compound within two days or else. Khattab came back on 18 September with fifteen armed men, entered the hospital compound, and reached a compromise with the staff on reducing the number of red crosses there.

One incident after another befell the hospital following the second visit. Random shots were fired at the compound; two doctors were kidnapped; supplies were stolen; the interpreter was kidnapped; Chechen staff members were beaten and warned not to work for the "infidels"; and Shirvani Basayev came and demanded (in good Chechen tradition) that only his relatives and friends be hired to work at the hospital.

After the murders, the Chechen prosecutor's office naturally wanted to talk to Khattab and wrote a letter to Khattab's official superior, Brigadier General Magomed Khambiyev, asking that Khattab be sent to the prosecutor general's office "to give testimony as a witness" by 22 June 1998. Khattab had never showed up, nor was he ever questioned by any investigator about the case. The request was either ignored by General Khambiyev or by Khattab himself. The prosecutor general never pursued the case and charges were never filed, leaving the case officially unsolved, though suspicion rests heavily on Khattab. The motive for the murders is unclear. Did the Red Cross symbols offend Khattab? Did Khattab, or whoever killed the ICRC workers, want to drive all foreigners out of Chechnya?

KHATTAB'S TERRORIST SCHOOLS

In September 1996, Khattab and his mujahideen established the Training Center of the Armed Forces of the Chechen Republic of Ichkeria in a former Soviet youth Pioneer camp in the village of Serzhen-Yurt on the left bank of the Khulkhulau River at the base of Chechnya's southern mountains. While the training center was officially subordinated to the commander of the Chechen armed forces, in reality it operated independently as Khattab's headquarters and his personal base of Wahhabi subversive operations in Dagestan as well as an international terrorist training camp.

Until the Russian Army closed them down in late 1999, Khattab and his Arab trainers operated at least four Wahhabi military/terrorist training camps in Serzhen-Yurt and another in Alleroi, which rivaled Osama bin Laden's camps in Afghanistan. Each camp was named after its Arab commander, with the central camp being commanded by Khattab himself. Camp Abu Jafar specialized in insurgency and guerrilla operations. Camp Yakub trained specialists in heavy armaments. Camp Abu Bakar trained terrorists ("saboteurs"), and Camp Dawgat trained ideology and propaganda specialists.

Khattab's students went through a two- to six-month regime of training in groups of five people. They learned the ideology of jihad and the honor of dying for the Wahhabi cause. After that, they studied guerrilla methods; how to operate in the mountains; tactics for attacking Russian armored columns; conducting ambushes and raids; taking and holding hostages; day and night shooting; hand-to-hand combat; communication training; mine laying; and survival training. The camps had tanks, APCs, and other armored combat vehicles.

Akhmed Magomedov, a Wahhabi preacher in Moscow and a frequent visitor to Khattab's camps, nostalgically recalls that Khattab's "students were real mujahideen, the warriors of Islam. In his camps they got what they missed in secular life: a common goal, a sense of community, and the spirit of masculine camaraderie."

All kinds of Islamic separatists and terrorists—Africans, Chechens, Chinese Uyghurs, Dagestanis, Malaysians, Russians, Tajiks, fighters from the Islamic Movement of Uzbekistan, and others—flocked to Khattab's camps for training. Some of the twenty-two men charged with the 16 February 1999 bomb attacks in Tashkent, Uzbekistan, were Khattab's alumni. Nugzar Chukhua, a Georgian citizen who participated in the attempted assassination of Georgian President Eduard Shevardnadze in February 1998, was trained in Khattab's camps. Khattab also made money by training international terrorists for Hezbollah, Hamas, and Osama bin Laden.

Until recently, video clips of Khattab's training could be seen on the Russian Web site www.intelnet.org/resources/chechen_terrorists/6.html. On the eve of Basayev's and Khattab's invasion of Dagestan in 1999, there were nearly two thousand fighters being trained there.

Besides his military schools, Khattab was active in the Wahhabi religious movement in Chechnya and received Saudi money to build Wahhabi schools, construct mosques, and establish a Wahhabi publishing house. Impoverished parents were paid stipends to educate their children in Wahhabi schools. Khattab's cadets went through Wahhabi indoctrination in his Caucasus Islamic Institute funded by the Muslim Brotherhood. At one time the institute boasted more than thirty Afghan and Arab lecturers, taught Arabic language and Shariah law, and propagated the idea of a unified Islamic state of the North Caucasus.

Khattab also wrote fighting and sabotage manuals and books. One of his most popular books is called *Twelve Methods of Self Sacrifice for Fighting and Killing*, which was published in the Chechen, Avar, Kurdish, and Armenian languages.

THE CLOSED CITY AND WAHHABI SUBVERSION

Between 1997 and 1999, Urus-Martan became the center of Islamic Wahhabi extremism in Chechnya and a place where neither President Maskhadov nor his law-enforcement organs were welcome. By 1999, nearly all the leaders of the political opposition to Maskhadov, some Wahhabi and some not, also found themselves in Urus-Martan.

After the 1994–1996 war, many Dagestani Wahhabis moved with their families to Urus-Martan. In 1997, a few hundred Wahhabis from Dagestan arrived in Urus-Martan, took over a school, built a mosque, and began recruiting young people for religious and military training in Khattab's camps. By 1998, Urus-Martan had become a closed city and, for a while, home to opposition leaders Basayev and Salman Raduyev—who were not Wahhabis—and Khunkar Israpilov and Arbi Barayev—who were. Wahhabis set up their own courts and security organs. Wahhabism was also strong in the Argun river valley, in Starye-Atagi, Shatoi, Yermolovskaya, and Bamut.

Wahhabis also became influential in the Chechen government. Acting President Yandarbiyev wanted to turn Chechnya into a pure Islamic state. In 1996, he decreed that all Soviet and Russian laws were invalid in

Chechnya and abolished the secular courts. A new Shariah criminal code patterned after the Sudanese model was implemented and a Supreme Shariah Court and regional structures were created. In August 1996, Yandarbiyev invited Bagautdin Magomedov, Dagestan's Wahhabi leader, to come to Chechnya to establish Shariah law.

Many of Khattab's friends subsequently moved into key government positions, especially in the courts, security, and military units under Yandarbiyev. Islam Khalimov, a doctor of medicine and an influential Wahhabi leader, was one of them. He became minister of Shariah state security and staffed his ministry with Wahhabis. Chechnya's Muslim cleric Mufti Akhmat Kadyrov would later blame Yandarbiyev of fusing a political time bomb with such appointments.

In early 1998, Wahhabi influence within Chechnya's government organs worried many. Raduyev used this fear in February to stir up more trouble for Maskhadov, while others outright declared Wahhabis to be enemies of the people.

Lecha Khultygov, director of Maskhadov's Chechen National Security Service, warned Chechens "not to let the [Wahhabi] camel get into our place." Khultygov also stunned the Chechen parliament with his revelations about hundreds of millions of dollars that Wahhabis were smuggling into the republic so agents of Muslim countries could destabilize Dagestan and Chechnya. And Khultygov expressed anger at Khattab's growing appetite for use of Chechen military resources—Khattab wanted the tank training range at Shali for his use too. Wahhabis were also implicated in the kidnapping and slave trade business.

Maskhadov had to do something. In May, he gave in to demands that he get rid of some of his Wahhabi ministers and sacked Khalimov, precipitating a huge Wahhabi protest in Urus-Martan. This protest frightened Maskhadov enough to reinforce Grozny with hundreds of his own loyal followers. Some of them suggested raiding Wahhabi headquarters in Urus-Martan, but Maskhadov wouldn't do it out of fear of starting a civil war.

On 13 July, what started out as a fist fight between Wahhabis and secular National Guards troops commanded by field commander Sulim Yamadayev soon escalated into a full-scale war. When Brigadier General Arbi Barayev (himself a fanatic Wahhabi warrior, head of the Special Purposes Islamic Regiment, and also deputy head of the National Guards) intervened on the side of the Wahhabis, backed up by Wahhabi armed units led by Amir Abd ur-Rahman (a Saudi spiritual leader of Wahhabis in Chechnya) and Brigadier General Abdul Malik Mezhidov (chief of the Executory Process Department of the Ministry of Shariah Security), the fighting got nasty.

For four days, both sides waged war on one another. The National Guards were supported by followers of the traditional Sufi Naqshbandi and Qadiri Islamic orders from outside Gudermes. Wahhabis accuse Sufi followers of deviating from pure Islam and Sufis accuse Wahhabis of sectarianism. More than fifty people were killed, thirty of them Wahhabis. Khattab did not participate in the fighting, but Basayev did intervene to get captured National Guards soldiers released.

The conflict spilled over elsewhere. On 17 July, somebody tried to assassinate the field commander of the National Guards units fighting in Gudermes. The next day, Wahhabi Shariah prison guards revolted and turned their jail keys over to thirty-two death row convicts. Shortly after that, a Wahhabi crowd gathered outside Yandarbiyev's home village of Starye-Atagi and asked him to lead their struggle against the authorities. But villagers warned that he would be evicted from the village if he did. The prosecutor's office of Chechnya also warned him against taking any action contrary to the Chechen constitution.

Maskhadov moved quickly to counter the Wahhabis. He went on television and declared them to be extremist forces that seek to seize state power in Chechnya and start a civil war in the republic. He disbanded the Shariah department that Mezhidov headed, and Barayev's Special Purpose Islamic Regiment. All involved in supporting the Wahhabis in Gudermes were relieved of their posts and stripped of their rank. Foreigners working in Shariah courts were declared persona non-grata. Three of Khattab's Jordanian colleagues in the Supreme Shariah Court were deported.

On 25 July 1998, Chechnya's muftiate stressed the need to forbid Wahhabism in the Caucasus and urged Maskhadov to "seize the literature which teaches radical Islam" being distributed by Khattab and others. That same day, a resolution was adopted by the Sufi Congress of the Muslims of the Caucasus that demanded that "Wahhabism, a movement new to our region, be banned through legislation; that the literature they distribute be confiscated; and that Chechen youth be protected from theological propaganda which teaches radicalism."

In the end, Maskhadov officially banned Wahhabism for splitting Chechen society and bringing the republic to the edge of civil war. The ban applied to all military units, political movements, and organizations as well as newspapers and television programs. Maskhadov told parents to pull their children out of Wahhabi schools to preclude Wahhabi propaganda from poisoning their minds. And he ordered Khattab to leave the country within forty-eight hours, decreeing Khattab's training camps and institute illegal.

"We are no longer going to tolerate in our land foreign nationals who are trying to enforce their rules," said Maskhadov. "All Arabs, Tajiks, Pakistanis, and others arrived in Chechnya not to promote the law of Allah in the republic but rather to split Chechen society into different groups, movements, and parties so as to prevent the building of an independent Chechen state. They will be expelled from the territory of Chechnya. We will not have a replay of the Afghan or Tajik scenario here."

However, Chechen Vice President Vakha Arsanov, a former Chechen traffic policeman, and Shamil Basayev thought Maskhadov had gone too far and personally came to the defense of Khattab. Basayev pointed out that the "peaceful" Khattab had no part in the Gudermes uprising: "Khattab and several other Arabs who have fought together with the Chechens against Russian troops now live peacefully with their families among the Chechens and do not interfere in Chechen internal affairs. He gives military training to young fighters on assignment from the Chechen leadership but, contrary to statements by his enemies, he does not teach them Wahhabism."

Khattab himself publicly pronounced that he had never meddled in Chechen affairs. But this time Khattab did—he defied the Chechen president by ignoring his decree of expulsion. Some say that he also threatened to kill Maskhadov over the incident.

In January 1999, there was another confrontation over the Wahhabi issue, only this time it involved Basayev in Urus-Martan, a place Maskhadov now described as "living by Wahhabi rules . . . and offering sanctuary to criminals who terrorize local people and attempt to prevent the establishment of law enforcement or governmental authorities."

On 22 January, Maskhadov's new Ministry of Shariah Security sent troops to Urus-Martan to investigate the abduction, murder, and beheading of four British Granger Telecom employees. Maskhadov's troops had come to arrest field commander Arbi Barayev, the godfather of the kidnapping business in Chechnya. Fighters loyal to both Basayev and Khunkar Israpilov patrolling the outskirts of Urus-Martan stopped the Shariah Security troops and refused to let them enter the city. Heated words were exchanged and another shootout ensued, killing one person and wounding several others.

The Maskhadov government labeled the incident yet another attempted coup d'etat but couldn't do anything further about it. For his part, Basayev, speaking on Udugov's Kavkaz television station, accused Maskhadov of "fanning tensions" in Urus-Martan and surrounds and "seeking a military confrontation" with the opposition.

Four days later, Basayev called an emergency meeting of all opposition leaders and anybody else interested. The meeting took place in Starye-Atagi.

All the notables were there. Khattab came with Basayev; Yandarbiyev showed up and so did Vice President Vakha Arsanov, Khunkar Israpilov, and the now-fired Foreign Minister Movladi Udugov. Even the previously neutral Ruslan Gelayev and others who had supported President Maskhadov came. Despite the seriousness of the situation, everybody decided against the use of force to oust President Maskhadov.

THE LITTLE WAHHABI REPUBLIC

A strange mix of Wahhabi militancy, romance, and marriage, an attempted assassination, a religious treaty of military alliance, and lots of political intrigue set in motion a series of events that, in 1999, led to the destruction of whole villages in the Russian Republic of Dagestan, terrorist attacks in the Russian heartland, and a brand new war in Chechnya. Khattab was a star character in this grim drama.

Dagestan, the center for Islam and Muslim education in the North Caucasus—and part of the Russian Federation that borders Chechnya—became the stage on which the first act of this drama played out.

Although radical Islamic ideologies had gained ground in Dagestan in the 1980s, a decade and a half later the number of Dagestani Wahhabi fundamentalists still only numbered 3 or 4 percent of Islamic believers in the Russian republic. Many lived in the villages of Karamakhi, Chabanmakhi, and Kadar in what became reverently known in 1998 as the "Little Wahhabi Republic," located in the heart of Dagestan. The Wahhabis—financed from Saudi Arabia and elsewhere—were politically active and very aggressive in proselytizing their beliefs. They were also antagonistic to non-Wahhabi Muslims who lived in the villages, demanding that everybody follow Wahhabi practices. It was a place where Dagestani police by mid-1998 dared not go. Karamakhi was a key Wahhabi stronghold.

Khattab was naturally attracted to the Little Wahhabi Republic, which refused to obey Russian laws. In late 1996, he spent a good deal of time there, and, in the new year, Karamakhi became his marital home. He established "blood relations" with the Karamakhi Wahhabi community when he and sixteen of his foreign mujahideen took Karamakhi girls for wives. Khattab married into a family that had one of the largest homes in the region. Later, Khattab took a second wife, a Chechen girl from Serzhen-Yurt.

Saudi-born Abu Omar al-Saif, known today as simply Sheikh Abu Omar, also married a Karamakhi girl. He was instrumental in creating the armed Wahhabi enclaves in Karamakhi and in Chabanmakhi, and is today the Wolves' spiritual leader. In his current capacity as chairman of the

Committee of Judges and Fatwas in the Wolves' Shariah government, he issues fatwas (theological decrees) to carry out acts of terrorism and blesses all terrorist operations. A second Abu Omar al-Saif was killed in 2001.

Khattab also established strong links with Wahhabi militants in the Little Republic. He strongly influenced them, conspired with them, armed them, and brought increasing numbers of them to train in his camps in 1997.

That year, political instability plagued Dagestan. Unidentified Chechen raiding parties and even Khattab's graduating students completing their "diploma defense" ambushed government vehicles, robbed shuttle traders, rustled cattle, stole automobiles, and kidnapped Dagestani police officers and the deputy minister of agriculture.

Violent clashes between Wahhabis and traditionalist Muslims in Dagestan started in May 1997. A month later, someone tried to assassinate Khattab. He was in a jeep near Benoi, south of Grozny, when a remote-controlled land mine buried in the road blew up early. Khattab was unhurt, but he blamed Russians and vowed to retaliate. He chose a convenient target—a large concentration of Russian troops stationed on Dagestani soil.

On 21 December 1997, Khattab and three platoons comprising 115 fighters from Chechnya, Ingushetia, several Central Asian republics, and Arab countries crossed the Chechen border and entered mountainous Dagestan by buses and trucks. Some militants from Dagestani Wahhabi villages joined him. An account of the attack was published on the Azzam Web site:

> Armed only with assault rifles, machine-guns and rocket launchers, they traveled many kilometers into Russian territory until they arrived at midnight, at their target destination—the Military Base of the 136th Motorized Rifle Brigade, the largest and heavily-armed armored Russian Army brigade in Buinaksk, Dagestan. At 0200, in the early hours of Monday, 22 December 1997, the Mujahideen platoons launched a full-scale raid of the base.
>
> The Mujahideen were able to take complete control of the entire base within the first five minutes of the operation, including the 300 Russian Army vehicles. All vehicles were destroyed, including 50 brand new Russian T-72 tanks. The Mujahideen were pursued as they headed back toward the border. On the way back, they ambushed Russian Army trucks, killing all occupants of the first truck. [Chechen] reinforcements arrived and they held the Russian forces off from 0500 that morning to 1500 the next day, when they broke away.

Khattab was able to escape only because twenty fighters of Raduyev's General Dudayev's Army led by General Magomed Khambiyev heard Khattab's distress call and rushed to the rescue. In the confusion that followed, Khattab and his men managed to escape. This demonstrated the close operational coordination between Khattab and Raduyev.

Russia says that it had three dead and sixteen wounded in the fighting. Khattab's official casualty count on his side was two Arab fighters lost. Thirty-six-year-old Egyptian Commander Abu Bakr Aqeedah, one of Khattab's most senior commanders who had fought alongside him in Afghanistan and Tajikistan, was among them. Fighting with his artificial leg, he died in the first few minutes of battle. Khattab himself was slightly wounded. Khattab's deputy Abu al-Waleed and Abu Omar also participated in the raid, but they were not hurt.

In leaflets dropped at the scene, the Central Front for the Liberation of the Caucasus and Dagestan claimed responsibility for the raid and announced that it was the beginning of a jihad in Dagestan. Militant Dagestani Wahhabis applauded the attack. They also issued a "Manifesto of the Jamaat of Dagestan to the Moslem World," accusing Dagestan's secular leaders of infringing on their beliefs and waging war on them.

A month later, the leader of the Dagestani Wahhabi community called for Dagestan to secede from the Russian Federation and create a new Islamic state of Dagestan. In December, he signed a "treaty of military mutual assistance" with Salman Raduyev. The document claimed that "the Islamic Jamaat of Dagestan and Dzokhar's Army represent forces which fight for a unified Islamic state in the Caucasus and for independence from Russia."

Khattab's Buinaksk raid was a prelude to a showdown with Russia over the forceful establishment of this unified Islamic state in Dagestan. For his part, though, Raduyev, "The Lone Wolf," would fail to live up to his end of the bargain when the real showdown did come.

III

TWO PRESIDENTS AND TWO ARMIES

> He is not a military authority or leader in the least. Who will follow him? Who respects him? He is needed by Berezovsky and Moscow to discredit Chechen authority and our policies. They give him money and he keeps his gangs. They don't know the "hero" of Pervomaiskoye, Raduyev, as I know him.
>
> President Aslan Maskhadov, 1999

RADUYEV, "THE LONE WOLF" TERRORIST

President Putin once called this Chechen warlord and terrorist "the most odious of all," and he was characterized by his own people as "uncontrollable," "irrational," "unbalanced," and "a bit deranged."

Salman Raduyev, nicknamed "The Lone Wolf," was a Chechen radical's radical. He was a renegade in the Chechen leadership who also had the distinction of being the first prominent field commander caught since Russia began its antiterror campaign in Chechnya in 1999. Raduyev was defiant of all authority. He never did what President Maskhadov told him to do, and most tolerated him for too long simply because he was a member of the powerful Gordali clan (teip) and his in-law was Chechnya's first President Dzokhar Dudayev.

Aslan Maskhadov never had much respect for him as a military leader either. Maskhadov says that Raduyev fought the Russians more for money than political ideals, but that is not true. However, Raduyev did rob trains, steal teachers' salaries, take more hostages than probably anybody else in modern history, blow up train stations, and make more threats and claim responsibility for more terrorist acts against Russia than anyone.

The village of Suvorov-Yurt in the Gudermessky district of Chechnya is Salman Salmanovich Raduyev's native home. He was born there on 13 February 1967, one of five children. His family later moved to Gudermes. Although his father was assassinated in April 1996, Raduyev always said that his parents, brother, and sisters "still live in Gudermes" and that "the Russian authorities treat them well." His second wife, Lida, and two sons now live in Turkey.

Raduyev studied in Secondary School #3 in Gudermes. He claimed that he finished with the grade of distinction in 1983, then went to work on a construction brigade of the city's government trade organization until he was drafted into the Soviet Armed Forces. During military service, he joined the Communist Party of the Soviet Union and afterward became head of the district's Komsomol committee (the Young Communist League).

Since he was prone to boasting, it is difficult to tell what higher education Raduyev had. Once, he told that he was a graduate of the Bulgarian Academy of Sciences' School of Management. Another time, Raduyev told *Moskovsky Komsomolets* (January 1996) that he had a degree in economics and was close to getting his Ph.D. at the Khasavyurt, Dagestan, branch of the San Remo International University. In 1997, Raduyev told another Russian newspaper that he was a graduate of the Rostov Institute of National Economy.

What is known with certainty is that in April 1989, he became head of the Gudermes Center of Voluntary Labor Associations. After he married President Dudayev's niece in 1993, he became prefect (mayor) of Gudermes.

Like Basayev, Raduyev organized an armed gang called the Presidential Berets. Its job was to protect the newly elected President Dudayev. This group later became the Sixth Battalion "Borz" (Wolves) of Dudayev's armed forces. It was dissolved by Maskhadov in June 1997 because, according to Maskhadov, "The leadership of the regiment has taken the path of illegal actions and some of its servicemen have been charged with criminal offenses including hostage taking and other outrages."

The Russian military had its first run-in with Raduyev in September 1992. Because of the fighting going on between the Ingush and Ossetians, Russian special forces blocked the Chechen-Dagestani border only to find themselves soon facing thousands of angry people and Raduyev's small army demanding that they leave. The situation was tense. Raduyev insisted that the Russian commander withdraw from the border area a few miles. Raduyev prevailed. The standoff resolved itself peacefully the next morning when Russian troops voluntarily withdrew from the border. For his part, President Dudayev called for a holy war against Russia for such incursions into Chechnya.

Raduyev saw little action in the first year of the war with Russia. From December 1994 through February 1995, he organized the defense of the Gudermessky district and rallied Chechens along the Dagestani border. But in February, he ran off to Turkey to participate in a meeting of the military organization Tigers of the Caucasus. Dudayev immediately removed Raduyev from his command of the Eastern zone of defense. Raduyev spent the spring and summer in the mountains and only got a command back in the fall as commander of the Eastern Direction.

WOLVES HAVE COME TO YOU!

Raduyev earned the label of terrorist barely seven months after Basayev's Budennovsk raid. Up to January 1996, he was known to Russia only as a close relative of Dudayev's and the Chechen field commander who briefly drove Russian forces out of Gudermes in December 1995, executing several captured Russian soldiers in the process.

Raduyev's path to terrorism began in December 1995, when Doku Zavgayev, the former Communist party boss of Chechnya who four years earlier had been beaten up and made to resign, returned to Grozny as head of the pro-Moscow Chechen government and decided to hold national elections to get himself legitimately elected president of Chechnya. The election was scheduled for 27 December, but Raduyev went on the offensive to disrupt the election in Gudermes, which happened to be under Russian military control. In an assault on the city with hundreds of fighters, Raduyev cut Russian lines of communication, surrounded the Russian military headquarters in the center of the town, and seized the buildings in which the polling was to take place. Raduyev also put himself on the election ballot for prefect of Gudermes.

The assault turned into a ten-day battle that was Raduyev's one real military success of the 1994–1996 war. This battle represented the first heavy fighting since the July 1995 peace agreement and signaled the resumption of a full-scale war with Russia. When Russian reinforcements showed up, Raduyev beat back a Russian tank and infantry counterattack, but, when helicopter gunships struck his positions, he lost 267 fighters.

Immediately after this battle, someone tried to assassinate Raduyev for the first time. Whether it was the work of Russian special services or people carrying out a blood feud as was rumored, or both, the house in Gudermes in which his first wife and kids were staying was blown up. Raduyev was not there when the bomb went off, killing all inside.

The enraged Raduyev vowed revenge. There was also pressure building on the Chechen side to mount a spectacular attack, so Raduyev decided to act on his own and assaulted the Russian military air base at Kizlyar,

Dagestan. He may have chosen this target because the helicopter attack on Novogroznensky originated there. In fact, his intention in attacking Kizlyar may have been much broader—that is, he may have wanted to widen the war, to drag Dagestan and eventually the whole North Caucasus into the fighting. What Raduyev ended up doing was an accidental copycat of Basayev's Budennovsk raid, but on a much grander scale. It was a daring raid and involved massive hostage taking against Dudayev's direct orders.

On 9 January 1996, Raduyev, Khunkar Israpilov, and two to three hundred fighters (including many of Israpilov's men, seven of Khattab's Arab mujahideen, and eight Chechen women) calling themselves "Lone Wolf" crept quietly across the border into Dagestan to attack the Russian military air base in Kizlyar, a city of about forty thousand people located seventy miles northeast of Grozny.

"Wolves have come to you!" Raduyev called out to Russian officers as he attacked the air base. However, Raduyev hadn't done all of his homework. Either his intelligence was poor or there was a spy in his ranks because the Russians seemed to know that he was coming. There wasn't much left at the airport to attack—just two helicopters, which he destroyed. Russian forces hit him back hard, and Raduyev's wolf pack withdrew to the city of Kizlyar itself. The military raid had failed and Raduyev had to look for a way out.

That night, Wolves assaulted the four-story hospital and maternity home and other strategic buildings in the city of Kizlyar. Breaking into apartments, they rounded up people by the hundreds and herded them into the hospital and other buildings until the hostage count numbered a satisfactory two thousand or so people.

Nina Moroz, who testified against Raduyev at his trial in November 2001, said that her husband was shot by a man who broke down the door to her apartment to take her family hostage.

Horrible things went on in the hospital too. Anna Romashchenko testified at Raduyev's trial that Raduyev killed her son Pavel, a policeman who was on duty at the hospital. He was murdered, savagely mutilated, and incinerated in the hospital's furnace. Larisa Fetisova's son's body was also found badly mutilated.

Once in the hospital, Raduyev followed Basayev's Budennovsk scenario as though he had carefully rehearsed it a hundred times. Raduyev mined all four floors of the building and demanded that Russian troops withdraw from Chechnya or he would shoot hospital patients. He promised to execute fifteen hostages for every Chechen killed if Russian forces tried to storm the building.

Thousands of Muscovites watched another Chechen drama unfold on their television screens as a defiant Raduyev told viewers, "We can turn this city into hell and ashes." He had already electronically disrupted police communications so they could not tactically coordinate battles with Wolves taking place in the streets. Raduyev's snipers also controlled a bridge across the Terek River as well as two high-rise apartment buildings near the hospital. The difference between Raduyev's raid and Basayev's assault on Budennovsk was that Raduyev's real priority was to get out of Dagestan alive.

The Kremlin dispatched extra security forces, and Interior Minister General Anatoly Kulikov and FSB chief General Mikhail Barsukov personally went to Dagestan. General Barsukov was in charge. Troops surrounded the central hospital complex and, in the exchange of gunfire that followed, more police and civilians were killed. Raduyev executed a police hostage inside to stop the Russian assault.

A negotiated settlement was reached, only this time the Russians did not have to make any political concessions like in Budennovsk, just let Raduyev and his men escape. Enver Kisrev, who observed and participated in the negotiations, later told a gathering at Harvard University that a delegation led by two Avar members of the parliament arrived at the hospital with several influential Chechens in tow. The delegation said it would hold the Chechens hostage until Raduyev was persuaded to release his hostages. They also promised that for every Dagestani killed in the hospital they would kill a Chechen.

In the end, the parliamentarians volunteered to become hostages themselves on Raduyev's escape buses. Raduyev agreed to let most of the hostages go if several high-ranking Dagestani officials would become his volunteer hostages to guarantee his safety out of Dagestan. The minister of nationalities affairs, the first deputy speaker of the Dagestani parliament, and several others volunteered to go too.

Basayev later told the *New York Times*'s Carlotta Gall that he was furious with Raduyev for leaving Kizlyar without getting something political out of it. "I tried to reach Raduyev, but he only answered after the first day of the assault [on Pervomaiskoye]. When he did I shouted at him: 'If you are going to take hostages you stay there.'"

Eleven buses and two large trucks were needed to transport Raduyev, his Wolves, and their hostages back to Chechnya. But near the border, the Russian military demanded that he stop the caravan and let the hostages go. This time the military wasn't going to let the Chechens get away as they had in Budennovsk. Raduyev refused to comply, saying that the agreement in Kizlyar allowed him to take the hostages to his final destination in Chechnya. A helicopter gunship answered with warning fire on the convoy, forcing Raduyev to take cover in the nearest village. He captured another two dozen or so police upon entering the village of Pervomaiskoye.

Russia was patient—for a while. Raduyev was given five full days with repeated appeals to free the hostages. Russian forces began their assault after the FSB spokesman on the scene mistakenly said that Raduyev had begun executing hostages.

A four-day bombardment of Pervomaiskoye using artillery and rocket fire, fighter planes, and helicopter gunships ensued until almost nothing was left of the village. One hundred and fifty-three of Raduyev's men were killed and twenty-eight more were taken prisoner. Fifteen hostages were killed and seventy-four wounded. One surviving hostage said that those who survived did so by digging trenches during the day and burying the bodies at night.

Raduyev tried once to break out of the encirclement but was forced back. He tried a second time and was successful in the early morning hours of 18 January. This time he had help. Maskhadov and Basayev had sent reinforcements—about four hundred fighters—which attacked Russian troops from the rear in a neighboring village just long enough to create a diversion so Raduyev could escape. Some of the sixty-five hostages found alive in Pervomaiskoye said that Raduyev and about seventy Wolves and sixty hostages escaped at 3 o'clock that morning.

Raduyev and his hostages made their way through minefields and Russian fire from three directions to Raduyev's underground hideout in Novogroznensky. Raduyev took sixty Russian and Dagestani hostages with him. They carried ammunition and Raduyev's wounded. Seventeen to twenty-two Interior Ministry troops were among the hostages. He later released five who were slightly wounded. Russia negotiated the subsequent release of the rest.

Kizlyar and Pervomaiskoye earned Raduyev the distinction of becoming Russia's Public Enemy Number Two, second only to Basayev, who immediately joined Raduyev in his underground hideout in Novogroznensky.

Raduyev boasted of beating the Russian Army, but Basayev chewed him out for not getting something tangible out of it. The only positive thing that Basayev could say about Kizlyar was, "Budennovsk and Kizlyar will repeat themselves again until Russia recognizes the Chechen republic."

Raduyev and his men had killed fewer than a hundred men but had set a new record in men lost in a single Chechen military operation. No wonder Maskhadov declared that Raduyev is not a military authority or leader in the least and denounced Raduyev's taking of hostages as damaging the separatist movement. President Dudayev announced that Raduyev had disobeyed orders and would be court marshalled. Instead, Dudayev awarded him the Komenci (Nations Honor) medal. Raduyev was not satisfied because Basayev had received the more coveted Hero of Chechnya medal for his work at Budennovsk.

Pervomaiskoye triggered a sympathetic international terrorist incident. Two Chechens and six Turkish citizens—including Muhammed Tokcan, a Turk of Chechen origin who had served with Basayev in Abkhazia and fought in Chechnya in the first year of the war with Russia— armed with shotguns and grenades hijacked the Black Sea ferry Avrasiya in the Port of Trabzon, Turkey. The ferry was carrying two hundred people. Tokcan vowed to blow up the ship if Russia did not halt the bombardment of Pervomaiskoye. They surrendered when Raduyev escaped from Pervomaiskoye. A sympathetic Turkish government convicted the hijackers but gave them light prison sentences. They soon escaped. Tokcan was even given amnesty by Turkey in 2000.

Basayev claimed the act of terror was intentionally planned well in advance. He told *Komsomolskaya Pravda* at the end of the month that the hijacking had been part of a plan to hijack a ship that he, Tokcan, and two of the other hijackers had worked out earlier: "We fought together in Abkhazia and they are old friends. They visited me and we developed a plan to seize a ship." Basayev was upset that they had surrendered early: "I don't know why they surrendered and didn't carry the plan through to the end." If what Basayev said was true, the hijackers' demands about Pervomaiskoye would have been a last-minute adjustment to their plans.

RISING FROM THE DEAD

Following Raduyev's dramatic attack, the Kremlin threw everything it had into killing or capturing him. Within five weeks, Raduyev took a bullet in the cheek while driving his car. It was a clean head shot, with the projectile exiting through Raduyev's left eye. He was left for dead. Russia said that other Chechens had killed him for messing up the raid on the air base at Kizlyar, but later a Russian sniper proudly claimed credit for the kill.

Raduyev remained "dead" for four months. Then on 11–12 July 1996, two bombs ripped through Moscow trolley buses—a familiar and scary Raduyev trademark. A bomb also went off in a subway train car between the Tulskaya and Nagatinskaya metro stops in Moscow, killing four people. "One of them was set off to mark my return," Raduyev proclaimed. Raduyev also claimed credit for the 19 July railroad station bombing in Voronezh, Russia, and the empty railroad car bombing in Volgograd on 25 July. Days later, bombs were also found on the railroad tracks near Smolensk and in a rail car in Astrakhan.

When Raduyev did show up again in Chechnya in July 1996, he looked very different—he was wearing dark sunglasses, his face was badly scarred, and it was obvious that he had had plastic surgery.

Raduyev's dramatically altered appearance inspired suspicion that this new Raduyev could actually be a double. That question kept readers of Moscow's newspapers riveted for a week. Everybody had their own ideas and theories. The debate was even televised, and it captivated everybody's imagination—mine included. How could he be the real Raduyev? Every feature of his face in minute detail was carefully studied and analyzed. Cartoons about him even appeared in the newspapers. Finally all agreed he really was Raduyev.

How did Raduyev do it? How did he return from the dead? Raduyev's men had taken him out of the emergency room at the Urus-Martan hospital, declared him dead "to fool the Russians," and rushed him to Chechen surgeon Dr. Khassan Baiev. Raduyev was in terrible shape. "His left eye was pulverized, and the left half of his skull fractured. Shards of splintered bone barely clung to the mangled flesh. His right eye remained intact, as well as a small portion of his nostrils," Baiev wrote in his 2003 book, *The Oath: A Surgeon Under Fire.*

Baiev performed an initial eight-hour surgery on Raduyev. He writes:

> We immobilized the upper jaw with semicircular splints, which we bolted down with titanium screws. To make sure the jaws would remain perfectly secure, I wrapped each tooth with inter-dental wiring and looped each wire around notches in the brace. I removed one lower front tooth so we could thread a feeding tube into his throat. Then we washed the viable slivers of both sinuses and the left cheekbone and began reassembling them like a jigsaw puzzle with the help of screw-down titanium strips. Finally, we repaired the defect in his face by rotating a skin flap from his forehead over the gap.

This use of titanium later earned Raduyev the nickname of "The Titanic."

Raduyev was subsequently evacuated to Turkey for recuperation and the fitting of a glass eye. He then traveled to Germany and, after signing an agreement promising not to kill his plastic surgeons if the operation did not go well, had further surgery. There is another version that says he was treated in the German BND federal intelligence service hospital near Munich and that the plastic surgery was also done by a BND department.

Despite the plastic surgery, Raduyev's face was a mess. But what worried everybody more was that he didn't seem to be in his right mind after his return in the summer of 1996. Chechen field commanders often commented on his post-recovery mental state. What made speculation worse was that he kept insisting that President Dudayev was still alive too. He was so persistent and convincing that many Chechens not only began to believe him but actually started to argue among themselves about the date of Dudayev's return.

After this, trying to assassinate Raduyev became an annual event, almost a sport. The bounty that Russia put on his head prompted would-be assassins three times in 1997 to try to kill him. In April, Raduyev was wounded again when his car was blown up. Sultan Miyev, his "military consultant," told journalists that a bomb had exploded under Raduyev's car on 9 April. He underwent surgery outside Chechnya on 12 April. In July, a van filled with explosives parked near his headquarters in Grozny detonated as Raduyev's car passed by. Three people were killed, but Raduyev escaped unharmed. He blamed the Kremlin. During an October assassination attempt, he was again wounded but soon recovered. He was again "killed" in 1998, but, within a month, photographed himself beside his own tombstone and published the picture on the Internet.

With a fresh lease on life in the fall of 1996—and despite Chechnya's agreement with Russia outlawing Chechen armed groups—Raduyev reorganized and renamed his army General Dudayev's Caucasian Liberation Army to more correctly reflect his pan-Caucasus aims. That December, he promised to use his army to fight Russia for the next forty-eight years if he had to because he regarded the interim peace agreements with Russia as treason. He also regarded the presidential election scheduled for January 1997 as a farce.

That same December, Raduyev returned to his specialty—hostage taking. This time he took twenty-seven police officers. On 14 December, Raduyev and forty of his Liberation Army fighters tried to cross the Chechen-Dagestani border but were stopped by border guards who refused to let them pass with their weapons. Raduyev disarmed them and forcibly took six Dagestani police and twenty-one Russian Penza OMON troops back to his headquarters in Noviye-Gordaly. Raduyev's men also seized a United Nations official and his interpreter but freed them within a few hours.

When asked why he took the OMON hostages, Raduyev said that it was to protest the illegality of the scheduled presidential election in January because "Chechnya already has a president, Dzokhar Dudayev." Raduyev made this statement nine months after Dudayev had been killed—surely Raduyev had lost his mind.

In the negotiations for the hostages, Raduyev agreed to let ten of them go, but first the Russian OMON commander would have to stand at attention in front of him and personally apologize for the border incident. The Russian officer refused.

The Kremlin warned Grozny that Raduyev's action put the Russian troop withdrawal process in jeopardy. This prompted the Chechen government to order Raduyev to drop all conditions and release the hostages at once. Foreign Minister Movladi Udugov condemned the incident as "a dreadful link in the chain of provocations aimed against the fragile peace in Chechnya" and as "disrupting the withdrawal of Russian troops."

For four days, Raduyev disobeyed everybody, saying that no one could tell him what to do: "No one has the right to change the state of war in the republic until complete victory—until Russia recognizes the independence of Chechnya."

THE THORN IN MASKHADOV'S SIDE

Aslan Maskhadov was elected president of Chechnya in January 1997, but the defeated and bitter outgoing acting President Yandarbiyev and his supporters soon staged public demonstrations at which they accused the new president of having taken Kremlin dirty money to finance his election campaign.

Raduyev went further. He flatly refused to recognize the legitimacy of Maskhadov's election. To Raduyev, Maskhadov's campaign statement that the deceased Dudayev should have been more "diplomatic and flexible" in negotiating with Russia bordered on treason. Maskhadov also called for a "common sphere" with Russia in economic, military, and educational matters, but this idea was not in keeping with the spirit of how Raduyev viewed Chechen independence either, so he rejected it too.

Raduyev repeatedly declared, "Only Allah and General Dudayev alone can order me to stop fighting." With a private army of nearly one thousand men and two hundred combat veterans on permanent alert, this was no idle threat. Raduyev's army was equipped with a few T-72 tanks and APCs and manned with special forces personnel and Dudayev loyalists. Deployed in southeastern Chechnya, they controlled the territory from Gudermes to the Dagestani border. This army was the focus of Maskhadov's June 1997 order to disband all private armies, an order Raduyev promptly ignored.

From Maskhadov's election forward, Raduyev became increasingly irrational, uncontrollable, and a source of serious aggravation for the Chechen president, Russia, and the peace process. Right after the election, on the first anniversary of Dudayev's death, Raduyev made the first of many threats to blow up three Russian cities. "We are declaring 21 April [1997] a day of national revenge," he proclaimed, "at least three Russian cities will go up in smoke. Revenge is inevitable. . . . I will stage a number of terrorist attacks in Russia."

Besides hostage taking and making threats against Russian cities, Raduyev engaged in a variety of common and not-so-common criminal activities. As early as 1996, acting President Yandarbiyev had accused him of robbing trains. He stole teachers' salaries too, extorted money from Chechen villages, absconded with government property, and blew up Russian train stations. For this, he had his own Kavkaz training center, which he opened with Khattab in September 1996. The Kavkaz camp was physically located alongside Khattab's camps in Serzhen Yurt.

Russian spies were everywhere in Chechnya in 1997, and Raduyev's elaborate plans to blow up Russian cities in April were either exaggerated or compromised. Instead, he ordered two female recruits of his newly formed special terrorist unit called Dzokhar's Way to blow up railway stations in two southern Russian cities. Raduyev billed these as "the beginnings of a series of strikes against Russian railroad stations and military installations."

On 28 April 1997, Aset Dadashyeva and Fatima Taimaskhanova planted bombs at the Pyatigorsk, Russia, railroad terminal, killing two people and badly wounding thirty. Dadashyeva testified at Raduyev's 2001 trial that she was personally instructed to carry out the attack by Vakha Dzhafarov, the headquarters commander of Raduyev's army. She was promised a three-room apartment and money for the mission.

When it came her turn to testify, Taimaskhanova said that she personally knew Raduyev and had even had her photograph taken with him. She had often visited Raduyev's office and saw explosive devices on his desk. She knew that he had planned a series of "actions" to "frighten Russia" and to mark the anniversary of Dudayev's death. Taimaskhanova confirmed that Vakha Dzhafarov had insisted that she and Dadashyeva carry out the attacks for Raduyev. She personally chose Pyatigorsk because she had lived there. She was also promised money.

Raduyev also claimed credit for the bombing in the village of Bira in the Khabarsky kray and the mine explosion in Armavir, Russia, on 23 April that killed three people. Vice President Arsanov, though, dismissed his claim, saying that Raduyev "is a medical problem and his statement should not be taken seriously."

It was at this time that Maskhadov—under pressure from the Russian Security Council, which was responsible on the Russian side for negotiating a peace treaty with Chechnya—began talking about taking possible measures against Raduyev, including arrest. However, nothing was done.

On 2 August 1997, Raduyev and former acting President Yandarbiyev (who only the year before had accused Raduyev of being a criminal) formed the Soldiers of Freedom movement made up of about one thousand war veterans. They vowed to resist any settlement that Maskhadov reached with Russia except full independence for Chechnya. Raduyev's Dzokhar's Way became the core of this new organization. On 16 November 1997, the movement passed a resolution declaring no confidence in President Maskhadov's domestic and foreign policies, demanding the resignation of the Chechen government and dissolution of the state commission on talks with Russia that was headed by propaganda guru and foreign minister, Movladi Udugov.

The following January, Maskhadov conceded to Raduyev's repeated demand to dismiss the cabinet and charged acting Prime Minister Basayev with forming a new government that would be more acceptable to the opposition. But this failed to mollify Raduyev.

The next month, in neighboring Georgia, on the night of 9 February 1998, men armed with rocket-propelled grenade launchers and automatic weapons attacked the motorcade of President Eduard Shevardnadze. The armor plating on Shervardnadze's vehicle saved him, but two of his body-guards were killed as well as one of the attackers, a Chechen.

Raduyev immediately claimed credit for the attack. Appearing on his own television station, Raduyev said that the attack was the work of a Chechen special operations unit called Wolves Without Borders, which had sentenced Shevardnadze to death because "he is a Russian agent" and because he "heads a bandit formation" in Georgia.

Reacting to these pronouncements, Basayev commented, "Raduyev's got plastic in his head instead of a brain as well as a bullet."

Georgia's investigation turned up evidence that Chechen mercenaries had indeed been involved; they and extremist supporters of deceased former Georgian President Zviad Gamsakhurdia, who was overthrown in a military coup in January 1992, had carried out the vicious attack.

Gamsakhurdia, who beat out the communists in the first democratic elections held in post-Soviet Georgia in 1990, was an eccentric and a cult figure among his devout followers. After being overthrown in 1991, Dudayev gave him political asylum in Chechnya. Raduyev befriended him, maybe because their characters were so much alike. It is said that Gamsakhurdia even converted to Islam under Raduyev's influence. In 1993, the former Georgian president made a last-ditch effort through insurgency to take back the reigns of power in Georgia but was either killed or committed suicide. After his death, Raduyev took in some of Gamsakhurdia's fighters and swore to help bring Gamsakhurdia's follow-ers back to power in Georgia. Nobody took Raduyev seriously though.

All of this caused the Georgian Security Ministry to take a closer look at a possible Raduyev connection. They found nothing. Chechen officials came up empty handed too. In the end, Maskhadov dismissed Raduyev's claim as simply the "ramblings of an unbalanced person" that somebody should do something about.

Basayev tried. On 21 February, Basayev called a meeting of field commanders to "sort things out with Salman Raduyev." Basayev said that the "Raduyev problem must be resolved" because "we are not going to tolerate any more of his provocative anti-state antics and attacks on the president and the government." Foreign Minister Udugov added, "We cannot have two presidents and two armies in the state."

The involvement of Chechens in the attack on President Shevardnadze did serve to discredit Maskhadov and briefly slow the momentum toward Chechnya's normalization of economic relations with Tbilisi. Raduyev's purpose had been served whether he was directly involved or not.

It was shortly afterward that Maskhadov banned Raduyev's Marsho (Freedom) television station from broadcasting antistate propaganda. Maskhadov was fed up with Raduyev's interference in Chechnya's external affairs, his persistent accusation that the Chechen president was caving in to Russia, neglecting the poor, and engaging in nepotism with appointments to government posts. Maskhadov also banned any kind of public strikes and demonstrations by Raduyev or his supporters. Maskhadov had a break in the spring while The Lone Wolf was in Pakistan, but things heated up between the two of them again in the early summer, finally coming to a showdown in mid-June.

SHOOTOUT AT TEATRALNAYA SQUARE

On 20 June 1998, The Lone Wolf organized a civil disobedience demonstration in Grozny. He went on television despite Maskhadov's ban and, using his uncanny ability to rally people, called out thousands of supporters who built a tent city in the middle of Grozny. That same night, Lecha Khultygov also went public, warning people not to participate in Raduyev's demonstration.

Khultygov's warning fell on deaf ears. The next day, a huge crowd showed up in Teatralnaya Square to hear Raduyev vehemently denounce Maskhadov for cheating the poor and betraying the legacy of President Dudayev. Raduyev whipped the crowd into a frenzy. Once sufficiently rowdy, he marched the mob to the government-run television station to demand air time. On the way, Raduyev accused Maskhadov of being an accomplice of those who tried to assassinate him in 1996 and those who killed Raduyev's father in April of the same year.

Raduyev ordered the seizure of the government television station and the mayor's office located in the same building, while Khultygov's security forces attempted to prevent the crowd from taking the building. Both sides hurled accusations of treason at one another, tempers flared, everything got out of hand, and the shooting started. When the smoke cleared, Khultygov, his bodyguard, Akhmed Basayev (a relative of Shamil Basayev'), and Vakha Dzhafarov were dead.

Khultygov may have been deliberately assassinated. Both Raduyev and Khattab had been gunning for him. Raduyev wanted revenge because Khultygov had earlier shot up Raduyev's television station and destroyed the tent camp. Khattab applauded his death because Khultygov had personally offended him and fellow Wahhabis with a vilifying article about them in the local newspaper and the allegations of a Wahhabi conspiracy that he had put before the parliament.

Maskhadov declared a three-day mourning period for those killed and on the third day imposed a state of emergency. He also filed charges against Raduyev with the Supreme Shariah Court for attempting to overthrow the government and ordered his arrest. But no real effort was made to apprehend Raduyev. Everybody knew that Raduyev was hiding with his deceased wife's relatives, but Maskhadov was reluctant to storm the house because any bloodshed would mean a revenge war with Dudayev's family.

There was talk at the time that Raduyev's actions were costing him support among Dudayev's relatives, making him and his army even more isolated and uncontrollable. But by the fall, he was organizing again against Maskhadov, only now with Basayev's help. Basayev's weight was significant.

Basayev gave the growing opposition more dignity and credibility. Along with Khunkar Israpilov, the head of the government's Antiterror Center, they methodically prepared and submitted a long list of charges against Maskhadov first to the Parliament and then to the Supreme Shariah Court in an attempt to impeach him.

Rallies and demonstrations that accused Maskhadov of running a dictatorship were still the order of the day, but now they were more orderly. One such demonstration took place in October while Maskhadov was in North Ossetia meeting with Russian Prime Minister Yevgeny Primakov. A gathering of four hundred people in Grozny called by Raduyev criticized Maskhadov's "willingness to rush to a meeting of the Russian premier with regional leaders at the first beckoning, forgetting that he is the president of an independent country," and demanded that Maskhadov be put before a Shariah judge.

Instead, in November, the Supreme Shariah Court tried Raduyev in absentia and found him guilty of attempting to overthrow President Maskhadov. He was sentenced to four years imprisonment and stripped of his military rank. Raduyev lashed out with threats of a civil war.

The Shariah Court left Raduyev a way out by offering to withdraw the sentence if he would undergo a medical exam that showed him to be in "poor health." He refused and promised to violently resist any attempt at arrest. He also lodged an appeal with the alternative Shariah Court set up the previous day by "field commanders" (himself, Basayev, and Israpilov). Raduyev added that the Commanders Council would ignore all future orders by Maskhadov.

The Commanders Council kept Raduyev's promise. In early February 1999, the council went ahead and organized the Congress of War Veterans that Maskhadov had demanded be canceled. The opposition to Maskhadov was now significant as evidenced by the warm reception that Raduyev received at the congress. It was attended by fifteen hundred war veterans who gave Raduyev a long and loud applause.

There was talk in the Commanders Council at this time of reconciliation with Maskhadov because he promised to create a Shura council and draft an Islamic constitution, but that was soon wiped away by his refusal to give up the powers of the presidency and another Raduyev-engineered kidnapping in the spring.

In March, Raduyev claimed responsibility for the kidnapping of Major General Gennady Nikolayevich Shpigun, an envoy plenipotentiary of the Russian Ministry of the Interior. On 5 March, gunmen in the back of the commercial plane carrying other passengers stopped the aircraft as it was taxiing down the runway at Severny airport in Grozny and removed General Shpigun from the plane. Abdul Malik Mezhidov was in charge of the physical kidnapping.

The act disgraced Maskhadov, who had personally guaranteed General Shpigun's safety. It also quickly halted political negotiations between Moscow and Grozny. Russian troops went on full alert and closed the border. Government representatives left Grozny, and Russia threatened an economic blockade, termination of air and rail service, and "limits" on energy supply if Shpigun was not released.

Maskhadov condemned the kidnapping and assured the Kremlin that he would track down those responsible and set Shpigun free within three days. He warned Russia not to use force to find Shpigun because it would only play into the hands of the opposition.

Ultimatums were passed back and forth as both sides talked of war, Chechnya mobilizing two thousand reservists.

The Russian interior minister, Sergei Stepashin, blamed Basayev for the kidnapping, but Basayev challenged the kidnappers to turn Shpigun over to him. He promised a sure death sentence to the Russian general in a Shariah court.

On 19 March, ITAR-TASS quoted a member of the Moscow Chechen diaspora returning from Chechnya as saying that Arbi Barayev was holding Shpigun in the town of Urus-Martan. The Russian prosecutor-general's office even thinks that Berezovsky ordered the abduction because Shpigun found out about Berezovsky's involvement in the kidnapping business of Raduyev, Barayev, and the others. Maskhadov, on the other hand, publicly blamed Khattab for kidnapping General Shpigun and "engineering clashes" among various extremist groups. Regardless of who was responsible, Shpigun's lifeless body was found in 2001.

Perhaps the Commanders Council was trying to precipitate a new war. If so, on 16 March, Russia's prime minister disappointed them when he announced that there would be no war. He refused to play into the hands of the opposition and declared his willingness to resume negotiations with Chechnya.

Maskhadov in turn condemned Basayev for supporting Raduyev and declared yet another government war on crime, blaming everything on the opposition and illegal Wahhabi activities. He named Basayev as one of those protecting and legitimizing the opposition: "Basayev is just a puppet in the hands of the opposition which uses him as power support in pursuit of its unseemly aims."

The president also lashed out at Saudi Arabia for financing the opposition and its bandit groups. "They try to turn us into an obedient weapon of the West in the Caucasus similar to the Afghan Taliban. We are Naqshbandi and Qadari Sufis. There is no place for any other Islamic sects in Chechnya."

Maskhadov wanted to create mobile groups in each Chechen village to combat the illegal activities of the now outlawed Wahhabis and local opposition branches. "Drive them from our villages! Restore order," he chanted—but he was powerless to do anything.

THE JAMAAT MILITARY ALLIANCE AND THE BEREZOVSKY HOSTAGE DEALS

Raduyev leaped at any opportunity to side with anyone or any organization willing to fight Russia. The signing of a military mutual assistance treaty in December 1997, with the Wahhabi Fighting Squads of Jamaat of Dagestan, is an example. He signed the treaty because "the Islamic Jamaat of Dagestan and Dzokhar's Army represent forces which fight for a unified Islamic state in the Caucasus and for independence from Russia."

Raduyev too supported the concept of a unified Islamic state of Chechnya and Dagestan, even though he had no particular ideological sympathies for the Wahhabis. In fact, the next month, he turned around and demonstrated in Grozny to kick Wahhabis out of Chechnya.

On 3 January, Raduyev rallied several thousand people in Grozny's Freedom Square and told them that certain high-ranking members of the

Chechen government supported the Wahhabi movement. Other speakers at the rally declared Wahhabis to be "enemies of the people." The crowd adopted a resolution calling on Maskhadov and the mufti of Chechnya to declare publicly where they stood on the Wahhabi issue. Raduyev even urged the Chechen parliament to outlaw the movement.

Finally, it appeared possible that Raduyev and Maskhadov had found common ground. However, Raduyev may have just been using the Wahhabi issue to stir up yet more trouble for Maskhadov. After all, Raduyev's army had rescued Khattab and his raiding party as they crossed the Dagestan-Chechnya border while being pursued by Russian forces after the raid on Buinaksk in December 1997.

Another example is Raduyev's support of the Khachilayev brothers (Magomed and Nadirshakh) who in early September 1998 were arrested for the May seizure of the Dagestani State Council and for carrying out a terrorist attack in Makhachkala on 4 September that killed eighteen people. Raduyev threatened terrorist attacks against Russia unless the brothers were freed. When his deadline passed, he said that he had been persuaded by the "national liberation forces of Dagestan" to put a temporary moratorium on attacks in hopes of their ultimate release.

Raduyev also gets credit for helping turn the people-for-sale trade in Chechnya into epidemic proportions. In January 1996, a kidnapper could get $2,000 from a grieving Russian mother for a living soldier with the rank of private. By midsummer, the price had gone up to $5,000 for that same soldier. A Russian officer brought $45,000. That price went up to $145,000 in 1997. Foreigners, aid workers, journalists, and high-ranking Russian government and military officers usually brought $2–3 million or more. Raduyev demanded $15 million for Shpigun. The bodies of executed soldiers also brought a price for return to their families. Raduyev found a niche here and in brokering deals for other warlords like Arbi Barayev for a cut of the take.

Like others in the business, Raduyev started off small. President Ruslan Aushev of Ingushetia observed that he "exchanges hostages for computers." He "has a whole house filled with [computers]; he is better equipped than some of Russia's special services."

Raduyev had a good partner on the Russian side—businessman and Deputy Secretary of the Russian Security Council Boris Berezovsky. Raduyev first brokered a deal with him by exchanging the Penza OMON policemen taken hostage in December 1996 for eleven Chechen prisoners of war held by Russia. After that, deals were made on such a regular basis that police and others suspected collusion between Raduyev and Berezovsky. Ruslan Aushev noted, "[Berezovsky] talks directly with Chechen field commanders, the same Salman Raduyev, and makes deals with them."

Berezovsky may have been playing the role of a "liberator"—that is, the role of a kidnapper's collaborator whose job it is to approach the victim's relatives and offer help in negotiating the ransom and getting the victim released for a cut of the money. Paul Klebnikov in his book *Godfather of the Kremlin* summed it up nicely when he wrote, "Berezovsky served as banker for the Chechen kidnappers, rounding up and transferring the ransom payments for the Russian side."

In September 1998, Raduyev personally turned over British citizens Camilla Carr and Jon James to Berezovsky for several million dollars ransom—although Berezovsky told the press he secured their release with computers and medical aid for Raduyev. Carr and James had been kidnapped in July 1997, by notorious kidnapper Arbi Barayev. Raduyev split the ransom with Arbi Barayev. Under British pressure, Maskhadov had tried himself to free the British couple, but the Chechen government's raid on Arbi Barayev's house failed because Raduyev's men drove off Maskhadov's troops.

The British couple had been held with Russian presidential envoy to Chechnya Valentin Vlasov, who was kidnapped in May 1998, probably to sabotage Maskhadov's plans to organize a Caucasian Common Market involving the construction of a new oil pipeline through Chechnya. Vlasov was released to Berezovsky in November of that year for $3 million. "By doing that they once again financed the Chechen criminal group," Nasrudi Bazhiyev, Chechnya's interior minister, noted.

Shortly after the Vlasov deal, a group of Russian POWs was set free through one of the Raduyev-Berezovsky deals. In December 1998, Vincent Cochetel, head of the UNHCR office in Vladikavkaz, was freed for $5 million, and Herbert Gregg, an American missionary, was freed in June 1999 for an unknown amount of cash. Others were not so lucky.

Berezovsky says that all together he helped free fifty-five people and never paid a single kopeck for them. But Maskhadov disagrees: "[Berezovsky] comes here [to Chechnya] with suitcases full of money and heaps of computers [to exchange for hostages], which discredits the Chechen nation since it only encourages the bandits."

According to rumors in the Kremlin in 1999, Berezovsky engaged in more then just brokering hostage release deals with his Chechen contacts. He employed them to discredit his political and business nemesis, Yuri Luzhkov, the mayor of Moscow, "by provoking a range of events that would destabilize the social and psychological situation in Moscow." The idea was that his Chechen friends would kidnap several famous people and carry out a series of attacks against commercial enterprises that Luzhkov owns. Some believe that the 31 August bomb that killed one person and wounded forty-one others in the underground Manezhny mall beside the Kremlin, Luzhkov's pet project, was part of this plot.

WHAT RADUYEV'S ISLAMIC MANIFESTO HAD TO SAY

Raduyev constantly worked at cross purposes to Maskhadov. Naturally, when somebody blew up Russian apartments buildings in Buinaksk, Moscow, and Volgodonsk in September 1999, killing more than three hundred people, Maskhadov and the Kremlin immediately suspected Raduyev, particularly since he jumped to claim credit for the bombings just as he had done for almost every bomb that went off in Russia since 1997. However, Khattab and Basayev were the guilty ones.

Raduyev's speech to a graduating class at his Kavkaz training camp in early 1999 implied that he may have been aware of a plan to attack Russian cities though. This is what Raduyev told the graduates: "You are graduating from our school today. . . . Those who will settle down in Russia and neighboring states will be expected to accomplish a special mission. You must destabilize the situation, the economy, and the financial system there. You must set up bases and select people. But you won't have to wait long. We are going to hit virtually all major cities if Ichkeria doesn't receive its complete freedom and independence by spring."

Maybe Raduyev was just boasting again. But as Yulia Karavayeva, who translated Raduyev's speech and published it in the Russian journal *Slovo* on 7 April 1999, said, "His words did not sound like the ravings of a madman."

In fact, Raduyev's detailed instructions to all students sounded more like a well-prepared manifesto of Islamic extremism. "Your teachers have trained you in the art of sabotage, corruption, and the circulation of rumors for four consecutive months. . . . Some of you will start your assignments tomorrow," Raduyev said. "You must:"

> Sow mortal terror among all those [Chechens] who have betrayed Allah. They must feel the cold hand of death every hour.
>
> Take the blood of those infidels not wishing to rally around Mohammed's holy banner.
>
> Instill fear and bewilderment among all [Russian] servicemen who are still stationed on our territory. Take them hostage and kill them.
>
> Compile a list of all officers, enlisted soldiers, and especially Cossacks who participated in the war [against us] to even the slightest extent. All of them must be killed.
>
> Smear all patriotic Russians who can be easily accused of fascism and nationalism.

To replenish your supply of weapons, Raduyev instructed, "Pay attention to those specific areas where Russian military units are stationed. Their hungry Russian officers and soldiers will sell just about any kind of weapon."

To replenish the ranks of the mujahideen: "You must expand the Moslem-school chain, accepting infidel children as well. Children amount to dough; that's why they will serve those who mould them. You must take advantage of Russia's lack of spirit."

To those given assignments to infiltrate civil institutions and organizations, Raduyev instructed:

> Pay attention to Cossacks who are our ancient and most terrible enemies, but Allah is merciful. Most Cossack atamans [chiefs] are corrupt and greedy. They can sell off their Cossacks and even their mothers for money. You must set up joint ventures in Cossack communities as you drag them into a financial pitfall. Some of the Stavropol territory's Cossack atamans are already working for us. Those of you who are going to work there have already received compromising materials on such atamans.
>
> You must sow ethnic strife on the territory of the national republics, putting local ethnic groups and Russians at loggerheads. Russians must be blamed for all trouble. Those nationals who don't want to live according to Shariah law must be killed and you must blame everything on Russians.
>
> Everyone who infiltrates federal agencies must demoralize such agencies. However, this must be done with Russian hands alone; let the Russians answer to their own law. You must not be suspected in any way.
>
> Those working at banks must exert every effort in order to delay wage payments and other settlements, the payment of pensions in particular, thus sowing discontent between Russians.
>
> Russia's state-power and financial structures are corrupt; many are penetrated by local mafias. We must assume leading positions inside mafia structures. While working in Russian regions, you must rely on Chechen, Gypsy, Dagestani, and Korean diasporas. You will be receiving all the required instructions and money from them.

Raduyev's prediction about a Chechen attack on Russian cities did indeed come true, not in the spring, but in September 1999. Just as Raduyev was making his speech, other Wolves were at work on plans to carry out terror attacks on three Russian cities in early September 1999.

IV

THE GODFATHER OF KIDNAPPING AND THE IDEOLOGIST OF APOCALYPSE

My attitude toward this [kidnapping] was negative, very negative. As much as possible we actively fought this. But then it became like an epidemic and we did not have any way to handle it.

Shamil Basayev, 2000

Udugov is a seasoned statesman who has done a great deal for Chechnya's nationhood . . . [but the] foreign minister should stick to the policy pursued by the president without undertaking stray actions which might complicate relations with foreign countries.

Chechen President Aslan Maskhadov, November 1998

PEOPLE FOR SALE

An unconfirmed story persists that Osama bin Laden paid Arbi Barayev, "The Wahhabi," $30 million to behead Granger Telecom workers Darren Hickey, Rudolf Petschi, Stanley Shaw, and Peter Kennedy. The Wahhabi chopped off the little finger tips of Adi Sharon, a twelve-year-old Israeli boy, and mailed them to the boy's father along with a ransom demand of $8 million. A seven-figure number in American dollars was paid to The Wahhabi for the release of Russian NTV journalist Yelena Masyuk and her film crew; $3 million for Valentin Vlasov, President Yeltsin's envoy to Chechnya; and several million for British humanitarian workers Camilla

Carr and Jon James. The Wahhabi wanted $1 million for Mishra Raghunatkh, an Indian student who had been studying medicine in Dagestan. Barayev sold two FSB agents back to Russia for $800,000.

Such was the multimillion dollar business that made Chechen warlord Arbi Alaudinovich Barayev and others like him wealthy, helped pay for a patron's presidential election campaign, drove foreigners and humanitarian aid workers out of Chechnya, further undermined President Maskhadov, and significantly contributed to the demise of Chechnya and the rise of a Chechen criminal state in the 1990s.

Nicknamed "The Wahhabi" for his religious fanaticism, Barayev was not typical of the many Chechen unemployed youth recruited and Wahhabi indoctrinated in the early 1990s. Powerful and feared, he was far more psychotic and maniacal, rivaling Raduyev and competing with Khattab in the torture and murder of Russian officials. He personally claimed credit for more than 160 assassinations. He murdered more than fifty people from his own village, including family members, that he suspected of treason or who refused to cooperate with him in crime. Little wonder that village people threw stones and refused to let him be buried in his hometown after he was killed by Russian federal troops in June 2001.

Born in Alkhan-Kala, Chechnya, in 1973, Barayev was strong and skilled in martial arts as a teenager. At the age of seventeen, his influential relatives got him a job as a traffic policeman. A year later, he became a personal bodyguard to his uncle, Vakha Arsanov, the future vice president of Ichkeria. He also protected Vice President Zelimkhan Yandarbiyev, with whom Barayev formed a close personal relationship, and Sultan Geliskhanov, President Dudayev's national security service chief.

Arbi Barayev was with Basayev in Budennovsk in 1995. After Dudayev's death, Yandarbiyev asked Barayev to organize a special Islamic regiment that became the feared Special Purposes Islamic Regiment. When the war was over, Brigade General Barayev kept the regiment as his own private army, employing it in, and supporting it with, his kidnapping business.

Maskhadov officially disbanded the regiment in 1998 for participating in the Wahhabi rebellion in Gudermes, but it continued to exist anyway as Barayev's private army. This is the same Special Purposes Islamic Regiment that the U.S. State Department placed on its global terrorist list in February 2003. Barayev turned each of his commands into his own personal criminal gang specializing in captives for sale, rent, or trade, and political kidnapping to discredit Maskhadov.

Urus-Martan served as Barayev's base of operations. He controlled the territory in north and northwestern Chechnya.

In the nineteenth century, the kidnapping of foreigners for ransom was a traditional cottage industry in Chechnya. But in the 1990s, it was so profitable that no fewer than sixty-two gangs with their private armies engaged in the kidnapping and captives-for-sale business. Barayev's was the biggest. He was the godfather of a $200 million racket that victimized thousands of Chechens, Russians, Jews, and foreigners. The business was so advanced that divisions of labor were even set up and religious contracts concluded between those who would do the physical kidnapping and the criminal and terrorist entities that provided the victim's transportation, security, and ransom negotiations. All of this was done in the name of Islam and formally written down on paper. (A typical contract appears in the photo insert.)

The epidemic of individual kidnappings in the mid- to late 1990s was preceded by several spectacular passenger bus hijackings for ransom in 1993 and 1994, which netted Chechen criminals $30 million. Typically, a Chechen gang would cross the border into Russia, seize a bus full of people, and demand $10–15 million ransom, weapons, and a helicopter to fly back to Chechnya in.

The first of these hijackings took place in December 1993 when four armed men burst into a school in the Rostov region of Russia and seized teachers and twelve students who were then taken in a stolen bus to a nearby military airfield. Russia paid the terrorists $10 million ransom and gave them a helicopter to escape back to Chechnya. They were caught four days later.

The following May, four more terrorists seized an excursion bus full of school children, parents, and teachers near the village of Kinzhal, in the Stavropol region of Russia. They demanded narcotics, a helicopter, $10 million in cash, and weapons. They freed all but four women hostages and then flew with their cash and their hostages to Chechnya. More examples are found in the "Chronology of Terror" at the end of this book.

When Russian antiterror forces began killing bus hijackers instead of paying their ransom demands, gangs switched to snatching individuals or smaller groups of people and taking them back to Chechnya where they were held for ransom.

These victims were generally chosen from the wealthy and strong, but not always. Russian children, like three-year-old Lena Meshcheryakova, could even be snatched from the arms of their parents. On 8 October 1998, at 5:30 a.m., four armed men burst into Lena's house in Grozny, stole her mother's gold earrings, and took Lena from her bed. Her kidnappers demanded $15,000 ransom, but, nine months later, reduced it to $1,000 because her mother could not raise the money. Relatives paid the final ransom for her release in July 1999.

Cruel Chechen women were involved in the business too. "Larisa hit me with a knife for losing a slipper," little Lena told her mother. At the time of her release Lena's ear was cut, she was emaciated, and she suffered from psychological trauma that will probably be with her forever.

Jewish children—and adults too—were singled out for kidnapping because of the belief that they would bring a higher ransom. Twelve-year-old Adi Sharon was kidnapped on 23 August 1999 while walking with his father in Moscow and held for months in a filthy dugout under floorboards of a village house before being rescued by the FSB in June 2000. Two of his fingertips were cut off.

The tips of two of Alla Geifman's fingers were cut off too, and a videotape was made of the amputation and sent to her father to hasten ransom payment. Alla, the thirteen-year-old daughter of banker Grigory Geifman, had been abducted in May 1999 near her house in Saratov, Russia, and taken back to Chechnya.

Another teenager, Laura Lichtman, eighteen, an Israeli citizen, was kidnapped that summer in the city of Nalchik, capital of the Kabardino-Balkaria Republic, when she went to visit to her grandmother.

Forty-year-old Oleg Yemelyantsyev, an Israeli citizen born in Russia, was kidnapped in April 1998 in southern Russia while trying to sell his apartment. He was taken to Chechnya and beaten with sticks, paralyzing one leg.

Jewish businessman Savi Azaryev was kidnapped in Volgograd, Russia, and imprisoned with Yemelyantsyev. His brothers paid his ransom after receiving a video of two fingers being cut off. Yemelyantsyev's family also received video footage of Yemelyantsyev's finger amputation. Another Jew, Lev Melikhov, fifty-two, taken from his house in Nalchik, was executed by his captors.

Not only children and Jews, but Russian soldiers and officers, clergy, journalists, professors, and foreign aid workers—anyone who could be sold or was capable of being put to work building mountain roads, houses, working in factories, or cultivating poppy and hemp for the Chechen narcotics trade—were abducted. More than three thousand Russian nationals alone were kidnapped for ransom or traded at a special slave market in downtown Grozny where it was possible to obtain lists of the names, occupations, and other information about people for sale. Russian slaves sold for a few hundred dollars and up, whereas foreigners cost much more at Grozny's International Friendship Square, nicknamed "The Square of Three Fools." People, like narcotics and arms, were also sold at the central square in Urus-Martan, right across the street from the Shariah police station.

Vadim Tsiputan from Russia's Nizhegorodskaya oblast is one of those who spent five years as a slave in Chechnya. He was abducted in 1995 and found in Dagestan in 2000. Russia told the Council of Europe in May of

2000 that forty-six thousand people had been abducted and enslaved in Chechnya between 1991 and 1999.

Mishra Raghunatkh, a medical student in Dagestan, is another one of those who became a slave. His father had sold a small family plot of farm-land in India for $3,000 so Mishra could study medicine in Dagestan. Arbi Barayev's men seized Mishra at a student party near Kizlyar, Dagestan, in October 1998. When his parents and then the Indian embassy refused to pay the $1 million ransom demanded, Barayev made Mishra his slave. He did dirty work, cooked, and carried weapons and Barayev's wounded under fire. Barayev frequently beat him and made him convert to Islam.

Arbi Barayev personally organized more than seventy abductions of foreign citizens, including Jews, journalists, businessmen, priests, and preachers. At one time, Barayev had so many captives that he didn't have enough room in mountain caves, empty wells, or basement cellars for them all, so he built a jail in a former Soviet "internat"—a special school for handicapped children—in Urus-Martan for them.

Not only was Barayev one of the few warlords who controlled this lucrative business, he franchised out to smaller operators who, for a fee, could receive special permission to use his name to kidnap and to extract bigger ransoms or higher fees for the sale of slaves. In the Chechen govern-ment's investigation of the industry, President Maskhadov claimed that The Wahhabi had received the personal blessing of Chechnya's Wahhabi religious leader himself to kidnap for ransom.

Barayev began his business by kidnapping twenty-nine Russian engi-neers from the TETs-2 heating plant in the village of Kirov near Grozny in January 1996. He then kidnapped to help pay for acting President Yandarbiyev's December 1996 election campaign. In October 1996, he handed Yandarbiyev $60,000 in cash he received for the return of a wealthy Chechen he had kidnapped from the village of Goiti Demelkhanov. Barayev kept the expensive foreign car that he got as part of the ransom deal for himself. The following month, Barayev kidnapped several Russian troops for ransom. The money he got for them went to Yandarbiyev's elec-tion campaign too.

After Yandarbiyev lost his election bid in January 1997, Barayev kid-napped to fund his own gangs. He initially specialized in taking soldiers for ransom but soon found more lucrative targets. He also became very wealthy and bought expensive real estate, threw lavish parties, and paid off corrupt Russian federal officials to look the other way.

In 1997, while Raduyev was busy blowing up train stations, Barayev was plotting the kidnapping of his first really big prize—Yelena Masyuk, a Russian NTV journalist and a personal friend of Maskhadov's. It didn't matter that she had just finished interviewing Raduyev and filming one of his famous anti-Maskhadov public rallies. On their way out of the country on 10 May 1997, Masyuk and her crew were snatched up and whisked away by six masked gunmen near the village of Samashki in western Chechnya.

"Money [ransom for Masyuk] was brought from Moscow to Nazran [the capital of the Republic of Ingushetia], and Ingush Interior Minister Daud Korigov and fifty policemen were sent to Chechnya with the money," the former President Ruslan Aushev of Ingushetia recalls. The Ingush president told the Russian newspaper *Obshchaya Gazeta* that he did not know how much was paid, but "money was given to some people, others were told not to interfere, and yet others were bashed on the head. There was a little bit of everything—money, force, and a desire to free the journalists. . . . Nasrudi Bazhiyev [Chechnya's deputy interior minister] and his boys did their job." NTV's chief, Igor Malashenko, later said that a seven-figure number in American dollars had been paid. Bazhiyev was assassinated shortly afterward by unknown assailants.

The Ingush police caught six of Barayev's bandits while they were attempting another kidnapping in the early summer of 1997. To get them back, Barayev attacked an Ingush militia outpost and took hostages for trade. He killed one of the hostages, a traffic policeman, whose death the policeman's family swore to avenge but never did. Barayev traded the remaining hostages for his men in July.

Two more of Barayev's men were caught kidnapping in Chechnya in early February 1998. This time Maskhadov went on television to talk about it and said that those arrested admitted that they belonged to Barayev's jamaat organization and had received special permission from him to kidnap. Now the spotlight turned to Barayev as the prime suspect behind the rash of kidnapping in Chechnya that had taken place.

Following Maskhadov's television revelation in March 1998, the still loyal head of the antiterror center, General Khunkar Israpilov, publicly accused the Special Purposes Islamic Regiment of several high profile kidnappings.

In addition to Masyuk, Roman Perevezentsyev and Vladislav Tibelius, two journalists from Russian ORT television, had been kidnapped on 19 January 1997. An Italian journalist, Mauro Galligani, followed a month later with a $1 million ransom demand. Nikolai Zagnoiko, an ITAR-TASS correspondent, and three employees of Radio Rossiya were also seized in the spring of 1997.

Barayev grabbed Ilyas Bogatyryev and his cameraman Vladislav Chernyayev in the early summer of 1997. Both worked for the Russian television program *vzglyad*. Several masked gunmen in two white Lada cars drove up, fired shots into the air, and then grabbed the two men while they were standing next to their Volga sedan on a busy Grozny street.

British citizens Camilla Carr, forty, and Jon James, thirty-eight, both psychologists working in Chechnya for the small United Kingdom–based NGO, the Centre for Peacemaking and Community Development, were taken in July; and in August 1997, four French nationals of the EquiLibre humanitarian organization were abducted.

Carr and James experienced a horrific fourteen months in damp cellars, were constantly moved from one group of guards to another, and at times were given little to eat. Camilla Carr was raped by her guard while Jon James was chained to a heating radiator in a nearby room. Both were beaten and tortured, and Mr. James was assured that his guards would cut off his fingers or he would be thrown into a cage full of poison spiders if he did not cooperate. He was also shown mock executions and made to wear a thick rag wrapped around his right hand to make it look like it had been cut off for a videotape sent to his relatives.

Israpilov specifically addressed the kidnapping of Camilla Carr and Jon James, who were helping children traumatized by the 1994–1996 war. Israpilov's public condemnation followed a failed raid on 16 March 1998 of Barayev's house to free the British couple that resulted in the death of three of Israpilov's men in a shootout with fighters belonging to both Barayev and Raduyev. This action indicated Raduyev's collusion with Barayev. Raduyev, who subsequently brokered the release of Carr and James with Berezovsky, was able to predict the "imminent release" of Carr and James weeks ahead of time. They were released on 20 September 1998.

At about this same time, an American colleague of mine was kidnapped for ransom in the Russian city of Volgograd. His armed abductors hid in the back seat of his car and grabbed him when he got into the car after leaving work late at night. They took him to a hideout outside the city, bound him, and left him alone in a garage. During the night, he untied himself, climbed out of the window, and walked back to town where he notified the police. Before daylight, an antiterror squad descended on the house where the four kidnappers were sleeping and brutally took them into custody. His kidnappers threatened to kill him if he testified against them in court. He left Russia for his own safety.

MUTINY IN GUDERMES

Barayev was a general in the Chechen armed forces commander of the Special Purpose Islamic Regiment and deputy commander of the National Guards when he kidnapped Carr and James. But it wasn't until July 1998 that Maskhadov dissolved Barayev's regiment and stripped him of his rank and National Guards post, not for kidnapping, but for disobeying the president's direct order to stop shooting National Guards troops in Gudermes.

The mutiny in Gudermes began on 13 July when Wahhabi soldiers of Barayev's Special Purpose Islamic Regiment got into an argument with two secular guardsmen from the Gudermes Regiment of the National Guards. Barayev was trying to establish Shariah law in Gudermes when disputes with local inhabitants and his own National Guards regiment escalated into a gun battle. His regiment, backed up by Wahhabi armed units led by Amir Abu ur-Rahman and Brigadier General Abdul Malik Mezhidov, chief of the Executory Process Department of the Ministry of Shariah Security who also mutinied, outright attacked the Gudermes National Guards. For four days as many as one thousand men waged war, killing at least fifty people. The Wahhabis suffered the most casualties. Despite Barayev's actions, President Maskhadov allowed him and his friends to negotiate their way out.

The next day, Maskhadov officially disbanded the Special Purposes Islamic Regiment and Mezhidov's Shariah security apparatus, busted Barayev and Mezhidov back to sergeants, and stripped them of their hero's awards from the first war. Though weakened, Barayev, like Khattab, had useful friends and allies in Yandarbiyev and Basayev who prevented him from being scooped up in Maskhadov's subsequent anti-Wahhabi drive.

An attempt was made on Maskhadov's life after the Gudermes gun battle. The Chechen government pointed an accusing finger at Barayev, Ramzan Akhmadov, and Yandarbiyev. The Shariah Court demanded that all three take an oath on the Koran, swearing that they had nothing to do with the assassination attempt. Yandarbiyev told the court that he was prepared to do that, so he was absolved. Barayev and Ramzan Akhmadov, though, never showed up for court.

It was at this point that Barayev declared open season on Maskhadov. Barayev made a second murder attempt on the president in August. Two months later, on 25 October 1998, Barayev went after the head of Maskhadov's new Administration for Combating the Abduction of People in Chechnya, General Shadid Bargishyev, killing him with a car bomb just one day after Bargishyev announced that the government would launch a full-scale operation to free the four Granger Telecom employees, Valentin Vlasov, and nearly forty other prominent kidnap victims still being held. General Bargishyev had given Barayev and other kidnappers twenty-four hours to free their captives.

Bargishyev's anti-kidnapping administration did subsequently make a few arrests. Apti Abitayev, who confessed to being one of the twenty men who did the physical kidnapping of the Granger Telecom workers, was picked up. Apti Kharayev, a commander of one of Barayev's units, was also arrested when he tried to carjack an Interior Ministry car and was charged with the murders of seven police officers.

A few minor captive traders, franchisees of Barayev's, were also arrested, and some more captives were freed, but no further attempt was made to go after Barayev himself. One of the reasons that Barayev was left alone was that he promised to start a new war on the territory of Russia if any attempt was made to apprehend him. Barayev had created the Supreme Council of Islamic Jamaats, and, on 13 December, the council vowed to launch combat operations across the Chechen border if Maskhadov used force against the Wahhabi jamaats in Chechnya, which the president said were complicit in the many kidnappings. Barayev's men dug trenches around Urus-Martan just in case. Barayev also kidnapped Mansur Tagirov, Chechnya's chief prosecutor investigating the four Granger Telecom murders.

Another reason Maskhadov did not go after Barayev was that the president simply did not have what he needed: "I have no specialist equipment. I am not able to intercept their telephone conversations, to react operationally to all the movements of bandits and hostages. I do not even have transport to pursue the terrorists. My people are not paid and they simply work out of enthusiasm. Tell me, how is it possible to wage war against crime under such conditions."

THE AKHMADOV BROTHERS

The Akhmadov brothers were Barayev's closest associates. They were a purely criminal gang of at least six brothers from the Taldy-Kurgan region of Kazakhstan whose sole source of income from 1997 to 1999 was the captives-for-sale business in Chechnya. Uvais Akhmadov, the oldest, born in 1952, was the corrupt Shariah police chief of the Urus-Martan district. Ramzan, the youngest, born in 1970, had served in Basayev's Abkhaz Battalion and was one of the most influential figures in Urus-Martan. Between 1997 and 1999, he kidnapped twenty people. In between were Rizvan, Ruslan, Apti, and Abu Akhmadov. All carried Ministry of Shariah state security identification, which gave them the power to arrest and detain anyone in Chechnya.

Only two of the brothers are still alive—Uvais and Ruslan. The latter was captured in mid-March 2001, along with Badrudi Murtazayev, an associate of Basayev's, as they tried to enter Azerbaijan on forged documents. Ruslan Akhmadov is charged with personally kidnapping and "illegally incarcerating for financial gain" thirty-four people. He is also charged with participating in the beheadings of the four Granger Telecom workers in Chechnya in late 1998. Murtazayev is charged with the 1996 abduction and murder of a Russian soldier based on videotape evidence that shows him and several of Basayev's fighters torturing and then executing the soldier.

Whereas Arbi Barayev focused on kidnapping high-priced people, the Akhmadov family specialized in lower-priced captives—Russian women, children, and clergy—and dealt in quantity. The Akhmadov brothers went to Moscow, Saratov, and other cities to find their victims or bought captives from other traders. In one case, a Russian soldier, Vasily Pinigin, sold a fellow Russian soldier, twenty-two-year-old Roman Tereshchenko, into slavery for a few hundred dollars. Russian Army officers in southern Russia also sold soldiers. In another case, a Russian sergeant traded a teenage recruit for heroine. These were good investments for the Akhmadovs since a Russian soldier could be sold back to his mother for $2,000 to $10,000.

Nineteen-year-old Russian Army private Yevgenny Rodionov was one of those sold back to his mother. His captors told her that they had kidnapped him for ransom, but they then murdered him because he refused to remove a silver cross from around his neck. The cross was still on his body when his mother exhumed the makeshift grave after she paid a ransom of several thousand dollars.

Mothers like Valentina Yokhina from Perm and Antonina Borshchova from Rostov-on-Don became captives themselves when they came to Chechnya in search of their missing sons.

For others like Polish citizens and biology professors Zofia Fisher-Malanowska and Ewa Marchwinska-Wyrwal, the fees for their freedom were on a par with what Barayev and Raduyev demanded—$2 million. The two women were abducted in Dagestan on 9 August 1999, along with their two male Dagestani colleagues, while studying a rare breed of mountain goat. They were transported back to Urus-Martan and put in Ramzan Akhmadov's custody. The war came along before Ramzan could collect his money for them, so when he fled Urus-Martan in October 1999, he took them with him. He abandoned the women when he became surrounded by Russian troops.

When Kiril Perchenko, a student and the son of a Moscow art dealer, was twenty years old, he was abducted in Moscow by a freelance kidnapper, transported to Chechnya in the bed of a cargo lorry, and sold to the Akhmadov family. During his six months in captivity, Perchenko saw the Akhmadovs routinely chop off the fingers and hands of captives while other captives were made to watch. The Akhmadovs had many rules; one was that captives were not allowed to look into the eyes of their guards. If kidnapped prisoners disobeyed, they were brutally beaten with wooden switches.

Perchenko was also an eye witness to Akhmadov family style torture and execution of a hostage. When twenty-five-year-old Dmitry Bobryshev, a Russian officer of the Russian Emergency Situations Ministry, interfered in the beating death of a fellow prisoner, four men threw him to the ground, rolled him onto his stomach, and held his arms, legs, and head from behind while two more men used a two-handled log saw to cut through his spine at the back of the neck and sever his head. The Akhmadovs liked this technique because it was more painful to the victim than a quick beheading with a sharp knife. One of the Akhmadovs played football with Bobryshev's head afterward. Oleg Yemelyantsyev witnessed a similar execution when a young Russian intelligence officer stabbed his guard during a mock funeral. "He was stretched between the trees and had his head sawn off while alive. His head was then hoisted onto a pole," Yemelyantsyev recalls.

When the second war with Russia started in October 1999, the Akhmadovs made their captives dig trenches, carry arms, and do other menial chores. Those who were too weak to keep up the grueling pace were simply shot. Perchenko and Alisher Orazaliyev—a twenty-two-year-old businessman from Kazakhstan—witnessed this kind of killing of fifty-one-year-old ITAR-TASS photojournalist Vladimir Yatsin, who had been kidnapped in Nazran, Ingushetia, by the Akhmadovs in mid-July 1999: "On 20 February 2000, we were being transferred to the village of Shatoi. Yatsin had health problems. He had bad feet and couldn't walk any longer, although we only had five kilometres to go. They shot him. We arrived in the village and were going to stay there, but then bombing started and we had to go down into the forest. On the way back we saw his body."

By the end of 1999, there were 506 ransom kidnap victims still being held in captivity in Chechnya. These included fifty-three women, eighteen children, and foreign nationals from six countries. Another 120 captives have been taken since then.

BEHEADINGS AND BETRAYAL

On 3 October 1998, the body of Russian envoy Akmal Saidov was found near a checkpoint on the Chechen-Ingush border. A note was attached that read, "To all Russians who are hostile to us. This will happen to anybody who works for the Federal Security Service." It was signed "The Wolves of Islam."

Chechen Wolves engaged in even more gruesome killing that month when they beheaded the four Granger Telecom employees. Darren Hickey, age twenty-seven, Rudolf Petschi, forty-two, Stanley Shaw, fifty-eight, and Peter Kennedy, forty-six, were installing a cellular phone system in Grozny when they were kidnapped on 3 October. Their severed heads were found on 8 December in a bag alongside a road, while their bodies were discovered eighteen days later in a forest outside Grozny.

Magomed Chaguchiyev is a Moscow mathematics professor who spent fifty-seven days in captivity with the four men. He told the *Sunday Times* (UK) during a June 2003 trip to London (to testify in a compensation claim against Granger Telecom) about the time they spent together. He describes the pit that they were held in with one hundred others, a pit with a reinforced metal door. When Darren Hickey, Rudolph Petschi, Stanley Shaw, and Peter Kennedy were brought in, they were badly beaten, disoriented, and depressed after being rousted from their beds by twenty armed men at 4 a.m. During captivity, they were repeatedly beaten with gun butts, truncheons, broken bottles, and chains, and shown videos depicting others who had been killed or were being executed. The only thing they had to eat was a loaf of bread once a week among the four of them. Their captors extracted a confession that they were really spies who had come to Chechnya to install a satellite system so British and Israeli intelligence services could listen in on telephone conversations and that their ultimate purpose was to stop the spread of Islam.

The Granger kidnappings were not merely a matter of economics—that is, letting two captives (Carr and James) go and taking four more. The kidnappings were sanctioned by elements of the opposition to further discredit Maskhadov. These kidnappings dealt a serious blow to Maskhadov's prestige in Europe, especially since he had just had a very successful trip to London. Maskhadov publicly announced that he would take personal control over the search for the hostages and punishment of their kidnappers. He even pledged blood vengeance against the kidnappers.

If Osama bin Laden really did pay money to have the four beheaded, that was not a purely business transaction either. Bin Laden's involvement was politically driven, but for different reasons. Barayev was known to sell any captive to the highest bidder—he often conducted such silent auctions for prize catches when he had two or more interested parties. He had been negotiating with Granger Telecom for the release of the four and may have reached a deal for around $10 million. But then Osama bin Laden is said to have stepped into the picture and outbid Granger Telecom.

A fellow hostage, Abdurakhman Adukhov, a government official from neighboring Dagestan, told the BBC's *Money* program his version of how Osama bin Laden won the competition. Adukhov said that Barayev personally told him about his links to al Qaeda and how his Arab friends intended to create a chasm between Islam and the West. But would killing these westerners by such gruesome means really do the trick? Tactically it would ensure that no more Western "infidels" came to Chechnya, would spoil Maskhadov's relations with Europe, and would further escalate tensions in the North Caucasus. Thus, it would contribute overall to Osama bin Laden's grand strategy of creating a clash of civilizations.

Autopsies of the four bodies confirmed that they had been starved, beaten with gun butts, and beheaded from the back of the neck with a large knife. Barayev did not act alone. The Akhmadov Brothers helped—if not in the kidnapping, then in the executions. Uvais Akhmadov personally delivered the heads to the roadside location where they were found.

The Chechen government reacted to the murders by announcing a thirty-day state of emergency, and Maskhadov for the hundredth time called for a mobilization of forces to combat terrorism. His new decree establishing the death penalty or life imprisonment for kidnapping would have been more useful, but nobody was ever convicted under the law.

Maskhadov publicly identified Barayev as the ringleader of the kidnapping gang that murdered the three Britons and the New Zealander. And Vice President Turpal-Ali Atgeriyev, who had been with Raduyev on his hostage-taking raid to Kizlyar, also pointed an accusing finger at Barayev. However, each attempt to bring The Wahhabi to Shariah court ended in protests by the Commanders Council and even physical resistance like that in January 1999.

On 21 January 1999, Maskhadov sent troops to Urus-Martan to bring Barayev in for questioning about the four murders. But fighters loyal to both Basayev and the deposed Khunkar Israpilov patrolling the border of the closed Wahhabi city refused to let them enter and even tried to disarm them. Another shootout ensued, which ended in one person dead and several wounded.

The actions of Basayev's men led Maskhadov's government to conclude that Basayev was intentionally protecting Barayev as he had Khattab. This was especially true after Basayev went on Udugov's Kavkaz television and accused Maskhadov of "fanning tensions" in Urus-Martan and seeking a military confrontation by "provoking various groups of people to attack one another."

Maskhadov responded by going on government television and saying that Barayev, like everybody else, had betrayed him by joining the opposition. First there was Basayev, many others in between, and now Barayev. "Everyone who was around, closest to me, are betraying me. Dudayev had his Labazanov [gangster and bodyguard who went over to the opposition], and I have Barayev playing this role now."

THE MANY FACES OF MOVLADI UDUGOV

"Movladi Udugov (Oudougov) is not a terrorist and he has no contacts whatsoever with Afghanistan or the al-Qaeda network." This May 2002

Udugov Internet statement is unconvincing. Whether or not Movladi Udugov ever personally planted a bomb or not makes little difference. Like Ivan Rybkin, the former secretary of the Russian Security Council who sat across the negotiating table from Udugov in 1997, told me, "[Udugov] has never had a gun in his hand, but the damage is the same."

Udugov threatens terror, and conspires with and represents those who do terrorize Russia. In 1996, he threatened kamikaze airplane attacks against the Kremlin. He propagandized the rash of 2000 suicide bombings against Russian forces in Chechnya, and he, too, engaged in the kidnapping for ransom business, handling negotiations on behalf of the kidnappers and even providing a holding cell in the basement of his own house. He also facilitated payment to those who blew up two Moscow apartment buildings in September 1999 and, by his own admission, negotiated with the Taliban for Osama bin Laden's political asylum to Chechnya in 1998. Udugov is wanted under Russian and international Arrest Warrant #279 "UKRF" dated 20 March 2000.

Udugov is today Basayev's (and when he was alive, Khattab's) propaganda mouthpiece—a role Udugov likes to describe as the "information part" of the present holy war against Russia. Indeed, this 1988 accounting degree graduate possesses such ability to craft effective propaganda and tell the "big lie" that the Kremlin long ago nicknamed him "Chechnya's Goebbels." Disinformation was his trademark in the first Chechen war with Russia. The Russian media marveled at his propaganda skills, and the Kremlin admits that Udugov single-handedly beat them in the "information war." Russia would be delighted to have him on its side. "Udugov alone is worth all the propagandists sitting in Moscow," Russian General Anatoly Kulikov once remarked.

But Udugov's personal contribution to the destruction of Chechnya is far greater that just his propaganda; he provided much of the ideological energy for it. In 1997, he initiated the Islamic Nations movement, which declared as its aim the unification of Chechnya and Dagestan into a new regional Islamic imamate in the North Caucasus—a concept often referred to as "Great Chechnya." A year later, he initiated the creation of a follow on Congress of Peoples of Chechnya and Dagestan, which declared its willingness to use force of arms to achieve their objective. The activities of Udugov and that congress led to an armed invasion of the Russian Republic of Dagestan, the forceful attempt to establish an Islamic state in that Russian republic, and an apocalyptic holy war with Russia in 1999.

Movladi Sandarbiyevich Temishev (he later changed his name to Udugov) was born in Grozny on 9 February 1962. Even as a boy, his passion was journalism. As a teenager, he worked on the district's *Komsomolskoye Plemya* newspaper and, later, helped edit the *Krasnoye*

Znamya paper. When he turned seventeen, he tried to enter the journalism faculty at Moscow State University but had to settle for studying industrial accounting in the economics faculty at Grozny University instead. He tried unsuccessfully to get the editor's job at the university's newspaper. In 1990, after he changed his name to Udugov, he got a job for a few months as a daily editor on one of the communist government's television programs. When he was fired, he edited the dissident *Orientir* newspaper until it was closed down by the local communist party.

Police records show that he served time in prison (under the name of Temishev) for theft from a state-owned store in the mid-1980s. The name Temishev appears on his birth certificate, but Movladi began using his mother's surname (Udugov) after being released from jail in order to hide his jail time so he could get a journalism job. There is a second version of this story that says that he was a bastard child and changed his name to be more acceptable to his clan.

Udugov denies the theft charge but says that he was sent to jail briefly in 1991, in connection with the fall of local communist authority and Dudayev's rise to power. Indeed, communist party boss Doku Zavgayev did accuse Udugov on television of committing cold-blooded murder.

As a member of the Presidium of the National Congress of the Chechen People and head of its information department, Udugov was an active participant in the Chechen revolution. In December 1991, he was appointed to the post of information and press minister. He was made a brigade general in October 1994 and was picked in February 1995 as Dudayev's personal press secretary.

Later, as head of Chechnya's Information Department and then first deputy prime minister responsible for "state politics and information" under acting President Yandarbiyev, Udugov was relentless in disseminating Chechen propaganda to Russia and the West. He understood the importance of keeping his door open to Russian as well as foreign journalists. He even arranged personal interviews with Chechen field commanders for them. Journalists felt comfortable around him, and he made them at ease with mujahideen field commanders too. Russian military officers, on the contrary, were usually suspicious of the media. He also paid off certain Russian journalists to write favorable stories about the Chechen side of the war.

Udugov was a relentless organizer of political congresses, information and media organizations, political parties, and Islamic movements. In September 1996, he organized the First World Congress of the Vainakh Diaspora. This was followed in December with establishment of the Union of Political Strength–Islamic Order and then a social-political movement called Ichkeria. He tried but failed to establish a Free Caucasus radio station in Poland. But he did set up the Chechenetz "scientific-analytical" political think tank. His Islamic Nations movement followed in July 1997, and, at the end of that year, he established two more groups: the Majlis, an ideological and political information group focusing on radio, television, and computer Web site propaganda dissemination, and another group to address Ichkeria's economic, social, safety, and foreign policy issues. His crowning achievement was the establishment in April 1998 of the Congress of Peoples of Chechnya and Dagestan.

UDUGOV'S RESPECTABLE DAY JOB

Udugov's 1997 presidential campaign had the slickest slogans, and his campaign posters were all genuine works of art. He appealed to radical voters who believed that only Islam could combat crime and ensure civil order in Chechnya. He also promised to make Chechnya a fully Islamic state if elected. Saudi money helped foot the bill for his election campaign. But not everybody subscribed to Udugov's fundamentalist views, and although he was an influential member of the Chechen government, his popularity and war record couldn't compare to that of Maskhadov and Basayev. Udugov captured only 1 percent of the vote in the January 1997 Chechen presidential election.

Though defeated in his presidential bid, Udugov immediately rebounded. Unlike Basayev, who announced that he could neither support nor oppose the new president but would wait to see what kind of policies Maskhadov adopted—or Yandarbiyev and Raduyev, who went into immediate opposition—Udugov pledged his unqualified support to Maskhadov. In April 1997, the new president rewarded Udugov by making him a first deputy prime minister with the "state politics and information" portfolio. He had earlier been chosen to head Chechnya's stellar team to negotiate a peace treaty with the Kremlin.

For the next twelve months Udugov would play the respectable role of Chechnya's senior negotiator to settle Chechnya's political status, which was left in limbo by the 1996 Khasavyurt agreement. He was no stranger to the role. As Yandarbiyev's deputy prime minister, Udugov had been a prominent figure and participated in nearly all negotiations with Russia.

The Russian security council secretary, Ivan Rybkin, leading the Russian side, would meet his match with Udugov. Rybkin described Udugov as a "cunning person" and an "extremely difficult negotiator." Udugov has also been described as having a "significant grasp of detail" and a "voracious appetite for tackling paperwork" and "producing quick comment" on draft documents in the negotiations.

Bilateral negotiations began in late February 1997. Udugov's priority was the conclusion of a peace treaty that would recognize Chechnya's independence from Russia. Only after that would he be interested in talking about Russian economic aid to rebuild the war-devastated republic. But Rybkin sought to put the economic cart before the political horse and offered a bilateral treaty like the one signed with the Republic of Tatarstan in 1994. That kind of an agreement would have given Chechnya maximum autonomy as an "associate" member of the Russian Federation, but Udugov rebuffed the offer. A stalemate resulted.

That spring, Udugov publicly condemned the rash of kidnappings in Chechnya as well as Raduyev's April bombings in Pyatigorsk and Armavir as seriously jeopardizing the peace process. When talks did resume, about as close as Udugov got Russia to recognizing the independence of Chechnya was the stipulation in the signed 12 May 1997 Treaty on Peace and the Principles of Mutual Relations Between the Russian Federation and the Chechen Republic of Ichkeria that each side would maintain relations in accordance with the "generally-recognized principles and norms of international law." That in itself was a significant accomplishment, but of course each side had different interpretations of what it really meant. To Maskhadov, it meant that the Kremlin had recognized Chechnya's independence.

Both sides agreed that economic and other agreements could be signed separately. On 3 June, Udugov and Rybkin came up with a unique plan to finance Chechnya's reconstruction based on the repayment of debts owed to Russia by former Soviet republics. Rybkin's 2002 plan was similar, only it proposed to finance reconstruction of Chechnya from the payment of debts owed by Western countries.

Rybkin's 1997 proposal gave Raduyev ammunition to loudly complain to the Chechen public that the Kremlin had succeeded in "buying off" Udugov and Maskhadov. That same month, Russian First Deputy Prime Minister Boris Nemtsov announced an agreement to export oil from Baku to Novorossiisk through Chechnya, lending credibility to Raduyev's argument.

In October, Udugov and Rybkin—and this time Rybkin's deputy, Boris Berezovsky—met near Sochi. Udugov proposed that an interstate treaty providing for the establishment of diplomatic relations between Chechnya and Russia be signed, but Rybkin refused, insisting that Chechnya was still part of the Russian Federation.

One might suppose that it was around this time that Udugov and Berezovsky got together and set up their own hostage-negotiating side business, but that is not the case. A November 1996 photograph shows them in deep, friendly conversation. Klebnikov writes in his book

Godfather of the Kremlin, "Berezovsky's relationship with Udugov was especially close," and he produces several recorded conversations likely relating to money transfers for hostages to prove it. Indeed, Udugov often boasted to friends of his ability to get money from Berezovsky on demand.

With considerable ingenuity, Udugov maneuvered diplomatically for international recognition of Chechnya as an independent country. He tried all kinds of tricks. As early as February 1997, he made foreign journalists obtain written permission from Ichkeria's Interior Ministry to visit the republic. He also told the OSCE that its Grozny mission would have to get formal written permission to stay in Chechnya because the mandate issued by the Russian Foreign Ministry had no legal power in Chechnya and "the independent Chechen state can no longer reconcile itself to judicial, legal gaps."

Udugov approached twenty countries to establish diplomatic relations, including Afghanistan, which responded positively. Journalists were often told that "several countries" had recognized Chechnya's independence (but Udugov wouldn't name them). In June, Udugov applied for Chechnya's membership in the United Nations. Udugov claimed that the May 1997 treaty between Russia and Chechnya had been analyzed by prominent international lawyers who all agreed that the treaty recognized the sovereignty of Chechnya. He highly publicized Grozny's acceptance as a member into the Saudi-based International Organization of the Capitals of Islamic States. He also tried to schedule a meeting with Louis Farrakhan, head of the Nation of Islam, during Farrakhan's brief private visit to Moscow. Why he wanted to meet with him is unknown.

Udugov was especially upbeat after Maskhadov's November 1997 trip to the United States. "I arrived in America on an official invitation" with "a diplomatic visa" and "as president of a free country," Maskhadov would tell doubters. Udugov praised the visit as a "diplomatic breakthrough" that would help Ichkeria become a "full-fledged subject of international law." Maskhadov echoed Udugov's claim that "many foreign states, beginning with the United States, are ready to recognize Chechnya's independence," but none did. Perhaps Moscow's threat to sever diplomatic relations with any country that dared recognize Chechnya as an independent country influenced some governments. All Udugov could do was to comment that Russia's threat was "ill timed and tactless."

In January 1998, Udugov became Ichkeria's deputy prime minister and minister of foreign affairs. Two months later, acting Prime Minister Basayev called for termination of talks with Russia. In his opinion, Maskhadov was only "pushing the republic back into the Russian Federation." By summer, Udugov publicly gave up too. In August, he claimed that no real progress had been made on defining the Chechen-Russian relationship since the

Khasavyurt agreement. He warned of destabilization in the North Caucasus, commenting to more than one person that a new war in Chechnya was inevitable.

THE GREAT CHECHNYA IDEOLOGIST

Udugov was right about a new war. Even if the Kremlin had recognized Chechnya's independence in 1997, the act of recognition would not have prevented a new war with Russia because Udugov and others were working against building the kind of genuine law-abiding Chechen state that would honor the territorial integrity of its neighbors.

While Maskhadov's foreign minister officially declared, "We want to live by the rules of the international community," privately Udugov devoted himself to the task of reuniting Chechnya and Dagestan. That proposition was not only totally at odds with Maskhadov's vision for Chechnya but could be realized only by force of arms in violation of international law. Udugov's unrelenting drive toward this end caused the Chechen president to charge him with "large scale ideological sabotage against the Chechen state," label Udugov a traitor, and kick him out of the government. It also led to holy wars with Dagestan and Russia.

Udugov never tried to hide his support and close association with the fundamentalist Wahhabi communities in Dagestan and Chechnya. His brother, Isa Umarov, was a Wahhabi leader. Udugov even received money from this small and secretive group of initially peaceful fundamentalists who at one time avoided open conflict with everybody.

Udugov was a strong advocate of the growing Wahhabi community in Chechnya, even using his position as minister of information to openly promote their beliefs. He arranged for regular television broadcasts of Wahhabi sermons through his own Kavkaz television station and strongly supported Wahhabi candidates like Islam Khalimov for high positions in the Yandarbiyev government. Even before the first Chechen war, Russia was calling Udugov the "ideologist of Wahhabism."

Like Basayev and so many others, Udugov reminisced of Imam Shamil's historical Dagestan. It therefore surprised few who knew him that in July 1997, Udugov announced his intention to establish an Islamic Nations movement to succeed his 1996 First Congress of the Vainakh Diaspora. Islamic Nations would bring together thirty-five Dagestani and Chechen Islamic political parties and religious and social movements, including Wahhabi, with the aim of "restoring Dagestan to its historical borders as it existed during the imamate of Shamil in the nineteenth century."

Udugov wooed the Chechen-Akkin people and local followers of Wahhabism in Dagestan, his lawyers justifying reunification of the two republics on the grounds that Chechnya had never seceded from the historical Dagestan of Imam Shamil in the first place. "Our aim," Udugov said, "is to prevent the splitting of the Chechens and the peoples of Dagestan on the grounds of ethnicity. . . . The Islamic Nation will orient itself toward restoring Dagestan to its historical boundaries."

Of course, there was a critical economic consideration behind Udugov's ambitions. "We want to preclude Chechnya from being isolated from Dagestan," he proclaimed. Indeed, by uniting the two republics, Chechnya would be able to breach the "Orthodox Christian blockade" imposed on the republic by Russia and Georgia. Sixty percent of Russia's Caspian oil shelf is located in Dagestan. If Chechnya had free access to Dagestan, then Chechnya's oil industry would become sufficiently independent, and Chechnya could separate itself from the Russian economic system. A unified Chechnya-Dagestan would bring Chechnya economic viability because it would have access to the Caspian Sea.

Udugov's Islamic Nations movement elected a representative body— the Majlis—which in turn elected Udugov its amir. Udugov also established the Chechen Islamic Order coalition in late July 1997, uniting some twenty Chechen political parties.

That fall, Amir Udugov increasingly spoke of the movement's need to fight for its aim of establishing a unified Islamic state. When Dagestani and Chechen Islamic Nations delegations traveled to Vedeno, the old capital of Shamil's imamate, to celebrate the Imam's two hundredth birthday in 1997, the slogans "Chechnya and Dagestan forever, together and free" and "Freedom is not given, it must be won" dominated the celebrations. Hadji Makhachyev, the leader of the Avar National Front, and Magomed Khachilayev, head of the Lak movement Kazi Kumakh, participated in the celebrations.

Throughout the fall of 1997, Udugov's unification rhetoric became increasingly militant. In November, he accused Russian intelligence services of intentionally aggravating relations between Chechnya and Dagestan by blaming Chechens and the Wahhabis for kidnappings and all the other troubles in Dagestan. Udugov repeatedly stated, "Grozny is ready to arm our Dagestani brothers for a joint struggle against Russia." He told a meeting of the Islamic Nations' Majlis, "The Chechen side has decided to help our Dagestani brothers so that armed Dagestan, together with Chechnya, could rise up against Russia."

While Udugov was propagandizing armed insurrection, Khattab was busy arming the Little Wahhabi Republic. But according to Udugov, it was Russia who was preparing to start a new war in the North Caucasus, as evidenced by the buildup of Russian military presence in Dagestan and the political and economic isolation of Chechnya.

In April 1998, Udugov took his Islamic Nations movement to the next level. He spent four months working with Dagestani and Chechen Wahhabi leaders, Basayev, and Khattab, organizing an Islamic Congress of Peoples of Chechnya and Dagestan under the aegis of the Islamic Nations' Majlis. The congress, which met in early April, consisted of 197 delegates from Dagestan, 186 delegates from Chechnya, and one hundred invited guests. The Dagestani government refused to attend, but Chechen Vice President Vakha Arsanov did participate. He promised that Maskhadov would come too, later in the afternoon, but he never showed up.

The congress made itself a permanent body, elected Shamil Basayev as its amir and Udugov its first deputy amir, and declared its intention to unify Chechnya and Dagestan into a single Islamic imamate by force if necessary. Basayev's leadership gave Udugov's unification movement significant impetus. It also became an active organizational force behind the Wahhabi uprising just months away in Dagestan.

Maskhadov was not happy with these developments, but all he could say was, "I will not allow any parties, movements, or congresses to heighten tensions in Chechnya and perform actions which can complicate relations with our neighboring states."

The Dagestani government wasn't happy either. It sent a statement accusing the congress of interfering in Dagestan's internal affairs. Even Magomed Khachilayev, who would himself in a month revolt and briefly raise the green Islamic flag over the Dagestani capital, signed the Dagestani government's letter of protest.

Udugov now explicitly warned that if Russian authorities moved to oppress Muslims in Dagestan, official Grozny "will assist in resolving the conflict by peaceful political means, but armed Chechen volunteers would be sent." He called for the formation of a special "Islamic peacekeeping brigade." This was officially constituted from Khattab's fighters and training graduates in June 1998, with the brigade carrying out its first "war games" under Basayev's leadership a month later. Udugov, who was present at the military display, told anxious reporters, "The brigade will show who really controls the Caucasus."

ANOTHER MASKHADOV BETRAYAL

Udugov did much to set the stage for future armed conflict with Russia. By the fall of 1998, he was also sitting squarely in the camp of the opposition to Maskhadov. Udugov, together with Vice President Arsanov and Zelimkhan Yandarbiyev, constituted in Maskhadov's own words "the Wahhabi bloc of the opposition." At one point in his rage, Maskhadov even labelled Udugov and Isa Umarov as "the main executors of the Chechen opposition."

In September 1998, Udugov's Kavkaz television repeatedly aired the litany of charges that Basayev, Israpilov, and Raduyev had brought against Maskhadov, causing the beleaguered president to pronounce Udugov's television station "a nest of evil and provocations" that "puts the Chechen people on the brink of a civil war." Maskhadov was especially critical of Kavkaz television's support of the unification congress and its aims. In early November, Maskhadov banned the television station for broadcasting "anti-state propaganda" and "the provocative statements of political parties, movements, and individuals." Udugov appealed to the Shariah court.

The Chechen president fired Udugov from his position as foreign minister on 30 October 1998. This was done as part of an agreement between Maskhadov and Russian Prime Minister Yevgeny Primakov in a "secret" meeting in Vladikavkaz on 29 October. In exchange, Primakov agreed to rebuild several enterprises, pay pensions and compensation to Chechen victims of the 1944 deportations, and establish cooperation between Russian and Chechen law enforcement bodies.

Maskhadov fired Udugov but was powerless to do anything more because "with the exception of Mufti Akhmat Kadyrov and the president, there are no people in the Chechen leadership who are against Udugov and the Kavkaz television company." *Nezavisimaya Gazeta* wrote, "Many members of the Cabinet shun from ideological attacks on their former comrades." Speaking on Kavkaz television in January 1999, Shamil Basayev, referring to the shootout between Shariah troops and his own men outside Urus-Martan that month, accused Maskhadov of fanning tension in Urus-Martan and adjacent areas and seeking a military confrontation.

Right after that, one of Maskhadov's gangs attacked Udugov's television station with grenade launchers. Nevertheless, in the emergency meeting of opposition leaders at Starye-Atagi that followed, Udugov voted not to oust President Maskhadov by force.

Udugov was therefore delighted with Maskhadov's 3 February 1999 decree announcing his intention to implement full Shariah rule in Chechnya because it meant that Maskhadov would finally relinquish his presidential power. Udugov reminded all that under full Shariah rule there are no such words as "president," "parliament," or "constitution" because all decisions are made by the collective Shura council. Movladi Udugov told radio Ekho Moskvy on 21 February that elections would soon be held for a new head of state and predicted that Maskhadov would win, but that the post would be "decorative."

In those last days of May 1998, Udugov flirted more and more with extremism. He more than toyed with the thought of bringing Osama bin Laden to Chechnya. The Arab-language *Al Hayat* newspaper reported in December 1998 that a Chechen official by the name of Ibragimov in charge of one of Chechnya's Foreign Ministry departments was negotiating with the Taliban in Kandahar to give Osama bin Laden political asylum in Chechnya. Yaragi Abdullayev, a former deputy of Udugov's, reportedly made a special trip to Kabul to further pursue the negotiations. Udugov publicly confirmed that the negotiations were taking place.

V

HOLY WARS IN DAGESTAN AND BOMBS IN MOSCOW

I think that the independent Chechnya should exist in its present boundaries, but Basayev thinks differently. He would like to try the Chechen experiment in other bordering territories, first of all in Dagestan, through which he can seek access to two seas, the Black Sea and the Caspian.

President Aslan Maskhadov, 29 October 1998

THE "BROTHERS" BASAYEV

It was Basayev's patronage that brought Khattab to Chechnya in the first place, and it was Basayev's political protection that made him untouchable by the Chechen prosecutor's office in 1996 and by the political and religious leadership in Grozny in 1998. It was also Basayev who made this Arab foreigner acceptable to Chechen society. Khattab's "adoption" by Basayev's father and acceptance as a "son" by Shamil's mother helped too.

Over the years, this brotherly relationship grew and matured through mutual respect and help, battlefield trust, shared political visions, and common hatreds. Khattab's battlefield experience and skilled foreign fighting force, his ties with the Afghan Alumni and al Qaeda as a source of fresh fighters, and especially his access to foreign money greatly benefited Basayev and gave Khattab significant influence within the ranks of the Chechen mujahideen.

In turn, Khattab was able to religiously influence Basayev, who belonged to the mystical Naqshbandi Sufi order and showed little interest in radical Islam in the early 1990s. Akhmed Magomedov, a Wahhabi preacher in Moscow, sarcastically recalls, "Shamil Basayev learned that he was leading a jihad from Russian NTV television. Only after being informed of this did he start reading religious books and making some progress in Islam." Khattab helped. But to this day, Basayev insists that he is not a Wahhabi—"None of us are Wahhabis."

In the spring of 1998, Basayev and Khattab entered into a fateful alliance that would forever change the face of the Chechen political struggle and even the physical landscape of Chechnya.

THE HOLY MISSION

Khattab believed that Allah had blessed him and Basayev with the holy mission of creating a new imamate in the North Caucasus that would stretch from the Caspian to the Black Sea. Khattab described this as "a pure Islamic land" governed by Wahhabi ideology, a land "which will be wiped clean of any kafir [infidels] or non-Islamic civilians." Furthermore, "Russians, Christians, and Jews" would be excluded from living in this holy land.

In April 1998, Udugov, Basayev, Khattab, and others went to work to create this new Chechnya. When the founding Congress of Peoples of Chechnya and Dagestan finished its first meeting, Basayev immediately called for the liberation of Dagestan, the first step in creating the new Islamic imamate. While Basayev said he hoped Dagestan's liberation could be done through political, not military, means, he began secretly burying stockpiles of war materials anyway.

Khattab was busier. In May 1998, he officially became Basayev's "advisor" and also began preparing for war. The following month, Khattab likely attended Osama bin Laden's worldwide Islamic League emergency session in Kandahar, Afghanistan, at which he must have laid out the idea of reuniting Chechnya and Dagestan by force and creating a new Islamic imamate in the North Caucasus. Osama bin Laden surely liked the idea; after all, he had been telling the delegates: "You cannot defeat the heretics with this book [the Koran] alone; you must show them your fist." At Kandahar or later, Khattab secured the Islamist commander in chief's personal guarantee of financial assistance for the project.

When Khattab got home, he immediately gave his fighting force a new name—the Peacekeeping Brigade of the Congress of Peoples of Chechnya and Dagestan—and an international "peacekeeping" mission. The brigade's initial strength numbered about seven hundred Chechens and foreigners.

That same month, local Dagestani Islamists led by Magomed Khachilayev and his brother Nadirshakh seized Dagestan's State Council building. The Khachilayevs got the unsolicited support of the Dagestani Wahhabi communities that Khattab had trained and helped arm. Militant Wahhabis used the opportunity to seize the police station in Karamakhi (killing one policeman), begin building fortified positions in the village, and establish a "checkpoint" along the highway connecting Buinaksk and Dagestan's mountainous districts.

When news of the Khachilayev revolt and the events in Karamakhi reached the Congress of Peoples of Chechnya and Dagestan, the congress declared its readiness to send Khattab's peacekeeping brigade to Dagestan if Russia intervened militarily. Raduyev jumped into the chorus too and threatened to start a war with Russia under the terms of the 1997 jamaat military treaty.

Maskhadov's patience was running short. He proclaimed that the Khachilayev brothers were in pursuit of their own clan interests and warned Basayev, Udugov, and Raduyev that Dagestan is a military adventure that they had better stay away from. As it turned out, neither Khattab's brigade nor General Dudayev's Army were needed because the Khachilayev coup fizzled on its own.

Then in June, Maskhadov's national security service director, Leche Khultygov, dropped a political bombshell when he told a stunned Chechen parliament that hundreds of millions of dollars were being brought into Chechnya from an Arab country to destabilize Dagestan and support the unification congress's activities. He said that it was Khattab and his Arab friends who were behind the conspiracy and warned that Chechnya had better put an end to the Wahhabis now before they got out of hand. "Our wolf is not getting into their Arab desert, so we must not let them get their camel into our place," he told the deputies. "It's time for Khattab to go home." That was good advice, but it was too late. A month later, Khultygov was shot dead at one of Raduyev's anti-Maskhadov rallies.

On 3 July, Basayev tendered his resignation as Ichkeria's acting prime minister "to concentrate on the work of the Congress." On 29 October 1998, President Maskhadov told Russian Prime Minister Yevgeny Primakov in Vladikavkaz what Basayev had meant in his short resignation statement: "I think that the independent Chechnya should exist in its present boundaries, but Basayev thinks differently. He would like to try the Chechen experiment in other bordering territories, first of all in Dagestan, through which he can seek access to two seas, the Black Sea and the Caspian."

Since Basayev had been appointed acting prime minister for a period of only six months, his term had expired anyway. In fact, a good deal of his popularity had been lost by his failing to keep his promise of improving the economy and reducing poverty and crime in Chechnya. He never did get the cooperation that he had asked for. Tax collection dropped and so did Chechnya's National Bank reserves, while the theft of petroleum products skyrocketed. Moreover, at the end of August, the Chechen parliament gave the work of Basayev's cabinets from December 1997 to July 1998 a failing grade and recommended that Maskhadov dismiss the entire government.

The day after his resignation, Basayev flaunted the congress's military muscle when he led showcase war games in Vedeno with about one thousand fighters of Khattab's peacekeeping brigade made up of Chechen, Arab, Dagestani, and even African fighters. Udugov made sure that reporters were given full access and told them that the games were meant to show Russia that any military measures against Wahhabis in Dagestan would not go unpunished. At the concluding ceremonies, Khattab symbolically awarded a sword to Basayev, who promised not to hang it on the wall but to use it to liberate the Caucasus. Udugov's personal appearance and his statements about the brigade's liberating mission in the Caucasus were also notable.

The following month, Maskhadov signed a decree releasing Basayev as deputy commander in chief of the Chechen armed forces after having appointed him to the position only three months earlier during the Gudermes uprising and the subsequent state of emergency in an attempt to calm things down.

August 1998 turned out to be a very busy month in both Chechnya and Dagestan. The mufti of Dagestan was killed in a bomb blast. He had been critical of the local Wahhabi community, which was suspected of the murder.

Also in August, the local governments of Karamakhi (which had lived its own autonomous life since May anyway), Chabanmakhi, and Kadar took the risky step of declaring the three villages "liberated Islamic territory." Shariah law replaced Russian Federation law in these areas. The Wahhabis also erected more of their own border posts, checkpoints, and signs warning that the territory was under Shariah Law.

That same month, Wahhabi representatives from these three villages traveled to Grozny to meet with Basayev, who gave them his word that he would send Khattab's "peacekeepers" to defend them if Dagestani authorities attempted to restore constitutional order in their "separate Islamic territory."

The 9 September arrest of Magomed Khachilayev brought a storm of protest from Basayev and Udugov's congress and a formal demand for Khachilayev's release. These demands were followed by Raduyev's own threats of terror against the Dagestani leadership if they did not free Khachilayev.

But neither Basayev nor Khattab got a chance to fight in Dagestan in 1998 because Russia decided not to resort to military force to reestablish law and order in Dagestan. After a brief personal visit to Karamakhi to get a look for himself, Russian Interior Minister Sergei Stepashin declined to crack down on the Wahhabi community.

GANGING UP ON MASKHADOV

Maskhadov had become disgusted by his associates' attempt to expand their struggle beyond Chechen borders. In August 1998, he choose to seriously interfere in the Dagestani plans of the Congress of Peoples of Chechnya and Dagestan. In the 25 August 1998 issue of *Nezavisimaya Gazeta*, Maskhadov's new First Deputy Prime Minister Turpal Atgeriyev (a relative) accused Basayev of inciting tensions in Chechen-Dagestani relations by his ill-conceived statements on behalf of the Chechen people in support of unification with Dagestan. Atgeriyev said that Basayev had no right to speak for the Chechen people or any Chechen governmental body in support of those who wanted to make Dagestan independent of Russia. Maskhadov followed by calling Basayev's and Udugov's plans "adventuresome." Until now, Maskhadov had been careful not to criticize Basayev publicly.

The attack called for a response. In mid-September, Basayev and his ally Khunkar Israpilov joined forces with the opposition being led by the not-quite-all-there Salman Raduyev for the purpose of forcing Maskhadov to resign as president. These defections immediately gave Raduyev's opposition power and new momentum.

Together, Basayev, Israpilov, Raduyev, and other members of the influential Commanders Council headed by Vakha Arsanov accused Maskhadov of violating Ichkeria's constitution along with a laundry list of other crimes. The list was sent to the Chechen parliament in mid-September 1998 for action.

Basayev's complaint said that Maskhadov had used cronyism and nepotism to pick candidates for office, held raucous celebrations, and built a sumptuous residence at a time when thousands of people in Chechnya were homeless. But more importantly, the president had:

- Usurped power and preempted the judicial system by depriving the parliament of its right to appoint judges.
- Implemented a Shariah legal system that ran counter to the republic's constitution and had provoked several armed conflicts.

- Knowingly obstructed the process of setting up a constitutional court in the republic.
- Violated the law by which the state sovereignty and independence of Chechnya could not be a subject of negotiation with other nations, including Russia.
- Received arms from Russia after his envoys had held secret talks with Russian Interior Minister Sergei Stepashin.

On 23 September, Chechnya's parliament considered the accusations with Maskhadov present. He persuaded the parliament to dismiss Basayev's charges.

At the end of September, the Commanders Council organized a congress at a sports stadium in Grozny to draw further public attention to its charges against Maskhadov. The event was attended by several thousand spectators. The presidium of the congress—namely Basayev, Raduyev, Ruslan Gelayev, Israpilov, and now the disloyal Vakha Arsanov—spelled out the charge that Maskhadov was trying to make the Chechen population into a bunch of slaves and was ruling the republic by dictatorship.

The event, chaired by Basayev, took and passed a vote of no-confidence in Maskhadov's ability to manage the country and demanded that he resign, threatening civil unrest if he refused to go.

The accused organized a counter-demonstration, a military parade on the other side of the stadium. He also retaliated by taking oversight of the oil industry away from Shirvani Basayev, who had been made chairman of the State Committee for Fuel and Energy by his brother in the cabinet reshuffle in January 1998. Maskhadov also proposed that Raduyev ought to be brought before a firing squad and shot.

Rumors of a coup circulated. Basayev, though, went to great pains in all public appearances to dispel such rumors by promising that the Commanders Council would seek the resignation of the president only by constitutional means. He even criticized Raduyev for suggesting there could be a coup. Basayev had repeatedly said since 1997 that he would use only legal means to oppose the president if that became necessary—even now he could not bring himself to start an armed struggle against Maskhadov.

In October, Raduyev revived the All National Congress of the Chechen People (OKChN) that had been earlier headed by Dzokhar Dudayev. Raduyev was trying to position himself as Dudayev's legitimate heir. Henceforth, in Raduyev's own words, "all anti-government activities will be carried out under the aegis of the OKChN." Was Raduyev trying to show Moscow that he was the one really in charge in Chechnya? After all, it was Raduyev who was able to get Camilla Carr and Jon James released in September 1998, when no one else could.

The next step was to broaden the base of the opposition. To that end it set up the Center for Social and Political Parties and Movements. This institution provided a broader forum in which anyone opposed to Maskhadov could join. Many people joined the center, which demanded Maskhadov's resignation as well as rejection of any talks with Russia until the Kremlin formally recognized Chechnya's independence.

In December, the opposition took its case to Chechnya's Supreme Shariah Court. On 24 December, the court—which consisted of Maskhadov appointees—found that the president had violated some laws. The judges accepted several of Basayev's arguments—including questions concerning the role of the country's secular parliament and the appointment to high offices of Chechens who had served in the pro-Moscow Chechen government during the 1994–1996 war—but rejected Basayev's call to make Maskhadov resign.

Early in the new year, the Shariah Court ordered the suspension of parliament for violating Shariah law. Parliament in turn declared the court's suspension illegal and proclaimed the Shariah Court unconstitutional because it had been set up by Maskhadov instead of the parliament as specified by the constitution.

The Commanders Council, which had only two weeks earlier itself called for dissolving the parliament and replacing it with a governing Shura council, now sided with the parliamentarians, shocking everybody. Basayev explained his reversal by saying that the Shariah judges had violated the Koran and Shariah when they voted to suspend the parliament because their action was taken to deflect the public's attention away from the charges being brought against Maskhadov.

At the end of January, the Commanders Council met and developed a set of measures to reorganize the state, but again they denied any intention of overthrowing Maskhadov. Their measures included curtailing the power of the president and the creation of a "Mehk Khel" (Shura council), which would collectively govern the country. On 1 February, they formally petitioned Maskhadov to adopt their proposals.

Maskhadov answered by going on government television on 3 February and reading a decree announcing full Shariah rule in Chechnya, suspending parliament as of 4 February, and creating a commission that would draw up a new Islamic constitution within ninety days.

This time Basayev, Udugov, and others were pleased. They concluded that Maskhadov had finally fully embraced Islam—he would soon cease to be the president because "he must turn over his power to the Shura." The creation of a Shura council, the supreme body of the state combining all the executive, legislative, and judicial branches of power, would be the final step in this process.

Maskhadov agreed to create a Shura all right, calling it the State Council, but he would personally appoint its members. He named Yandarbiyev, Basayev, Israpilov, Arsanov, and others to the council, but they refused to accept his appointments because the council was not to have governing powers over the Chechen Republic of Ichkeria. In short, Maskhadov still did not want to give up his presidential powers.

Maskhadov left the opposition no choice. On 8 February, Basayev dissolved his Party of Freedom on grounds that there should be only one party in Chechnya—the "party of Allah." The following day, the Commanders Council convened its own Shura and eleven days later elected Basayev leader of Ichkeria's thirty-five-member Mehk Khel, which stood as a rival government to President Aslan Maskhadov's now isolated government.

The Mehk Khel declared itself the highest authority in the land. Former acting President Yandarbiyev and even former allies of Maskhadov joined the body. Maskhadov was invited to join too, but he refused. Opposition Shura centers run by field commanders were opened in most of the republic's districts. Khamid Basayev, Shamil's younger brother, became deputy head of the Main Staff of the Ichkerian Shura.

Chechnya now had two governments, Maskhadov's and an alternate Islamic government headed by Shamil Basayev. In the spring of 1999, Shamil Basayev was the most powerful leader in Chechnya.

ESTABLISHING THE NEW IMAMATE

While Basayev and Udugov engaged Maskhadov, Wahhabi political unrest in Dagestan festered. Basayev and Khattab fed it by agitating, arming, and training more Dagestani Wahhabi militants in Khattab's camps despite President Maskhadov's 1998 summer decree outlawing the camps.

At the end of the year, rumors began to circulate about an impending Wahhabi attack on Dagestani authorities. In part, the rumors were fueled by leaflets circulated in some Dagestani villages saying that there would soon be a war to liberate Dagestan from Russia and establish an Islamic state. The leaflets were signed "The Congress of Chechen-Dagestani Nations" and "The United Dagestani-Chechen Jamaats." They were Udugov's handiwork.

By early 1999, armed Dagestani Wahhabis led by Brigadier General Jarull Rajbaddinov from Karamakhi completely controlled the Little Wahhabi Republic. Then in March, the Wahhabi *Khalif* newspaper published in Grozny announced the formation of the Islamic Army of the Caucasus. By now, weapons from Chechnya were freely flowing into Karamakhi, Chabanmakhi, and Kadar.

By the summer of 1999, there wasn't anybody in Chechnya who didn't expect something to happen in Dagestan soon. Mairbek Vachagayev, Maskhadov's representative in Moscow, later said that Basayev's and Khattab's military actions in Dagestan in August 1999 came as no surprise to him or, for that matter, to most Chechens: "Everyone who watched Movladi Udugov's Kavkaz TV channel expected something like this to happen." This is what Maskhadov meant when he told German Die Deutsche Welle radio that the 1999 war with Russia was "masterminded by Basayev and Udugov."

"We asked Basayev not to attack Dagestan—we said that we should first show the world that we are an Islamist state and let them see for themselves that everything is OK," Magomed Khambiyev, Ichkeria's minister of defense, told a *Vlast* Russian correspondent after he surrendered in April 2004.

Then why didn't Maskhadov, Khambiyev, and the others stop Basayev? "If we had done something against Basayev, the Chechen people would not have understood. Forty percent of the people supported him; he is, after all, a hero of Ichkeria. People saw him as a liberator after the first war," Khambiyev explains. Moreover, Maskhadov depended on Basayev. "Without Basayev, Maskhadov didn't have enough money, arms, or people," Khambiyev elaborated.

For a month and a half before entry into Dagestan, Basayev and Udugov tried to rally the support of the whole Dagestani Wahhabi community, inviting Taifura Eldarkhanov, Bagautdin Magomedov, and Adolla Aliyev to Chechnya with rewards of oil riches. Khattab also recruited five hundred Dagestanis in the Botlikhsky district and paid them $150 each to agitate. Dagestani fighters were also recruited with promises of $700 each and a $1,500 pension to the family if the fighter was killed in combat. Money was also paid out to collect intelligence on the deployment of Russian forces. Then Basayev brought in two religious higher-ups, one from Saudi Arabia and one from Pakistan, with signed "fatwas" (religious decrees granting permission) to launch the holy war against Dagestan.

Nikolai Zhitch, a Russian Chechnya analyst, writing in *Versiya* on 8 June 1999, predicted a Chechen invasion of Dagestan in the middle of that month. "Khattab is just waiting to graduate another class of 1999 in June," he wrote. Zhitch estimated that "66 percent of all Chechen guerrillas will move into neighboring [Dagestan] by mid-June to take part in hostilities. At the same time, those particular forces controlled by President Aslan Maskhadov will remain in Chechnya."

Zhitch was two months off in his estimate. In the last weeks of July 1999, Dagestani police and Russian federal forces surrounded Wahhabi villages and established their own checkpoints. When skirmishes broke out, the militant Wahhabi leaders who had visited Basayev in Grozny in July called on him for help. The leadership of the Congress of Peoples of Chechnya and Dagestan met on 24 July to officially "discuss the situation" in Dagestan.

On 7 August, Basayev and Khattab, supported by a fresh group of Khattab's training camp graduates and seasoned warriors from the Wahhabi community in Urus-Martin and elsewhere in Chechnya, launched their holy war against the Dagestani government. Basayev told *Lidove Noviny* that he crossed the border because "many Dagestani political parties and movements are fighting for Dagestan's freedom nowadays. Some of them have asked me to take up the command of the Mujahideen United Armed Forces of Dagestan." He also pledged to cleanse Dagestan of Zionist influences, a theme that was echoed by Udugov, who said that the mujahideen were fighting "world Zionism" and that their ultimate goal was to liberate Jerusalem.

Khattab described his role as the "military commander of the operation" and Basayev as the "overall commander in the battlefield." Arbi Barayev and Abdul Malik Mezhidov participated too. So did Shirvani Basayev and about two thousand Chechen, Turkish, Pakistani, Saudi, Dagestani, and other fighters armed with APCs, antitank guns, air defense systems, and the very best in other modern Russian fighting equipment.

Numerous times during the assault, Basayev made the point that this was a truly international Islamic army entering Dagestan: "It is not a Chechen army, but an international corps comprising Chechens, Dagestanis, and other nationals." This international army was Khattab's Peacekeeping Brigade of the Congress of Peoples of Chechnya and Dagestan, later called the Islamic International Brigade—the same Islamic International Brigade that the U.S. State Department put on its terrorist list in February 2003.

One of Basayev's fighters was a British citizen of African descent known as Amir Assadula. He converted to Islam in the early 1990s, went to Chechnya after the first war, and joined Khattab's foreign mujahideen forces. When he was killed in the Vedensky district in July 2002, a video-cassette that he had recently made to recruit foreign fighters was found in his belongings.

There were many others: Colonel Abu Khakhim, Khattab's first deputy; Xavier Djaffa, a Frenchman; Abu Abdullah Jafar (also spelled Dzhafar), a Pakistani; Sheikh Abu Musab from Algeria (an instructor in Khattab's Caucasus Islamic Institute); and others like Masood al-Benin.

Masood al-Benin was born in France, graduated with a degree in mechanical engineering, and then went on to do an MBA in London. There, he was recruited for training in Afghanistan but, at the last minute, decided to go to Chechnya with two friends. Benin arrived in Chechnya at the end of the 1994–1996 war, later trained in Khattab's camps, and became a religious instructor and a reporter for qoqaz.net. He died fighting in Shatoi in the spring of 2000. His obituary published by qoqaz.net says, "The [videos] edited by Masood are currently in circulation all over the world."

Basayev's international army immediately occupied thirty-six villages, seven of them (Ansalta, Rokhota, Shodroda, Ziberkhali, and Tando in the Botlikhsky district, and Gagatli and Andi in the Tsumadinsky district) without a fight.

Local Islamic governing bodies were hastily set up and the Islamic Shura of Dagestan was established as the governing body of the new Islamic imamate. On 10 August, the Shura government declared Dagestan independent of Russia in a formal Decree of Independence that was announced to the world on the kavkaz.org Web site. At the same time, the Shura proclaimed the necessity of "liberating the Islamic territory of Dagestan from age-old occupation by Russian rebels." To do that the Shura officially declared a second holy war, this time on Russia. This declaration was also published on the kavkaz.org Web site.

Thus Basayev and Khattab not only precipitated an act of war on Russia by invading Dagestan, but their new Islamic government officially and publicly declared war on both Dagestan and Russia.

The Shura further introduced by proclamation Shariah law across the whole of Dagestan and ordered the arrest of the Dagestani president as a traitor to the cause of Muslims.

Sirazhdin Ramazanov, the prime minister of the new Islamic Dagestan, announced that he had started "consultations" to form a government. His first appointment was that of Magomed Tagayev (the author of several books calling for a holy war in Dagestan) as minister of information.

An Islamic Shura of Dagestan decree issued on 10 August asked Basayev to be the military amir of the United Forces of the Dagestani Mujahideen. The next day, Basayev named Khattab commander of the Shura's Islamic Army of Dagestan and proclaimed that the international forces in Dagestan "would fight until the full victory of Islam in the world."

Meanwhile, Movladi Udugov, as the spokesman for the Congress of the Peoples of Chechnya and Dagestan, reported from Chechnya on the progress being made in establishing the new Islamic state. On 29 August, Maskhadov fired Udugov from the Chechen National Security Council for this and "large scale ideological sabotage against the Chechen state."

For the two weeks that they were in Dagestan, Basayev and Khattab exposed whole villages and their populations to Russian military bombardment. Basayev warned the residents of Ansalta and elsewhere and entire villages were evacuated. Russian air and artillery bombardment began on 10 August. Several villages were completely destroyed as fighting spread from Botlikhsky to the Tsumadinsky and ultimately to the Buinaksky districts.

If Basayev and Khattab ever did expect overwhelming support from those elements of the population that wanted to rid Dagestan of Russians, they never got it. Basayev and Khattab were not welcomed as liberators by anybody except Wahhabi militants, and the behavior of some of Basayev's men irked devout villagers: "I saw these so-called believers. They don't take their shoes off in the mosque. They don't know how to pray and they drink vodka by the glassful." Some residents even asked Russian authorities to give them guns so they could defend themselves.

By mid-August, things were not going well for Basayev. Two Russian divisions (one army and one Interior Ministry) plus about one thousand Dagestani police engaged his international army. On 14–17 August, Basayev's forces were driven out of the Tsumadinsky district. On 15 August, he appealed to the Dagestani people: "For 140 years Islamic Dagestan has been occupied by the Russian kafir. For 140 years Islamic Dagestan has been ruled by the law of Satan and his servants. We want victory or Paradise! And, God willing, we will free Dagestan from the kafirs. Drive the Russian aggressors and their hangers-on out of your villages and cities. Establish the Shariah of Allah, and perhaps you will be saved."

Three days later Basayev returned to Chechnya and summoned a "congress" of field commanders to appeal for help. Maskhadov and Yandarbiyev attended, and so did Raduyev and others. Basayev called on them to support "the struggle of faith" in Dagestan, but all except Israpilov condemned the action. It's true that Raduyev considered helping Basayev. Had the smell of blood brought him back from Pakistan? Maybe, but in the end, Raduyev decided to get even with Basayev for earlier calling him a "hysterical woman." To the surprise of many, Raduyev was perfectly calm and logical at the meeting, simply saying that he was categorically opposed to Basayev's actions in Dagestan.

It took two weeks of Russian heavy aerial bombing, rocket attacks from Russian helicopter gunships, and artillery assaults to dislodge Basayev and Khattab from Dagestan. Conventional weapons did little good. It was the use of devastating fuel air explosives (vacuum bombs) that did the trick. On 22 August, Russian air forces and artillery also hit Kenkhi, Komsomolskoye, Vedeno, Gudermes, Sovetskoye, Urus-Martan, Serzhen-Yurt, and other towns and villages in Chechnya that Russia believed were supporting Basayev. Udugov says that Khattab's camps were the first to be targeted during the battles in Botlikh and, as a result, Chechen fighters had to relocate their bases in the mountains.

On 23 August, Magomed Tagayev announced that Basayev had ordered his mujahideen to fall back into Chechnya to prepare for the "second phase of the operation."

Of course, Masood al-Benin filmed the whole thing. Until it was disabled, pictures could be seen on the qoqaz.net Web site. In an interview with Azzam Publications on 27 September 1999, Khattab said that his forces shot down several helicopters (one with three senior Russian generals in it), two attack planes, and destroyed eighteen Russian Army vehicles. He claimed his fighters killed five hundred Russian soldiers. Udugov's Kavkaz television reported that Basayev and Khattab lost only thirty-two of their own men with sixty-two wounded in the operation. Russia counted more than five hundred mujahideen killed. The Kuwaiti newspaper *Al-Sharq Al-Awsat* said that at least forty Arab volunteers died in Dagestan. Two of them were Hakhim al-Madani and Sheikh Al-Tabuki. Khattab was slightly wounded.

Basayev and Khattab, though, miraculously escaped. How was this possible? Anne Nivat, a Moscow correspondent for the French daily *Liberation* who covered the war, tells that she learned from eyewitnesses that Basayev and Khattab left the battle zone along a safe corridor at night in cars with their headlights on with no attempt at concealment. *Novaya Gazeta* on 6 September 1999 reported a similar story.

A third version published in the Russian magazine *Profile* says that Basayev and Khattab were escorted back to the Chechen border by two armed Russian helicopters. Another version based on an account by a Dagestani policeman published in the German book *Der Krieg im Schatten* (2003) says that the retreat took place in "broad daylight," and that "they used the main road to Chechnya and were not fired at by our combat helicopters. . . . We received express orders not to attack."

It is probable that Khattab and Basayev bought their way out. Khattab himself said in a 20 November 1999 interview published on qoqaz.net, "The Russian Army is prepared to sell everything for a price"—even safe passage out of Dagestan.

President Maskhadov condemned Basayev. There were other people too who were very unhappy with Basayev when he got home. One of them was Magomed Khambiyev, who accused Basayev of starting an apocalyptic war. A gunfight broke out between Basayev and Khambiyev. Basayev got mad and drew on Khambiyev, shooting him in the leg. Khambiyev picked up his own gun and got a shot off too, slightly wounding Basayev in the side. "We never got along," Khambiyev recalls. "We argued in 1994 and in 1998 too."

KHATTAB'S BOMBS IN MOSCOW

Already in May 1998, just a month after the Congress of the Peoples of Chechnya and Dagestan declared its aim of uniting the two republics, Khattab laid the religious groundwork for using terror on Russian civilians to achieve the congress's objectives: "The Almighty doesn't order us to kill peaceful civilians (irrespective of their religious faith and nationality) because all peoples and all persons depend on the will of the Creator. However should the infidels confront or threaten the Moslems in any way, then the Moslems shall have a moral-legal right to fight them with all means at their disposal."

Hard lessons had come out of Dagestan. Basayev and Khattab would now ratchet up the holy war against Russia. In an e-mailed statement to Azzam Publications on the day after he left Dagestan, Khattab announced, "The second stage of the operation is under way." But this time the tactics would be different: "The Islamic fighters have decided to adopt completely different tactics to avoid being targeted by mass bombing as in Dagestan. Purely military methods are giving way to military-political ones."

Terrorism was on his mind. On 31 August, somebody put a bomb in Moscow's prestigious underground Manezhny mall beside the Kremlin. It exploded, killing one and injuring forty-one other people. Two days later, Khattab promised, "The mujahideen of Dagestan are going to carry out reprisals in various places across Russia." Events soon proved that Khattab planned to keep his word.

On 4 September, a bomb tore through an apartment block housing Russian military staff in Buinaksk. The watermelon truck wired with explosives killed sixty-four people and wounded 174 others. A second truck bomb was found on the military base the same day, but it was dis-armed after someone saw two wires hanging suspiciously from under the vehicle.

The Buinaksk bombing was later tied directly to Khattab. The March 2001 trial of Isa Zainudinov, Alisultan Salikhov, and four accomplices for the Buinaksk bombing revealed that Khattab had promised them $300,000 to do the job.

On 5 September, Basayev and Khattab and the congress's peacekeep-ing brigade returned to Dagestan for another round; this time, they went to the Novolaksky district with one thousand fighters. A seven-day siege ensued. Udugov's role in helping plan the Novolaksk operation resulted in a Russian warrant for his arrest on charges of violating the "armed revolt" article of Russia's criminal code.

That same day, Dagestani OMON forces unsuccessfully assaulted Karamakhi. A few days earlier, Khattab's father-in-law had been caught trying to escape wrapped in a rug in the back of a truck. In the days that followed, federal forces bombarded the village, which finally surrendered on 13 September. Karamakhi, including Khattab's in-laws' home, was completely destroyed.

Earlier, a dispute had broken out between Basayev and Nadirshakh Khachilayev over the failure of Khachilayev's detachment to support Basayev. Despite earlier agreement, Khachilayev refused to order his men into battle. Basayev threatened his associate with assembling a Shariah court that would sentence Khachilayev to death if he did not immediately begin combat operations in Novolaksk. Khachilayev, who had been hiding in Chechnya from Russian authorities and had joined Barayev's Supreme Council of Islamic Jamaats, was expelled from the republic. He went into hiding in Karamakhi.

Khattab's Islamic Army of Dagestan finally retreated back into Chechnya on 12 September. Khattab claimed that two hundred more Russians were killed, while the losses on his side were sixty. Yeltsin publicly vented his anger at the Russian military's inability to immediately repulse Khattab.

In the meantime, the first Moscow apartment building at house #19 Guryanova Ulitsa was blown up two seconds before midnight on 8 September, killing ninety-four people and wounding more than two hundred.

The following Monday, 13 September, another basement bomb went off. The carnage shown on television from the explosion at house #6 Korpus 3, Kashirskoye Shosse—where 124 men, women, and children were killed in their sleep at 5 a.m.—was wrenching. I remember the events vividly—we could not sleep for many nights after that, wondering if our building would be next.

On Tuesday, 14 September, police found and defused a third bomb at another apartment building on Borisovskiye Prudy Ulitsa.

The following Sunday, 16 September, at 5:58 a.m., a truck bomb blew the facade off an apartment building full of sleeping people in the Russian city of Volgodonsk. Phone calls were made to families living at house #35 Octyabrskoye Shosse, just before the blast, the caller asking, "How can you sleep with death just around the corner?" Eighteen people were killed and sixty-nine hospitalized. Altogether, 342 were wounded.

On 9 September, Basayev told the Czech newspaper *Lidove Noviny* that the bombing in Moscow had been "the work of Dagestanis—not our work." On the one hand, Basayev denounced terrorism. One the other, he said that Russia's military actions justified it: "For the whole week, Army and the Interior Ministry units have been pounding three small villages [in

Dagestan]. This [terrorism like in Moscow] will go on because those whose loved ones, whose women and children are being killed, will also try to use force to stop their adversaries."

Khattab told *Al-Watan Al-Arabi* that the war "had shifted to all Russian cities and would be directed against all Russians." When specifically asked, he refused to condemn the Moscow bombings. Vyacheslav Izmailov, a respected news commentator on Chechnya, thought that he knew why Khattab reacted this way.

Going on Russian NTV television, Izmailov said that very reliable sources in Chechnya had told him that Khattab, just after his initial defeat in Dagestan, recruited former Russian military personnel for a terror campaign across the Russian Federation. The men were divided into four teams to carry out bombings in Dagestan, Moscow, St. Petersburg, and Rostov-on-Don. Each team was given money to buy what it needed and to rent premises to hide explosives intended for the bombings.

On 15 September, the Islamic Liberation Army of Dagestan claimed responsibility for the Moscow bombings. Was this the same Islamic Army of Dagestan that Khattab was in charge of? The Russian government's case says it is.

The Russian federal prosecutor's office alleges that Khattab paid Chechen national Achimez Gochiyayev, thirty-one, $500,000 to carry out the attacks at Guryanova Street, #6 Kashirskoye Shosse, and Borisovskiye Prudy, and then helped hide Gochiyayev and his accomplices in Chechnya.

Gochiyayev, the mastermind, was a terrorist sleeper. Born in 1970 and raised in the Karachaevo-Cherkessia Republic, in 1997, he closed down a construction business in Moscow and went to Chechnya to train in Khattab's camps. After graduation, he went back to his home in Karachaevo-Cherkessia, where he established and ran his own Wahhabi jamaat (Muslim Society #3) until Khattab activated him. Gochiyayev, using the alias Mukhita Laipanov, rented the basements of the three apartment buildings in Moscow for "commercial storage."

Five of Gochiyayev's fourteen accomplices have been caught and charged with transporting the truckload of sugar sacks filled with explosives (hexogen) to Moscow. The route the explosives took to get to Moscow was from Urus-Martan to a food warehouse in Kislovodsk, where the hexogen was stored in a rented truck until late August. Ruslan Magiayev, Timur Batchayev, Yusuf Krymshamkhalov, and Adam Dekkushev then transferred the explosives to another vehicle and drove them to Moscow. There, Gochiyayev registered in a hotel using his brother-in-law's name (Taukan Frantsuzov) and then supervised placement of the explosives in the rented basements of the three apartment buildings.

Adam Dekkushev was caught by Georgian security services and handed over to Russia in 2002. He confessed that Abu Omar instructed him on how to organize and carry out terrorist acts, while plans of the apartment building bombings were developed by Khattab personally. In early December 2002, Batchayev was killed in a Georgian raid on the Pankisi Gorge while Yusuf Krymshamkhalov was apprehended and extradited to Moscow. Magiayev was apprehended by Russian police in Mineralnye Vody. Gochiyayev remains on the loose.

In court, Adam Dekkushev said that he, along with Yusuf Krymshamkhalov and Batchayev, prepared the explosives, transported them to Volgodonsk, and randomly picked the apartment building on Octyabrskoye Shosse to blow up. Abu Omar had promised to pay him for the job, but Dekkushev never got a single kopeck. Dekkushev's appeal to Abu Omar for material help for his family was also rejected. And according to Dekkushev's court testimony, it wasn't the FSB who ordered the bombing of the building as Berezovsky alleged, but the CIA.

The 4 September Buinaksk bombing has been solved too and tied directly to Khattab. Six men arrested in Azerbaijan were convicted of the bombing in March 2000. One of them admitted that he worked for Khattab but claimed that he did not know that the explosives he transported in his truck from Khattab's camp to Dagestan were intended to blow up the military apartment buildings. Khattab promised the bombers $300,000 to drive their truck bombs into the center of the compound, which would have destroyed four apartment buildings simultaneously. They parked on an adjacent street instead and blew up only one building. They complained at the trial that Khattab had not given them all the money he owed them.

The evidence that Khattab was responsible for the apartment building bombings in Moscow is clear. Of course there is also the now well-known story told by Berezovsky too. I remember that the story began to circulate in Moscow almost immediately after the bombings.

Berezovsky says that the FSB, working on behalf of the then newly appointed prime minister and KGB veteran Vladimir Putin (but without Putin's knowledge), blew up the apartment buildings to consolidate Russian society around Putin's candidacy for president prior to the presidential elections by creating the pretext for restarting the war in Chechnya. The idea was that this would ensure Putin's presidential election victory.

There is a second fantasy version that says that Basayev and his brother Shirvani are really long-standing GRU agents and that the bombings were not planned by radical Islamists at all, but by Russian military intelligence. According to this account, all the details of the attack were worked out in the summer of 1999 in a villa in the south of France with the participation of Basayev and the head of the presidential administration, Aleksandr Voloshin. Furthermore, it is alleged that the explosive materials used were not supplied from secret bases in Chechnya but from GRU stockpiles near Moscow.

Basayev's declarations of war and terrorism in Russia ignited the apocalyptic war in Chechnya in the fall of 1999. Russian Prime Minister Vladimir Putin declared on 27 September, "We are now the victims of the aggression of international terrorism." A day later he proclaimed, "It is clear we cannot simply drive them out of one spot and draw a line.... The whole world knows that terrorists have to be destroyed at their bases." Two days later, Russia responded with one hundred thousand troops and brutal military force to eliminate "foreign terrorist bases" from the North Caucasus.

VI

THE WARS THAT SHAMIL STARTED

In this war, we are fighting under the banner of Islam. Our
objective is to raise the word of Allah and establish Islamic rule
everywhere.

Ramzan Akhmadov, September 1999

A WAR TO ESTABLISH ISLAMIC RULE EVERYWHERE

Finally, the opposition got what it wanted—war. People in Chechnya were
saying, "Shamil went to Dagestan to take war by the hand and led it back
to Chechnya."

Everybody went to the trenches, but, this time, Chechens would fight
for many different reasons. Maskhadov would fight because he had to, for
self-preservation and for the independence of Chechnya. Raduyev would
fight for the thrill of it. Basayev, Khattab, Udugov, Barayev, the Akhmadov
brothers, and many others would fight to establish Islamic rule in the
North Caucasus. Ramzan Akhmadov explains: "In the first war, we fought
under the banner of 'freedom [for Chechen independence] or death.' In
this war, we are fighting under the banner of Islam. Our objective is to
raise the word of Allah and establish Islamic rule everywhere."

Faced with an advancing Russian Army in late September 1999,
Maskhadov and those who still followed him were forced into an alliance
with Basayev to fight Russia whether they liked it or not. Maskhadov's only
other choice was to accept the Taliban's offer of political asylum. Of
course, that's not how Maskhadov tells it. He says that Basayev, Raduyev,
Israpilov, and others came to him and pleaded that he forget their past dif-

ferences. "'You know that you can count on us,' [they said]—and I thought to myself, where else can I get soldiers to fight this war?"

There was a positive side of this new war, too, for Maskhadov. He got to play the role of president and commander in chief of the Chechen armed forces again, though from the beginning Basayev and other field commanders never really took orders from him. When Basayev stated that fact publicly in a 2001 interview, Maskhadov said that Basayev must have had a "headache" at the time of the interview. But Khattab confirmed what Basayev had said. Later on, Maskhadov was more honest when he said that field commander Ruslan Gelayev was absent without leave and he didn't know where he was.

Basayev, commanding the Chechen Eastern Front, engaged Russia's 58th Army in conventional fighting in the village of Goragorsky, west of Grozny, as the Russian Army advanced on the capital. But General Vladimir Shamanov, commander of the 58th Army, mistakenly reported in October 1999 that he had Basayev cornered and that "[Basayev] is running around like a mad dog."

In Gudermes, Raduyev and Barayev put up a hard fight against Russian forces, but, in the end, they had to abandon the city. Then on 26 November, General Dudayev's Army mounted a significant counteroffensive and retook Novogroznensky. Raduyev pounded the town with GRAD missiles and then went in on foot. He wasn't able to hold the city for long, though.

In October, the kidnapper Arbi Barayev, fighting with a head wound and leading a detachment out of the four hundred fighters under his command, attacked a column of one hundred Russian armored vehicles near the village of Pobedinskoye, destroying four tanks. Despite being a criminal and terrorist, Barayev was a skilled military leader and would chalk up several victories against Russian forces before being killed in June 2001.

In January 2000, Barayev was falsely reported killed by the Russian side in heavy fighting. Earlier that month, a blood feud started between him and field commander Ruslan Gelayev.

Gelayev had been besieged by Russian forces in his native village of Komsomolskoye, but he and the remnants of his detachment managed to escape and hide in the mountains. He had earlier prepared an escape route for his men and others, but Barayev, who was also hiding in the mountains, independently paid a guide to lead only him and his men out. He was spotted by Russian forces and lost half of his fighters—two hundred men—to land mines. This prevented Gelayev's immediate escape, causing his men to eat horseflesh and freeze to death for nearly a week. Dying from starvation and untreated wounds, they tried to escape anyway but found themselves blocked by Russian forces and minefields. Gelayev blamed Barayev for this trouble and vowed revenge.

There is a second story that says that after Barayev escaped, he telephoned and told Gelayev that he had sent buses to evacuate Gelayev's wounded. But when the relieved Gelayev led his men out of the forest to meet the buses, he ran head on into the Russian Army.

In March, Gelayev blew up Barayev's expensive house in Alkhan-Kala and, in early summer, attacked Barayev in Grozny. They clashed again in July 2000 in the village of Shalazhi, killing forty mujahideen. Gelayev took refuge in the Pankisi Gorge soon afterward.

In January 2000, Barayev's kidnapping accomplice, Ramzan Akhmadov, became the mujahideen commander responsible for Shatoi, Sharo-Argun, Atmikily, and Tembly. He saw action on 19–21 January when he attacked the 58th Russian Battalion command center with mortar bombardment.

WOLVES ARE TRAPPED

Three thousand fighters defended Grozny in December 1999. Basayev commanded nearly half of them in the Octyabrsky district. Ruslan Akhmadov and Israpilov had another eight hundred in defensive positions in the Zavodsky district, while Aslambek Ismailov led three hundred in the Leninsky district. Another six hundred were spread evenly between the Staropromyslovsky and Chernorechnye districts.

Three times the Chechens employed chemical weapons in defense of Grozny. They detonated reservoirs of chlorine and ammonia in the eastern suburbs, leaving a green poisonous cloud over the city for days. By mid-December 1999, Russian ground forces took the eastern suburbs anyway and began their breakthrough to the city's center. The going wasn't easy. Chechen rocket-propelled grenades killed 115 Russian soldiers in two days alone.

On 10 January, Basayev announced that the Chechen State Defense Committee had a plan to block the Russian advance. It did hold them back for a while. In the weeks of street-to-street fighting that followed, key buildings and suburbs often changed hands. Basayev's forces fought fiercely, using burning oil wells to obscure vision, booby trapped structures, and snipers on rooftops and in buildings, hidden in open trenches and in pits covered with concrete slabs that were fully raised when they could see the whites of the enemy's eyes. "We knew the city like the back of our hands and killed inexperienced [Russian] soldiers like grouse in their mating ground," one Chechen fighter recalls.

Nevertheless, by the end of the month, Basayev, Barayev, Ruslan Akhmadov, Israpilov, and other key Chechen leaders and their forces found themselves trapped and in trouble in Grozny. At the end of January, in contradiction to Maskhadov's order to hold the city until 23 February, Basayev ordered a general withdrawal through a special corridor in the direction of Alkhan-Kala.

As in Dagestan, Basayev thought that he had bought his way to safety, but an FSB agent posing as a greedy Russian military officer tricked him. The agent let it be known through Barayev's people that safe passage out of Grozny could be bought for a fee of $100,000. The money was paid in cash, but Basayev should have heeded his own earlier remarks about Winston Churchill not trusting the Russians. A few miles short of Alkhan-Kala, Basayev walked straight into an ambush.

Basayev, Lecha Dudayev (a nephew of Chechnya's first president), Khunkar Israpilov, Abdul Malik Mezhidov, and Ruslan Gelayev headed the column, which was preparing to cross the bridge over the Sunzha River. "We walked into a minefield . . . then they started shooting at us from their armored personnel carriers and with their machine guns and grenade launchers," a survivor recalls.

Nearly half of the three thousand fighters, officials, refugees, and others attempting to escape Grozny were killed, among them Khunkar-Pasha Israpilov, Lecha Dudayev, Aslambek Ismailov, and many other prominent people.

Basayev was severely wounded: "The front part of my foot was injured by a butterfly mine during our withdrawal from Grozny. What hit us during withdrawal were not land mines but butterfly mines that are deployed by aircraft. These mines do not need to be buried in the ground as they resemble the color of earth. The wound became infected and the lower part of my foot was amputated."

Dr. Baiev did the amputation at the hospital in Alkhan-Kala. Baiev vividly recalls that moment in his book: "[Basayev] had probably lost 50 percent of his blood; another half hour, and he'd be dead. I had to work fast. He was suffering oxygen starvation as a result of failing circulation. Under the dirt and gunpowder, his skin was paper white, contrasting with his full black beard. I removed what remained of his combat boots. The sole of his right foot was shredded, hanging by tendons and soft muscle tissue, exposing shattered fragments of the tibia and fibula."

"I'm going to have to amputate your leg above the ankle," Baiev told his patient. The videotaped amputation was shown on Russian television.

The Russian military operation, code-named "Wolf Hunt," was a huge victory for the Russian side. "Frankly we did not expect the bandits to swallow the bait, least of all did we expect them to be in such large numbers," commented General Shamanov.

Khattab had not been in Grozny, but his situation in the Vedensky district was equally as dire. The Russians drove the mujahideen out of Urus-Martan in December 1999. One of Khattab's Arab fighters in the new year reported:

> The situation here is very bad. The Russian Army is everywhere, except for some remote areas in the mountains they find hard to access so far. Our former experience of fighting against the army of the communist regime in Afghanistan, or the army of the Serbian government, is of little use. In Chechnya we deal with an enormous and powerful military force. The Russian troops keep chasing us all over the place. We are waiting for the snow to melt and open up the paths in the mountains. At the moment our people can do little more than just sleep up there.

PLANNING HOW TO FIGHT THE JIHAD

By the end of February, Chechen fighters had redeployed to southwestern and southeastern Chechnya. Fighters carried Basayev on a stretcher part of the way and he rode horseback the rest. Recovery from the loss of his leg would take a while. He couldn't fight, so he engaged in polemics and planning how to fight the war.

Basayev verbally attacked the Palestinian ambassador to Russia, Hairi al-Oridi, for remarking in Moscow that Chechnya is part of Russia and the Chechen problem is Russia's internal problem. Basayev didn't like the ambassador's unkind words about Khattab either. The ambassador had called Khattab a "traitor of Muslim interests since he undermines Russia, which has always been a true ally of the Arabs," and accused Khattab of playing into the hands of Israel.

In an open letter to the PLO leadership, Basayev called them hypocrites and traitors who love Russian pagans and prefer Pepsi to fighting for Palestine. Basayev suggested that the Palestinian leadership step aside and let a younger generation who will do the job right take over.

No wonder the Palestinians rejected Basayev's October offer to send 150 mujahideen to "perform jihad in Palestine." Basayev's Military Command Council proclaimed, "These Mujahideen are prepared to leave at any time. Even with the current situation that the Republic of Chechnya lives in, our hearts are still thirsty for jihad in Palestine." The next month, Hamas leader Sheikh Ahmad Yassin told Chechen Wolves to "stay in their land and continue their sacred fight against the Russians."

Once Basayev linked up with Khattab, the days were spent planning how to fight the war. There wasn't much debate. On the one hand, the mujahideen would switch from the trench warfare that they had fought in Grozny to hit-and-run guerrilla tactics in fighting Russia on Chechen soil. On the other hand, terror, both in Chechnya and in Russia proper, would play an equal role in the holy war. An information holy war run by Udugov would be conducted too.

Basayev recalls that they had an especially hard time in February and March 2000, when they were forced to abandon trench warfare for partisan tactics. "We survived two encirclements and reached the plains, sending fighters to villages in order to prepare bases for partisan activities." Mujahideen split up into packs of fifteen to twenty men and blended so well into the local population that a Russian military spokesman had to admit, "It is impossible to say how many gunmen are in this or that populated area."

The decision to switch to guerrilla warfare was passed in a formal resolution of the Chechen State Defense Committee on 9 February 2000 and announced by Basayev on Udugov's kavkaz.org Web site: "Until now we have not applied hit and run tactics in full force. We have employed conventional tactics that involve defending fixed lines and facing the enemy head on. We will now expand our guerilla tactics that do not involve defending fixed positions and rely on mobile strikes against the enemy behind their lines and in unexpected circumstances."

Coordination of the various mujahideen groups to fight the guerrilla war was carefully considered too. Basayev and Khattab created the Mujahideen Military Command Council—a central command—to do that. Khattab described its structure: "The Council presides over 70 commanders of various units. The members of the Council are made up of the principal commanders of the Chechen war and are, of course, leading participants in the actual fights."

Field commanders were assigned to every district of Chechnya and were responsible for the coordination of guerrilla operations within their district.

The replacement of foreign mujahideen killed and the training of new Chechen recruits to replace the initial heavy losses of men posed a problem. In May, Basayev announced that one hundred more Dagestani Wahhabis had joined up, while 150 experienced foreign fighters from Afghanistan had just arrived in Nozhai-Yurt.

Russia had quickly closed down Khattab's training camps so new recruits were trained on the run. In March, the Pakistani journal *Al-Irshad* reported that a Pakistani militia training officer named Hidayatullah had been dispatched to Chechnya to help out. Chechen fighters would also be sent to Osama bin Laden's training camps in Afghanistan. President Maskhadov facilitated coordination of that by opening an embassy in Kabul after the Taliban government officially recognized Chechnya as an independent state in January 2000.

A few hundred fighters were subsequently trained in Osama bin Laden's camps. That summer, President Putin threatened to bomb these camps. The United States joined Russia in issuing a joint statement warning the Taliban to "dismantle the terrorist infrastructure that sends fighters to Chechnya and Kashmir."

Getting weapons and explosives to fight the new war did not present a problem. Field commanders took what they needed from dead Russian soldiers and OMON police. Raids on Russian camps like the one near Starye-Atagi in June 2000, by one of Khattab's special units of the Shura of the Muslims of Ichkeria and Dagestan commanded by Abu-Yakub, sometimes netted a large cache of weapons. Basayev later confirmed that the "Russians are giving us practically everything we need. Hit them slightly on the head and they leave everything. Most arms and ammunition we have captured."

If the mujahideen needed more weapons, they simply bought them from Russian soldiers. There was plenty of precedent for this. At the beginning of the first war with Russia in 1994, a renegade group of Soviet Army generals sold arms from Soviet Chechnya's military depots to Dudayev. Khattab often publicly stated, "There is continual availability of weapons and equipment which are bought from Russian soldiers themselves." Raduyev said the same thing in his speech to the graduates of his school in February 1999 and even named the bases where mujahideen could buy weapons.

Sometimes, fighters made the trip across the mountains to Georgia to buy guns. For a long time, the Georgian government openly accused Russian soldiers of engaging in a thriving arms trade in the Caucasus from the Russian base in Vasiani, Georgia. Once, Georgian state security tracked a truck loaded with antitank weaponry, automatic rifles, and rocket-propelled grenades with a street value of $90,000 leaving the base headed for Chechnya. The driver was a Russian serviceman. It was easy to find an intermediary in Tbilisi who could arrange a sale from the Vasiani base.

The Russian base in Georgia has since been closed, but the sale of arms and ammunition by corrupt Russian soldiers from other bases has not stopped. Even as late as June 2002, several senior Russian military officers were arrested for selling the land mine to the Dagestani terrorist linked to Khattab who killed forty-five people during the 9 May 2002 Victory Day celebrations in Kaspiisk, Dagestan.

BASAYEV'S "BEE STING" GUERRILLA TACTICS

Basayev described his perpetual hit-and-run guerrilla tactics as "incessant little bee stings" (Basayev kept bees in his youth) that would ultimately overwhelm the enemy by sheer numbers. Indeed, over the next two and a half years, such "bee stings" would claim the lives of more than eight thousand Russian military and police personnel. Even at the official Russian count of fifty-two hundred personnel killed, Russian losses in Chechnya are greater than the average annual Soviet Army losses in Afghanistan in the 1980s. On the other side, the Russians say they have killed fourteen thousand Chechen and Arab mujahideen, but these figures may be inflated.

From cities and villages to tactically advantageous mountainous heights, the Chechens daily hunt down and kill Russian federal forces in ambushes using Kalashnikovs, grenade launchers, light mortar, flamethrowers, land mines, suicide bombers, and whatever other weapons they can buy, steal, capture, or dig up from secret hiding places.

In early March, Chechen fighters nearly wiped out the Russian 6th Company Pyskov paratrooper division in an ambush in the Argun Gorge, killing eighty-four paratroopers, most under the age of twenty. Only six survived.

By mid-March 2000, Basayev and his mujahideen were still concentrated in the Vedeno Gorge. Russia suspected that he would try to flee Chechnya in a small plane that would land on the frozen surface of Lake Kazenoi-Am to pick him up, so Russia bombed the ice-covered lake. But Basayev assured them that he was staying put in a secret location, that he was "recovering well," and that his "leg is healing surprisingly fast." Until a professionally made artificial limb came from abroad, Basayev had a local carpenter fashion a temporary wooden leg made from a crutch in which his knee rested on the handle and the top part of the crutch was strapped to his leg with a belt.

At the end of the month, Basayev's forces ambushed Russian troops near Vedeno, while three to five hundred mujahideen under Khattab's command fought in Sharo-Argun. Fighters then broke out of the mountain region and headed toward the Chechen plains.

Meanwhile, Barayev reentered Yermolovskaya in March with little Russian resistance and stayed there until early May when he again became surrounded. Barayev and all except one of his units got out of the encirclement alive.

Telephone intercepts between Basayev and Khattab at this time provide a rare glimpse into the conduct of the war and the logistical difficulties they were having.

In one, Khattab complains that the Russians are traveling by helicopter. Basayev responds that "two or three machine-gunners placed at different routes" and Strela surface-to-air missiles would come in handy. Basayev also complains that his leg is giving him trouble again and then asks if Khattab knows that the Russians have found the ammunition and arms cache buried in the cemetery.

In another communication, Basayev says that if only he had a surface-to-air missile, he could have shot down a Russian landing party: "I have two projectiles, but no launcher." Khattab promises to buy a launcher and deliver it in a few days.

In a mountainous area of the Shalinsky district, Russian troops destroyed a makeshift airfield and a second aircraft that Russian intelligence believed was going to fly Basayev to Azerbaijan for medical treatment.

At the end of May 2000, the Russians launched a large-scale offensive in the Southern Mountains near Vedeno and Nozhai-Yurt with the objective of killing fighters under Basayev's command. The Russian side reported Basayev killed, but, on 27 August, he felt well enough to challenge President Putin to a personal dual. "You are so desperate to shape the destiny of Russia and determined in your struggle against international terrorism that I have decided to help you," Basayev wrote to Putin. "I would like to challenge you to a duel. All our commanders will guarantee you maximum security. You can even choose the weapon. I'm not the best sportsman, but you're not bad. So, do you agree? The dual would benefit both our peoples and the rest of mankind too."

The Russian president answered by ordering Russian air crews to paint Basayev's name on the next load of bombs destined for Chechnya.

In June 2000, a unit led by Arbi Barayev entered an industrial section of Grozny and, in two hours of fighting, killed another fifteen Russian soldiers. The following month, Barayev launched two more attacks in Grozny. There were numerous hit and run attacks in June as well as a five day battle in the southeastern region of Chechnya.

By the early summer of 2000, Russia was declaring a military victory, but Basayev had a different perspective. In his July 2000 Azeri television interview, he assessed the situation that summer as being much better than at the beginning of the year when, he concedes, "We had a rough time." He said that eighteen hundred mujahideen had been killed since the war in Chechnya began, most of them in Grozny, but that many fighters who had quit in February were now coming back, enabling the mujahideen to carry out thirty attacks daily.

July was a busy month. In addition to Basayev's suicide bombers targeting military installations that month, fighters under Ramzan Akhmadov's command carried out guerrilla actions in Urus-Martan while

Arbi Barayev launched more attacks in Grozny. There were also multiple actions in Argun, Vedeno, Kurchaloi, the Black Mountains south of Urus-Martan, Gekhi, and Chiri-Yurt.

A month after Basayev's Azeri interview, Russian troops claimed that they wounded him and killed thirty-five of his fighters. That same month, Khattab was filmed busily preparing his mujahideen for a big guerrilla offensive in the fall. A 10 August videotape shot by Khattab's cameraman shows The Lion of Chechnya, strong and healthy, briefing his mujahideen. Attacks were planned on Gudermes and Argun.

Throughout 2001, Chechen and foreign mujahideen engaged Russian troops with those incessant little "bee stings," which claimed an average of three to four Russian lives daily. While Russia controlled territory by the day, the mujahideen ruled the night, coming out of hiding and laying mines and preparing new ambushes for the next day.

On 1 January 2001, Barayev engaged in new fights in Grozny. His death six months later had a significant impact on Chechen guerrilla, as well as terrorism, capabilities. On 27 January, a squad of Ramzan Akhmadov's Islamic Brigade attacked a military convoy near the village of Chechen-Aul, killing sixteen and capturing a military transport truck. Two days later, Chechen mujahideen and Arabs ambushed four FSB employees in their car on the road from Kalinovskaya. On 14 March 2001, Khamid Basayev was killed fighting in the Vedensky district.

Mujahideen actions continued in the summer of 2001, while the biggest guerrilla offensive of the year came in September 2001. Six days after Osama bin Laden attacked the United States, three hundred fighters assaulted and seized most of the city of Gudermes, while other fighters hit checkpoints and convoys, took back a mountain village, burned an administrative building in Serzhen-Yurt, attacked Shali, Kurchaloi, Starye- and Novye-Atagi, and shot down a military helicopter in Grozny, killing two generals and eight colonels. One of the Russian generals, General Anatoly Pozdyakov, had been responsible for planning all military operations in Chechnya. A surge of fighting took place. Udugov claimed that two thousand mujahideen were involved. This was the biggest setback for the Kremlin in months.

TARGETING CIVILIANS IN THE TERROR WAR

The capture of Raduyev in March 2000 finished his plans—if ever they did exist—to attack Russian nuclear facilities. But just as Raduyev was being locked up, Basayev and Khattab were finalizing their own war terrorism plans that, if successful, would plunge Russia into a state of political chaos by the end of the year. Their initial laundry list of terror against civilians, federal forces, and politicians included more apartment building bombings; bomb attacks on markets and stores in neighboring Russian republics and metros and train stations in Moscow and elsewhere; multiple suicide bomber attacks in Chechnya; kidnappings; and possibly the assassination of President Putin.

In June 2000, the Chechen High Command announced on Udugov's Web site that mujahideen would attack targets within Russia proper. "We will destroy Russian forces in Chechnya. But our operations will not end at the borders of Chechnya, they will also be conducted regularly in Russia."

That same month, the Russian police in Stavropol caught five of Khattab's graduates red-handed with explosives, detonators, and equipment they were readying for more apartment building bombings in Moscow and Saint Petersburg. The police found additional explosives already in Moscow. A Stavropol court tried and sentenced them on conspiracy charges. However, Achimez Gochiyayev, the group's ringleader and the man who orchestrated the bombings in Moscow in 1999, escaped capture.

A month later, on 9 July 2000, a bomb put under a car in the crowded Vladikavkaz market in North Ossetia killed nine people. This wasn't the first bombing in the market. In March 1999, an explosion there had killed sixty-seven people. The city of Vladikavkaz is the capital of North Ossetia, which borders Chechnya and is home to a large Russian military base. The market is a frequent target of Chechen attacks.

Also on 9 July, a second bomb destroyed a shop in Rostov-on-Don, claiming four lives. It was never determined whether the Rostov bomb was related to the war or was vengeance for a business dispute.

Likewise, was the blast in the Pushkinskaya Square underground pedestrian passageway in Moscow in August 2000, which killed thirteen people and hospitalized 118 others, part of Chechen war terrorism, a random act of hooliganism, or the result of a business dispute? The bomb was packed with screws inside a briefcase and plastic handbag left on the floor of the passageway at a busy pedestrian intersection during the evening rush hour.

Udugov claimed that the "government in the Kremlin" was behind the August terror attack. This was still a popular Berezovsky theme left over from the Moscow apartment building bombings the year before. But the FSB says that terrorists sent by Basayev and Khattab are responsible. The timing of the attack provides the best clue as to who was responsible. The attack coincided with the first anniversary of Basayev's and Khattab's invasion of Dagestan. They stormed into Dagestan on 7 August a year earlier, and the bomb in the Pushkinskaya Square passageway was put there on 8 August.

A small marble monument with the inscription "To those who died and suffered in the terror act of 8 August 2000" today stands in the place where the bomb went off.

Were the eleven pounds of explosives and detonators found at the Moscow Kazanskaya train station the day after the Pushkin Square bombing the work of the same people or others?

The Ostankino television tower—a prominent Moscow landmark and the world's second largest television tower, which is always crowded with Russian tourists—was set on fire in August 2000. An electrical fault was given as the official reason for the fire, but Udugov's Web site said that Basayev paid $25,000 to an Ostankino employee to torch the tower. Rescuers found four bodies at the bottom of the elevator shaft, including the body of a firefighter and a twenty-four-year-old woman.

On 12 September, a truck bomb in the Oktyabrsky market in Grozny killed a woman and her daughter.

On 6 October, the Pyatigorsk railroad station was bombed again, killing two women. Chechen resident Ilyas Saralyev and a former Pyatigorsk policemen, Vladimir Mukhanitz, were arrested in 2003 for the Pyatigorsk terror attacks. Saralyev paid Mukhanitz less than $200 to carry out the attacks. Other bombs in the city's administration building and in the Kazachem market in nearby Nevinnomyssk went off too, killing seven more people. Three days later, police defused a bomb in the Prikimsk Hotel in Budennovsk.

In November 2000, five more people were killed and more than forty injured in another Vladikavkaz market bombing. Two more car bombs killed seven and wounded forty-four in an outdoor market bombing in Pyatigorsk on 7 December 2000.

The following month, twenty-four of Barayev's men went to the Volgograd region to disrupt the regional governor's election there. On election day, police found a bomb planted at a crowded polling station and disarmed it before voters showed up.

The new year of 2001 saw new kidnappings too. Wolves targeted the famous Medecins Sans Frontieres (MSF)—also known as Doctors Without Borders—humanitarian organization that was working in both Chechnya and Dagestan. On 9 January, Kenneth Gluck, director of MSF in Nazran, Ingushetia, was returning home in a four-car unarmed and unescorted convoy from Starye-Atagi when he was kidnapped by seven fighters on orders from field commander Abu-Bakar Dzhumayev. Twenty-six-year-old Magomed Khussein Gakayev and thirty-two-year-old Ayub Katayev have been charged with Gluck's kidnapping and went on trial in May 2003. The other five kidnappers are dead. Gluck was the first American to be seized since Fred Cuny disappeared in 1995.

The motive for Gluck's kidnapping was his exchange for Dzhumayev's fighters held by Russia, but then Dzhumayev was killed in combat. Another version is that Gluck was seized because his captors believed he was a Western spy collecting information on them.

Gluck was treated comparatively well. He was held in a dark basement, hit in the head only once, and fed three meals a days during his captivity. No demands were ever made of MSF and, strangely enough, it was Ramzan Akhmadov who recommended that "the American be set free because he has asthma problems and needs care."

On the twenty-sixth day of his captivity, Gluck's captors returned his documents and money to him, stuffed a note from Basayev in his pocket saying the kidnapping had been a mistake, blindfolded him, and drove him back to the hospital in Starye-Atagi. Gluck declined to testify against his abductors out of fear for his life and retribution against Arjan Erkel, another MSF employee, kidnapped in August 2002.

In January 2001, a small bomb went off in an apartment building elevator shaft at house #3, Starozukovsky Parad, in Moscow's northern administrative district. In February, Chechen Hazmat Zuziyev was arrested in Moscow with two bombs that he planned to detonate on the day marking Stalin's 1944 deportation of Chechens.

On 5 February, a small bomb under a bench exploded in Moscow's Beloruskaya metro station during the evening rush hour, hospitalizing ten people. That same day, an artillery shell car bomb equivalent to seven pounds of TNT and reinforced with 7.62 mm ammunition, nails, and ball bearings was found and defused in a busy residential neighborhood in Kizlyar, Dagestan.

Three days later, at 4 a.m., a bomb exploded inside the courthouse in Shali, Chechnya, partially destroying the building. Also in February, Russian railroad engineers found a homemade bomb containing three large caliber artillery shells like those found in Kizlyar and an electronic detonator under the railroad tracks near Gudermes. Was General Dudayev's Army back at work again?

March 2001 was a big month for war terrorism too. Three bombs went off in the Stavropol region and in the Karachaevo-Cherkessia republic. Twenty-one people were killed and 150 others injured. One bomb exploded in a crowded market in the city of Mineralnye Vody, another at a police station, and a third in a car as the police were trying to defuse it.

That same month, on Khattab's orders, Supyan Arsayev (brother of Aslambek Arsayev, the former Chechen minister of Shariah security during the Gudermes uprising) and his two teenage sons, one sixteen and the other nineteen, hijacked a Russian Vnukovo Airlines flight leaving Istanbul, Turkey, bound for Moscow with 172 other passengers aboard.

Using knives and the threat of a bomb, the Arsayevs took control of the plane, which was forced to land in Medina, Saudi Arabia, because of a fuel shortage.

The hijackers said they would free the passengers only when the war in Chechnya ended. Saudi negotiators succeeded in getting forty-seven women and children released in exchange for refuelling the aircraft, which the hijackers wanted to fly to Kandahar, Afghanistan. When the hijackers threatened to blow up the plane and the youngest of them slit the throat of a stewardess, Saudi special forces stormed the aircraft. The senior Arsayev was killed instantly. A Turkish passenger was shot and killed too.

Maskhadov denied the Chechen leadership had anything to do with the hijacking, but Atfayva Fariza, a representative of Chechnya in Jordan, identified the hijackers and said that their purpose was to attract world attention to the Russian atrocities in Chechnya. The teenage Arsayevs were tried in Saudi Arabia.

In July, Chechen Sultan Said Ediyev hijacked a bus en route to Stavropol from Nevinomyssk, Russia, demanding the release of Basayev's friends who had participated in the 1991 airliner hijackings from Mineralnye Vody in exchange for the release of the thirty-seven passengers.

That September, unidentified mujahideen kidnapped a wealthy Russian businessman and his employee and held them in an oil refinery in the Selsky district of Grozny. In July 2002, the businessman was rescued as he was being transported in the trunk of a car to a new location, but his employee has never been found.

Also in September 2001, a car bomb in Argun, intended for the pro-Moscow Chechen head of the local administration, destroyed the local administration building and injured one person. On 9 November 2001, Wolves paid Ruslan Chakhkiyev and Movsar Temirbiyev $1,000 to put a bomb in the Falloi market in Vladikavkaz.

On 28 April, the Vladikavkaz market was the target of yet another bombing following the FSB's killing of Khattab. Eight people were killed and thirty-seven wounded in a blast caused by a time bomb filled with nuts and bolts in a long pipe used as a barrier to block the market's entrance.

Also in April, police made a horrifying discovery at a new gravesite in a cemetery across from the landing flight path at Vnukovo Airport in Moscow. They found a cache of missiles and a launcher waiting to be dug up and used against an incoming aircraft. Vnukovo Airport services both domestic and government flights in and out of Moscow.

The following month, a large remote-controlled land mine hidden along the parade route for the WWII Victory Day celebration in Kaspiisk, Dagestan, killed forty-five people and wounded ninety others. The bombing was in retaliation for Khattab's assassination in March.

Collaborators were executed too in 2002. In May, a local Chechen by the last name of Simbarigon suspected of being a Russian informer was murdered. His decapitated head was found near the local administration building in Mesker-Yurt; his skinned body was found on the outskirts of the village. The U.S. State Department's *Country Reports for Human Rights Practices, 2002* reported that other civilians who refused to assist Wolves were also assassinated; civilians were made to build fortifications and used as human shields; and Russian civilians were murdered—some with food poisoning.

In June 2002, three local Chechen officials from the Nozhai-Yurtkovsky district were kidnapped. A month later, Nina Davidovicha, director of the Russian humanitarian NGO Druzba (friendship) in Chechnya was abducted. And in August, Medecins Sans Frontieres was targeted again, this time in Dagestan. Arjan Erkel, a Dutch national and an employee of MSF's Swiss branch, who headed the organization in Dagestan, was kidnapped.

These monthly terror attacks preceded the summer 2002 reorganization of the Chechen armed forces and the creation of a new terror strategy that included seizure of the Moscow Dubrovka theater and nearly one thousand hostages that October.

BASAYEV'S SECOND SUICIDE BATTALION

Suicide bombings targeting police and Russian military troops began in January 2000, when a bomber walked up to the Russian embassy in Beirut, Lebanon, and detonated his explosives, leaving one policeman dead and several others wounded. A note reading "I martyred myself for Djokhar [Dzokhar]" was found in his clothing.

Two months later, a half dozen of Gelayev's fighters became trapped in Komsomolskoye. They concealed live grenades in their pockets and walked over to the Russian side to surrender. Several Russian soldiers were killed.

As early as March 2000, Russia had accused Basayev of training women for suicide bombing missions. He delivered in June. On 9 March, a nineteen-year-old Chechen woman by the name of Khava Barayev, Arbi Barayev's cousin, and her best friend Luiza (Kheda) Magomadova drove a stolen truck loaded with explosives into the Alkhan-Yurt OMON commandant's headquarters. Udugov claimed that twenty-five Russian policemen were killed but Russia said that only two died.

"I know what I am doing," Khava Barayev told her relatives. "Paradise has a price and I hope this will be the price for paradise."

Her suicide was meant to inspire Chechen men to jihad. "We hope that those who claim to be men will follow in your footsteps and go to jihad without hesitation," Arbi Barayev told Khava in a videotaped ceremony as she prepared for her death. Turning to the camera, Khava implored Chechen men to "not take the woman's role by staying at home." She continued, "A large number of women are involved in jihad now, and I hope that all men will go for jihad too. If you go for jihad it does not necessarily mean you are going to die; you will only die at your appointed time. So why don't we choose the best way to die—martyrdom, the highest, most eminent way?"

Luiza then took her turn in front of the camera to urge more Chechen women to join the jihad: "Do not stay at home, go for jihad for the sake of Allah. . . . It's time for women to be fighting alongside the men. . . . Going to the battlefield with the mujahideen brothers will be support for them and victory will come sooner. Insha'Allah!"

This was the first suicide bombing in Chechnya by women. More suicide bombings by men, women, and children would come. Like Khava's, many would be preceded by a videotaped ceremony, with the women wearing long black dresses and their faces covered with a veil.

On 11 June, a man and a woman blew themselves up at a vehicle checkpoint in Grozny, killing two. But the real terror came at the beginning of July 2000. For two days in early July, Basayev and Ramzan Akhmadov threw the Kremlin and Russian forces in Chechnya into a state of terror panic.

On 2 July, a truck filled with explosives tried to crash through the gate at Russian military headquarters in Urus-Martan but was stopped by small-arms fire before it could reach its target. It nevertheless killed two soldiers besides the bomber.

That same Sunday evening, a truck bomb was driven into a police station in Gudermes, killing eleven. This was the first of two bombs in the city that day.

Basayev warned publicly of more attacks if Russia did not free women and children being held in one of the Russian detention centers. He also made statements that the bombings would stop if Russia handed over Russian Colonel Budanov for raping and murdering an eighteen-year-old Elza Kungayeva.

Early Monday morning on 3 July, a truck bomb killed twenty-five Russian MVD troops and wounded eighty-one in Argun. In another suicide attack, three people were killed and twenty others wounded in a truck bombing in Novogroznensky. A sixth attack took place in Naibyora.

One smart suicide bomber claims that he got the job done without killing himself. He says he was told to drive a truck filled with explosives hidden under bags of flour through the main gate of the military base in Argun. But when he saw that the gate was blocked by armored vehicles, he just drove up and down the highway in front of the target until he was stopped. He was escorted back to the commandant's office for questioning. Because he didn't have his driver's license or any vehicle documents with him, he simply agreed to pay the soldiers one thousand rubles if they would let him go. He didn't have any money with him either, so they told him he could go get the money but he would have to leave the truck with them. He asked that they park his truck under shelter in case of rain, and they obliged. Once outside the gate, he met his partner and detonated the explosives by remote control.

Basayev said that these suicide attacks were meant to disprove the claims being made by the Kremlin that the war in Chechnya was over and to demonstrate that Russian military forces were not in control of the republic after all. Udugov said that more than six hundred soldiers were killed in this series of suicide bombing attacks; Russia's official casualty count was thirty-three dead, eighty-four wounded, and three missing.

On 2 August, another suicide car bomber killed the deputy head of the Russian administration in Urus-Martan. Other suicide car bombings that month in Khankala, Argun, and elsewhere killed at least thirty and wounded fifty. Ramzan Akhmadov, who commanded the suicide operations, publicly proclaimed, "These were planned actions to carry out terrorist acts." Udugov threatened to extend the bombing outside Chechnya.

Suicide bombers—Basayev and Udugov said there were as many as five hundred bombers—volunteered, were paid, or were coerced into becoming martyrs in the name of Allah. Old women, children, and teenage girls were recruited to carry out suicide missions in Chechnya. The *Newsday* videotape taken from an al Qaeda hideout in Afghanistan in 2002 shows a Chechen boy suicide bomber sitting in a room. The narrator says, "This young boy loses his life in a suicide attack for his beliefs." The boy prays, and then the film shows his suicide attack in Gudermes.

Sixteen-year-old Mareta Dudayeva also tried to take her life and others in December 2000, when she nearly drove an Army URAL truck into a Leninsky district police station in Grozny. But guards opened fire on the cab of the truck, wounding her and stopping the truck in the nick of time. "Everything will blow up now," Mareta screamed as she bolted from the cab and tossed a grenade after herself. But the half ton of explosives failed to detonate.

There were more suicide bombings in 2001. In September, a suicide bomber blew himself up at a Russian checkpoint in Argun.

Aizan (Luiza) Gazuyeva wasn't quite seventeen when she killed the harsh Russian military commander of one of the most horrible places in Chechnya, Urus-Martan, the former stronghold of the Wahhabis. Her husband, Zelimkhan, who the FSB believed was a fighter, was taken in one of the frequent cleansing operations in the city and never heard from again. Aizan tried desperately to find out what had happened to him but was always told, "Nothing is known about you husband's fate."

One day she decided to solve the problem herself. On 29 November 2001, she walked up to General Geidar Gadzhiyev on the street and asked: "Do you remember me?" "Get out of the way, I'm not going to talk to you!" he retorted. That's when she detonated the explosives under her clothing. Days later, the general died from his wounds.

In February 2002, fifteen-year-old Zarema Inarkayeva tried to deliver a bomb to a Grozny police station, but it failed to go off. The girl said that she had been kidnapped and told that her family would be killed if she didn't go through with the bombing.

In another case, a Russian soldier gave a hungry eleven-year-old girl on the side of the road some food. She asked if she could come into the armored transport to warm up. The soldiers let her in and she blew herself up.

DID BASAYEV REALLY SINK THE KURSK?

In the days following the tragic sinking of the Russian Navy's nuclear submarine, the *Kursk,* in August 2000, Basayev announced that it had been no accident, but an intentional act of sabotage orchestrated by the Chechen High Command and an Islamic crew member to destroy the submarine and kill its crew of 118.

Information posted on Udugov's Kavkaz Center Web site stated that a Dagestani member of the crew had gotten in touch with the Chechen Military Council in June 2000 to express his desire to help fight the Russians. He said that he could sink the submarine and was willing to die for Allah in order to help his Islamic brothers.

This claim raised the question of whether or not Dudayev's 1995 plans to hijack a nuclear submarine had been resurrected and modified. The FSB investigated to find out. They learned that a new torpedo built by the Dagdizel Defense Plant in Kaspiisk, Dagestan, was being tested aboard the submarine and that the torpedo's designer was on board to monitor the tests. Senior Lieutenant Arnold Borisov, a Dagestani, and a second Dagestani, Chief Engineer Mahmed Gazhiyev, were also on board. Gazhiyev's job was to test the torpedo's new hydrogen peroxide propulsion system. A third Dagestani, senior warrant officer Abdul Kadyr Eldarov, was a member of the crew. However, the FSB concluded that none of them were terrorists. Another name, Jad Jayev Muhammad, was published on the Muslim Brotherhood Web site.

The Web site of the Ukrainian political association Brotherhood offered the explanation that two explosive devices had been planted on the submarine during installation of the new torpedo and repair work in Dagestan and that Chechens associated with field commander Ruslan Gelayev were responsible. It is also conceivable that Dagestani workers assembling the new torpedoes powered by volatile hydrogen peroxide sabotaged one of them so that it would explode upon launch.

The Russian Navy concluded in its three-year investigation that it was an exploding torpedo that set off the explosive chain reaction that sank the submarine, but that it was an accident caused by a defect or damage to the torpedo's propulsion system. It was learned that one of the torpedoes had been dropped and damaged as it was being transported to the submarine, but, for some reason, the shift supervisor insisted that it be loaded on board anyway. "Why would they let a malfunctioning torpedo on board?" Ekaterina, the mother of a *Kursk* sailor, asked.

ASSASSINATION TERROR

A plot to assassinate Russian President Putin was timed to take place during his visit to Yalta for a Commonwealth of Independent States summit on 18–19 August 2000. However, the plot was foiled by the Ukrainian security service, which arrested four Chechens and their Arab accomplices.

That same month, Azerbaijan's Ministry of National Security uncovered a well-organized second plot to assassinate President Putin during an official state visit to Azerbaijan later that year. This sophisticated plot was tied to Arbi Barayev.

The would-be assassin was an ethnic Kurd and an Iraqi citizen named Kianan Rostam. He was an explosives instructor who had been trained in Afghanistan, came to Chechnya in 1997, and fought in one of Arbi Barayev's units at the outset of the new war in 1999. He was linked with terrorists in Afghanistan who helped him get everything ready for the assassination. Rostam got to Baku by marrying an Azeri woman and entering the country in early 2000 on a false Russian passport. That fall, he prepared explosive devices at his home with the help of six Arab colleagues.

Azeri security learned of Rostam's intentions through an intercepted telephone conversation with an Afghan called Samsir who had also fought in Chechnya. Transcripts of Rostam's phone calls show that he discussed the final details of the assassination with Arbi Barayev in November 2000.

With just ten days left before President Putin's visit, the Azeri security ministry intercepted a package of explosives on its way to Rostam. He was arrested three days later at his home, where police found another 105 pounds of explosives and enough sophisticated radio control equipment to detonate multiple bombs simultaneously. Rostam, who was sentenced to ten years in prison by an Azeri court in October 2001 for plotting with Barayev to kill President Putin, was undoubtedly after the $7 million bounty that Basayev had put on President Putin's head.

The assassination of pro-Moscow Chechens began in 2000. In July of that year, two powerful bombs were defused near the pro-Moscow Chechen administration building in Gudermes. One contained thirty-three pounds of ammonite inside a 125-millimeter artillery shell. Another was inside a metal pipe. Also in July, the residence of Mufti Akhmat Kadyrov, the Kremlin-appointed head of the pro-Moscow administration, was shot up by gunmen. He was not home at the time.

In November, Ibragim Dudayev, a member of the Akhmadov brothers gang under the command of Abu al-Waleed, murdered the administrative head of Mesker-Yurt.

Assassinations also became a significant feature of the 2001–2002 terror war. If Chechens couldn't get Putin, terrorists would assassinate his pro-Moscow Chechen administration. Barayev, before he was killed, as well as Khattab, carried out a wave of assassinations of pro-Russian civil servants, religious leaders, and informants. Eighteen district and town administrators, five religious leaders, and a host of Chechen police officers, teachers, civil servants, and informants were killed in 2001.

In April 2001, a bomb exploded in the Vedensky district administration building. Barayev's mujahideen were responsible for a series of bomb attacks in Grozny, Gudermes, and Argun in June in which several Russian officers and senior pro-Moscow Chechens were killed. After his death, Barayev's men also carried out several retaliatory murders of pro-Moscow Chechen officials in Barayev's name—each with a note reading "For Barayev." The heads of some of those killed were severed and stuck on stakes to warn others of the consequences of collaboration or informing on the whereabouts of mujahideen.

In early June 2001, Arbi Barayev's Special Purposes Islamic Regiment executed a village mayor and, a month later, a resident of Alkan-Kala for treason.

More assassination attempts were made on Kadyrov. The closest came on 3 September 2001, when a powerful bomb ripped through the heavily guarded and fortified Russian government building in Grozny. The bomb went off in a second-floor toilet located under the conference room where Kadyrov, Chechen Prime Minister Stanislav Ilyasov, and the heads of districts in Chechnya were conducting a meeting. Kadyrov described the bombing as yet another "link in the chain of assassination attempts." His attempted assassination was part of a plan Khattab had put together called "Kafir 1," which targeted Kadyrov and other Sufi elders for assassination.

This continued in 2002. Pro-Moscow Chechen police officers and members of their families are regularly assassinated. In one case, the son of a police officer was tied to a concrete post and blown to bits. "We are targets," says Salam Salamov, deputy head of the Chechen Interior Ministry. "They know where we live. Our families, our parents live in fear." More than three hundred Chechen police officers have been killed since 2001.

On 18 April 2002, a bomb blast killed sixteen pro-Moscow Chechen police officers. The blast came a few hours before Putin made his annual television state of the nation address in which, for the second year in a row, he said that the war in Chechnya was over.

UDUGOV'S INFORMATION WARS

Chechen access to the Russian media at the beginning of the second war with Russia was almost nil. Russian First Deputy Press Minister Mikhail Seslavinsky warned the Russian media that providing any platform to Maskhadov, Basayev, Khattab, or Udugov would be tantamount to treason. Russia jammed Chechen radio and television broadcasts and imposed a further information blockade to seal the republic off from the outside world when Russian troops moved back into Chechnya.

Nearly every means of Chechen communication to the outside world was cut off, so the master Chechen propagandist resorted to that which Russia couldn't easily control—the Internet. Udugov established www.kavkaz.org, which hosted the Kavkaz-Center News Agency. This venue became the principal propaganda organ of Basayev, Khattab, and the Islamic extremists associated with them.

In October 1999, Udugov told the Web site Transitions On-Line that kavkaz.org was originally set up by a group of young computer programmers in Grozny earlier in the year and operated on a shoestring. He gave them a little money and lots of "analytical material" from his think tank, the National Center for Strategic Research and Political Technologies. Saudi donations later picked up funding of the Web site which, along with Kavkaz television, became the propaganda organs of the Congress of Peoples of Chechnya and Dagestan.

Udugov describes his Web site as a "private, independent news agency" that "does not reflect the viewpoints of any particular country or any governmental structures of the Chechen government." He denies that it is a terrorist Web site, nor is it affiliated with any terrorist network. Information is presented in Russian, English, Turkish, and Arabic and is updated every few days. It was renamed kavkazcenter.com after the

Dubrovka theater siege because its U.S. registration was suspended. Udugov's Web site can no longer operate in the United States.

The Web site portrays the war in Chechnya as a religious war in which Russia is leading a Christian crusade against Islam, a position that before the summer of 2002 caused Maskhadov to repeatedly deny any association with the site. It routinely exaggerates Russian war casualty figures, but then Russian Web sites exaggerate Chechen losses too and minimize their own. And sometimes the material is downright ridiculous. For example, after Osama bin Laden's attack on America, Udugov published a Basayev statement that not only declared solidarity with the Taliban but said that the attack was not the work of Osama bin Laden at all, but that of "the international financial mafia," "the military-industrial mafia," or maybe the Moussad. The Moussad is well known and it is doubtful that they had anything to do with the attack on the United States on 11 September 2001, but Basayev didn't say who the other two entities were.

Kavkaz.org had already caught Russia's attention months before the second Chechen war started. When Basayev and Khattab crossed the border into Dagestan in August 1999, kavkaz.org became their official mouthpiece and the only alternative information source to the Dagestani government's official Web site, kavkaz.com.

Udugov portrayed the declaration of holy wars against Dagestan and Russia as a Dagestani liberation struggle against a corrupt state government in Makhachkala and "Russian bandits." His Web site published all press releases from the newly established Islamic Government of Dagestan as well as dispatches from Basayev and Khattab on how they were doing in fighting the holy wars.

Not all of the information was accurate. Dagestan's Defense Ministry accused Udugov of inventing information and telling lies about federal military operations. But his propaganda was effective. It was precisely this propaganda that got him kicked off the Chechen National Security Council on 29 August. In Maskhadov's words, Udugov had "turned himself into the principal conductor of a full-scale ideological diversion against the Chechen state" and "endangered our friendly relations with Dagestan."

Kavkaz.org soared in popularity in Russia in the summer of 1999, ranking in the top thirty (based on the number of hits) of search engine Rambler's list of Russia's top one hundred Internet sites. By comparison, the Dagestani government Web site wasn't even in the top one hundred list. Several Russian newspapers also praised Udugov's site for its "professional approach to information." Its popularity was probably helped by the fact that it is constantly being hacked.

Russia has tried to put the site out of business through both hacking and diplomatic action. The first step was to remove kavkaz.org from Rambler and List.ru. Then Russian hackers began with small things. They posted a picture of Mikhail Lermontov (the famous Russian poet who fought in the Caucasus War in the nineteenth century) holding a Kalashnikov with the message "Misha was here" on the main page. Elsewhere, they posted messages like, "This site has been closed down at the request of Russian citizens." And, "This is what will happen to all Web sites of terrorists and murderers." Images of gravestones inscribed with "Kavkaz-center" were put on the main page. Sometimes visitors were diverted to the Russian Information Center Web site. Sometimes the site was down, but it usually came back within a day or so. Hackers signed their messages "the Siberian Web Brigade."

In conjunction with hacking efforts, Russia also launched a diplomatic campaign against kavkaz.org by having it removed from its U.S. server located in Southern California. The server removed the Web site on grounds that it contained terrorist propaganda and hate material. The site has moved several times since with locations in Tbilisi, Georgia, Qatar, Lithuania, and elsewhere.

Udugov's site now operates as kavkazcenter.com. Until February 2003 it was hosted by Microlink Data in Lithuania. Russia pressured the company to close the site down. In February, it moved to www.Storman.e in Tallin, Estonia. Russia has put pressure on the Estonian government to close it down, but the prime minister said that since it is not a government site, he could not interfere. Udugov apparently got another server in Lithuania because he announced on his site on 22 June that "Lithuanian security had seized the Lithuanian server."

In late 2000, Udugov also set up a Chechen Information Center in the Pankisi Gorge near the village of Duisi. The radio broadcast was called "Free and Independent Ichkeria-Caucasus." The center broadcasts audio-taped news bulletins in Chechen and Russian and also religious texts in Chechen. The broadcasts are said to be "in the spirit of the fighters' chief propagandist, Movladi Udugov."

The Wolves' internal propaganda committee does a good job of keeping the Chechen population and the refugee community in Ingushetia well informed. News is spread by word of mouth. But Maskhadov also has a mobile television broadcasting unit and broadcasts irregularly in short segments. On 21 September 2002, Maskhadov captured a local television station in Samashki and interrupted the regular broadcasting to make a long speech about resisting Russian forces. Maskhadov packed up the television equipment and took it with him when he left.

Maskhadov made another televised broadcast on 2 February 2003. This time it was an hour-long program broadcast to Western Chechnya and the Ingush border area denouncing the March 2003 constitutional referendum scheduled by Moscow. He promised to launch a fresh offensive against Russian troops in Chechnya before the event: "All that we are waiting for is spring." A follow-up broadcast showed mujahideen training for the spring offensive.

Maskhadov also has his own Radio Ichkeria, which amounts to little more than a collection of home radio operators using homemade equipment to transmit pre-recorded audio programs that are sent to them. In late September, Chechen mujahideen also captured a local radio station in the Nadterechny district and stole the equipment.

Besides television and radio, Wolves use a variety of underground channels to get the message out; one of those is a newspaper called *Ichkeria*. Radio Free Europe/Radio Liberty Russian Service reporter Musa Khasanov (based in Grozny) says that it is now common to find a copy of *Ichkeria* on your doorstep in the morning. The newspaper is likely printed abroad, smuggled into Chechnya, and then photocopied. *Ichkeria* publishes stories about Russian cleansing operations; corruption in the pro-Moscow Chechen administration; foreign commentary about Chechnya; and orders, edits, appeals, and commentary by Maskhadov.

THE MASKHADOV-UDUGOV INTERNET WARS

The sparring between Maskhadov and Basayev and company did not stop when Russian troops entered Chechnya. Initially, both sides denied the persistent rumors of difficulties between them as simply FSB disinformation. But by the spring of 2000, everything was out in the open, starting with Maskhadov's attack on Udugov and his Web site.

In a telephone interview with German radio Die Deutsche Welle in April, Maskhadov condemned Udugov as a "nobody," a "private person," a "provocateur," and a "warmonger" who should not be taken seriously. "I once again declare that Mr. Udugov and Kavkaz Center are persons and structures hostile and in opposition to the president and to the government." Maskhadov concluded. Basayev and Khattab also received the honor of being called warmongers.

Maskhadov's representative in the United States, Lyoma Usman, condemned kavkaz.org and Udugov as not representing Chechen interests because they portray the war with Russia as a "religious one between Islam and Christianity, which we cannot accept."

Of course, the FSB did all it could to exploit and promote the dissension. On 23 January 2001, *Nezavisimaya Gazeta* quoted a Stavropol FSB official as stating that Udugov met secretly with Lord Frank Judd, the head of the Parliamentary Assembly of the Council of Europe delegation, when Judd visited Chechnya on 15–16 January to persuade him to break off contacts with Maskhadov and acknowledge Basayev as the sole representative of Chechen fighters. Udugov denies this ever happened.

On 5 March 2001, Maskhadov was back at it again, criticizing "private information agencies" that "do not cover the events in Chechnya in the interests of the Chechen state" and "that clearly have an anti-Chechen character and [do] irremediable harm to Chechen independence." He repeated his earlier statements that none of these private agencies "have my authorization to perform the functions of [official] information agencies" with clear reference to the Kavkaz-Center News Agency.

The next day, Maskhadov's spokesman issued a statement that tied this criticism to an article that kavkaz.org had published about "the Judeo-Christian pagan alliance's" concern over the Taliban's plans to destroy ancient Buddhist monuments in Afghanistan. Maskhadov's spokesman emphasized that "the Chechen leadership has no connection to Kavkaz Center, an Internet site that supports the intentions of the Taliban to destroy these historical monuments." And he repeated earlier statements that before the war "Maskhadov had accused Movladi Udugov—the founder of the Kavkaz television station and of the Kavkaz Center Internet site—of anti-Chechen subversive activity." Only this time he called Kavkaz Center the "Kremlin's mouthpiece which is trying to convince the world that Russia is not conducting a colonial war of conquest, but is indeed confronting some sort of international force."

On 7 March, kavkaz.org published Maskhadov's statements in full without refuting the charges. This was not surprising because the Web site often prints criticism of itself, which is what gives the site credibility. Kavkaz.org followed with quotes from an "interview" with Udugov, who completely agreed with Maskhadov that the Web site "is not a government information agency, and never was," but an "independent Islamic agency, which covers events not only in Ichkeria and in the Caucasus generally, but throughout the Muslim world." Moreover, Udugov smugly pointed out that "Kavkaz Center does not hide its support for the Chechen mujahideen and tries to be as objective as possible in its coverage of the Russian aggression against the ChRI."

In July, Maskhadov struck out again after Kavkaz Center and Lenta.ru published interviews with Udugov and Yandarbiyev in which they claimed that there was no place for Maskhadov in any future Chechen government. Maskhadov did not have nice things to say about them:

These traitors preferred to leave their people for foreign countries to save their bacons. From luxurious villas in the intervals between plentiful meals they've been crying about their outstanding merits and contributions they've made for Ichkeria. They've been writing books and giving interviews, thus teaching those who have been sacrificing their lives for the freedom of Great Ichkeria how to fight. They've been collecting money for an alleged support of our fight. However, most of the donations tend to accumulate in their own accounts, the accounts of their close relatives and friends. Now and again they've been sending dollars to support our jihad.

Other Chechen Web sites published calls by extremists for Maskhadov to be ousted by force if necessary. In one, Khattab described Maskhadov as a "vile jackal spreading lies," while Maskhadov's Chechenpress countered with reports that Turpal Movsayev, head of Chechen special forces, was planning to assassinate Khattab.

The attacks back and forth halted with the summer 2002 reorganization of the Chechen armed forces and reconciliation between Basayev and Maskhadov. Udugov now has Maskhadov's approval to publish "official materials" on his Web site.

VII

THE CHECHEN MONEY TREE

Many people today are taking an interest in where we are getting funds; they are making up stories that people ranging from
[Osama] bin Laden to [U.S. President] Clinton are helping us.
Ordinary Muslims, ordinary people are helping us. Not a single
government in the world is helping us.

Shamil Basayev, ANS TV, Baku, July 2000

Basayev says he budgeted $25,000 for his 1995 raid into Russia. He spent
huge sums of money to "liberate" Dagestan in 1999. Khattab agreed to pay
bombers $300,000 to blow up Russian military housing in Buinaksk and
$500,000 for apartment buildings in Moscow. At $300 per month, The
Black Arab also paid his fighters well by Chechen standards. In 1998,
Basayev valued his own personal property, house, and several foreign cars
at $600,000. "Not a single government in the world is supporting us. . . .
We only get money from ordinary Muslims, ordinary people," Basayev
declared to his Azeri television audience in July 2000. He said that a little
Saudi girl sent him one thousand Saudi dinars, students in the United
States and England sent $1 to $1,000, and an old lady from Qatar sent
$2,700.

But it takes a lot more money than that to train, arm, feed, and pay a few
thousand fighters; buy expensive real estate; run presidential campaigns; put
money away in foreign bank accounts; hide your family abroad; make life-
time annuities to families of killed and wounded mujahideen; bribe Russian
officials; pay bounties to kill Russian soldiers and blow up tanks; organize
terror and conduct multiple jihads. The money to do all that comes from a
vast financial enterprise that enjoys a disparate range of revenue sources.

THE CHECHEN MAFIA BRANCHES

Powerful Chechen criminal groups operate in cities all across Russia. Besides running prostitution, drug, gun, oil, and auto-theft rings, they control "protection" security firms, small outdoor food markets, hotels, taxi companies, and several thousand other commercial firms as well as some banks in the country. A percentage of the money that these businesses generate flows back to Chechnya and to the field commanders they sponsor. Basayev, for example, has links to the Moscow Chechen mafia.

Investigations by Russian federal tax police, anticrime, and antiterror agencies going back to 1991 have uncovered sophisticated credit and financial banking schemes—including federal budget debt liquidation and debt repayment through insolvent banks—that have enabled the Chechen mafia to collect and launder huge sums of money. The "Aviso" scheme, in which thousands of fake business promissory notes were used to collect funds from Russia's Central Bank, is one of the biggest bank fraud cases in Russian history. Between 1992 and 1994, roughly $30 million in rubles was stolen from Moscow banks. Although some of the promissory notes (avisos) were Chechen originated, President Dudayev denied that his government had anything to do with originating them. More recently, complex money-laundering channels have been found in banks in Moscow, Krasnodar, Stavropol, the Rostov region, and elsewhere, yielding some $0.6 billion in profits annually. In another scheme, nearly $3 billion was transferred to offshore banks as "payment for [fictitious] services."

While their hands are tied by weak domestic money laundering laws, Russian law enforcement agencies have gone after these banks when they could. In 1999, the Sodbusinessbank was indicted on charges of supporting terrorists. In early 2000, Russia also investigated the Trust Credit, Khleb Rossii, Irs, and other financial organizations for laundering Chechen terrorist money. Russian banks have also accused the French Credit Agricole Indosuez bank of having close links with Islamic fundamentalists in Chechnya because the bank is used to transfer cash money to the accounts of Al-Haramein, a Saudi-based charity that finances Arab fighters in Chechnya. The Russian tax police also periodically conduct midnight raids on Chechen businesses suspected of funding terrorists.

OIL THEFT, NARCOTICS, AND COUNTERFEITING

The theft of oil was a big earner for field commanders until the Russian Army moved back into Chechnya in 1999. Chechen fighters in the first war with Russia moonlighted by selling home-distilled petrol made from stolen crude oil. This was the only source of fuel for most drivers.

Oil theft, particularly from holes drilled in the Baku-Novorossiisk pipeline passing through Chechnya, expanded after the first Chechen war. Basayev did little to stop the theft of oil during his reign as first deputy prime minister. In fact, theft went up. Eighty percent of the oil produced in Chechnya since 1996 has been stolen. In one Chechen government crackdown in December 1997, two hundred large trucks full of stolen petroleum and one thousand tons of crude oil were confiscated. In 1998, receipts from the illegal refining of stolen oil grossed an estimated $3 million a month.

Illegal oil extraction, refining, and sale of oil are still huge problems in Chechnya. Corrupt Russian federal officers and pro-Moscow Chechen police make lucrative incomes from protection money paid by the many illegal micro-refineries that exist.

Evidently legal oil production is presently funding Wolves. Without naming any specific company or companies, Russia's MVD minister said in 2003 that some Russian "structures" operating in the territory of the Southern Federal Okrug (Dagestan, Chechnya, Ingushetia, Kabardino-Balkaria, Stavropol, and elsewhere) are under the control of criminal elements that are funding fighters in Chechnya.

Narcotics was also a big cash producer before the fall of 1999, netting about $0.8 billion annually. In 1995, Basayev openly acknowledged, "We cultivate marijuana." He manufactured heroin too! By 1999, drug production in Chechnya was on full industrial footing, with heroin factories operated by Udugov, Basayev, and Khattab. One factory was located at middle school No. 40 in Grozny, another in the Energetik sanatorium in the Shali district controlled by Basayev, and a third in the Zorka children's camp run by Khattab.

To supply the busy narcotics factories, poppy as well as marijuana and other narcotic plants were grown on Chechen plantations worked by slaves kidnapped by Arbi Barayev and others. The intricate web of smuggling routes used to bring foreign fighters and weapons into Chechnya were also used to smuggle drugs out to European drug dealers. Helicopters, small airplanes, and foreign flag ships were used to transport shipments to foreign countries. Basayev bought several single-engine Cessna airplanes for this purpose. Chechnya also acted as a transit route for drugs from Turkmenistan, Iran, Pakistan, Turkey, and Afghanistan bound for the Baltics and Western Europe. *Al-Sharq Al-Awsat* wrote that Basayev also controlled the "Abkhaz heroine road," which the Taliban used to transport heroine to Europe.

Chechen mafia organizations handle drug distribution in Russia. On 22 December 2000, the Russian prosecutor's office in Ryazan arrested twenty-six-year-old Umar Vakhidov, a relative of Basayev's, who controlled drug sales in the Ryazan region and who was responsible for transporting drugs from Chechnya to Russia and returning the money to Chechnya. Vakhidov visited Chechnya every three to four months and freely traveled the republic.

The counterfeiting of American dollars is a third big producer of cash. Printing operations began in 1996 in Argun and Grozny as well as outside Chechnya. Within two years of starting up, Chechen-counterfeited U.S. dollars flooded banks in Siberia, the Far East, and the Volga regions. The Russian government had to take one million counterfeit U.S. dollars in 1996 $100 bills out of circulation in the Primorsk region of the Russian far east and $100,000 in the Magadansk region of eastern Siberia. Both counterfeit American dollars and Russian rubles showed up in street kiosks, small stores, and supermarkets in the Amur, Ivanovo, Vologda, Moscow, and Tyumen regions, as well as in the Republic of Karachaevo-Cherkessia.

Chechnya's counterfeiting operation was closed down when the Russian Army moved back into the republic in 1999. One of the production houses in the Shatoisky district was destroyed, but the plates to make U.S. dollars were never found. New counterfeit U.S. dollars are now being produced. In the summer of 2002, Moscow police seized $100,000 of the new counterfeit U.S. dollars. In 2002, police reported as much as a 50 percent increase in counterfeiting in Russia, much of it attributed to Chechen counterfeiting. Some of the counterfeit money was being used to buy weapons and even pay the salaries of Chechen fighters. In 2001, a huge ruckus erupted when mujahideen found out that much of the several million in U.S. dollars that had been received to pay them was in fact counterfeit.

EMBEZZLEMENT AND THE SALE OF NUCLEAR MATERIALS

If, in 1997, The Lone Wolf robbed trains and stole teachers' salaries, then others too have stolen from Russian federal funds meant for Chechnya. Money from the Russian federal budget to pay for administrative costs, reconstruction, pensions, and welfare benefits is regularly embezzled by Chechen government officials or mysteriously disappears en route to Chechnya. Alexei Arbatov, a member of the Russian Federation State Duma committee responsible for reviewing federal budget expenditures allotted to defense and security matters, says that the equivalent of $1 billion for programs to restore Chechnya's economy "simply vanished" in the first Chechen war and early postwar period.

President Maskhadov often talked about this problem. The Chechen minister of interior ordered the arrest and extradition of seventy people from Russia for embezzlement in 1997 alone. Acting President Yandarbiyev had taken government money for personal use but was never prosecuted. Chechen Vice President Vakha Arsanov told the Chechen parliament that embezzlement was even taking place right under Maskhadov's nose in "the upper echelons of power" in Chechnya. Others accused Maskhadov himself of pumping money from the Chechen pension fund into his own personal bank account abroad. Ichkeria's president and others embezzled Russian health-care funds and children's allowances for Chechnya. Money and goods from foreign charity organizations for refugee relief are particularly vulnerable to embezzlement and theft. Only in magical Chechnya can whole railroad cars of humanitarian aid, spare parts, and even oil disappear into thin air without a trace.

Embezzlement schemes still flourish. In May 2001, Hazmat Idrisov, the pro-Moscow Chechen prime minister, was arrested for embezzlement. Russian auditors have also uncovered large-scale corruption and theft of Russian funds for reconstruction in Chechnya. Chechen civil servants claim that Moscow's money was used to repair two thousand homes in Grozny, but a close audit discovered that most of the repairs were paid for by homeowners themselves and the money was stolen, an undetermined amount of which went to fund the Wolves' jihad. Double billing Moscow for reconstruction work is common. So is phony documentation of work completed. Builders use every scheme imaginable to steal government funds.

In 2001, the equivalent of $18 million in Russian rubles was embezzled from federal funds meant to rebuild Chechen schools, hospitals, and other infrastructure. In one case, $2.4 million earmarked for reconstruction of schools and hospitals was stolen. In another, $838,000 was embezzled from a fund to improve Chechen education. Aslanbek Aslakhanov, a Russian State Duma Chechen deputy, says that only about 10 percent of the money destined for reconstruction ever gets put into projects and "the rest is invisible."

Maybe this is why Vice President of the Chechen Republic of Ichkeria Akhmed Zakayev says, "Money for our armed forces comes from Russia, it comes via [President] Kadyrov's administration itself. There is not one minister, manager, or village head who does not give us money. As long as the Kadyrov administration continues, we will never have trouble with our finances."

Early on in the Dudayev years, Russian trains were robbed too. In the first six months of 1993 alone, more than 450 trains were robbed and goods from containers stolen, with losses amounting to seven million

(1993) rubles. Salman Raduyev became a notorious train robber in 1996–1997.

The theft of millions of dollars in property—farm land, animals, machinery, and automobiles—not only from Dagestan but in the neighboring Stavropol region, was also a source of income in the interwar years.

History of the sale of stolen nuclear materials and radioactive waste dates back to 1992. That year, 669 pounds of low enriched uranium was stolen from the Cheptsk Mechanical Plant located in the Republic of Udmurtiya, Russia. Chechen criminals may or may not have been involved in the theft, but a portion of the haul was brokered in Grozny that year to Azeri nationals who resold it to Iran for $15 million. Grozny also brokered a subsequent deal for an unspecified sum.

Nuclear smugglers from Kazakhstan reportedly approached Chechen Wolves in the summer of 2002 with an offer to sell them osmium-187, one of the required components for making mini-nuclear bombs. Osmium brings a high price on the black market. Chechens might have been interested in buying it for their own use or resale to al Qaeda. Osama bin Laden's representatives have approached mafia groups in Russia to discuss buying nuclear weapons and nuclear materials. They have made the same offers to Wolves. While a few cases like the 1992 theft and sale of nuclear materials are documented, there may be others that have gone undetected and have served as a source of income for some Chechen or foreign field commanders.

THE CAPTIVES-FOR-SALE AND BEREZOVSKY BRANCHES

The $200 million kidnapping, captives-for-sale, and slave-trade business made Arbi Barayev and his close associates very rich people and put nice sums of money in the pockets of Salman Raduyev and businessman Berezovsky too. Berezovsky is wanted by the Russian federal prosecutor's office as a conspirator in the captives-for-sale business.

There is also an outstanding arrest warrant for Berezovsky for handing over bundles of Russian federal budget money to Basayev and others. Basayev's business ties with Berezovsky go back to 1990 or earlier. In 1997, Berezovsky's envoy and business partner Badri Patarkatshvili went to Ingushetia with a few million dollars in a big suitcase and gave it to Basayev in the presence of then Ingush President Ruslan Aushev and Vice President Agapov. That may have been the $2 million that he gave to Basayev to rebuild the cement factory in Chiri-Yurt. Vice President Arsanov later said that Basayev gave Maskhadov $1 million and kept the rest for himself.

Two years later, in the summer of 1999, Badri flew to Kabardino-Balkaria's Nalchik airport and passed another $1 million to Movladi Udugov. Russia says that this money was given to Udugov specifically to buy arms so Basayev could invade Dagestan that summer. This wasn't the only instance in which Udugov received money from Berezovsky.

President Maskhadov was very vocal about Berezovsky's financial support of Raduyev, Basayev, Udugov, and others in the opposition: "He's hatching plots and linking up with the opposition . . . paying for their television, their Internet access, and their satellite telephones." Maskhadov frequently declared, "He's playing a very important role."

In January 2002, the FSB opened a new investigation against Berezovsky for his involvement in "the financing of illegal armed formations and their leaders." Fourteen months later, the British police arrested Berezovsky on new Russian charges alleging that he defrauded the government administration of the Samara region out of $30 million between 1994 and 1995.

Berezovsky maintained close ties with Basayev, Udugov, and others in Chechnya to further his own business interests. This continues today. Charles H. Fairbanks Jr., director of the Central Asia Caucasus Institute, says that his institute has interviewed Chechens who received money from Boris Berezovsky through Chechen Islamic extremists.

PAKISTAN AND THE "NOBLE CAUSE OF THE CHECHEN MUSLIMS"

Sergei Yastrzhembsky, President Putin's spokesman on Chechnya, said in early 2003 that there are no longer any foreign governments providing direct financial support to Chechen fighters, but that has not always been the case—and organizations and foundations in many countries, including Pakistan, still provide support. Raduyev promised subversive school graduates in February 1999 that money will come from some European countries, as well as Pakistan, Afghanistan, and other countries. "They will furnish us with money, weapons, and equipment for our army."

Pakistan has been a major sponsor of "the noble cause of the Chechen Muslims." Pakistan's Inter-Service Intelligence decided early on to support Basayev. Both Russia and China have complained about Pakistan's "nurturing and dispatching" of militants to Chechnya and Muslim parts of China. Many teachers in Pakistani madrassas (religious schools) are Pakistani veterans of the wars in Chechnya. In 1999, Lashkar-e-Tayyiba, one of Pakistan's largest militant organizations, signed up several hundred men to fight Islamic holy wars worldwide. Some of them were sent to

Chechnya. That fall, Russia protested to Pakistan that Abu Abdullah Jafar, a Pakistani, had led a two-hundred-man Arab battalion of fighters into Dagestan in 1999. Jafar was a member of the terrorist group al-Badr (Full Moon) and was also one of Khattab's financial agents. He was killed in Chechnya in May 2001.

The Pakistani journal *Al-Irshad* reported that in March 2000, a Pakistani militia officer by the name of Hidayatullah was also sent to Chechnya in a training role. The journal estimated that a couple dozen Pakistani fighters had already been martyred while fighting in Chechnya.

Pakistan's Islamic political parties also send money and military supplies to Chechnya. On his fund-raising trip to Pakistan in 2000, Yandarbiyev expressed his delight with the fact that "fraternal Pakistan has promised us every support."

The Pakistani Islamic religious establishment has been heavily involved too. Preceding Basayev's entry into Dagestan in August 1999, three Pakistani Wahhabi preachers conducted a special prayer service in Chechnya during which they read out to Basayev, Khattab, Jafar, and others a fatwa (permission) from Wahhabi religious leaders to establish an Islamic state in Dagestan.

The Al-Rashid charity in Pakistan has funded Chechen fighters. In 2000, it sent $750,000 in cash after alleging that aid sent to Chechnya for refugee relief through the United Nations failed to reach its destination. This new influx of money was simply handed over to an unidentified "religious group" in Chechnya. President Bush froze the assets of this charity in the United States after 11 September 2001, and so did Pakistan, but not before Karachi gave advance notice of its intent, thereby giving the charity time to withdraw funds from all of its bank accounts.

SAUDI AND JORDANIAN BRANCHES

President Maskhadov often tongue-lashed Saudi Arabia for providing financial aid to the Chechen opposition. The U.S. State Department says there is evidence of "substantial financial support" reaching "Chechen and Dagestan rebels" from the Arab world. One senior U.S. State Department official estimated that about $100 million has been sent to Chechnya since 1996. That is probably a conservative figure. A former Chechen financial official estimated that before August 1999, over $1 billion had come into the republic from the Middle East. In late June 2002, Russian Defense Minister Sergei Ivanov produced accounting ledgers seized in a raid on Maskhadov's headquarters that showed Chechen financial sources in Qatar, Jordan, and Turkey. Around $6 million a month was reaching

Chechnya in 2000, but that sum had been reduced to about $2 million just before the 2002 summer reorganization of the Chechen armed forces. It is more now since the Dubrovka theater siege and the series of successful suicide bombings in Chechnya beginning in December 2002.

In August 1999, Russia accused Saudi Arabia of funding Basayev's and Khattab's Dagestani venture. On 20 September 1999, the state-run Saudi Press Agency denied Russia's claim. But deep Saudi public sympathy for Chechens does motivate the Saudi government, Saudi Islamic foundations, as well as private Saudi citizens to donate large sums of money for Chechen religious purposes and refugee relief, undetermined amounts of which falls into the hands of Arab and Chechen field commanders in Chechnya. In 1998, Maskhadov loudly complained about Saudi financing of "certain opposition elements" and "bandit groups."

In 1991, a Saudi businessman went to the city of Ulyanov, Russia, to finance the building of a mosque. He brought a large bundle of cash with him and met with Russian Islamic leaders, including the mufti of the European section of the Muslims of Russia organization. The businessman left Russia satisfied that the mosque would be built, but it never was, and the huge sum of money he left behind disappeared. Some believe that muftis took it, while others say that the Chechen mafia in Ulyanov got hold of it and sent it to Chechnya.

Presidents Dudayev, Yandarbiyev, and Maskhadov all used Saudi money, which also helped finance Movladi Udugov's election campaign in 1996. Saudi funds helped finance Udugov's kavkaz.org Web site too. Khattab received Saudi donations to build Wahhabi schools as well as money to pay parents to send their children to study in those schools, construct mosques, and open Wahhabi publishing houses. Khattab once personally asked a Saudi official for financial help in purchasing ammunition and developing camps to train fighters.

After the second war in Chechnya started, King Fahd in December 1999 made a donation of $5 million for Chechen Muslims within the framework of the campaign organized by the Joint Saudi Committee for the Relief of Kosovo and Chechnya. The Saudi television Chechnya Relief Campaign in December 1999 and January 2000 raised another $13 million. Did some of this money trickle down into the pockets of certain field commanders?

Islamic charities are commonly used as fronts to fund the Chechen mujahideen. The Saudi-based religious charity Al-Haramein Islamist Foundation was one of Khattab's principal financiers. Al-Haramein was originally set up to support the Afghan mujahideen but today finances the militant wing of the Wahhabi movement worldwide. The foundation began funding militant Dagestani Wahhabis as early as 1997 through its branch in Baku, Azerbaijan. Azerbaijan's Ministry of Justice subsequently closed down Al-Haramein's office on grounds that its "activities did not conform to its charter." Al-Haramein also established a special fund called the Foundation Regarding Chechnya, a branch of which opened in Azerbaijan at the end of 1999 and sent "operatives" out to establish secure supply routes for Khattab and Basayev. Al-Haramein emissaries also made arrangements with Taliban contacts in Pakistan to acquire weapons and combat gear and to recruit mercenaries who would be sent to Chechnya through Turkey and Georgia.

One of those mercenaries was Abu Darr, a Saudi citizen, who was a close friend of Arbi Barayev but who went to Khattab's command after Barayev was killed by Russian forces. In late June 2000, Darr and his unit of Arab fighters were encircled by Russian forces near Serzhen-Yurt, but they broke through the encirclement and escaped after week-long combat.

In December 1999, Russian intelligence intercepted a message from an unnamed Al-Haramein operative in Chechnya to Saudi Arabia specifically requesting field hospitals, medicine, and medical equipment, as well as facilities for evacuation of the wounded to Georgia at an estimated cost of $3 million. The money to pay for this was to be channeled to Chechnya and Georgia via Turkey. Another intercept said, "Sheikh Jamal is sending you three surgeons with Turkish and Pakistani assistants. The planes with the above on board are on their way to Georgia where they will land in 2–3 hours."

Schools in Saudi Arabia collect money for the jihad. In his July 2000 Azeri television interview, Basayev told the story about an eight-year-old girl who brought her doll to sell at a school auction for the North Caucasus jihad. "The doll costs ten dinars. She brought the doll, the most precious thing to an eight-year-old girl, to sell it and send money for the jihad. And a businessman bought the doll for one thousand dinars and she sent this money and also a letter."

Saudi Arabia has also provided medical help for seriously wounded fighters and plays a delicate diplomatic balancing act in its political support for Chechnya. In June 2002, Saudi Arabia refused to condemn terrorism against Russian forces in Chechnya. The Saudi ambassador to Russia said that it was necessary to distinguish terrorism against civilians and terrorism against military occupants of a country. Saudi money also supports Chechen refugees in Georgia's notorious Pankisi Gorge. In 2002, Saudis built a brand-new mosque in the village of Duisi.

The fact that Movsar Barayev made cell phone calls to Saudi Arabia, Qatar, and the United Arab Emirates during the October 2002 Dubrovka theater siege raises deep suspicion that Persian Gulf money was pledged or helped finance the siege. During one of the FSB-intercepted calls, an unidentified person on the other end of the line asked for a video of the scene inside the theater and was told that it would cost him $1 million.

Pressure by both Presidents Bush and Putin on the Saudi government in November 2002, and Saudi promises to pull in the reigns of Saudi Islamic charity organizations to slow down the flow of money to terrorist organizations, will hopefully put the squeeze on some of the funds flowing to Wolves.

Fighters have also come from Saudi Arabia. The Islamic Observation Center in London says that "hundreds of Arab Muslims, mostly from Saudi Arabia and other Gulf countries," have gone to fight in Chechnya since 1995.

Jordan has an old and well-established Chechen community numbering around fifteen thousand people. There are many Chechens in high positions in the security forces and intelligence departments of the government. This community, the second largest abroad, has contributed large sums of money to Chechnya—reaching at one point $20 million annually according to the Russian Interior Ministry.

Jordanian Chechens early on established close ties with President Dudayev—two of them even served as his foreign ministers. Another Jordanian, Ipak Fath, an elderly Chechen-Jordanian Wahhabi activist, returned to Chechnya and brought with him funding to help arm, feed, and dress many Chechen fighters during the first war with Russia. After Dudayev was killed, Wahhabi money from generous givers in Jordan and Saudi Arabia was funneled through acting President Yandarbiyev and then President Aslan Maskhadov until he fell out with Basayev and Khattab. All of them used Khattab's financial channels.

In the first Chechen war with Russia, Jordan provided medical help to seriously wounded Chechen jihad fighters. Aukai Collins wrote in his book *My Jihad* that he went to Jordan to have a nerve in his foot reattached after receiving initial medical treatment in Azerbaijan. "Once I got to Jordan I was taken to the best hospital in Amman and was scheduled for surgery with a military surgeon. . . . I underwent a five-hour operation."

CHECHNYA'S TURKISH COMMISSARS

Turkey, a predominantly Muslim country, is the gateway to the Chechen jihad. The traveler to Istanbul in 1995 could not miss the green Chechen flags and Dudayev's portraits in shops, and, at least once, the visitor was asked to donate to the Chechen cause.

Two diaspora organizations, the Committee for Cooperation with Chechnya and the Cooperation with the Peoples of the Caucasus, served as financial conduits for money collected during the first war. These organizations funneled $1 million into Chechnya in the first few months of 1995. At the end of 2002, Russia complained to Ankara about some eighty organizations providing aid to Chechen fighters, demanding that the Turkish government immediately close down these organizations, which the Kremlin believes helped finance the October 2002 Dubrovka theater siege.

It's not surprising that Turkey is a principal financial supporter of Chechen mujahideen since seventy thousand Chechens live in Turkey, the largest Chechen community abroad, and another ten million Turks trace their family heritage back to the Caucasus.

Mosques contribute money too. The Fatih Mosque, one of the oldest in Istanbul, routinely collects for Chechnya and organizes political demonstrations in support of Chechen independence. It has also recruited fighters. Likewise, the Beyazit Mosque has organized demonstrations in support of Chechnya. Istanbul is also home to numerous aid and humanitarian organizations that help Chechnya. Kafkasya Yardimlasma Dernegi is a well-known Chechen aid organization that is suspected of funneling funds to Chechen fighters.

Early on, Turkey provided much covert support to Dudayev, serving first as a conduit for the flow of Libyan money to Chechnya and then buying weapons and providing training to fighters destined for Chechnya. Libyan leader Muhammar Gadafi donated millions to Dudayev, clandestinely transferring this money through the Libyan intelligence service at the Libyan embassy in Ankara to the Turkish Refah Party. The party in turn laundered the money and passed it on to Usman Imayev, the Chechen minister of justice and head of the National Bank of Ichkeria. This worked until Imayev started skimming off the top for himself.

Dudayev soon learned of Imayev's compulsion. To fix the problem, the president told Imayev that instead of taking cash he must persuade the leadership of the Refah Party to buy weapons with Libya's money. The party agreed. Turkey used the money to buy old Soviet-era weapons from former East German arsenals and allowed Dudayev to send planes to Turkey to airlift the weapons to Chechnya.

But not all of the money given to the Refah Party ended up in Chechen hands. In August 1997, the Turkish State Security Court launched an investigation into Chechen claims that $10 million of Chechnya's money disappeared while in the hands of Refah officials. Maskhadov sent a representative to Necmettin Erbakan, leader of the Refah Party and then prime minister, to find the money. Erbakan could not account for it, but he did give $2 million from a slush fund to Maskhadov's man, promising to hand over the balance later.

More than once, Russia has accused the Turkish government of tacit complicity with Chechen terrorists, and for good reason. When Basayev hijacked the Russian airliner to Turkey in 1991, Ankara proclaimed it to be a "protest act" and let him leave with the plane and passengers for Chechnya. All of the nine people who hijacked the Black Sea ferry *Avrasiya* in 1996 received light prison sentences and then quickly escaped from jail. One was later rearrested and then given amnesty, only to take hostages again. Hospitals in Turkey have also provided medical assistance to wounded Chechen fighters. Dudayev's son received medical treatment there after being wounded in the first war with Russia. Turkey is also used as a safe haven. "All of us spent some time in Turkey as well as in Georgia and Azerbaijan," says a former Chechen fighter. Both Zelimkhan Yandarbiyev and Udugov took temporary refuge there. Raduyev's wife and children live there.

For a long time, Islamists who wanted to fight in Chechnya could receive training first in the Chechen-populated town of Ducze, Turkey, the epicenter of a devastating earthquake in 1999. Mustafa is a Turk of Albanian origin who trained in Ducze and later lost his leg fighting in one of Khattab's units in Chechnya. In 2001, he told CNN Italia interviewer Ali Isingor that when he decided to go to Chechnya he got in touch with a friend who was a former member of the Turkish Grey Wolf terrorist organization. His friend in turn contacted the ultranationalist branch of that movement known as Nizami-i Alem Acaklari. They organized everything for him and put him in a training camp where he was taught how to fight and shoot. Nizami-i Alem Acaklari also made the arrangements for him to get to Chechnya.

Ramazan Aydin, a waiter from Ducze, is another fighter who trained at the Ducze camp, went to Chechnya in the first year of the war, then hijacked a Turkish plane to Germany in early 1996 to draw international attention to the war in Chechnya.

In January 1996, the Kremlin lodged an official complaint with Ankara about the Chechen diaspora sending fighters like Mustafa and Ramazan to Chechnya. There were others who followed them. The Turkish Federal Justice Ministry reported in August 1999 that at least seventy Turkish nationals were in Chechnya—some participating in Basayev's actions in Dagestan. Mairbek Vachagayev says that the "preferred route" of fighters like Mustafa and others from Turkey was through Georgia. "They also went to Chechnya by simply passing through Moscow, then going down to the Caucasus," Vachagayev told *Le Monde* in December 2002.

Judge Jean-Louis Bruguiere, a French investigative judge in 2002 looking into the recruitment of French nationals to fight in Chechnya, confirmed that he found French citizens entering Chechnya through Istanbul and then Georgia.

AZERI TRADITIONAL ROUTES

Azerbaijan is a traditional route used to move fighters, money, drugs, weapons, and materials into and out of Chechnya and the Caucasus. The country was once a true safe haven for Chechen fighters. Both Basayev and Khattab fought on the side of Azerbaijan against the Armenians in 1992, and the Azeri people are generally sympathetic to the Chechen fighter.

In the 1994–1996 Chechen war with Russia, Azerbaijan provided much support to Chechnya. Baku's hospitals treated many wounded Chechen fighters. The Chechen mafia helped get fighters across the border and made the necessary arrangements with hospitals for medical treatment for the wounded.

A host of charity organizations like the Benevolence International Foundation (BIF), Al-Haramein, the Kuwait Society for the Revival of the Islamic Heritage, and others set up regional offices in Baku and opened local bank accounts to facilitate the flow of funds to Chechen field commanders. In Baku, Al-Haramein worked in cooperation with the Al-Baraka bank, a business of the transnational Dailah Al-Baraka Group whose head helped sponsor President Maskhadov's trip to the United States. Russia says that the Al-Baraka Investment and Development Company has also funded Chechen fighters.

At one time, Basayev also used Azerbaijan as a staging area, with Turkish-piloted helicopters flying materials and foreign fighters to Chechnya.

Support in the second war has been less. Under Russian pressure, the Azerbaijani Ministry of Justice closed down many branch offices of these charities in 2001 and 2002 on grounds that their activities did not conform to their charters. Bank accounts of suspected terrorists and terrorist groups were also carefully monitored and, in some cases, seized. Azeri security forces even captured terrorist Ruslan Akhmadov and turned him over to the Russians. Nevertheless, right up to his death, Khattab kept his private mailbox in Baku, and his courier made frequent runs back and forth carrying money, usually in amounts of $200,000 to $300,000.

In 2000, Russia complained that arms and ammunition were again being shipped to Chechnya through Azerbaijan, and, during his October 2001 visit, Russian Interior Minister Boris Gryzlov said that Chechen terrorists were using Azerbaijan for drug trafficking. He also warned Azerbaijan that it still ran the risk of Chechen terrorists hatching plots on

Azeri soil like the one to assassinate President Putin during the Russian president's visit scheduled for late 2000.

Azerbaijan also provides medical treatment for wounded mujahideen. In January 2000, under the terms of a 1997 agreement between Azerbaijani and Chechen health authorities, one hundred mujahideen wounded in a Russian artillery attack were treated in Baku.

THE SHEVARDNADZE TRAIL

If Vietnam had its Ho Chi Minh Trail, then Chechnya has its Shevardnadze Trail. That's what the Kremlin calls the eight-mile-long stretch of no-man's-land in eastern Georgia known as the Pankisi Gorge, a lawless area that Georgia is unable to totally control and that has served as a conduit for financial and logistical support and fighter reinforcements into Chechnya since the early 1990s.

The Pankisi Gorge is accessible only through treacherous mountain passes and is closed by snow from October through May. Nevertheless, for a long time, it was home to an assorted collection of murderers; terrorists; drug runners; kidnappers; arms traders; Islamic holy warriors; a few thousand Chechen refugees; Saudi Wahhabi preachers; Arab school teachers; and several thousand ethnic Georgians and Kists (local Chechens). In late 2001, it also became a temporary home to al Qaeda fighters fleeing Afghanistan. Deserting Chechen field commander Ruslan Gelayev hid there from late 2000 until the summer of 2002, and other Chechen fighters periodically flee into Georgia to hide, rest, recover from their wounds, form new units, and go back into Chechnya. Arab instructors under Khattab also trained terrorists and new foreign recruits in the gorge. Until late 2002, there were up to eight hundred Chechen and foreign fighters in the gorge.

Complaints about the "constant flow of money and materials" passing through the gorge to Chechnya were overshadowed in the late summer and fall of 2002 by allegations that the gorge was being used as a springboard for new guerrilla and terror attacks on Russia, causing the Kremlin to threaten Georgia with war. A few hundred fighters did return to Chechnya following the Wolves' 2002 summer reorganization and Maskhadov's call for them to resume the fight at home. Clashes with them on the Russian border continued into September, including the late September battle with Gelayev's forces in Galashki, Ingushetia, resulting in the death of sixteen Russian soldiers.

Intense Kremlin and U.S. pressure on Tbilisi has produced some results. A Georgian December 2002 military raid on the Pankisi Gorge

Djokhar Dudayev, former Soviet Air Forces general and
Chechnya's first president. *Author's collection.*

Shamil Basayev (right) conferring with Aslan Maskhadov (left). *Author's collection.*

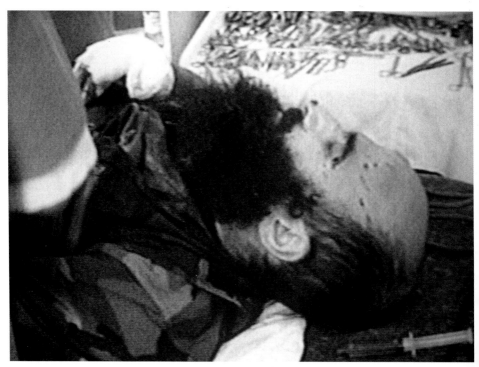

Shamil Basayev—Interpol Fugitive Arrest Warrant #14843—on the operating table during his foot amputation. A Russian mine blew his toes off while he was fleeing from Grozny. (2000) *ITAR-TASS.*

Shirvani Basayev, Shamil's brother, demanded that only his relatives and friends be hired to work at the International Committee Red Cross hospital in Novye-Atagi. (1996) *Author's collection.*

Movladi Udugov, Chechnya's "Goebbels" (left), confers with Shamil Basayev during better times. *Author's collection.*

The early face of Chechnya's fighting forces. *Author's collection.*

"Commander of the Islamic Army of Dagestan" Khattab. His real name was Samir Salakh al-Suweilem, a Saudi professional Wahhabi Islamic warrior with ties to Osama bin Laden. *Author's collection.*

People trader and executioner Arbi Barayev was nicknamed "The Wahhabi" for his religious fanaticism. *ITAR-TASS.*

A classic kidnapping contract. The translated Russian text reads: "Praise be to Allah and mercy and benevolence on the slaves he has chosen. We the witnesses, Abdu-Rashid, Seiffulakh, Khamza, and Abu-Umar, swear to the contract which is concluded between us and Yasir of Syria representing the side of Dzhuneid, concerning the seizure of a kafir for ransom and division of the money between the two sides as follows: 45% for the side of the kidnappers (8 people) and 55% for the side in Chechnya (2 persons/Dzh, Yas) responsible for transportation, security, and (ransom) negotiation. And may the Almighty bear witness to our words.
Abdu-Rashid, (signatures)
Seifullakh,
Khamza,
Abu-Umar

بسم الله الرحمن الرحيم

Хвала Аллаху милость и милосердие тем рабам которых он выбрал.
Мы свидетели Абду-Рашид, Сейфуллах, Хамза, Абу-Умар свидетельствуем о договоре, который был между нами и Ясиром Сирийским представлявшим сторону Джунейда о захвате кафира для получения выкупа и раздел денег между двумя сторонами: 45% процентов для стороны которая захватывает ('8 человек) и 55% для стороны которая в Чечне (2 человека(дж, Яс)) за перевозку, охрану и посредничество
И Аллах тому, что мы говорим свидетель.
Абду-Рашид
Сейфуллах
Хамза
Абу-Умар

This Russian man's head was held on a stump and cut off with a hatchet while Barayev's cameraman videotaped the slaughter. Beheadings were common if a victim's family failed to pay the ransom demanded. *Author's collection.*

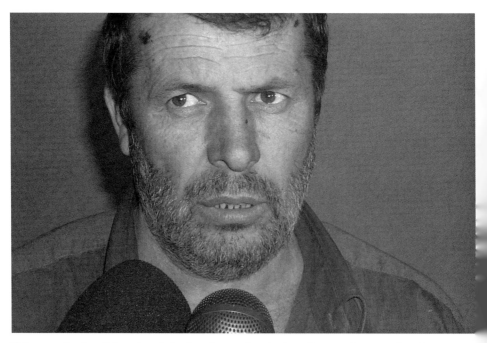

Kidnapper Ruslan Akhmadov, forty-six, a "man of agriculture," answering questions in Dagestan after his capture. (March 2001) *ITAR-TASS.*

Aslan Maskhadov at Zemlikhan Yandarbiyev's house on 5 January 1997 for a meeting of the top five contenders for the Chechen presidency. Movladi Udugov, Akhmed Zakayev, and Shamil Basayev also attended. *ITAR-TASS.*

President Putin once described Salman Raduyev, "The hero of Permomaiskoye," as "the most odious of all." *Author's collection.*

Newspaper cartoons and television programs about Raduyev's "rise from the dead" entertained Muscovites in July 1996. *Author's collection.*

House 19, Guryanova Ulitsa, Moscow, September 1999. "Chechen wolves have declared war on us," President Boris Yeltsin proclaimed to the world after basement bombs leveled two Moscow apartment buildings full of sleeping families. *Author's collection.*

Doka Dzhatemirov, twenty nine, procured the surface-to-air missile which shot down the giant Mi-26T helicopter killing 127 people in August 2002. *Author's collection.*

Khattab's burial somewhere in the mountains of Chechnya. (2002) *Author's collection.*

"It was a dream come true," twenty-three-year-old Movsar Barayev told reporters about the siege of the Dubrovka theater. (2002) *Author's collection.*

ВЕЧНАЯ ПАМЯТЬ
ЖЕРТВАМ ТЕРРОРИСТИЧЕСКОГО АКТА
В ТЕАТРАЛЬНОМ ЦЕНТРЕ НА ДУБРОВКЕ
ОКТЯБРЬ 2002 Г.

This placard bearing the names of those killed at the Dubrovka House of Culture was erected at the theater's entrance on the first anniversary of the hostage siege. *Author's collection.*

A dead Black Widow at Dubrovka, killed by a single gunshot to the head. *Author's collection.*

The corpse of a Dubrovka terrorist awaits disposal. *Author's collection.*

Peering through his courtroom cell, Alikhan Mezhiyev denied at his 2004 trial that he had left a bomb in the car parked beside the Yugo Zapadnaya McDonald's restaurant in Moscow or facilitated the siege of the Dubrovka theater. *Grigoriya Tambulova.*

A page from the diary of Tushino's Black Widow Zuilkhan Elikhadzhiyeva reads: (top) "the mountains of Chechnya," (middle) "the Caucasus," and (bottom) "We cannot escape death; it doesn't matter where we go or how far we go, it will get us. It's a shame that my loved one won't be with me no matter how much I want it. Insha'Allah, I will become a shakhida, [word unintelligible] will be eternal [unintelligible] to us. Insha'Allah. *Author's collection.*

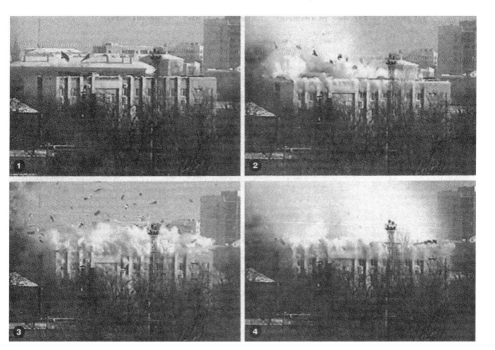

Frames from a video tape show the exploding Chechen government administrative building in Grozny. Basayev says he pushed the detonator button himself on the suicide truck bombs. (December 2002) *Author's collection.*

Police and a spectator carry a body from the "Wings" rock concert and beer festival at Moscow's Tushino airfield. The Black Widow attack in July 2003 left fourteen dead. *Iliya Pitalyev.*

In separate incidents in September and December 2003, railroad track bombs and suicide bombers blew up trains carrying students and commuters in southern Russia, killing forty-five and wounding 154 others. *Author's collection.*

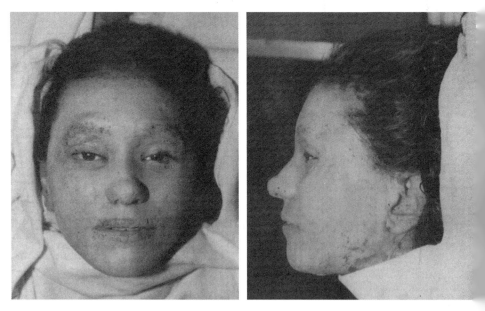

"The Head"—all that remained of the Black Widow who killed six people in front of Moscow's plush National Hotel in December 2003. *Author's collection.*

Фоторобот предполагаемого террориста.

Police sketch of the 6 February 2004 Moscow subway bombing suspect. *Author's collection.*

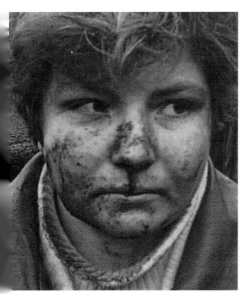

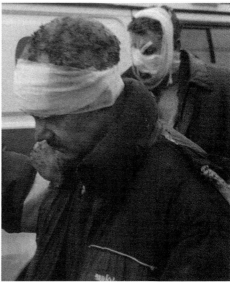

he luckiest survivors emerged with only bloody faces, multiple lacerations and singed hair rom the February 2004 Moscow subway tunnel terror which killed more than fifty people. *uthor's collection.*

Saudi-born Abu al-Waleed (left) and amir of the Riyadus-Salikhin Reconnaissance and Sabotage Battalion of Shakhids, Shamil Basayev, in the mountains of Chechnya. (2003) *Author's collection.*

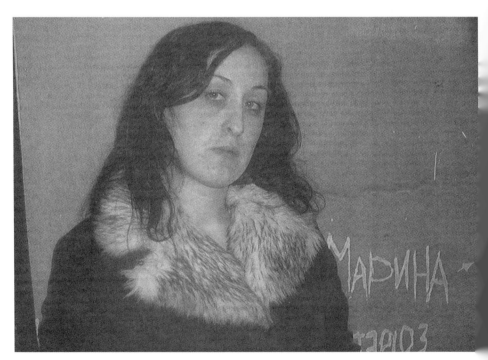

Teenage Chechen girls in Moscow say that twenty-two-year old Zara Murtazaliyeva wanted to recruit them to become suicide bombers. (March 2004) *Author's collection.*

killed five Chechen mujahideen and resulted in the capture and extradition of Yusuf Krymshamkhalov, wanted for the 1999 bombings in Moscow. Georgia also uncovered an al Qaeda run "biological training academy" in the Pankisi Gorge. The U.S. ambassador to Russia has also acknowledged that there have been terrorist training camps there, camps that were subsequently linked to a plot to attack the Russian embassy in Paris in December 2002.

Georgia has also extradited some of the thirteen Chechen mujahideen caught reentering Georgia in August 2002. However, a Georgian Supreme Court in May 2003 refused to extradite three more, which again raised the ire of the Kremlin. Some two dozen or so foreign mujahideen of different nationalities, including French, Arab, and Japanese, were also deported. Georgia also turned over a dozen Arabs directly to the United States.

The new president of Georgia, Mikhail Saakasvilli, is cooperating with Russia. A few more of the thirteen Chechens caught in August 2002 have shown up in Russian custody, leading to speculation that Chechens are now being unofficially extradited to Russia. Three of Gelayev's men who miraculously reached the Georgian border after their bloody raid into Dagestan in December 2003 were promptly caught and handed over to Russia.

INTERNATIONAL ISLAMIC BRANCHES AND OTHER ASSISTANCE

The Fund of the Muslim Brotherhood, a pan-Arab group headquartered in Egypt, raises money for Wolves under the guise of aid to Chechen refugees. The Brotherhood's literature and Internet postings have championed the cause of establishing a North Caucasus Islamic imamate. Russian intelligence says that Sheikh Abu Omar in Chechnya is an "emissary" of the Muslim Brotherhood and an "operative" of Al-Haramein, and today focuses on obtaining financing for terrorism through his contacts in the Arab world.

Until 2001, pro-Chechen organizations in London also provided some sources of funding, but these international Islamic groups reduced or cut off their funding to Chechnya in order to increase funding for Palestinian groups fighting Israel. More recently, the FSB detected contact with representatives of Hamas and the Islamic Jihad, which Russia believes is related to providing material support (like explosive suicide belts) and financial assistance to Wolves.

In October 2000, the FSB searched the Moscow offices of the Kuwait-based Society for Social Reforms, which is accused of funding Chechen fighters and having ties with Osama bin Laden. Russia suspected the society was financing "bandit formations" as early as 1993. The FSB in 2000 said that its investigation showed that the society was really the Moscow branch of the Muslim Brotherhood.

Russian intelligence believes that the Islamic Relief Organization (IRO) headquartered in Birmingham, England, is funded by the special services of Saudi Arabia and Kuwait and provides financial assistance specifically to Maskhadov. Soon after the organization moved into Grozny in 1998, the IRO's home office deposited a large sum of money into its Russian "Sbergbank" account for the declared purpose of feeding Chechen refugees. Subsequent auditing found that while some money was spent on food, most of it was simply withdrawn and disappeared.

Local IRO Chechen managers were arrested, convicted on embezzlement charges, and given three to five years suspended sentences. But Russian economic crime experts say that this is a typical scheme to fund Chechen fighters. The money in the bank account is converted into cash and "embezzled" by the local manager, who takes his cut and then transfers the rest to the right people. Because only the local manager is charged and convicted of embezzlement, the organization is able to continue operating with a new local manager and a new embezzlement scheme.

Russia says that the Islamic Liberation Party (ILP), a radical Islamic organization set up in the 1950s by Palestinians with branches now in Russia, Central Asia, and the Ukraine, has financed Wolves. In June 2003, the FSB arrested fifty-five ILP members in Moscow, some of whom were said to be in possession of small amounts of plastic explosives.

After the 11 September attack in 2001, Russia offered to provide the United States with intelligence in exchange for American intelligence and help with cutting off the sources of Chechen terrorist financing. Russia publicly announced in July 2002 that it was very pleased with the U.S. response.

In October 2001, President Bush froze the assets of Al-Rashid. A month later, the United States froze the assets of the Chicago-based Benevolence International Foundation (BIF) Islamic charity. In April 2002, the head of the charity was arrested by the FBI for lying to a grand jury investigating his ties to Osama bin Laden. Mr. Arnaout claimed that he had never provided support to "people or organizations known to engage in violence, terrorist activities, and military organizations of any nature." But the judge ruled that the evidence presented was enough to warrant the perjury charges. According to the FBI's warrant, in 2000 qoqaz.net designated the BIF a "trustworthy charity with experience of working in the Caucasus, through which those wishing to donate money to Chechen fighters should act."

The FBI later turned up documents showing that BIF had bought antimine boots for Chechen mujahideen in 1995. That same year, BIF opened an office in Baku, Azerbaijan, and delivered an X-ray machine to a Chechen representative there who signed a receipt stating that the unit would be transported to Chechnya for use by the Chechen mujahideen. During one trip to Chechnya, BIF officials were given a shopping list of military supplies needed. The organization subsequently bought $90,000 worth of shoes from a UAE company; spent $66,000 for military uniforms; and spent another $34,000 on boots for mujahideen in Chechnya. BIF spent $1.4 million in Chechnya in 1999.

The United States also found correspondence from Osama bin Laden in BIF's Bosnia branch office with the comment, "The time has come to attack Russia."

Before his death in March 2002, Khattab was the chief financial officer of the North Caucasus jihads. He received foreign monies and, in consultation with Basayev and Maskhadov, funneled these funds to various field commanders and their mujahideen. Deciding exactly how to divide up the money after Basayev was seriously wounded in December 2001 led to friction and bad blood between Khattab and Maskhadov and between foreign mujahideen and Chechen field commanders.

The United States has worked since September 2001 to cut off Khattab's sources of funding. Alexander Vershbow, the U.S. ambassador to Russia, says that the U.S. government has been successful at doing this. Khattab's death in March 2002 further helped to cut off foreign financing of the jihad.

The German-Caucasian Society in the Federal Republic of Germany promotes cultural ties with the Caucasus republics. The society's involvement in training "Chechen military engineers" in Germany to detect and defuse land mines caused a huge scandal and political protests from Russia. In February 1999, the Russian Foreign Ministry complained to the FRG's embassy in Moscow about the practice. Russia's concern was that while Chechens were being trained how to defuse mines, they were also learning how mines work and are installed. They could become mine layers themselves. The FRG confirmed that training was being done as "specialized humanitarian assistance." But Russia questioned why citizens of Russia were being taught a military occupation without agreement from the Russian side. The practice was subsequently stopped.

Similar criticism befell the British anti-land mine charity Halo Trust. It went to work in Chechnya shortly after the first Chechen war ended. In November 2000, the trust was accused of carrying out secret training in Chechnya of "specialists in mines and explosives" and of spying on Russia. Halo denied the charges.

Belarus, a former Soviet republic that ended up with a large stockpile of conventional Soviet weapons and is today one of the world's top arms exporters, Moldavia, and the Ukraine have all shipped arms to Chechnya. On 11 January 2002, *Jane's Intelligence Digest* reported that Victor Sheyman, the former head of the Belarus Security Council, coordinated the arms shipments through former members of the Belarussian Almaz antiterrorist squad who had become mercenaries in Chechnya. They served as intermediaries for the delivery of these weapons. Many of the surface-to-air launchers and missiles in the hands of Chechen forces that are used to shoot down Russian helicopters in Chechnya come from these former republics.

INTERNET, PERSONAL APPEALS, AND VIDEO SALES

Basayev said in his 2000 Azeri television interview that he does not solicit funds, but there have been times when others close to him have. In August 1999, the Web site of Azzam Publications ran an interview with Khattab in which he urged every Muslim to send "aid, trained fighters, money, and equipment" so the mujahideen could "complete the job of driving the Russians out of the Caucasus."

Khattab cautioned, however, that only those who know how to get the money directly to the mujahideen should send money. "Do not," he warned, "give large sums of money to anyone claiming to get the money to the mujahideen in Chechnya unless they can guarantee to provide you with a written, signed, and dated receipt from Khattab."

Azzam's Web site IslamicAwakening.com in January 2000 put out an appeal to Muslims worldwide for money, medical expertise and supplies, and fighters: "For those who are able, get to Chechnya to give physical and financial assistance." But the Web site advised fighters to join only Khattab's or Basayev's forces because they are the only ones that are "trustworthy and aligned to Islam." The Web site advised, "Doctors and medical personnel should endeavour to make their way to Chechnya through aid organizations and join the fighting units of Ibn al-Khattab."

With regard to those who want to help by raising finances, the Azzam Web site advised them to collect "as much money as possible from friends, families, relatives, and contacts in mosques, centers, and everywhere" and "leave this money with a trustworthy individual in your community . . . until we post the details of the aid organization able to collect the donations, and then send your money to them."

Azzam publications continue to raise money for the North Caucasus jihads. Such appeals by Azzam Web sites operating in Nevada and Connecticut will surely result in the filing of U.S. federal charges against

Azzam principals for "providing material support" and "conspiring to launder money in support of terrorism."

High-ranking members of the 2002 Majlis ul-Shura, like Sheikh Abu Omar, have appealed through Kavkaz Center for "assistance in the informational, social, and military realms."

In 1997, Maskhadov toured several Middle Eastern countries to secure loans to rebuild the Chechen economy, but Basayev said that he came back empty-handed. Similarly, Yandarbiyev visited Pakistan, Turkey, and other countries in 2000 seeking financial support. He had better luck there. But Maskhadov, in March 2001, accused Yandarbiyev and Udugov of "accumulating most of the donations into their own accounts and the accounts of their close relatives and friends. . . . Now and again they've been sending dollars to support our jihad." More recently, Maskhadov imposed a "presidential tax" on Chechen businessmen to raise money for himself.

Web sites like qoqaz.net and others supported by diasporas in Turkey, Jordan, and elsewhere also solicit donations and even advise to which charities "with experience working in the Caucasus" to give the money.

The sale of war videos, particularly Khattab's tapes, continues to be a source of funding. One potential buyer was told that a tape of the Dubrovka theater siege would cost him $1 million.

THE OSAMA AND AFGHAN BRANCHES

The holy war against Russia has not been conducted in isolation of the financial, material, and manpower support from Khattab's home base of Afghanistan and the supreme Islamic commander in chief himself, Osama bin Laden. Indeed, the Osama bin Laden branch of the Chechen money tree has contributed millions of dollars to the North Caucasus jihads. That is why Sergei Ivanov, the Russian minister of defense, likes to say that "Afghanistan and Chechnya are two branches of the same tree."

It is difficult to determine the exact amount of Osama bin Laden's contribution. The United States will say only that it has been "a substantial amount of money." Osama bin Laden himself admits to personal investment in the North Caucasus jihads. He told a Pakistani journalist in 1999 that it is his "moral duty to provide [Chechen fighters] with every kind of help."

This statement followed a visit by a Chechen delegation almost certainly led by Khattab to Osama bin Laden in Kandahar to finalize a June 1998 agreement to provide military, financial, and other assistance. The Islamic Salvation Fund in Pakistan, a bin Laden fund set up to finance mujahideen worldwide, in turn helped finance the 1999 "liberation" of Dagestan and later provided funding, weapons, volunteers, and training in al Qaeda camps.

The Spanish newspaper *El Mundo* quoted a Lebanese-born al Qaeda contact as saying that Osama bin Laden sent $10 million to Chechnya in 1999. This may have been the $10 million that Russian intelligence learned Osama bin Laden gave Basayev by intercepting a conversation between an al Qaeda Lebanese commander and the official in charge of the al Qaeda branch in Italy. Another source said it was not $10 million but $25 million that was sent. Other sources say that Khattab personally got $15 million from Osama bin Laden in 1999 for the jihad in Dagestan. Some of the $30 million that Osama bin Laden paid for the four decapitated heads of the Granger Telecom workers, if he did buy them, would have been spent on the jihad too.

Confirmation of financing, material, and fighter support to Khattab and others has come from several sources, including Osama bin Laden associates. In 2000, an associate named Abu Daoud told the Associated Press that Osama bin Laden had sent four hundred Arab fighters to Chechnya with explosives and weapons. On 26 January 2000, the Taliban government officially recognized the Chechen Republic of Ichkeria. Udugov said the next step would be a bilateral accord on financial and military assistance. Six days later, Afghanistan announced that it had dispatched a contingent of Taliban fighters to Chechnya. One of those was Afghan Abu Said al-Kandagary, who was killed on 28 June 2000. A military instructor in al Qaeda confirmed that Osama bin Laden sent an unspecified number of fighters to Khattab in the late spring of 2000.

Foreign fighters killed in Chechnya are seldom positively identified, but, by the end of 2001, the FSB had produced a list of seventy-five it had been able to identify. The country of origin for nearly a third of them could not be determined; the rest came from Afghanistan, Algeria, Egypt, France, Kuwait, Lebanon, Morocco, Saudi Arabia, Turkey, the United Arab Emirates, and Yemen. At least five were from Yemen. It's not known how many of these were dispatched by Osama bin Laden or al Qaeda.

More recently, al Qaeda urged Islamic organizations in Kuwait to provide $2 million to Wolves, and President Putin confirmed in February 2003 that Osama bin Laden is still funding Wolves in Chechnya.

One possible scenario is that Osama bin Laden's financing has been done in exchange for help in trying to acquire nuclear materials. A story that Osama bin Laden had acquired Soviet nuclear warheads with Grozny's help surfaced in the fall of 1998. That is what *Al-Hayah* and another Arab language newspaper, *Al-Watan Al-Arabi,* reported. The deal was reportedly brokered by Grozny and clinched in September 1998 for $30 million in cash and the equivalent of $70 million in heroin. Some of the warheads were old Soviet suitcase bombs that Russian General Alexander Lebed in 1997 told the U.S. Congress had gone missing.

In his 1999 book, *Osama bin Laden: The Man Who Declared War on America*, Yoseff Bodansky, director of the U.S. Congressional Task Force on Terrorism and Unconventional Warfare, says, "There is no longer much doubt that bin Laden has finally succeeded in his quest for nuclear suitcase bombs" and that the "evidence of the number of nuclear weapons purchased by the Chechens for bin Laden varies between 'a few' (Russian intelligence) to 'more than twenty' (conservative Arab intelligence services)."

A 2002 book entitled *Through Our Enemies Eyes* by an anonymous U.S. "senior intelligence officer" discusses this same episode but says only that the story is "to an extent, plausible," that it "has the ring of plausibility, perhaps even echoes of truth." According to *Al-Watan Al-Arabi*, these warheads came from arsenals in the Ukraine, Kazakhstan, Turkmenistan, and even Russia, and ended up in storage in some deep tunnels near Khost, Afghanistan.

Maybe more realistic is a third version of the story, which says that a deal for twenty nuclear devices was in fact made for $30 million and a couple of tons of narcotics, but that the FSB got wind of it and foiled delivery of the goods.

These events preceded a statement by then Russian Prime Minister Putin that Osama bin Laden visited Chechnya in 1999 to check on his investments. Other information had Osama bin Laden paying Khattab to train new al Qaeda recruits after the United States bombed his own training camps in Afghanistan in 1998, and spending a week inspecting Khattab's training camps before the August 1999 Dagestan invasion.

VIII

HUNTING DOWN
TERRORIST WOLVES

If [the wolf] loses the struggle, he dies silently, without expression of fear or pain. And he dies proudly, facing the enemy.

Chechen myth

SINKING THE "TITANIC"

Russian General Shamanov said that his corridor operation in February 2000 was only a tiny fragment of a much larger "Operation Wolf Hunt." Hunting down and assassinating Wolf pack leaders was part of Operation Wolf Hunt too, although the existence of a "death list" was not made public until almost a year later after responsibility for the war in Chechnya had been transferred from the Russian Defense Ministry to the FSB. Six Wolves topped the list: Raduyev, Basayev, Khattab, Barayev, Maskhadov, and Ruslan Gelayev.

Russia caught The Lone Wolf without firing a single shot within six months of beginning Operation Wolf Hunt. Exactly how the FSB nabbed Salman Raduyev in March of 2000 is still a secret, but Raduyev, his chief bodyguard, and a financier were all quietly grabbed by FSB agents in occupied Novogroznensky. The head of Russia's intelligence service will say only that the operation was well planned and based on totally reliable intelligence, and that they managed to avoid a shootout with Raduyev's nearly one hundred bodyguards. Raduyev didn't offer any personal resistance, either—he was reportedly sitting on the toilet and was too much in a state of shock and disbelief when he was grabbed. Given his pride, death probably would have come easier to him than this humiliation. "He couldn't speak for several hours. He just kept silent," his captors said. "He does not really understand what has happened to him."

When Raduyev did come to his senses he swore that he had been betrayed, not by subordinates but by a competitor, although he never did say who it was. Maybe it was Maskhadov. The president was probably glad to finally be rid of the disobedient Raduyev—even in wartime, he had refused to follow Maskhadov's orders. But it is unlikely Maskhadov turned him in. Maskhadov says that Raduyev turned himself in: "He believed Russia's promises [of money] and surrendered to them."

Kommersant Daily speculates that the "pro-Basayev camp" gave Raduyev up, but it is unclear what Raduyev had done to warrant this. Raduyev did call Basayev's actions in Dagestan "perilous for the Chechen people" and Basayev a "traitor." And at his court trial, Raduyev condemned the invasion of Dagestan as "a tragic mistake," but hadn't it been Raduyev who always said that war with Russia should never end?

A story published in the January 2000 issue of *Nezavisimaya Gazeta* lends credibility to *Kommersant Daily*'s theory. The newspaper printed a "Judas" offer addressed to Russia's commander of the Eastern Front in which Raduyev said he would execute Basayev in return for personal amnesty for himself and his people and $1 million in cash. The letter read: "We will stop this war that Shamil Basayev started. He was the one who invited Shiite [Wahhabi] extremists to the Caucasus and took their advice to attack our ethnic brothers in Dagestan. The criminal must be punished. I have men ready to execute Basayev or hand him over to the Russian Army."

Maybe Raduyev did lack principles after all and was just trying to save his own skin. Alexander Gurov, head of the Security Committee in the Russian State Duma, characterized Raduyev as just a "bloodthirsty bandit working for money; not fighting for any ideals" and trying only to find a way out when things got really nasty. But the Judas letter could just as well have been an FSB fabrication. If that were true, though, surely Basayev would have seen though the ruse.

Other information says that a businessman working for an FSB informant helped find Raduyev, while another version of his apprehension says that several people suspected of being members of illegal armed formations were detained and forced to tell where Raduyev was hiding.

Another FSB source said, "We knew people who were closely connected with Raduyev, so we contacted them and, after some negotiations, they promised to transport Raduyev to Novogroznensky where we caught him. . . . We knew that his fellow-fighters wanted to get rid of him, so we appeared with our proposition."

A fourth version says that Raduyev was offered a huge sum of money by FSB agents posing as foreign donors wanting to support the Chechen jihad. Raduyev traveled across Chechnya with his financial manager to retrieve the money, only to fall into the FSB trap.

Raduyev's capture was wildly celebrated in Moscow. It was a media event that again caught everybody's attention. But this time, Raduyev, instead of looking fearsome as usual, appeared thin and frail, even ill. He looked subdued and powerless without his black beard and trademark sunglasses to hide his horrible facial scars and glass eye. Television carried the initial interrogation footage, and all the Russian newspapers had stories about Raduyev with past and present photographs of him. The publicity boosted Russian troop morale, and it wasn't bad for Putin's presidential candidacy either since the election was only a few weeks away. "[Raduyev] is in prison, which is the right place for him. We would like to think that this is just the beginning," acting President Putin said.

There could have been other reasons for the timing of Raduyev's capture too. In February 1999, he had threatened to attack Russian government targets using "radiological materials." He didn't carry out the attacks, although he had free access to such materials from the same place that Basayev got his in 1995. Instead, right on the heels of Khattab's last retreat from Dagestan in September 1999, and after the apartment building bombings, Raduyev resurrected Dudayev's 1995 plans to attack Russian nuclear facilities. Russian intelligence developed credible information that Raduyev had prepared fifteen-person squads of saboteurs to attack Russian nuclear installations, including nuclear power plants. The Ural region, in particular the Chelyabinsk oblast with its numerous nuclear facilities, was a likely target. The threat was widely published in Russian newspapers.

Since these attacks didn't take place either, the plan was either fabricated or Raduyev changed his mind because the element of surprise was gone and security around nuclear facilities had become too tight. Raduyev even denied that he would do such a horrible thing because "it would result in a catastrophe with unpredictable consequences." Instead, he promised to sabotage "strategically important military installations." But Russian defense ministry officials right up to Raduyev's capture were still saying that he was planning large-scale terrorist attacks inside Russia and that they thought it would be against nuclear facilities.

It is difficult to gauge the impact Raduyev's capture had on Chechen guerrilla fighting capabilities. Russian analysts took the view that he wasn't making much of a contribution to the Chechen side in the war anyway; that he never had been a fighter of Basayev's caliber; and that his absence would probably have little real effect on Chechen capabilities. "Raduyev was created by our mass media. He is a second-rate figure. . . . His capture has no importance or impact on the development of the military campaign," concluded Mahmut Gerayev, president of the Academy of Military Science in Moscow. *Nezavisimaya Gazeta* added, "We should not exaggerate the real weight of Raduyev." He is not missed much.

THE TRIAL AND SENTENCING OF RADUYEV

Before going to trial, Raduyev spent eighteen months in the FSB's infamous Lefortovo maximum security prison in Moscow. Things haven't changed much at Lefortovo since the time that political prisoners were rehabilitated there in the Soviet era, but Raduyev says that his treatment in Lefortovo was "like I was a general or something. It was very correct."

The positive effects of Lefortovo were apparent during much of Raduyev's trial. Contrary to being characteristically defiant, belligerent, and boastful, Raduyev's courtroom manner was pleasant and respectful, even cooperative. In prison, he abandoned his no-compromise, fight-to-the-end principles in favor of Chechen accommodation of Russia. "In politics I'm [now] a realist. . . . I'm sure that it is possible to find a peaceful settlement in which we can live together with Russia; the honor of the Chechen people will not suffer from it," Raduyev told *Dagestanskaya Pravda.*

How strange it was to hear such words on Raduyev's lips, but then he said other strange things too that made you think he really had lost his mind. He said that he believed President Dudayev was still alive because "no one has shown me his grave" and "my father and mother still live in Gudermes, and Russian authorities treat them well."

The evidence contained in the seven-hundred-page indictment against Raduyev for eighteen violations of the Russian Criminal Code filled 129 thick notebook binders. The case even included details of the medical examinations of those killed during the raid on Kizlyar and Pervomaiskoye. Raduyev was charged with mass murder; the organization of illegal armed formations; abduction; banditry; and terrorism. There were three other men on trial with him, all of them accomplices at Kizlyar and Pervomaiskoye: Aslanbek Alkhazurov, Turpal-Ali Atgeriyev (former Chechen prime minister and head of Shariah state security), and Hussein Gaisumov.

The closed but televised trial began in mid-November 2001 at the Dagestani Supreme Court building in Makhachkala under intense security. Streets were blocked off, Russian snipers manned the rooftops, and police and FSB agents flooded the town looking for terrorists. There was significant local opposition to the trial being held in Dagestan, most of it generated by fear of a terrorist attack. Many of Raduyev's victims at Kizlyar refused to testify against him for fear of reprisals. The Interior Ministry of Dagestan was very concerned too, estimating that as many as five terrorist groups were operating in the republic. One of these groups sent by Khattab was apprehended at the Chechen-Dagestani border. Ultimately, security concerns caused the trial to be moved behind concrete walls and a barbed wire fence at the Makhachkala SIZO #1 detention center.

Raduyev and his accomplices were transported to court in an armed convoy. He wore a black baseball cap, mirrored sunglasses, and a dark coat, and, together with the other three men, sat in the usual steel cage in the court room. He had grown his beard back. He smiled as court officials began reading the indictment against him.

Russian Prosecutor General Vladimir Ustinov personally prosecuted the case. When he asked Raduyev to state his occupation, Raduyev told the court that he was commander of the northeast sector of the armed forces of the Chechen Republic of Ichkeria.

Testimony from witnesses was laborious. Magomed Omarov, Dagestan's deputy interior minister, told the court that in January 1996, he saw several local policemen gunned down in cold blood as they responded to Raduyev's siege on the hospital, while Dagestani political figures who volunteered to take the place of some of the hospital hostages were themselves taken hostage without Raduyev letting any of the original hostages go. Raduyev testified that he led the raid on Kizlyar but maintained that he was only following President Dudayev's orders and that he did not intend for it to become violent.

Raduyev pleaded not guilty to the 28 April 1997 Pyatigorsk railroad station bombing and all the other charges. But it was the testimony of Aset Dadashyeva and Fatima Taimaskhanova, both female members of Raduyev Dzokhar's Way terrorist unit, that convicted Raduyev for the Pyatigorsk bombing.

The court found Raduyev not guilty on the counts of organizing and participating in illegal armed formations but guilty as charged on all other counts. Sentencing came in late December. Since Russia had placed a moratorium on death sentences in 1996, the death penalty could be ruled out. Everybody expected life imprisonment, though, and Raduyev himself was prepared for life behind bars: "I couldn't care less if I get a life sentence . . . I have died three times already, I can spend my life in prison, I have no regrets." He got life in a "special-regime correctional colony."

Atgeriyev received fifteen years in prison, Alkhazurov eight years, and Gaisumov five years. All but Gaisumov appealed.

In April, Raduyev, Alkhazurov, and Atgeriyev were moved from Makhachkala to the Presnensk transfer prison in preparation for the 11 April Supreme Court trial. Raduyev took part in the Supreme Court proceedings via televised hookup. In excerpts shown on Russian television, Raduyev's attorneys argued to the Russian Supreme Court that the Kizlyar raid was not a criminal act but a military operation carried out during a war between two independent states, Russia and Chechnya. Raduyev characteristically gestured as he asked the court to commute his sentence. However, since Russia had never recognized Chechnya as an independent state, the Supreme Court did not buy the argument that he should receive protection under international law. "The soldier from Ichkeria will have to serve out his sentence," the Court concluded. In addition, all of Raduyev's property would be confiscated, and he would have to pay damages in a civil suit brought against him by Dagestan.

Raduyev and his companions spent the next year in Lefortovo prison. But in May 2002, the lawyers for the trio could not find their clients; they had vanished. Raduyev's attorney learned at the beginning of May that all three had left Lefortovo under heavy guard bound for Makhachkala, probably for the civil suit trial, but they never arrived in the city. When pressed for information about Raduyev, the Russian Justice Ministry would only comment that "other competent authorities deal with this case."

Raduyev was not heard from again for seven months. But on 14 December 2002, he died from "natural causes" (internal hemorrhaging) in the maximum security prison in Solikamsk, Russia. His wife, Lida, sons Dzokhar and Zelimkhan, and elder brother who live in Turkey wanted to bury him in Chechnya, but a new law passed by the Russian Duma following the Dubrovka siege prohibits the bodies of terrorists from being returned to their relatives. Turpal-Ali Atgeriyev died from a stroke in prison five months earlier. Udugov alleges that Raduyev was tortured to death because he refused to testify against Akhmed Zakayev in the latter's extradition trial in London. Maskhadov says only that Raduyev "was violently killed in prison."

DANCING WITH WOLVES

In the summer of 2000, ordinary Chechens became suspicious of the odd behavior and unusual lifestyles of the kidnapping godfather and the Akhmadov brothers who were again living in their own homes, strolling freely about town, even driving around the republic in their own expensive cars without any interference from Russian forces. In short, they were living too freely and too well off to be wanted Chechen generals and terrorists. At first, there were just rumors that Barayev had some kind of "informal relations" with "sources" close to Moscow, then people started talking, field commander Gelayev among them, that Barayev and the others had all become Russian spies.

On 8 August, Sanobar Shermatova writing in *Moskovskiye Novosti* tried to make some sense out of it all. She found out that Barayev and the Akhmadov brothers were not even on Russia's most wanted list and that the Russian Army's General Staff had even provided the Kremlin with evidence that Barayev and the Akhmadovs were in possession of FSB Associate identification cards, making them untouchable by the Russian military. An official investigation into the charges placed the blame on Yunus Magomedov, the FSB's man in charge of the Urus-Martan district. Even though Magomedov was fired, Barayev and the Akhmadovs continued to live their unusual lifestyle. Barayev even got married and threw a lavish wedding reception guarded by Russian federal troops.

A subsequent article in a Moscow newspaper, giving as its source Russian military intelligence, revealed further strange details that led Shermatova to conclude that there was an interagency rivalry going on between the FSB and the GRU—a not uncommon phenomenon in Russia. Other sources said that Barayev was in possession of a "special pass" issued by the Russian military command and that in early November 2000, he even traveled to Moscow. Barayev's sighting in Moscow was reported in some Moscow newspapers. Moreover, in mid-November, Barayev and two other field commanders were detained by Russian spetnaz troops in Grozny but were mysteriously released.

These strange events are what led Shermatova to conclude, "This fight among the special services in Chechnya led to the most important Chechen commanders being left in peace—including such generals and slave-traders as Barayev and the Akhmadov brothers."

In 2003, Shermatova said that she turned up new evidence that the GRU was involved all right, but that Barayev's death was the result of traditional Chechen blood payback for the 1999 murder of Ruslan Azerkhanov, the administrative head of Barayev's hometown. It seems that Azerkhanov's relatives just happened to be members of a GRU "special Chechen unit" that determined that Barayev was responsible for his death. This unit was made up of relatives of people kidnapped or killed by Wahhabis under Arbi Barayev and the Akhmadov brothers.

Hunting for Azerkhanov's murderer, the special Chechen unit had earlier detained Islam Chilayev, Barayev's deputy, for interrogation. But

Chilayev proved his innocence and offered up Barayev as Azerkhanov's shooter, thus precipitating a war between the GRU unit and Barayev that likely resulted in Barayev's death and, later on, the revenge killing of six members of the unit.

Arbi Barayev's older brother, Buharu, denies that Arbi was ever a spy or an agent for Russia and says that the whole story was simply made up by the FSB to sow discord among the mujahideen. But back in July 2000, Basayev had confirmed in his Azeri television interview that "the majority of people who were engaged in the most notorious cases of kidnapping of journalists and foreigners are all on the Russian side now."

Still other sources say that the decision to eliminate Barayev was taken only after the personal intervention of President Putin at a special meeting of the Russian Security Council.

The joint FSB–Interior Ministry operation got under way in the early morning hours of 19 June 2001 and finished in the evening of 24 June. FSB and Interior Ministry troops focused their house-to-house search in Alkhan-Kala and Kulary. Twenty houses were destroyed in the search. Finally, the house that Barayev and eighteen of his men were hiding in was completely surrounded. No attempt was made to take him alive; Russian troops simply opened fire, immediately killing fifteen fighters. Barayev, wounded, tried to escape but fell in the yard outside. The two surviving mujahideen attempted to carry him away but managed only to hide his body in a pile of bricks before fleeing themselves. He was found a few days later.

Barayev's body was turned over to his mother-in-law, his new wife, and nephew Movsar Suleimenov. When they showed up in Alkhan-Kala with Barayev in the bed of the truck taking him to the cemetery, angry townspeople armed with pitchforks, spades, sticks, and stones met the convoy and refused to let it pass. Pelting the truck with stones, the mob yelled, "Take him to the dump." Traditional Chechen law prohibits burying murderers in cemeteries.

KHATTAB'S LETHAL LETTER

In the summer of 2001, the FSB began work on a secret plan to quietly eliminate Khattab. The task was much more complicated than the Raduyev and Barayev operations and involved the use of agents, foreign agents, double-crossers, and a highly lethal and invisible biological warfare killing agent.

Russia learned that Khattab's mother sent letters to him through a secret post office box in Baku, Azerbaijan. One option was to intercept a letter, contaminate it with a lethal agent, and then slip it back into the secret mailbox. Khattab's courier, Ibragim Alauri—a close and trusted Dagestani friend—would pick up the letter and personally deliver it to Khattab as he had done hundreds of times before. Option two was to recruit Ibragim as a double agent and doctor the letter once he took it from the mailbox.

But a lot of people thought the FSB had already lost its chance to get Khattab. When the U.S.-led war on terrorism started in Afghanistan, it was rumored that Khattab and several hundred Chechen fighters had gone to Afghanistan to fight American soldiers. Northern Alliance General Mohammed Daoud himself said that Khattab was leading a force of one thousand fighters belonging to al Qaeda in Kunduz. On 23 November, Russian RTR Television also quoted "unofficial sources" as saying that Khattab had arrived in Kunduz by way of Azerbaijan and Pakistan. The strana.ru Web site on 23 November quoted ITAR-TASS as saying that Osama bin Laden had personally asked Khattab to take charge of the defense of Kunduz.

They were all wrong. Some of Khattab's fighters went to fight in al Qaeda's elite 055 Brigade in Afghanistan in 2001 and were killed and captured in Afghanistan. But Khattab stayed in Chechnya. Lieutenant General Valery Baronov, the Russian commander in Chechnya, was right when he said that Khattab was still in Chechnya and "has a well-organized system of guerrilla units under his command."

While the FSB worked out the details of its secret plan to assassinate Khattab, military forces hotly pursued him. They got very close. In the early winter of 2001, he was wounded in the shoulder and the leg in the Vedensky district, and three of his fighter units were wiped out. Russian troops also found and destroyed another one of Khattab's secret hiding places containing explosives, large amounts of weapons and ammunition, computers, and Wahhabi literature.

Soon after that, in December, Basayev was seriously wounded and evacuated abroad for medical treatment. Before leaving, he passed the sword of leadership on to Khattab, but things began to go wrong shortly after that. There was less cohesiveness between the mujahideen than before. Squabbles between Chechen field commanders and the Islamic units under Khattab's command broke out. There were also arguments between Khattab and Maskhadov on how to split the money coming in from abroad. Cooperation deteriorated, which meant fewer attacks against the enemy.

All of this made it easier to track Khattab. In the new year, Russian forces thought for sure they had him cornered. They knew that he was in the village of Bachi-Yurt in the Shali district. Elite troops were sent in to track him down. Snipers were dispatched, but he was not found, elusive as ever. He had been there, though. Seven of Khattab's men were captured, including Khattab's deputy Abu Sayak, who later died from his wounds.

After so many attempts to capture or kill Khattab, it seemed that he would remain elusive forever. Nothing seemed to work. Huge rewards had not helped to snare him because Khattab executed anyone suspected of cooperating with the Russian authorities. In December 2001, Khattab executed the Sadayev brothers, two of Basayev's closest and most experienced field commanders, because he suspected them of spying for Russia. Khattab's men threatened or beat village elders or members of their family if they tried to convince them to leave to save their village from Russian bombardment. Khattab was able to move about freely because he had instilled so much fear in the population that nobody would dare disclose his whereabouts lest their head end up on a stake.

Offers to negotiate had not helped either. Chechen leaders who wanted peace had tried to reason with Khattab and Basayev. Russians and Chechens alike called Khattab and Basayev "the incorrigibles" who want only "endless war." President Putin understood this and believed that it was pointless to pursue a negotiated peace settlement in Chechnya because neither Basayev nor Khattab was interested, and there was nobody in Chechnya who could bring them under control, certainly not Maskhadov.

By the early spring of 2002, the FSB had everything in place for execution of its plan to kill Khattab. In early March, Ibragim went to the Baku mailbox and picked up a package from Saudi Arabia containing a new Sony video camera, a wristwatch, and a letter. On 19 March 2002, he went back to Khattab's hideout in Chechnya and personally handed the package to Khattab, who took it and disappeared into his shelter. When Khattab came out half an hour later, he looked like he had seen a ghost. His face was white and he rubbed his eyes with the stubs of his fingers. Khattab momentarily fainted into the arms of his bodyguards but recovered long enough to tell Ibragim, who had been detained, he could go. It took another hour for the poison to do its work, then Khattab fell dead into the bushes.

Of course, there are other versions and theories about how and why Khattab died. One says that he was poisoned by bad food at a party. Khalid Yamadayev, a former field commander who is now deputy military commandant in the pro-Moscow administration, says that he believes Maskhadov may have bribed a member of Khattab's entourage to poison him because they had often squabbled and Khattab's reputation as a terrorist tainted the Chechen independence movement. Yet another theory is that Khattab came into conflict with his deputy, Abu al-Waleed, in the summer of 2001, after Khattab decided to personally pocket a $170,000 donation made by the Muslim Brotherhood to help finance the jihad.

There is no confirmation about the type of biological agent used to kill Khattab, but the agent's quick reaction suggests that it was botulism toxin.

Khattab's people would not confirm that it was the FSB who killed him. A video shot by mourning comrades showing Khattab's body in a freshly dug grave was victoriously touted on Russian television as another FSB success. But why was the video shot and how did the FSB get hold of it? The Command Headquarters of the Chechen Mujahideen says that it filmed his burial for Khattab's relatives to show that he was buried with the observance of all customs and according to Shariah laws. The FSB acquired the video after it was taken off the body of the fighter who had filmed the burial.

Many people, though, doubted the authenticity of the video. There were no visible bullet holes in Khattab's head, nor any blood, and Khattab's people initially denied that he was dead. His people later explained that they delayed the announcement of his death "in order to give us time to properly bury Khattab and to avoid possible defiling of his grave." On 1 May 2002, the *Al-Sharq Al-Awsat* published a letter from Khattab's family acknowledging his death and releasing an obituary with facts about Khattab that were previously unknown.

Khattab's real name was Samir bin Salekh al-Suweilem. His brother wrote that Samir had been inspired to stay on and fight in Chechnya by the plea of an old Chechen woman who had told him, "We want [the Russians] to leave our lands so that we can return to Islam." That meeting was, his brother said, a turning point in Khattab's life—"He sobbed until his beard became soaked with his tears."

His brother said that Khattab had been an ambitious child who had dreamed one day of owning a castle with "a garage big enough for five cars." As he grew older, Khattab shed his fantasies and refused to go home, even after his father promised to buy him a house. Nevertheless, Khattab had been a good son. He always telephoned his mother in Saudi Arabia before he went to kill Russians. Khattab left three children by his Karamakhi wife.

DEATH OF THE MESSENGER AND TERROR RETRIBUTION

Ibragim may have been an unwitting messenger of death or an agent working for the FSB. Regardless of his complicity, retribution was swift. Al-Jazeera television was the first to report his execution. Leaflets telling that Ibragim had been executed and why were also circulated in Grozny.

Kavkaz.org confirmed that "the traitor had been gunned down for treason and cooperation with the Dagestani secret services." Khattab's own people searched for him in Baku for weeks, only to find out that Basayev had already beat them to the punch by ordering Ibragim's execution. His body was found bound, with five bullet holes in the head, in a ditch on the outskirts of Baku. Basayev claims that a second person was involved too. He is being hunted.

Now that Ibragim had been taken care of, Senior Commander Abu al-Waleed, Khattab's successor, promised terror against Russia for killing Khattab. Al-Waleed is the nom de guerre of Abdel Aziz al-Ghamidi. A year younger than Khattab, Abu al-Waleed (also spelled Walid), the son of a Saudi imam, was born in Al-Hall, Saudi Arabia. He had also trained with Abdullah Azzam (1986–1987); fought in Afghanistan, Bosnia, and Tajikistan; and was one of the original band of five Afghan veterans who accompanied Khattab to Chechnya in 1995. He fought in the first Chechen war, helped Khattab set up his training camps after the war, and was with Basayev and Khattab in Dagestan in 1999. He is a devout Wahhabi extremist.

Two days after the FSB aired the film footage of Khattab's dead body on Russian television, eight people were killed and forty-five injured in a bomb blast at the crowded Vladikavkaz market in North Ossetia. The blast was caused by a time bomb filled with nuts and bolts that had been placed in a long pipe used as a barrier to block the market's entrance. But this was only a "diversionary action."

The big blast came eleven days later on 9 May as President Putin was speaking at the annual World War II Victory Day celebration in Moscow. A Dagestani Wahhabi terrorist used a remote-control device to detonate an MON 90 large land mine hidden under a parked bus along the main street in Kaspiisk, Dagestan. The mine blew up as the long parade celebrating the Soviet Army's victory over Berlin in World War II passed by, killing forty-five people (including six children and several Russian Army colonels in the military band) and sending one hundred others to the hospital. The bombing sent a terrifying message that there will be terror even in the absence of Khattab.

Field commander Rappani Khalilov, a relative of Khattab's wife who was later reported killed in fighting, ordered the bombing. He was one of Khattab's senior lieutenants who commanded "a combined detachment of saboteurs." He did not act alone. His accomplices included Dagestani nationals Artur, Zaur, and Shamil Mamayev; eight Russian military personnel from the 136th Motorized Rifle Brigade stationed at Buinaksk; Abdulkhalim Abdulkarimov; Murad Abdurazakov; Kazim Abdurakhmanov; and several Dagestani police officers.

The FSB quickly traced fragments of the mine back to the military engineering unit at the Russian military base in Buinaksk; an inventory check was done and several MON 90 mines were found missing. Seven subordinates and Lieutenant Colonel Nikolai Yamkovoy, head of the brigade's engineering service, were charged with illegal possession and sale of munitions to terrorists. The Russian officers are all on trial as are the Mamayev brothers and several police officers. Yamkovoy had six more MON 90 mines at home and was running a comfortable little side business selling arms. Abdulkhalim Abdulkarimov videotaped the massacre and was sentenced in April 2004. Abdurakhmanov is still on the loose.

IS BASAYEV DEAD OR ALIVE?

Basayev became the next priority target on the Russia's death list. But no one even knew if he was dead or alive. He hadn't been heard from since he was wounded in December of 2001. Some thought that Basayev was abroad recovering from his wounds. However, Russian doctors speculated that he had succumbed to gangrene poisoning in his leg. After Khattab's death, the Russian Army general in charge of Russian forces in Chechnya even declared that Basayev was dead too, but admitted that his body had not been found. The Russian general later retracted his statement, saying that it was based only on the fact that Basayev hadn't been heard from in any kind of communication for a long time. The FSB, on the contrary, continued to maintain that there was nothing to indicate that Basayev was dead. The hunt went on.

IX

NORD OST

Do not assume that we consider you a peaceful population. We do not. To us you are unarmed military men, because those who by a majority approve the genocide of the Chechen people cannot be peaceful civilians. According to Shariah law, mere verbal approval of war puts peaceful citizens in the ranks of the enemy. You are just the unarmed enemy.

Shamil Basayev, Prima News Agency Interview, May 2002

A LEADERLESS JIHAD

While the debate raged about whether Basayev was dead or alive, Aslan Maskhadov attempted to rally the divided and weakened Chechen and foreign fighters by calling an "emergency meeting of field commanders." The April 2002 meeting set up a new Supreme Military Council, which looked very much like the one that Basayev and Khattab had established earlier but that was now defunct. Maskhadov hoped that his council would lessen infighting, promote cohesion, and result in better coordination of attacks against the "occupiers." It didn't.

In mid-May, Basayev decided to go public and once and for all settle the debate about the state of his health. He did so in a proxy interview with the Moscow-based Prima News Agency. The interview at first revealed a demoralized Basayev. He confirmed that Khattab had been killed—"They slipped him a poisoned letter"—but more importantly, he acknowledged, "The jihad proceeds in a haphazard manner." In Basayev's view, it had become essentially leaderless: "Mujahideen know what to do, and neither I nor other leaders are needed very much now."

This seemed like an honest and realistic assessment of the military situation in Chechnya. Chechen fighters were ideologically divided and had suffered tremendous losses in a little over two and a half years of war with Russia. The death of Khattab was a great personal loss for Basayev and devastating to Chechen guerilla and terrorism capabilities too, not to mention the damage it did to the smooth flow of finances from Osama bin Laden and the Gulf states. Nevertheless, such negative words coming from Basayev seemed odd. Maybe his spirit really had been broken.

By the end of the interview, though, Basayev had pulled himself together. He even talked enthusiastically about terror against Russia, seeming to give it priority in future Chechen actions: "We intend to pay every house of yours a visit, for all of Russia is at war. . . . Do not assume that we consider you a peaceful population. We do not. To us you are unarmed military men, because those who by a majority approve the genocide of the Chechen people cannot be peaceful civilians. According to Shariah law, mere verbal approval of war puts peaceful citizens in the ranks of the enemy. You are just the unarmed enemy."

This promise of new terror would take the shape of a suicide squad seizing a packed Moscow theater six months later. But were these seemingly contradictory messages in May—a leaderless jihad, on the one hand, and promises of new terrorism in Moscow, on the other—meant to intentionally confuse the FSB? Maybe.

On 9 June, police in Moscow uncovered something very disturbing. Acting on an anonymous telephone tip, they dug into a shallow grave at a cemetery located in the village across from and directly under the landing flight path of Vnukovo Airport—the airport that is used for domestic and all kinds of charter and government flights. What they found stunned them. It was not a decaying body in a casket, but a grave filled with horror—surface-to-air missiles and a launcher. Somebody intended to shoot down an airliner in Moscow.

Maybe the jihad wasn't so haphazard after all. Fragmented pieces of intelligence began to provide clues that the missiles in the Moscow graveyard were part of something bigger.

In faraway Georgia, police observed the movement of two to three hundred armed Chechens leaving the relative safety of the Pankisi Gorge in groups of four and five and heading for the mountains of Chechnya. Georgian state security estimated that there were about one hundred Arab and eight hundred Chechen fighters in the Pankisi Gorge before the exodus began. Weeks earlier, Maskhadov had called on all Chechen and foreign fighters in the Pankisi Gorge to return to Chechnya to resume the fight. Some were now heeding the call as well as responding to significant Georgian military pressure on them to leave.

Three days before the Moscow graveyard discovery, Maskhadov called a second commanders' military conference. This time Basayev was notably present and so were important foreign Islamic spiritual leaders. Deliberations of the conference were kept secret except for the closing resolution "to increase guerilla warfare on the entire territory of the ChRI [Chechnya]" and undertake "certain other important military measures."

The following day, Maskhadov made a surprising announcement to the Chechen public, hinting at cooperation with Basayev and his forces: "I positively declare that we have sufficient forces and facilities in order to punish the Russian war criminals. Summon up your patience and Insha'Allah, with the help of Allah, the all-merciful and omnipotent, we will force the Russian occupiers to leave our long suffering land."

A secret report on the conference and its decisions was sent to "the countries of the Middle East and Turkey." This was done to raise money, but money for what? At the same time, there was a marked increase in the assassination of Chechen pro-Moscow local officials. The administrative head of the village of Bachi-Yurt was gunned down outside his quarters; the house belonging to the duty officer of the local police station was attacked with a grenade launcher; two other senior officials were killed in their homes; and two Chechen employees of the Russian Army commandant's office in Shali were murdered. There was also an increase in bounty money to anyone willing to kill Russians and Chechen collaborators; to blow up a Russian APC or tank; or to shoot down a helicopter. One hundred U.S. dollars would now be paid to kill a Russian soldier, $1,000 to $1,500 for an officer, and $3,000 to $5,000 to shoot down a helicopter. The only catch was that the attack must be videotaped.

Russian police also suspected that mujahideen were infiltrating the new Chechen security organs hurriedly being put together by the pro-Moscow Chechen government. Only two personal references are required to become a policeman, and serious background checks are not made. Some Russian law enforcement agencies working in Chechnya believe that whole Chechen Interior Ministry directorates are controlled by men who are mujahideen and should not be trusted.

Russia's spies were also reporting that the Islamic mujahideen were accumulating weapons in Grozny, Gudermes, and Argun. Police in the three cities were being watched more than usual—in some cases, there was around-the-clock surveillance of Russian checkpoints. An increase in the male population in these three cities was also detected.

In mid-June, the Georgian police apprehended a Georgian state security ministry officer and a Russian national bound for Chechnya with a load of antitank shells, missiles, and other weapons valued at $500,000. This was one of the most valuable arms hauls ever confiscated.

These were all warning indicators that something big was about to happen. At the beginning of July, Defense Minister Sergei Ivanov announced what the fuss was all about. A Russian Army raid on Maskhadov's headquarters on 24 June uncovered an elaborate plan to assault Grozny with combined fighting forces (Maskhadov's and Basayev's) totaling more than one thousand fighters. The assault was to have taken place on 25 June, but, Ivanov said, "We . . . foiled the operation."

THE SUMMER OF RADICALIZATION

Details about the 6 June military conference cementing an alliance between Maskhadov and Basayev only began to emerge in mid-October 2002. Basayev says that he and Maskhadov spent twenty days together hammering out the details of a new unified military structure, discussing and developing a unified plan of combat operations, and even signing an oath of allegiance to a Majlis ul-Shura, which was described as a "combined executive and legislative body to regulate issues of the state."

Had Basayev and Maskhadov finally put aside their ideological differences and feuding and reached some kind of middle ground? Who had the upper hand with ultimate authority and oversight of "military operations," Maskhadov or Basayev?

Despite Basayev's new commitment to cooperate with Maskhadov, there was nothing on Udugov's Web site to indicate that Basayev had softened ideologically. And Ivan Rybkin told me on 24 October 2002 that he had found no indication in his new search for a negotiated settlement on Chechnya that Basayev was willing to reasonably talk peace.

On the contrary, Maskhadov has clearly shifted ideologically toward Basayev and an extremist outlook. There is plenty of evidence to support this. First, Maskhadov now describes the war with Russia as a religious one—something for which he used to criticize Basayev and Udugov not long ago. Second, he also now endorses war terrorism, although publicly he continues to reject terror as a means to end the war. Third, Maskhadov retracted his earlier accusations that the amir of the Majlis of Muslims of Chechnya and Dagestan (Basayev) had driven a wedge between the mujahideen and was doing irreparable harm to the Chechen separatist movement. Maskhadov also rescinded his earlier punitive decree removing Basayev as commander of the Eastern Front for "actions which alien-

ate and disunite us," "for spreading rumors and gossip," and for "sabotag-
ing [Maskhadov's] instructions and actions."

In June 2002, Maskhadov could claim success in unifying all Chechen
and foreign forces in Chechnya fighting Russia, but he had to give up an
awful lot to do it. In the new political-military decision-making structure
that was set up, Maskhadov is still the president of the Chechen Republic
of Ichkeria and commander in chief of the Chechen forces, but only nom-
inally. He does not have the final say because Basayev's 1999 Shura structure has been resurrected to make collective decisions for Ichkeria. Before
his death, Khattab spent a lot of time working out the details of the new
structure. "So did our brothers abroad," Sheikh Abu Omar says (but he
doesn't tell us who they are). The Majlis ul-Shura reasserted the Wolves'
goal of "creating an Islamic state and Shariah rule" in the North Caucasus.

In short, what Maskhadov refused to do in February 1999, he agreed
to do in 2002. His voice is now only one among equals. Sheikh Abdul
Khalim ibn Adbus-Salam, the chairman of the Supreme Shariah Court of
the Chechen Republic of Ichkeria and chairman of the Shura's Committee
on Judges and Fatwas, explains that "the Amir [Maskhadov] consults the
[Majlis ul-]Shura and adopts the [collective] decisions made by the
Majlis." Ichkeria's constitution was amended to reflect these changes.

The new Shura established several committees, which are said to func-
tion as ministries and "manage the day to day affairs of the Chechen state."
Basayev, who became the deputy commander in chief of the Chechen
forces, heads the most important one, the Military Committee.

In the military reorganization that was done, Basayev appointed his
own commanders to the top positions in the new military structure.
Fronts under the command of the Military Committee were created—the
Northern, Western, Eastern and Southwestern fronts—each with a "sec-
tor" and "direction," and each headed by a Basayev loyal commander.
Many are Arab. Khattab's replacement, Abu al-Waleed, was appointed
commander of the Eastern Front. Dokka Umarov is in charge of the
Southwestern Front.

A Financial Committee was also set up to centralize financing and
decide on the dispersal of funds. A Social Committee was established to
solve refugee problems, provide help for the wounded, and care for the
families of those martyred. An Information Committee will handle propaganda, and a Committee of Judges and Fatwas will address legal and religious questions.

The Russian media correctly described the new alliance as a
"Maskhadov defeat" and the military reorganization as done "on Basayev's
terms." While Basayev is formally Maskhadov's subordinate in the new

structure, in realty Basayev dominates the decision-making process, thereby further radicalizing the Shura.

If in the spring of 1999, Basayev was the most powerful leader in Chechnya, that again became true in the fall of 2002. Russian journalist Anna Politkovskaya, who reports extensively on the war, often critical of Russia, put it nicely when she wrote in *Novaya Gazeta* in late October 2002, "Any more or less reasonable men close to Maskhadov have been pushed into the background, while Shamil Basayev has moved into the spotlight." Udugov reported in April 2003 that Basayev commands about three thousand mujahideen, a figure that roughly coincides with that given by then Chechnya's Prime Minister Anatoly Popov.

Udugov and Zelimkhan Yandarbiyev were brought into the fold too. Udugov became head of the External Subcommittee of the Information Committee while Yandarbiyev became the "special representative of the president of Chechnya to the Muslim countries."

It is difficult to determine what motivated Maskhadov to concede so much; maybe it was the money. With financial resources drying up since 11 September 2001 and the financial flow from abroad further disrupted by Khattab's death, Basayev and the extremists were getting the bulk of the money reaching the republic from abroad. Naturally, Maskhadov wanted his cut too. But more importantly, recasting Maskhadov as having seen the light and now fighting a religious war would also build a good case for increased financial support from abroad. That is why there were foreign Wahhabi spiritual leaders in attendance at the June reorganization conference and why a "secret" report on the conference's proceeding was sent to the Middle East and Turkey.

There were other reasons too. Maskhadov's Chechen Press Agency earlier said that the unification was forced on them by Russia's refusal to enter into negotiations with the president of the Chechen Republic of Ichkeria. Maskhadov might have calculated that he could maneuver himself into a better negotiating position with Russia. For a long time now, the Kremlin has been saying that it is senseless to negotiate with him because he cannot control Basayev. Akhmed Zakayev specifically addressed this question in an interview with *Kommersant Daily* on 29 August 2002 when he said, "Maskhadov has demonstrated that he is in control of the situation. He has united all those who keep resisting the Russian troops. It is clear that if Russia intends to begin a political dialogue, Maskhadov is the only possible negotiator."

In the final analysis, though, Maskhadov may have simply had little choice if he wished to go on fighting.

MILITARY OFFENSIVES AND PLANNING TERROR

Despite the 25 June setback, the fruits of the Chechen summer reorganization soon became apparent. In mid-August, Basayev reported that combat operations had become more coordinated and effective since the reorganization. The increase in Russian and pro-Moscow Chechen casualties since the summer reorganization bore this out.

The Majlis ul-Shura also adopted a strategic plan of operation that included a change in military strategy and a terror strike at the heart of Russia by the end of the year. Guerrilla warfare would be waged with "large scale" military offensive operations.

The shooting down of a giant Mi-26T Russian transport helicopter killing 127 policemen, FSB, military personnel, and children in mid-August was a huge Chechen success and, in a way, made up for the lost opportunity to storm Grozny at the end of June. In what he called Operation Jihad, Mairbek Vachagayev, Maskhadov's spokesman, claimed credit for the single largest loss of life on the Russian side since the second Chechen war began. The operation was carefully planned, well executed, and even videotaped.

Twenty-nine-year-old Doka Dzhantemirov procured the Igla surface-to-air missile used to shoot down the helicopter, organized the terror act, and personally videotaped it, but an accomplice pulled the trigger on the missile launcher. Both, and a third accomplice, have been tracked down, tried, and sentenced.

Dzhantemirov's video shows the Russian helicopter with its right engine on fire. The tape then cuts to footage of Maskhadov showing the film to fighters and commenting that the helicopter is burning and falling near Khankala.

On 1 September, another surface-to-air missile shot down a second helicopter, an Mi-24, in the Nozhai-Yurt district. These attacks signalled an intensified battle against Russian air mobility.

Shura mujahideen also launched coordinated attacks against several villages in southern Chechnya; ambushed Russian checkpoints, local police, and military commandants' headquarters; and raided houses of pro-Moscow officials. In one twenty-four-hour period, they attacked sixteen positions, including a military convoy in the village of Dyshne-Vedeno and a police patrol in Gudermes.

The summer reorganization—as well as intense Georgian military pressure—also triggered a second stream of fighters returning to Chechnya from the Pankisi Gorge. More than sixty Chechens attempted to cross the border in July but were ambushed by Russian forces on the Chechen side because a Georgian shepherd turned them in. Thirteen of them fled back to Georgia but were captured by Georgian border guards. Late August saw another fierce battle between Russian border guards and Chechen fighters. On Tuesday, 24 September, another four fighters were detained by Georgian border guards as they attempted to cross into Ingushetia. Clashes with fighters from the Pankisi Gorge became so frequent in August and September that Russia came close to going to war with Georgia over them.

In late September, a detachment of Ruslan Gelayev's forces numbering around three hundred mujahideen left the Pankisi Gorge and attacked the village of Galashki, Ingushetia. Several days of fighting followed. On the Russian side, sixteen soldiers were killed, and a local woman, Fatima Ozdayea, was murdered. Gelayev had several surface-to-air missiles with him, which also enabled him to shoot down two Russian helicopters.

The Russian commander says that his troops killed forty-four of Gelayev's mujahideen, including several foreign fighters. Gelayev was wounded, but he promptly telephoned Kavkaz Center to refute Russian reports that he had been killed.

Gelayev too had reached some kind of agreement with the Majlis ul-Shura. It had been almost two years since Ichkeria's commander in chief had busted General Gelayev back to the rank of private for mismanagement of troops, the wrongful death of mujahideen at Komsomolskoye, displaying cowardice, and being AWOL. Now, the Shura collective asked Gelayev to return home.

That agreement, though, came later in the summer, because in mid-June Maskhadov said in a tape-recorded interview with Thomas de Waal that Gelayev had "long been absent from Chechnya" and that "I have not given him any order to leave the territory of Chechnya and I await his explanations." In January 2003, Gelayev publicly affirmed his allegiance to the Shura.

A documentary video shot by freelance journalist Roderick John Scott, who was with Gelayev's fighters and was killed in Galashki, shows that Gelayev's group had left the Pankisi Gorge about a week and a half earlier to make the march through the treacherous mountainous terrain. Seven of Gelayev's fighters who were captured went on trial in North Ossetia in October 2003.

Moscow has long accused Georgia of protecting Ruslan Gelayev after President Shevardnadze rescued him from the Kodori Gorge while fleeing hostile Abkhaz forces in October 2001. Georgian President Shevardnadze long ago acknowledged that Gelayev was on Georgian soil but said that he was "not a bandit but a normal man with a higher education." Gelayev was trained as a history professor.

More Chechen military assaults came in late September. On 21 September, Maskhadov captured a television station in the town of Samashki not far from Grozny. He interrupted the regular broadcasting to make a long speech about resisting Russian forces. Maskhadov took the television equipment with him when he left.

Two days later, Chechen mujahideen captured a local radio station in the Nadterechny district of northern Chechnya. They threatened to kill employees of the local pro-Moscow administration, police, as well as local residents if they further cooperated with Russian authorities.

Basayev's fighters also attacked a convoy near the Bass River Gorge. Skirmishes occurred in Alleroi, Gansolchu, Shirdi-Mokhk, Agishbatoi, Bamut, and Achkhoi-Martan. Twenty fighters attacked Meskerty in the Kurchaloevsky district, blew up the administration building, assaulted the police department, and took three policemen hostage.

In late September, mujahideen also entered the village of Jurgurty and, without firing a shot, disarmed the pro-Moscow Chechen police as well as persuaded the entire Chechen administration to resign, threatening to come back and kill them if they ever cooperated again with Russia.

On 29 September, a Ural truck carrying eighteen Russian troops was attacked near Kurchaloi, and, in Shali, the police station and the Russian commander's office were assaulted.

Commenting on the terror component of the Shura's strategic plan, Maskhadov cryptically announced in August, "We will be able to change the situation by the end of the year and force the enemy to leave our land."

At an August Shura planning session, Basayev proposed a terror attack on the "lair of the enemy in the heart of Moscow." There was agreement that the attack should be more spectacular than the apartment building bombings in 1999, involving larger numbers of Russian civilian casualties.

In mid-July, an opportunity apparently presented itself to acquire valuable materials that could be used to make a small nuclear device. Nuclear material smugglers from Kazakhstan reportedly approached the Shura with an offer to sell osmium-187. Osmium isotopes are one of the required components for making mini-nukes because osmium increases the destructive power of the explosion. With osmium, the device can be very compact.

This incident coincided with the 18 August disappearance of Professor Sergei Bakhvalov, a prominent Russian nuclear chemist whose mutilated body was found on the outskirts of Krasnoyarsk, Russia, ten days later. He chaired the Department of Physical Chemistry at Krasnoyarsk State

University. The professor was one of the world's leading specialists in extracting plutonium and had been recently honored for dismantling the nuclear reactor of the *Kursk* submarine.

Bakhvalov's abduction was part of somebody's plot to steal Russian nuclear technology. Maybe Wolves kidnapped Bakhvalov to assemble nuclear materials somewhere outside Chechnya, but he refused and was killed. Maybe they or others kidnapped him with the intent of selling their catch to Osama bin Laden or other international terrorists interested in acquiring a nuclear device and the deal went sour.

Basayev could be working to acquire a small nuclear bomb, but, for his next terror act, he decided to rely on what he knew best and what had worked for him in the past: spectacular hostage taking.

This time, Basayev conceived of a plan to establish a special suicide unit called the Riyadus-Salikhin (Fields of Righteousness) Reconnaissance and Sabotage Battalion of Shakhids (martyrs) to do the job. To facilitate easy entry into Moscow, the unit was much smaller than the one Basayev organized in 1995. Members went to Moscow not as a group, but instead individually infiltrated the city. Nearly half the unit was young women, which also facilitated infiltration since women are seldom stopped by the Russian police for document checks. Seasoned fighters completed the other half of the battalion.

Roughly $225,000 was budgeted for the operation. The battalion spent three months in intense preparation. Russian passports and other personal identification documents were bought or made for those who were hunted by Russian authorities, and the men shaved their beards well ahead of time.

Much of the preparation for the attack had to be done in Moscow, including the acquisition of schematic drawings; the collection of critical security information; visits to the target site; and even dress rehearsals. Those trusted sleeper agents that Raduyev spoke about in 1999 took care of the logistics and other support. Some even participated in the siege.

One of those who helped was twenty-one-year-old Chechen Alikhan Mezhiyev, who bought cars for "diversionary explosions" and mobile telephones. Another was Usman Tatayev, who acquired the three minivans used to transport the terrorists to Dubrovka. He participated in the siege too. A doveronist (legal permission given by the registered owner) to operate the three vehicles was found in his pocket at Dubrovka. A third was forty-three-year-old Yakha Meferkhanova, a resident of Moscow, who participated in the siege. It's not known what other role she had.

Using the alias Khava Erbiyeva, forty-two-year-old Yassira Vataliyeva (one of Basayev's female fighters in the first war) rented three apartments (at house #22, Vorontsovskaya Ulitsa; #15, Festivalnaya Ulitsa; and #4, Korpus 1, Yelevatornaya Ulitsa,) for "relatives coming from Dagestan for medical treatment." She used the Kalita-Grad Moscow realty firm—the same firm used fourteen months later to rent an apartment for those dispatched by Basayev to blow up two natural gas pipelines in the Moscow oblast on 15 March 2004.

"We spent all summer working on it. . . . Two months alone were spent in Moscow getting prepared," a participant recalled.

The original target was the Russian parliament and its two houses, the State Duma and the Council of the Russian Federation. But three alternative targets had to be chosen when the field commander that Basayev had picked to lead the siege was killed in combat in Chechnya. The new targets were the Moskovsky Dvorets Molodyozhi (MDM) theater, where *42 Street* was playing; the Estrada theater; and the Dubrovka theater. Some sources say the Kurchatov Institute was chosen too. Yassira scouted out the targets and videotaped everything, but the final selection of Dubrovka was made by Ruslan Abu-Khasanovich Elmurzayev, who was already in Moscow and who orchestrated things there. He made his appearance as "Yassir" and Abu Bakar at Dubrovka.

Yassir recalled, "We choose the [Dubrovka] theater because it is in the center of the city and there were a lot of people there."

Dubrovka terrorists coming to Moscow used different means to get to the capital. Barayev came by train from Mineralnye Vody. At least three came on the bus from Khasavyurt, Dagestan, on 17 October. Some took the bus from Makhachkala, Dagestan. Others came by various overland routes. One flew from Ingushetia. Most arrived only a few days before the siege.

At least some of the women who came to Moscow using their real passports moved freely about the city in the days before the siege. Two made notes to attend a meeting at the Luzhniki sports stadium on 21 October and another used Moscow's subway at 9:30 p.m. the night before the siege.

THE DUBROVKA SIEGE

At 9:15 p.m. on Wednesday, 23 October 2002, Wolves struck. At least twenty-two men and nineteen women bounded from three vehicles and charged through the front entrance of the House of Culture theater center at the corner of Dubrovskaya and Melnikova streets in an industrial suburb of Moscow. The men, wearing camouflage military fatigues, and the women, in long back robes with their faces veiled, dispersed according to their well-rehearsed scripts, each taking his or her predesignated position in the balcony, the hallways, and the main auditorium for the spectacular finale of the evening.

The second act of the musical *Nord Ost* had just opened, and the theater's video camera was rolling when the first camouflaged Chechen jumped onto the stage and ordered the stunned cast to get off. Spectators thought that it was a joke—just part of the second act—since the cast was dressed in 1940s style camouflage, until a terrorist fired shots into the ceiling. Another hit an actor on the head with a gun butt.

"You are hostages. . . . We've come from Chechnya. This is no joke. We are at war," Movsar Barayev, the leader, shouted.

From the beginning, the siege had Shamil Basayev's imprint all over it, his guidance based on the lessons learned at Budennovsk and Kizlyar apparent, including hostage control inside the theater. People were ordered to stay calm, to obey orders, to put their hands on top of their head. Those with mobile phones were told to call and inform their relatives and the media that they had become hostages. Later on, hostages were made to throw their telephones and handbags on the floor.

Male hostages were separated from the women, foreigners from Russians. Sandy Booker, the forty-nine-year-old American electrical engineer who died from the knockout gas later used by Russian forces, had left his passport in the hotel. He could not prove he was an American. But his fiancée, Svetlana Gubaryeva, and her thirteen-year-old daughter, Sasha, managed to convince Barayev that they were an American family. "This is my papa," Sasha told Barayev. Sandy and his family were placed in the foreigners' section. Later on, an agreement was reached to release the Booker family at 8 a.m. on 26 October, but the storm came two and a half hours earlier. Sasha and Sandy died in the storm.

The first execution came at 11 p.m. Twenty-six year-old Olga Romanova appeared in the theater out of nowhere. Barayev demanded answers. "Who are you?" "Why did you come here?" "What are you up to?"

She started shouting insults at Barayev: "You think you're so high and mighty, but your position means nothing to me." He told her to sit down and shut up, but she kept it up. "What is this masquerade? And you even brought your machine guns with you!" Then she turned to the hostages and screamed, "Why are you sitting here? What are you afraid of? Why don't you just get up and go!"

Witnesses say that she was drunk, or on narcotics, and wanted to die. Maybe she was an FSB agent. Udugov's Web site later said that she was.

A terrorist in the balcony with the women and children yelled, "Shoot her." "Go ahead, go ahead and shoot me!" she dared them. So they did. They took her behind the door and put four bullets into her. Barayev said he wasn't fooled: "The same thing was done at Budennovsk [just before the Russian storm of the hospital]."

Surviving hostages told this account of the first execution to Russian writer Eduard Topol, author of *o lubov i terror ili dvoye v Nord Oste* (*About Love and Terror, or Two at Nord Ost*), an excellent book about the theater siege and Svetlana Gubaryeva's romance with Sandy Booker.

Barayev, Yassir, and their helpers checked passports and other identification to determine how many police and military personnel were in the audience. One police official managed to cut the carpet and hide his police identification. He lived. The press reported that a GRU officer who did not have time to conceal his identify was executed. Even so, Barayev let an MVD major general he found in the theater live.

Muslims and Georgians were told they could leave. A few foreigners were released, and children were told that they could leave too. Fifteen did go shortly after midnight of the first day. And Barayev released twenty-five-year old Oksana Ignatovskaya, who was nine months pregnant. Some of the *Nord Ost* cast escaped by climbing out of a third-floor restroom window.

Al-Jazeera television broadcast a prerecorded videotape of the terrorists' demands, confirming that the operation was being done "on orders from the Chechen republic's military commander."

Basayev must have been especially proud at that moment. This time, the Hero of Budennovsk really had succeeded in getting a suicide mission all the way to Moscow. If Basayev had been physically capable, he would have led the operation himself. But his artificial leg slows him down, so he picked the twenty-three-year-old field commander Movsar Barayev, nephew of The Wahhabi, to command it. Basayev says that he chose Movsar Barayev only after several other more senior commanders had been killed in combat.

Far from being inexperienced, Movsar (born in 1979, with the birth name Mansur Salamov, but he also went by Suleimenov) was seasoned in both combat and terrorism. He had been a Wahhabi since childhood and, in his late teens, was trained by Khattab in explosives and sabotage techniques. Movsar became one of his uncle's bodyguards and a common criminal, active in his uncle's kidnapping and people-for-sale business too. Russian NTV television has archived video footage showing Movsar in Chechnya clowning with a knife and threatening to cut the throat of an unidentified woman. Other footage shows him beheading a Chechen woman accused of being a spy for Russia. Arbi Barayev was his role model. All Movsar ever wanted to be was a copy of his uncle. People used to laugh at Movsar when he would answer the phone using Arbi Barayev's name in his uncle's absence.

Movsar commanded an Argun "sub-unit" of his uncle's "special units" after the second war with Russia began. He also organized the July 2000 suicide attack on Argun. When Arbi Barayev was killed in June 2001, Movsar assumed command of his uncle's Islamic Regiment. It was then that he dropped the name Suleimenov and took his uncle's last name.

Movsar was part of Khattab's inner circle, entrusted with distributing funds to fighters. But his skimming off the top brought him into conflict with field commanders. In 2001–2002, Movsar paid his own people more than a half million dollars. On 26 June 2002, he murdered Rizvan Akhmadov in an argument over $45,000.

It was a surprise to see Movsar Barayev in Moscow. He was earlier reported under arrest, and the Russian military twice reported him killed, once in August 2001 and again a few weeks before the Moscow siege. In 2001, he was the only one out of five to escape alive from a Russian spetnaz attack on his car in Argun. Just before Dubrovka, it was rumored he had been wounded and went to Azerbaijan for treatment.

Thirty-two dead Dubrovka terrorists have been positively identified by valid passports found on their bodies, the names revealing that the siege was very much a family affair, with sisters, aunts and uncles, cousins, husbands and wives, in-laws, and best friends participating. The fact that thirty-two of the terrorists traveled on their real passports indicates that they felt safe enough to do so because they were not wanted. Ages of the hostage takers ranged from sixteen to forty-three. Four teenage girls participated, two of them only sixteen.

Movsar Barayev said that his "aunt"—Arbi Barayev's sixth wife and widow, "Zura"—commanded the female terrorists at Dubrovka. The only Zura on the official list of killed terrorists at Dubrovka was attractive Zura Bitziyeva, twenty-two. Using her real passport, this professionally trained business executive assistant "who could easily fit into a miniskirt or tight jeans" had come to Moscow on a bus from Makhachkala on 16 September, more than a month ahead of the others, indicating a role in organizing the siege.

Zura left this note behind for a friend: "By the will of Allah, I left for you know where. . . . I couldn't eat or communicate with anyone. . . . I have but one request, please believe in this to the end. Allah willing, we will soon meet in paradise."

Fatima Ganiyeva, twenty-seven, and her younger sister, sixteen-year-old Khadichat (Milana) from the Chechen village of Assinovskaya, were there too. Both were sisters of Rustam Ganiyev, one of Basayev's field commanders whom the Russian press reported sold his sisters into certain death for $1,000 each. A third sister, Raisa, a student at Grozny University, was allegedly sold too but reportedly asked for federal protection when it came her turn to die. They came from a strict Wahhabi family.

The credibility of this brotherly betrayal story is in doubt because of what Zarema Muzhikhoyeva, the 9 July 2003 Tverskaya bomber, had to say about Raisa Ganiyeva sixteen months after the Dubrovka siege. In an interview with *Izvestiya* reporter Vadim Rechkalov from her prison cell in early February 2004, Zarema, who also lived in Assinovskaya, told the newspaper that it was this same Raisa Ganiyeva who had put her on the road to becoming a suicide bomber. Raisa was well connected. "Everybody knew she had connections with fighters, she was special, and she didn't try to hide it," Zarema told Rechkalov. Zarema naturally went to Raisa when she decided to become a suicide bomber. Raisa was very helpful. She gave the aspiring suicide bomber the handbook *The Moment of Death* and other Wahhabi literature, coached her, and then turned her over to Rustam, who introduced Zarema to Basayev.

Sixteen-year-old Aiman Kurbanova (not on the official list of dead terrorists), the pretty girl with the doll-like face from the village of Staraya Sunzha near Grozny, was the youngest female terrorist at Dubrovka. She was strict and stern with the hostages, her pistol always at the ready. "She was raised on Allah. . . . Give her the order to detonate her bomb and she will do it immediately—that would be her ultimate joy," another terrorist at Dubrovka warned a hostage. Aiman's older sister, Raiman, thirty-eight, was there too. "Both are pregnant," Barayev told a hostage, and both husbands (with different names) were also in the theater.

Aishat (Luiza) Bakuyeva, twenty-six, a successful pharmacist from Grozny (who was not on the official list either), had come to Moscow after losing all her family but her mother to war. Four brothers, including the well-known Baudi Bakuyev, who belonged to Arbi Barayev's gang, had been killed in nearly three years of war. Neighbors say that she had become distant and would no longer cry at funerals after she found the body of her youngest brother, fifteen-year-old Daud, who had been taken into custody as a suspect in a bomb blast in Grozny. Aishat sold her small business in Grozny, packed a suitcase, and told friends that she was moving to Moscow to start a new life. Major Igor Alyamkin of the Nizhegorodsky Moscow branch of the OVD completed the paperwork for her Moscow registration on 20 August 2002. His failure to check her family's background and corruption charges have landed him in jail.

A sixth woman, Sekilat Aliyeva, twenty-five, came from a Wahhabi family that lived the Oktyabrsky district of Grozny. "She was an actress and is the sister of a friend of my uncle's [Arbi Barayev]," Movsar Barayev told a hostage. She had recently worked as an assistant in the history department at Grozny's university. In 1998, she studied at the Islamic University in Grozny and began wearing a veil. She came to Moscow from Khasavyurt on a bus ticket purchased on 17 October. She left a note behind too, promising to save a place in paradise for her mother.

Sekilat's deceased brother, a former member of Arbi Barayev's gang, had been married to Maryam Khadzhiyeva, twenty-two, who was reported by Sanobar Shermatova to have been in the theater. However, her name is not on the official death list.

Aiman Khadzhiyeva, twenty-eight, and her sister Koku, twenty-six, however, are on the list. A subway ticket used at 9:30 p.m. the day before the siege was found on Koku's body at Dubrovka.

On 29 September, twenty-six-year-old Zareta Bairakova left home after a knock at the door and a brief visit by an older woman. Zareta's mother was in prayer and did not hear the conversation but remembers that her daughter left with the stranger and never came back. On 17 October, Zareta bought a bus ticket in Krasavyurt leaving for Moscow two days later.

Forty-three-year-old Yakha Meferkhanova, a resident of Moscow, was the oldest female terrorist at Dubrovka.

All of the Chechen women in the theater were vocal about their desire to die. "It would be a present for me if I died for Allah now," one told a hostage. Another confirmed that she didn't want to die, but "I am ready to do it for Allah." A third said, "It doesn't matter if I die here or there [in Chechnya]. . . . My husband and children have been killed, so I have nothing to live for." "We will all die," they told hostages.

Basayev's deputy—or the real leader of the siege—a man who called himself Abu Bakar but was addressed as "Yassir" by his accomplices in the theater, turned out to be a Chechen resident by the name of Ruslan Abu-Khasanovich Elmurzayev. Like Barayev and the others who were hunted by Russia, he had a false passport. The one found at the theater belonged to a deceased resident of the Karachaevo-Cherkessia Republic that had been bought from the man's wife six months earlier. Initially, people thought that Abu Bakar must be Arab. There have been at least five Abu Bakars in Chechnya; two (one of whom was Turkish) were killed in May 2001, and a third (an Egyptian) took a Russian bullet six months later. Seda Elmurzayeva, eighteen, Elmurzayev's wife or sister, was in the theater with him.

Barayev said that he was on a suicide mission to stop the war in Chechnya and would "go all the way" if President Putin did not meet his three demands: an antiwar rally was to be arranged near the theater; a second rally was to be organized on Red Square; and Russian troops were to withdraw from Chechnya by Saturday morning, 26 October. Should Russia fail to meet any one of those demands, Abu Bakar promised to "do what Hitler couldn't" and warned that there were other "suicide squads all over the city" just waiting for his signal.

Earlier, he had ordered Alikhan Mezhiyev to take two Chechen women suicide bombers to Pushkinskaya Square (a busy park in Moscow across the street from Moscow's main McDonald's restaurant). The women were to blow themselves up there. Alikhan said in his March 2004 court trial that Abu Bakar had called him on the mobile phone and asked to be picked up at the Kristall Casino on Proletarskaya Ulitsa because he had been in an automobile accident. But there was no accident. When Alikhan arrived, Abu Bakar instructed him to deliver the women to the square. On the way there, Alikhan heard the news about Dubrovka over the radio. For unknown reasons the women did not go through with their terror act. Alikhan says that he talked them out of it; he took back their suicide belts and put the women on the train back home to Ingushetia.

The mission of the two women at Pushkinskaya Square was to have been part of a series of planned "diversionary" explosions in Moscow to coincide with the theater siege. Basayev had picked Aslambek Khaskhanov from Urus-Martan to lead this "diversionary group," which was to carry out several small-scale terror acts in Moscow to cause public panic. The 19 October car bomb that killed one person and wounded eight on Pokryshkina Ulitsa adjacent to the Yugo Zapadnaya McDonald's was part of this plan. The Moscow prosecutor's office has criminally charged Khaskhanov and four others—Aslan Murdalov, nineteen, the brothers Alikhan and Akhyad Mezhiyev (seventeen), and Khanpash Sobraliyev—in the McDonald's case.

Another bomb was in a car that the group had parked near the Mayakovskaya metro stop's Tchaikovsky concert hall. Police say they discovered the bomb (with a defective clock alarm timer) in the car at the concert hall, found another car bomb at the Pyramid café, and a third at a bus stop. Other reports say that someone from Khaskhanov's group (perhaps Abu Bakar himself) removed two of the cars and abandoned them in a car storage lot on Leninsky Prospekt where police found them on 16 January 2003. Russian television broadcast news of their discovery.

Alikhan said at his trial that he took Khaskhanov immediately to the airport after the explosion at the Yugo Zapadnaya McDonald's; that he (Alikhan) didn't know there had been a bomb in the car that he had parked there; and that he called Abu Bakar to tell him that the car he had left at the Mayakovskaya metro stop (at the request of Khaskhanov for a prospective buyer to look at) might also have a bomb in it. Abu Bakar told Alikhan not to worry, that the bomb had failed to go off because of a defective timer.

Investigators say that this same group had planned car bombings at the State Duma and at the Pushkinskaya Square McDonald's (located at 29 Bolshaya Bronnaya Ulitsa) in 2001, but the bombs had failed to go off.

The Dubrovka hostages were repeatedly threatened with certain death. Barayev, in a personal interview at the theater, told the *Sunday Times* reporter Mark Franchetti, "Our dream is to become shakhidi, martyrs of Allah. We are more than determined to die here. Allah has already fulfilled our dreams by just allowing us to come to Moscow and mount this operation successfully."

Hostages were shown that the building was rigged with explosives and assured that no one would escape alive. Barayev and company had a small arsenal, with easily enough explosives to bring the entire building down and kill everybody inside. They brought twenty-five explosive belts, two eighty-eight-pound homemade bombs that looked like large diver's tanks, thirty mines and booby traps, 114 hand grenades, fifteen AKSU-74 automatic rifles, and eleven pistols. There are rumors that the weekly bus from Grozny brought the explosives to the capital, the bus being stopped by police for document checks several times but let go each time after a bribe was paid.

The terrorists placed their bombs in strategic locations throughout the theater, with explosives reportedly being wired to a stage switch and other electrical power sources. Every time a hostage escaped or was released, after a television interview, or after negotiations with those who were allowed to enter the building, explosive charges would be moved to new locations.

The Chechen women wore explosive belts packed with ball bearings and bolt nuts strapped around their waists. The "Black Widows" (as the Russian media dubbed the Chechen women) mixed with the hostages to ensure maximum control and casualties when they detonated their bombs. "They work in shifts," Barayev told Mark Franchetti. "Those on duty have their finger on the detonator at all times. One push of the button and they will explode."

Barayev knew how to manipulate the hostages, some providing important communication links to the media and the authorities outside. One hostage pleaded live on NTV for security forces not to storm the building. Another was given her phone back to convey the message that Barayev would start shooting hostages if Russia failed to take his demands seriously. A third told television audiences that Barayev was ready to kill ten hostages for every one of his number shot by Russian security forces. Yet another said that Barayev would trade ten hostages for a State Duma deputy. Maria Shkolnikova was allowed to briefly come out of the building to say that the terrorists had a large amount of explosives with them and that the police should not storm the building. She also asked that the international community and journalists get involved. Several hostages were ordered to call their relatives to organize demonstrations against the war. Others secretly called relatives to ask them to look after their children, to tell them where their money was hidden at home, to ask for forgiveness, or to report the location of bombs in the building.

Of course, Udugov cranked up his propaganda machine. He provided Al-Jazeera satellite television with the terrorists' prerecorded tape of demands. He also called the BBC to inform them of the theater siege, and the kavkaz.org Web site said that Russia must begin a military withdrawal from Chechnya or everybody in the theater would die.

Barayev and his "assistants" stayed in constant touch with Kavkaz Center by cell phone. On 24 October, Barayev telephoned Udugov four times, and other hostage takers made at least five calls, all of which were published as exclusive Kavkaz Center interviews. The Web site also published Barayev's 24 October, 3 a.m. statement that the building had been mined and that he was holding more than a thousand people who would die if any attempt was made to storm the building.

Yandarbiyev talked with Barayev twice on 25 October, once in the morning and again in the afternoon. The purpose of the conversations is unclear. He did not tell Barayev to cease and desist, though. Barayev told Yandarbiyev that Basayev had sent him and repeated several times that Maskhadov did not know about the operation, but on "one occasion [Barayev] said that maybe [Maskhadov] did know since Basayev is his subordinate." These conversations resulted in a Russian arrest warrant for Yandarbiyev and an 8 May 2003 arrest and extradition appeal to Qatar (where Yandarbiyev lived until he was assassinated by a car bomb in February 2004).

The next forty-eight hours at Dubrovka were eventful and tragic. There were talks with Russian State Duma deputies Boris Nemtsov, Aslanbek Aslakhanov, Irina Khakhamada, and Grigory Yavlinsky, as well as with journalist Anna Politkovskaya. Doctor Leonid Roshal was also let into the theater to treat the hostages.

Politkovskaya entered the building at 2 p.m. on 25 October. "Does your mother know about this?" she asked her young terrorist escort. "No, but we have gone past the point of no return. Either the war ends, or we blow up the hostages," he told her. She proposed to Barayev that he "let the [hostage] teenagers go," but he answered with an emphatic "No!" "At least let us feed the children," she countered, but Barayev said no to that too: "Our children are hungry, so let yours also go hungry." The only agreement was that Politkovskaya would come back with enough water and juice for seven hundred people.

The release of a few more children—the youngest, five and six-year-olds—did come after the visit of Politkovskaya and the others, but so did the deaths of two more hostages.

A girl attempting to escape was shot. A man who entered the building looking for his son was executed too. How he got past the police cordon outside is a mystery, but he entered the building and said that he was looking for his son, Roman. Barayev was convinced the man was an FSB agent. Yassir asked the age of the boy, but when he could not find the sixteen-year-old, Yassir hit the man on the head. "Well, should we shot him here or not?" someone asked. "No!" hostages screamed. Then he was taken away and executed.

Two brave teenage girls jumped out of the second-story bathroom window to escape. They were shot at, but a young policeman danced in the window of the building across the street to divert the terrorist, giving the girls, one with a broken leg, time to get away. The terrorist shot himself in the foot in the process. "If you don't take this bullet out of my foot, I'll send ten of your people to Allah," he told the visiting doctor. After that, people were made to use the orchestra pit as a toilet.

The Russian hostage rescue operation that began early on Saturday morning, 26 October, may have been triggered by the belief that the terrorists had begun to execute the hostages as the dawn deadline approached. The evening before, Barayev had told Politkovskaya that he would "wait only a little while longer" (until 6 a.m.) before killing the hostages, just long enough to give President Putin time to declare publicly an end to the war and withdraw troops from one district of Chechnya as a sign of good will. This was reinforced by a phone call from a hostage who said that Barayev had promised to begin killing everybody at dawn.

Facts about what happened next are sketchy. Viktor, a man in his early twenties, sitting at the back of the theater, bolted from his seat, threw a Coca-Cola bottle at a terrorist, and ran down the aisle toward the exit shouting, "Mama, I can't stand it anymore." A Black Widow opened fire but missed her target, the bullets hitting a man in the eye and a woman, Tamara Starkova, in the side. This was the gunfire heard from inside the building between 1:15 and 1:30 a.m.

Surviving hostages say that Barayev was distraught about the shootings. He told a hostage to call the emergency squad to come and get the wounded. Forty to forty-five minutes later, the wounded man and woman were evacuated from the building. The man later died. Viktor lived.

Barayev then announced that he had three messages for the hostages. The first was that there had been negotiations with the Russian government and that General Viktor Kazantsyev (President Putin's official negotiator and his plenipotentiary representative in the Russian Southern Federal District) would fly from Grozny and be at the theater at ten in the morning. If Kazantsyev failed to show, Barayev would shoot one hundred hostages. Secondly, Barayev said that he had given Russia a list of Chechens who should be brought to the theater and exchanged for some of the hostages. And thirdly, he had been given a "green corridor" out of Dubrovka.

At 3:08 a.m., there was a grenade explosion inside the theater. There was also gunfire just before the storm, which might have prompted Alexandr Machevsky, the senior Russian official in charge, to give the signal to storm the building. Russian special forces pumped a sleep-inducing gas, later described as probably being fentanyl, into the theater through the ventilating system to stop "the women and younger boys" in the concert hall from setting off the bombs. The police had determined through listening devices that most of the women and some of the younger terrorists were in the concert hall, others were on patrol in the hallways, and Barayev and his deputies were in a separate room on the second floor looking at the video film of the theater seizure.

The gas pumped in under the stage knocked out only those in the concert hall, but not everyone immediately. When the twelve Alfa and Vympel federal antiterror units entered the building, they engaged the terrorists in close-quarter combat in the corridors and on the stairs. Russian snipers took out those terrorists standing near windows. A diversionary force drew the terrorists' gunfire and then broke through the hallway, while a second group went straight to the room where Barayev and his assistants had been trying to splice together the videotape of their entrance onto the stage.

If Barayev and his shakhidi intended to kill everybody in the theater, why didn't they detonate the bombs when the storm began? Electronic jamming may have prevented Barayev from communicating the order. Then too, the Black Widows would not have acted without direct orders from Barayev or his men. A few hostage survivors remember seeing some terrorists scrambling around looking for gas masks. Other terrorists may simply have decided to draw as many Russian spetnaz into the theater as possible, fight to the very end, and then detonate the bombs. However, one hostage concluded, "It was clear that they were not shakhidi—they wanted to live."

Basayev says that there was another reason they did not detonate their bombs—the detonators inside the theater (as well as those with the women suicide bombers outside the theater) were "nonfunctional." He believes that someone sabotaged them, and he is looking for the guilty parties.

Akhmed Zakayev claims that the Barayev group was infiltrated in Moscow by an FSB agent. Anna Politkovskaya says that it was a GRU agent. Both name a certain Chechen journalist, Khanpash Nurdyevich Terkibayev, as one of the Dubrovka terrorists. Zakayev says that Terkibayev, who had served as Maskhadov's representative in Jordan but had been fired a year earlier because he was suspected of being a Russian agent, slipped out of the theater just before the hostage rescue operation began.

It is a fact that a Khanpash Terkibayev also traveled to Strasbourg as a representative of the Russian delegation to the Parliamentary Assembly of the Council of Europe in the spring of 2003. That raised calls for a government explanation. These ranged from the stinging accusations made by Politkovskaya in a 28 April 2003 *Novaya Gazeta* article to a 29 April open letter to President Putin from three Moscow civil rights groups demanding an investigation of these strange circumstances. Terkibayev, who was killed in an auto accident in Grozny on 15 December 2003, denied his involvement in the theater siege.

Two hundred troops were involved in the rescue operation, which took no more than fifteen minutes. When it was over, Movsar was on the floor in a pool of blood and broken glass with three bullet holes in his forehead, and the Black Widows lay slumped in their red plush seats in the auditorium, each with a single bullet hole in the head.

Some terrorists may have escaped. The deputy interior minister initially said that an unknown number had fled, but that one had been picked up standing among a group of journalists. Other police sources say that about ten got away. Several press reports say that Elmurzayev (Yassir) was one of those. In 2003, a Russian intelligence officer swore that he saw Elmurzayev alive in Chechnya. But the official prosecutor general's version is that none escaped, that there were no more than forty-one terrorists to begin with and that all were killed.

No fewer than 130 hostages also died, most within hours or days later from failure to get timely and adequate medical treatment after being gassed. Transport to hospitals was inadequate and disorganized. There was no medical professional to coordinate on-site care, and the authorities took forever to tell doctors and hospitals what kind of gas had been used. Negligence on the part of those officials responsible for organizing emergency care was the principal cause of death for most.

Debate is still raging about the gas used. Many Western experts doubt that it was fentanyl. There was initial speculation that a nerve gas had been used because hostages reported that the vapor had a bitter, kind of peppery smell. Someone else speculated that it was BZ, a colorless, odorless substance with hallucinogenic properties that was used by the United

States in Vietnam. A veteran of the Soviet chemical weapons program thought that it was "Substance 78," which he said is something like BZ. Sickness symptoms among the hostages included an inability to walk, memory loss, fainting, heartbeat irregularities, and vomiting. Some blood and urine samples also showed traces of halothane, a gas used as an anesthetic that is inhaled. Whatever kind of gas it was, its effects were worsened by the poor physical condition of the hostages; the lack of water, food, and sleep; severe psychological stress; and existing medical problems that many suffered from.

How did Maskhadov react to all this? On 26 October, he found himself engaged in serious international political damage control. The West immediately asked if Maskhadov had known about the attack beforehand. If he had known, it would be difficult for any democratic country to further support him as someone with whom the Kremlin should negotiate.

Maskhadov said that he had no prior knowledge of the attack, though under close scrutiny this claim is suspect. He denied that he knew Barayev, but a fall videotape made before the Dubrovka siege shows footage of Maskhadov, Barayev, Basayev, Yassir, and Sheikh Abu Omar sitting together and talking. Maskhadov is heard saying, "I don't have any doubt that in the final stage, we will conduct an even more unique operation than Jihad [Jihad is short for Basayev's 1995 Operation Jihad].

Basayev tried to give Maskhadov's story credibility by going public with a personal confession that he had carried out the operation behind Maskhadov's back. Basayev took the entire blame in a published confession on Kavkaz Center and asked Maskhadov's forgiveness as well as the forgiveness of "my fellow fighters for the fact that I hid the planning and carrying out of this operation from them."

To make his confession even more plausible, Basayev officially tended his resignation from all posts in both Ichkeria's Majlis ul-Shura and the Islamic Shura set up in Dagestan in August 1999. He said that he would still command the Riyadus-Salikhin Reconnaissance and Sabotage Battalion of Shakhids, though.

This maneuver was meaningless in reality. If he really did resign, his resignation was either not accepted or didn't last very long because he is still the most powerful leader in Chechnya, even chairing sessions of the Majlis ul-Shura like the one held the day before suicide bombers blew up the Nadterechny district government administration building in early May 2003. Moreover, Abu al-Waleed has told Al-Jazeera television that "not a single leader in Chechnya remains outside the Shura."

TERRORISTS KILLED AT DUBROVKA:
THE OFFICIAL LIST (WITH ITEMS FOUND ON BODY)

1. Abdulsheikhov, Arslanbek Alimpashayevich
   (Абдулшейхов Арслан бек Алимпашаевич)
   Male; Dob: 5 April 1967; Found: valid passport.

2. Adilsultanov, Muslim Salmanovich
   (Адилсултанов Муслим Салманович)
   Male; Dob: 1 May 1981; Found: valid passport.

3. Akhmatkhanov, Khamlkhazhi Akhmarovich
   (Алиев Али Максудович)
   Male; Dob: 1978; Found: valid passport.

4. Akhmetov, Akhmed Mumadiyevich
   (Алиева Секилат Увайсовна)
   Male; Dob: 6 September 1983; Found: valid passport.

5. Aliyev, Ali Maksudovich
   (Алхазуров Идрис Махмудович)
   Male; Dob: 1 May 1965; Found: valid passport.

6. Aliyeva, Sekilat Uvaisovna
   (Ахматханов Хамильхажи Ахмарович)
   Female; Dob: 2 Jan 1977; Found: valid passport; Khasavyurt-Moscow
   bus ticket purchased 16 October 2002 with 17 October departure.

7. Alkhazurov, Idris Makhmudovich
   (Ахметов Ахмед Мумадиевич)
   Male; Dob: 7 February 1974; Found: valid passport.

8. Baikhatov, Arsen Nazhmudinovich
   (Байракова Зарета Долхаевна)
   Male; Dob: 16 February 1981; Found: valid passport.

9. Baikhatov, Rashid Savatdiyevich
   (Байхатов Арсен Нажму динович)
   Male; Dob: 1982: Found: valid passport.

10. Bairakova, Zareta Dolkhayevna
    (Байхатов Рашид Саватдиевич)
    Female; Dob: 3 April 1976; Found: valid passport; Khasavyurt-
    Moscow bus ticket purchased 17 October 2002 with 19 October
    departure; paper with a note for a meeting at "Luzhniki" (sports stadi-
    um) on 21 October 2002 scribbled on it.

11. Barayev, Movsar Bukharovich
     (Бараев Мовсар Бухарович)
     Male; Dob: 19 October 1970; Found: forged passport in the name of
     Akhmatkhanov, Shamilkhazh Akhmarovich (Ахматханов
     Шамиль хаж Ахмарович).

12. Bicultanova, Marina Nebiyullayevna
     (Бимурзаев Магомед-Эмин Сайданович)
     Female; Dob: 21 December 1983; Found: valid passport.

13. Bimurzayev, Magomed-Emin Saidanovich
     (Бисултанова Марина Небиюллаевна)
     Male; Dob: 23 March 1979; Found: valid passport and driver's license.

14. Bitsiyeva, Zura Pezvanovna
     (Битева Заира Башировна)
     Female; Dob: 22 April 1980; Found: valid passport; Makhachkala-
     Moscow bus ticket with 16 September 2002 departure; confirmation
     of Grozny Professional School No. 3 diploma.

15. Bityeva, Zaira Bashirovna
     (Бициева Зура Резвановна)
     Female; Dob: 17 May 1978; Found: valid passport with the words
     "Israpilova Kagmara from Rubezhnoye" written on the cover.

16. Dugayeva, Madina Movsarovna
     (Дугаева Мадина Мовсаровна)
     Female; Dob: 13 January 1978; Found: valid passport with four tat-
     tered photographs; two postcards with the messages "To my sister
     Madina from your favorite, one and only unforgettable sister Iman, 27
     April 2001" and "I wish you happy birthday, with much happiness,
     Amina and mama, 13 January 2002"; identification as "assistant" in
     the Department of Acting Arts at the Chechen state university, issued
     27 April 2001.

17. Dzhabrailov, Salgir Isayevich
     (Джабраилов Салгир Исаевич)
     Male; Dob: 1976; Found: valid passport.

18. Elmurzayev, Ruslan Abu-Khasanovich
     Male; Dob: 5 January 1976; Found: forged passport in the name of
     Kzhabrailov, Sapgir Isayevich (Джабраилова Сапгира Исаевича).

     Elmurzayeva, Seda Seitkhamzatovna
     (Эльмурзаева Седа Сейтхамзатовна)
     Female; Dob: 1984; Found: valid passport.

20. Ganiyeva, Fatima Sulumbekovna
    (Ганиева Фатима Сулумбековна)
    Female; Dob: 1975; Found: valid passport.

21. Ganiyeva, Khadchat Sulumbekovna
    (Ганиева Хадчат Сулумбековна)
    Female; Dob: 1 April 1986; Found: valid passport.

22. Gasanov, Nizami Isa-ogly
    (Гасанов Низами Иса-оглы)
    Male; Dob: 1962.

23. Gishmurkayeva, Aset Vakhidovna
    (Гишмуркаева Асет Вахидовна)
    Female; Dob: 15 August 1973; Found: valid passport.

24. Khadzhiyeva, Aiman Vagetovna
    (Хаджиева Айман Вагетовна)
    Female; Dob: 26 July 1974; Found: valid passport; Khasavyurt-Moscow bus ticket purchased 16 October 2002 with 17 October departure; note for a meeting at "Luzhniki" (sports stadium) on 21 October scribbled on the ticket.

25. Khadzhiyeva, Koku Vagetovna
    (Хаджиева Коку Вагетовна)
    Female; Dob: 9 April 1976; Found: valid passport and metro ticket used at 9:30 p.m. on 22 October.

26. Khamzatov, Turpal Kamiyevich
    (Хамзатов Турпал Камиевич)
    Male; Dob: 5 September 1978; Found: valid passport; three thousand rubles; $340; Khasavyurt-Moscow bus ticket with 19 October 2002 departure; sports log book for "Master Boxer" with the sport club "Vainakh."

27. Khunov, Fuad Shakhambiyevich
    (Хусаинов Расча Сайдаминович)
    Male; Dob: 13 December 1964; Found: valid passport.

28. Khusainov, Rascha Saidaminovich
    (Хусаинов Расул Сайдаминович)
    Male; Dob: 15 December 1977.

29. Khusainov, Rasul Saidaminovich
    (Хунов Фуад Шахамбиевич)
    Male; Dob: 1976; Found: valid passport.

30. Khusenova, Liana Musayevna
    (Хусенова Лиана Мусаевна)
    Female; Dob: 1979; Found: valid passport.

31. Kurbanova, Raiman Khasanovna
    (Курбанова Райман Хасановна)
    Female; Dob: 18 February 1964; Found: valid passport.

32. Magerlamov, Oleg Alaidarovich
    (Магерламов Олег Алаидарович)
    Male; Dob: 29 November 1965; Found: valid passport.

33. Meferkhanova, Yakha Khamidovna
    (Меферханова Яха Хамидовна)
    Female; Dob: 1959; Found: Moscow registration.

34. Mugayeva, Malika Daydovna
    (Мугаева Малика Даудовна)
    Female; Dob: 30 October 1971; Found: valid passport; Makhachkala-Moscow bus ticket departing 22 October 2002.

35. Musayev, Ibragim Adlanovich
    (Мусаев Ибрагим Адланович)
    Male; Dob: 17 May 1977; Found: valid passport.

36. Mutayeva, Malizha Daudovna
    (Мутаева Малижа Даудовна)
    Female; Dob: 1971; Found: valid passport.

37. Shakova, Fatimat Mukhamedovna
    (Шакова Фатимат Мухамедовна)
    Female; Dob: 6 May 1977; Found: valid passport with evidence of Moscow registration; small prayer book in Arabic in passport.

38. Shidayev, Magomed Abuyazidovich
    (Шидаев Магомед Абуязидович)
    Male; Dob: 16 June 1975; Found: valid passport; tour contact issued by ZAO "Turuniversal," Makhachkala; work pass from Mintopyenergo, a state-owned company, Grozny region, which had the telephone number of a Moscow taxi cab company written on it.

39. Tagirov, Lecha Gapurovich
    (Тагиров Леча Гапурович)
    Male; Dob: 20 July 1954; Found: valid passport and Khasavyurt-Moscow bus ticket purchased 16 October 2002 with 17 October departure.

40. Tatayev, Usman Alaudinovich
    (Татаев Усман Алаудинови)
    Male; Dob: 1979 or 1970; Found: valid passport; "doverennost" (legal permission) to operate three vehicles (used to transport terrorists to Dubrovka) and doverennost for a VAZ-21099 registered to Kristina Valerevna Yakubovska, Moscow.

41. Yupayeva, Zaira Bashirovna
    (Юпаева Заира Башировна)
    Female; Dob: 1978; Found: valid passport.

X

THE THIRD WAR

This is essentially a war declared on us. It is a war without fronts
or borders, a war without a visible enemy, but a war all the
same. This is a new war of the twenty-first century.

Sergei Ivanov, minister of defense, Russia, October 2002

A NEW TERROR WAR

Dubrovka was a watershed event. The theater siege failed to force Russia
out of Chechnya, but it did effectively end the second Chechen war and
begin a new one—a third war—with the attendant reshaping of military
doctrine, strategy, and tactics on both sides.

On the Chechen side, Dubrovka created a new dynamic with two fun-
damental and qualitative changes taking place. First, terror is clearly now
the strategic weapon of choice, taking precedence over guerrilla actions.
Second, Basayev has escalated the war by adopting the Palestinian model
of suicide terror against civilians. A third dimension, international terror
operations, is also being added.

Terror is now the Chechen force multiplier because other options are
limited; because it costs less than guerilla warfare and attracts bigger foreign
investment; because Basayev's physical health and political power are
stronger now; and because Basayev and Maskhadov have become impatient.

Wolves continue to have good access to conventional weapons—this is
especially true about surface-to-air missile launchers that they buy from
the former Soviet republics—but they have been complaining for some
time about shortages of ammunition. Most importantly, though, they

simply do not have the numerical fighter strength needed to drive the eighty thousand Russian federal troops out of Chechnya. Moreover, Basayev says that he is through making specific demands of the Kremlin: "The next time we won't be making any demands! There won't be any more hostage taking [either]." Instead, Basayev promises to "extract maximum damage" on Russia through other, more serious, means of terror.

"I swear to Allah, if Russians or Americans will give us cruise missiles or intercontinental ballistic missiles, then we will not be using suicide attackers or trucks loaded with explosives," Basayev proclaimed on 2 June 2003. He may not have such missiles, but Basayev does have a comparatively rich variety of other terror options, certainly more than most terrorists.

There is a history of Chechen theft, smuggling, and dealing in stolen nuclear materials and radioactive waste going back to 1992, when low enriched uranium was stolen and brokered in Grozny for resale to Iran. This is one of a dozen or so cases where nuclear materials in Russia have been stolen. The security of these nuclear materials is now a grave concern to both Russia and the United States, especially since Wolves have conducted surveillance of Russian nuclear warhead storage facilities and transport trains at least a half dozen times in the past two years. Colonel General Igor Volynkin, who is in charge of Russia's nuclear security, says that in 2001 terrorists tried twice to penetrate bunkers storing nuclear arms. He believes that Basayev wants to get his hands on a nuclear warhead.

Even if Basayev doesn't get hold of a nuclear bomb anytime soon, he likely does still have access to nuclear waste materials. In addition to materials from the previously mentioned radon facility, Chechens may also have acquired some of several hundred missing lead-shielded boxes containing cesium-137 that were used in Soviet agricultural experiments. Only nine boxes have been found. Indeed, radioactive waste originating in Chechnya continues to turn up. Just days before the Dubrovka siege, Russian border guards caught a Chechen smuggling a 2.2-pound container of radioactive waste material into Azerbaijan. Two small metal boxes containing radioactive materials were also found in a taxi in Tbilisi, Georgia, in June 2003.

Basayev isn't the only Chechen to have built a dirty bomb. In 1998, someone, probably Raduyev, attached a mine to a container of cesium-137 and left it on the railroad tracks outside Argun, Chechnya.

The detonation of a dirty bomb using only a few ounces of powdered cesium-137 could spread a low level of radioactive fallout over many city blocks. Casualties would be concentrated in the immediate blast area, but the psychological effects and cleanup of contaminated areas would go on for years. Even today, some people who live near Moscow's Izmailovsky

Park are convinced they were somehow contaminated by the cesium that Basayev put there in 1995.

In late 2002, I told Russian embassy officials in Washington, D.C., about my concerns of an attack on the Moscow subway system using a dirty bomb. Moscow takes the threat of a dirty bomb attack seriously. City security officials in mid-January 2003 announced that they had intercepted some "twenty serious signals" of a terrorist attack targeted against Moscow's huge underground metro system. Anatoly Kotelnikov, the Russian deputy minister of atomic energy, believes that a dirty bomb attack against the metro at rush hour is a highly likely scenario.

Basayev says that the use of chemical and biological weapons against Russia is a good idea too, and claims that he has access to such weapons. Old Soviet artillery shells containing nerve agents like sarin are stored in a dilapidated facility in Shchuchye, Russia. If Basayev got his hands on one of these shells, he could kill hundreds of people. While Shchuchye is Russia's largest facility, there are other places where the remainder of forty thousand metric tons of warfare chemicals are stored awaiting disposal.

It was only ten years ago that Basayev received training in chemical weapons in Afghanistan. More recently, Wolves may have received special chemical weapons training in Iraq. Yossef Bodansky told a U.S.-Russian public forum on terrorism in Washington, D.C., in September 2002 that Chechens had recently trained with al Qaeda in Iraq on chemical weapons. The Russian side, though, was surprised by this information. It's not known what Russian intelligence subsequently turned up.

Moscow police believe that they probably thwarted a small chemical attack when they caught Sergei Krym-Gerei, one of Basayev's Wolves, with a large bottle containing almost eighteen pounds of liquid mercury during a police dragnet at the time of the Dubrovka siege. Mercury, a neurotoxin, acts as a poison to the human central nervous system and can be absorbed into the body through the skin, the respiratory, or the gastrointestinal tracts. It can easily be used to contaminate the environment, food, and water supplies, causing severe sickness and even death. Children are particularly susceptible. In 1978, the Arab Revolutionary Council used mercury to contaminate Israel's citrus fruit exports to Europe. The poisonous metal was simply rubbed onto the skin of the fruit. Children in West Germany and Holland got sick, and Israel's orange exports dropped by 40 percent.

Basayev does not rule out a biological attack on Russia either. In 1995, he threatened to unleash germ warfare on the Russian city of Yekaterinburg: "We could put a biological weapon in Yekaterinburg and let the people who live there all get sick." Basayev said in March 2004 that he still "reserves the right to use chemical and toxic weapons against Russia."

The Russian State Research Center for Applied Microbiology in Obolensk, fifty miles south of Moscow, has one of the world's largest collections of anthrax, but Russia's chief medical officer Gennady Onishchenko assures the Russian public that the theft and trading in the bacteria from this and other such facilities is impossible. However, in May of 2002, an American team of scientists from the Pentagon's Threat Reduction Agency went to Vozrozhdeniye Island in Central Asia's Aral Sea to dig up and kill over one hundred tons of military-grade anthrax that had been buried at the former Soviet field-testing facility for biological warfare in 1988. The purpose of the trip was to prevent Basayev and other terrorists from getting their hands on live anthrax spores, but people have been scavenging the island for junk and whatever else they could sell for years anyway.

Basayev would not have to steal anything from Obolensk or elsewhere because it is easy to make different kinds of primitive biological weapons in the field. It does not require sophisticated laboratories, only simple materials, knowledge, or instructions of what materials to use and how to mix them. Al Qaeda ran such a laboratory in the Pankisi Gorge in 2002.

In August 2001, ITAR-TASS reported that the FSB had intercepted a communication in which Chechen General Rizvan Chitigov asked Chechen field commander Hizir Alhazurov how to make "homemade poisons" that could be used against Russian soldiers. The FSB raided Chitigov's home and seized instructions on the manufacture of homemade toxic agents for contaminating consumer goods, a primitive chemical laboratory, and explosives. The materials seized also contained instructions on how to make ricin.

Toxins in the possession of terrorists arrested in Great Britain and Paris at the end of 2002 and beginning of 2003—as well as remnants of a "biological terrorist academy" uncovered in the Pankisi Gorge—show that al Qaeda recently trained Wolves in the Pankisi Gorge on how to make biological warfare agents. Production equipment, agents, and handwritten instructions on how to mix ingredients were unearthed near an abandoned building in the gorge. Traces of ricin that were found there have been linked to four North Africans arrested in Great Britain. The Pankisi discovery is also linked to a December 2002 plot to attack the Russian embassy in Paris. At least one unidentified al Qaeda trainer in biological and chemical warfare was in the Pankisi Gorge in late 2002. President Shevardnadze concedes that "one or two people" who specialized in making poisonous toxins were in the Pankisi Gorge, but he says they are no longer there.

Large KamAZ trucks laden with explosives and operated by both men and women "kamikaze" drivers worked well against Russian forces in

Chechnya in the summer of 2000 and will surely be used again, only this time against political and economic targets too, resulting in large numbers of civilian casualties, both Russian and Chechen.

Basayev will deploy more female suicide bombers too. At the time of this writing (2002), he was training a new group of thirty, some as young as thirteen. Female suicide terrorists will probably outnumber their male counterparts.

With regard to likely targets, Basayev said in a November 2002 open letter to NATO, "All military, economic and strategic properties on Russian territory are legitimate targets. . . . Chechens reserve the right to attack any facility in Russia." "Strategic properties" would include government administrative buildings in Chechnya or anywhere in Russia, even the Russian parliament.

Chechen leaders associated with Maskhadov have said that an attack against a Russian nuclear power station is a likely scenario. Both Mairbek Vachagayev and Akhmed Zakayev say that such an attack would extract the kind of maximum damage that Basayev is looking for. "The Russians should thank God that [Barayev and his unit] just seized a house of culture and not a nuclear power station," Vachagayev says. Zakayev is more direct: "We cannot exclude that the next such group will take over some nuclear facility." Zakayev concludes, "The consequences would be catastrophic, not only for Russian and Chechen society, but for the whole of Europe."

The idea would be to create another Chernobyl. The 1986 explosion at the Chernobyl nuclear power plant in the Ukraine left hundreds near the plant dead and sick from nuclear radiation and exposed several European countries to increased levels of radiation.

For these reasons, maximum security should be standard at Russian power plants, but that may not be the case. Security has improved since 11 September 2001, but two top Russian regulation officials say that it is still not good enough. Oleg Sarayev, general director of Rosenergoatom, the agency responsible for the generation of power at several plants, will not rule out the possibility that terrorists could penetrate the security of a Russian nuclear power plant. Yuri Vishnevsky, head of Gosatomnadzor, Russia's nuclear regulatory agency, said in November 2002 that security at Russia's plants is still far from perfect.

A recent event at one power plant near Moscow proves just how vulnerable they really are, especially to an inside threat. Just weeks after Dubrovka, a captain of security at the Kalinin Nuclear Power Plant in the Tver oblast, north of Moscow, was arrested and charged with terrorist collaboration. He was caught red-handed with classified plans of the facility in his possession and coded telephone numbers of Chechen Wolves in his pocket.

Security at the Kalinin site has since been overhauled, and a high-security regime is in place at another forty or so power plants and nuclear facilities in Russia. In Moscow alone, there are more than thirty nuclear reactors functioning in research institutes.

New security requirements have also been put in place for rail transport of radioactive waste and nuclear reactor fuel to power plants in Russia and Iran. Nevertheless, people are still nervous. "I have talked to many, many facility directors in and around the Moscow area and all of them—and they tell me this point blank—are worried about the truckload of Chechens pulling up to their gate," Rose Gottemoeller of the Carnegie Endowment for International Peace said in January 2003.

Yuri Vishnevsky says that there, in fact, have been attempted terrorist penetrations, but he will not say whether he was referring only to the Kalinin incident or others. He will say only that "every so often Basayev and others declare that attacks on nuclear facilities are inevitable," so security is being beefed up. Special attention has been given to protecting the two plants nearest to Chechnya, the Rostovskaya and Novoronezhskaya nuclear power plants.

RECOGNIZING TERROR AS THE GREATEST THREAT TO NATIONAL SECURITY

Russia is redesigning its national security posture and military doctrine based on the Kremlin's conclusion after Dubrovka that terrorism represents the greatest threat to Russian national security. President Putin has ordered Defense Minister Sergei Ivanov to draw up a new national security concept that will take into account this new reality.

A key change in the new concept will be Russia's right to execute pre-emptive strikes against "ideological and financial" targets abroad that support terror against Russia. This could be used to justify the assassination of Udugov or Yandarbiyev in Qatar. Defense Minister Ivanov is also promising to build a contract-based Russian Army with fewer servicemen, all of whom would be equipped with new precision weapons for use against terrorists in densely populated areas. Attractive ads for contract recruits are already being run on Russian television. But the modernization of the Russian Army will not happen anytime soon. "We still need a long time before we can begin supplying the Russian Army with new equipment and weapons so that the army can adequately and effectively react to arising threats," Russia's Prime Minister Mikhail Kasyanov told a Russian cabinet ministers' meeting in February 2003.

The FSB will continue to bear the prime responsibility for combating terrorism, but the Russian Army and airborne troops will assist the FSB and the Interior Ministry in interdicting terrorists.

Combat training is also being modified to take into account the lessons learned at Dubrovka and elsewhere. Russian tactics are changing too. Russia is now borrowing heavily from the Israelis in dealing with Chechen and foreign terrorists and their families. For example, Defense Minister Ivanov announced in early January 2003, "We use the wholly Israeli method when we know the exact composition of a [terrorist] cell, and we do not let go until the entire cell has been eliminated. If there is a cell of ten people and we have eliminated nine out of ten, we will pursue the tenth until his elimination."

Employing the same tactics as Israel, Russia demolished the family homes of those involved in the Dubrovka siege. The apartment buildings around Khankala air base that were earlier used as cover by Wolves to launch surface-to-air missile attacks against Russian helicopters taking off and landing at the airbase have also been demolished.

Russian retaliation in Chechnya after Dubrovka was expectedly severe. There were more terrible "cleansing operations" as well as Russian fuel air bombardment of the Vedeno Gorge in hopes of killing Basayev. President Putin also promptly suspended an earlier decision to reduce the eighty thousand troops in Chechnya.

On the political front, the Kremlin has ruled out any talks with the "nonexistent President [Maskhadov] of a nonexistent republic [Ichkeria]," instead scheduling a constitutional referendum for 23 March 2003 and presidential and parliamentary elections in Chechnya by the end of the year.

Russia also launched a diplomatic offensive to persuade Washington under U.S. Executive Order 13224 to designate several Chechen structures as terrorist groups. On 14 February 2003, the U.S. secretary of state added three groups to the State Department's terrorist list, all of them linked to the Dubrovka theater siege. They are Basayev's Riyadus-Salikhin Reconnaissance and Sabotage Battalion of Chechen Martyrs (Shakhids); the Special Purposes Islamic Regiment (a.k.a., Islamic Special Purposes Regiment; a.k.a., Islamic Regiment of Special Meaning; a.k.a., the Al-Jihad-Fisisabililah Special Islamic Regiment) that Movsar Barayev took command of when his uncle was killed; and the Islamic International Brigade, formerly the Peacekeeping Brigade of the Congress of Peoples of Chechnya and Dagestan (a.k.a., International Battalion; a.k.a., Islamic Peacekeeping International Brigade; a.k.a., the Peacekeeping Battalion;

a.k.a., the International Brigade; a.k.a., the Islamic Peacekeeping Army; and a.k.a., the Islamic Peacekeeping Brigade).

These names have also been added to the U.S. Treasury Department's Office of Foreign Control Assets SDN list as "Specifically Designated Global Terrorists." Any assets they have in the United States are now frozen, and U.S. citizens and organizations are prohibited from making contributions or receiving any funds, goods, or services for the benefit of these groups.

The United States, the United Kingdom, China, and Spain have also joined Russia in asking the United Nations 1267 Sanctions Committee to put the three groups on its consolidated terrorist list. France will also support the designation. All UN member states are obligated to impose arms and travel sanctions and to freeze the assets of these groups in their countries.

Basayev's public reaction to the U.S. freeze was indifference: "I have no bank accounts there, and feel neither hot nor warm over it." But he did strongly object to the State Department's blacklisting: "We too can list [the United States] among our categories." He never explained what he meant by "categories."

Russia also made diplomatic appeals combined with stern warning to Georgia and the Gulf states to cut off the flow of money, material, and fighter resources to Chechnya. Russia is still not satisfied, though, with the progress being made in Georgia. Sergei Ivanov says that "Chechen rings" continue to operate in Georgia and are trying to seize control of Georgian companies involved in the shipment of international cargo for their arms, drug, and fighter trade in support of their holy war. He also says there are still many Wolves in the Pankisi Gorge, but Georgia's President Shevardnadze disagrees.

Moscow is counting on its improved relations with Pakistan to reduce the number of fighters coming from that country to Chechnya or joining terrorist cells abroad.

WHO ARE THE REAL MASTERS OF CHECHNYA?

Exactly two months and four days after Dubrovka, Basayev's Riyadus-Salikhin Reconnaissance and Sabotage Battalion struck again, only this time they were not taking hostages, just as Basayev had promised.

In the early afternoon on Friday, 27 December, three suicide bombers crashed a large KamAZ truck and a jeep loaded with huge amounts of explosives through quadruple security barriers and into Akhmat Kadyrov's Chechen government administrative building, the most heavily guarded structure in Chechnya. The first explosion left a twenty-foot-wide crater; the second was closer and tore off the entire facade as well as collapsed several floors of the newly renovated four-story complex in Grozny.

Forty-eight people died instantly. Many others were trapped beneath the rubble. Within days, the death toll climbed to eighty-three with more than 150 people in the hospital, many missing limbs or crippled for life.

Stunned, Kadyrov, who was in Moscow at the time of the attack, commented: "Terrorists act as if they are the masters of Grozny." They were that day. The suicide bombers used vehicles bearing Russian military license plates. Eyewitnesses say the drivers wore Russian military uniforms, looked "Slavic," spoke Russian, and flashed Russian military IDs and documentation as they passed through numerous security checkpoints on the way to their target.

Basayev tells a different story. "Yes . . . those behind the wheel were dressed in military uniforms," but a Chechen family—a man forty-three years old, his son (seventeen), and daughter (fifteen)—carried out the bombings. The father, Gelani Tumriyev, and his daughter were in the KamAZ truck, which was carrying four metric tons of explosives, while the boy drove the jeep loaded with nearly three hundred pounds of explosives in it. Several years earlier, Tumriyev had abducted both children from their mothers and kept them prisoner in Achkoi-Martan.

Basayev says that "[the bombers] ran though the first two checkpoints at full speed, and everyone simply ran away at the third and forth ones. Not a single shot was fired." But that's not all. Basayev personally pushed the button on the remote controlled bombs: "I did not only take part in that blast, I pushed the button on the remote control explosive devices that were in the vehicles. I was watching from a distance, and when the vehicles disappeared from eyesight and entered the premises of the puppet administration compound, I pushed the button."

Basayev had planned the operation for 23 or 24 December, but, for technical reasons, he put it off for three days. "We had information that Kafir-ov [Kadyrov] would not be there, but at the same time we learned that Babichev [Kadyrov's deputy], Ilyasov, and Kazantsyev's deputy, Korobeinikov [in other words, the pro-Moscow Chechen leadership minus Kadyrov], would be." Basayev timed the attack to take place during a scheduled meeting, but it was delayed; consequently, "We failed in our ultimate objective, which was [to] bury all the scum."

In London, Akhmed Zakayev went to the press to tell that Chechnya had turned into a second Palestine. This was a good tactic. Maskhadov, for his part, played Arafat's role well in quickly denying that the president of the Chechen Republic of Ichkeria had anything to do with the Grozny bombing.

The denial of the Muslim Brotherhood was equally swift. Since the FSB has accused Abu al-Waleed (who is a senior member of the Muslim Brotherhood) of putting together the Grozny operation, the Brotherhood stands accused of complicity in the attack. There is another reason the FSB is pointing a finger at Abu al-Waleed. He has replaced Khattab as "commander of the Arab fighters" in Chechnya and Basayev's principal advisor on terrorism. Basayev knows him well. He was Khattab's deputy and is present in most of the early photographs taken of Basayev and Khattab together.

The December Grozny bombing was not meant to be an isolated act. Wolves had planned two more terror attacks in Russia—and one in Europe—to coincide with the Grozny bombing, but all failed for different reasons.

Two Wolves with explosives were arrested in a Moscow outdoor market packed with holiday shoppers. Both men in their twenties, one from Gudermes and the other from the Nadterechny district, entered the cramped outdoor market next to the Yugo Zapadnaya metro stop carrying explosive material and ball bearings in plastic containers attached to their trouser belts. They also had several grenades. An anonymous caller tipped the police to the pair.

A terror attack in Voronezh, Russia, also failed. In November, Dzhabrail Abdulazimov, leader of the Saratov Wahhabi jamaat, dispatched Khanpasha Israilov, a Chechen Grozny resident, to Voronezh to blow up the movie theater or the outdoor Yarmarka market near the Voronezh-Kursky railroad station. Israilov had been trained as a sniper and mine layer in Khattab's camps and had fought in Dagestan in 1999. He had also been a people trader. Israilov's handler had instructed him to wait in Voronezh until he was contacted by two other Chechens and an "Arab," who were to provide him with explosives and instructions. When they failed to show up, Israilov returned to Saratov, where he sold arms and narcotics to feed himself until the police caught up with him.

A week before the Grozny bombing, nine members of a new Wolves' terrorist cell in France fell into the hands of French counterintelligence. They were in the final stages of putting together an operation against the Russian embassy in Paris. The leaders of the cell (which the French are calling the Chechen Network) confessed that they intended to target the Russian embassy to avenge the deaths of Khattab, al-Moutana (an unknown Arab mujahideen killed in Chechnya), and Movsar Barayev.

If the year wasn't bad enough for Russia, Udugov promised new "kamikaze operations" early in the new year. Basayev would deliver big time in May 2003, but not before completing the training of a fresh squad of suicide bombers and executing several guerilla actions and smaller scale acts of terrorism—acts that nevertheless claimed the lives of sixty more people.

A bomb hidden in a couch killed Dzhabrail Yamadayev, the commandant of a special pro-Moscow Chechen military group in the Gudermes district and a member of the powerful Yamadayev brothers clan from Gudermes. Basayev's feud with Yamadayev dated back to 1997, when Yamadayev ousted the Basayev-appointed head of the Gudermes city administration. But it was only after Dzhabrail and his five brothers encircled a schoolhouse full of Wahhabis and killed them during the July 1998 uprising in Gudermes that the Basayev family declared a blood feud against them. When Dzhabrail Yamadayev went over to the Russian side in 1999, Basayev put him on his traitor hit list. Sulim Yamadayev points the finger at Basayev for killing his brother.

Maskhadov's fighters attacked Kadyrov's motorcade in Argun, killing three Russian soldiers and four bodyguards. Kadyrov escaped unharmed, though. Then, two days before the 23 March constitutional referendum in Chechnya, Wolves from the Central Sector of the Eastern Front kidnapped a half dozen policemen from the village of Yalkhoi-Mokhk. And on the eve of the referendum, two policemen were killed, eleven polling stations were shot up or set on fire, and a joint session of the President, Parliament, Government and the Supreme Court of the Chechen Republic of Ichkeria officially sentenced referendum organizers to death.

On 23 March, Wolves slept while voters cast their ballots to remain in the Russian Federation, but the killing started again soon after. April was an especially bloody month. Early in the month, a mine in a garbage pile destroyed a minibus full of construction workers. Wolves also assassinated Akhmed Zavgayev, Doku Zavgayev's brother, head of the Nadterechny district government administration, and a remote-controlled land mine taped to the bottom of a manhole cover in downtown Grozny killed five policemen and three civilians.

In the middle of the month, Wolves detonated a powerful remote-controlled mine on the road from Khankala airbase, blowing up a minibus and killing fifteen people inside. A video shot by Basayev's cameraman shows the blue bus being split into two pieces by the explosion. One survivor walks away, but a second explosion, timed to coincide with the arrival of rescue workers, kills two more.

At the end of April, locals in the village of Michurina outside Gudermes found three pro-Moscow Chechen officials who had been kidnapped days earlier while on a hunting trip. They had died from gunshot and knife stab wounds. Wolves also disarmed a group of riot police in

Grozny and abducted a police official from a city café. The bodies of two more police officers were found in Nozhai-Yurt at the beginning of May. Wolves also kidnapped Alkhazur Musalatov, the vice president of Chechen Academy of Sciences. He has yet to turn up. Twenty-one more people died in other attacks.

Basayev put the finishing touches on his 2003 terror master plan—code-named "Operation Whirlwind"—in early May, just in time for the Victory Day celebrations in Chechnya. Minutes before the annual Victory Day parade started at Grozny's Dinamo Stadium on 9 May, police spotted a bomb along the parade route. One Chechen policeman was killed trying to disarm it, and two others were wounded. Akhmat Kadyrov was supposed to attend the celebration but changed his mind at the last minute.

Basayev's big surprise came three days later in what had been a relatively calm district of Chechnya until Wolves assassinated Akhmed Zavgayev there the month before. At 10 a.m., two men and a woman, Zarina Alikhhanova, crashed another explosives-laden KamAZ truck into the metal barrier protecting Nadterechny's district government administrative building in the village of Znamenskoye (Chulgi-Yurt). The explosion (caused by a bomb made from a mixture of agricultural nitro, cement, and aluminum power) left a crater sixteen feet deep and thirty-three feet wide and completely destroyed the district's building, most of the adjoining FSB building, and eight nearby village houses.

The force of the explosion and the casualty count compared to that of the December Grozny bombing. Fifty-six people died instantly. Some of those who had luckily survived the December Grozny bombing died in this attack because their offices had been moved to Znamenskoye. The death toll quickly rose to sixty.

It seems implausible that it was still possible to fill a huge truck full of explosives and drive across Russian territory without the assistance of greed and corruption at security checkpoints. Kadyrov demanded answers: "Where did the explosives come from?" The police and the Russian military had stopped the truck more than once to check the driver's documents, but "no one bothered looking in the back." The story was a familiar one. A later official government version said that the explosives had been hidden under bags of cement, and that is why they had not been found.

The next day, Kadyrov himself was again the target of Black Widows. Bodies were still being collected in Znamenskoye when one to three of Basayev's women approached Kadyrov during an afternoon religious festival attended by fifteen thousand people outside a mosque in Ilisk-han-Yurt. The media reported that the women, dressed like journalists, approached a security cordon as Kadyrov was sitting down to talk with VIP guests. Media reports say they had press passes and shoulder bags along with a microphone and a video camera.

"Let us through, we want to catch [Kadyrov's] final words," one of the women shouted as Kadyrov's personal bodyguards intercepted them about ten feet from their target. That's when a woman who was identified as Larisa Musalayeva, thirty-one, pushed a detonator button, setting off the nail bomb around her waist. The explosion left only her head and killed twenty-six other people, including a second Black Widow, Zulai Abdurzakova. One hundred others were wounded. Though drenched in blood, Kadyrov, shielded by his bodyguards (four of whom were killed), again walked away unscathed. The media says that the shakhida carried out the bombing in retaliation for the death of her brother a few weeks earlier.

Like before, Maskhadov played Arafat's role by denying any responsibility for the pair of attacks: "The Chechen President does not lead people who blow up themselves and others." But Basayev does, and he proudly claimed credit for them: "By the grace of Allah, mujahideen fighters from our suicide . . . brigade carried out two successful operations against the Russian occupiers and their local lackeys."

Basayev proclaimed, "We are the warriors of Allah," and promised, "This [terror] whirlwind will soon be everywhere." Twenty-one days later, on 4 June, it touched down at a bus stop near the Prokhladny Russian air forces base in Mozdok, North Ossetia, killing eighteen people. This time the amir of death dispatched a young woman, Lidiya (Lida) Khaldykhoroyeva, to target a bus carrying helicopter pilots flying combat missions into Chechnya. For two days, she patiently stalked her target, deliberately passing up opportunities to strike other military targets. When the regularly scheduled base bus carrying the pilots stopped at a railroad crossing to pick up its last load of passengers, the girl, wearing a light overcoat with her shrapnel-filled bomb hidden underneath, asked to be let on. The driver refused and she detonated her bomb.

Why are these Chechen women killing themselves, and why do some Chechen mothers send their children to death? Is it out of sheer desperation and revenge because they have lost their men folk and whole families have simply given up? Some psychologists tell us that this can be the only explanation because suicide and the concept of using Chechen women in combat are alien to Chechen culture and society. But that is not true. During the nineteenth century Caucasus wars, Chechen women pounced on the backs of Russian soldiers at the battle of Badi-Yurt and threw themselves off the cliffs into the ravines below. Basayev had female fighters (two) with him at Budennovsk, and so did Raduyev in Kizlyar (six of them died and two escaped.) The Lone Wolf also employed female terrorists to bomb railroad stations. Chechen women have commanded units of fighters and have been killed in combat too. Some also reconnoiter, set mines at night, smuggle arms, and plant bombs in buildings.

Abu al-Waleed says that Chechen women are getting even with those they blame for the loss of their children, brothers, husbands, and uncles. Wolves aggressively promote this image because it conveniently puts the blame back on Russia for the terror. But Atle Takayev, a Chechen police chief in Grozny, says, "They're not black widows at all; they are just making up these stories about themselves!" Some women, like Aizan Gazuyeva, might genuinely feel they have nothing left to live for and become shakhidas specifically for that reason, but they appear to be few in number.

Al-Waleed says that others are killing themselves because Russians are raping, humiliating, and threatening them in their homes. These accusations are difficult to prove, and there is no evidence that rape by a Russian soldier has motivated any suicide bomber.

Money motivates others. Like so many other things in this war, this is about the money too. Since the Majlis ul-Shura will pay an award of $1,000 or more to families of martyrs, suicide bombing is a way to provide for families and loved ones left behind.

Other Chechen women are sacrificing themselves because of forbidden love, or maybe because Basayev has personally asked them too. It is an honor to die for him.

And there are those like Khava Barayeva who are truly religious zealots. Khava's logic makes sense to them. Even if these women aren't zealots, they may be convinced that becoming a shakhida is a guaranteed way of getting to paradise.

Still others may be killing themselves because they have been kidnapped and raped by Wolves and are redeeming themselves after being shunned by their family. The idea is that undertaking jihad in this way will purify one's spirit. Such may have been the case with an unmarried twenty-two-year-old woman who died in a Grozny hospital after a shootout with police on 24 June 2003. The woman and two Chechen men dressed in camouflage fatigues were in a Russian Army minibus headed for their target in Grozny when they were ambushed by OMON police. The woman lived long enough to tell that she had been kidnapped five months earlier and had been in training for four months in a special camp for shakhids. She was wearing a suicide belt filled with four pounds of explosives and shrapnel but did not say what her target was. The woman, who gave her name as Luiza Asmayeba, was four months pregnant.

"For me, death is the only way out. . . . Nobody needs me now. They [the handlers at the suicide camp] told me I was unclean and should do my duty," she said in videotaped testimony on her deathbed.

There can be no explanation for a mother sending her children to their death. Chechen children have become martyrs to save their parents, though. Fifteen-year-old Zarema Inarkayeva agreed to blow up a Grozny police station after she was told by her kidnappers that they would kill her mother if she did not cooperate.

Basayev's terror whirlwind touched down three more times in June. On 13 June, a bomb smuggled into the nearly completed multi-story Gudermessky district traffic police building left nothing but a pile of rubble. That same day, Basayev's men abducted Sirazhdin Zamayev, the pro-Moscow Chechen principal of a high school in Basayev's home district, and murdered him on school grounds.

A week later, Wolves targeted a second multi-story police (MVD) building right around the corner from the procurator's offices in the heart of Grozny, but this time unsuccessfully. The suicide scenario was the same as in Grozny and Znamenskoye. A man and a woman crashed an explosives-filled military KamAZ truck through the outer perimeter metal fence but failed to penetrate the large concrete barriers providing a second defense perimeter around the building, falling short of their target by three hundred feet. Police gunfire into the truck detonated more than a metric ton and a half of explosives. Besides leaving a huge hole in the street and breaking glass everywhere, the blast killed six people and wounded another thirty-six, mostly residents of adjacent apartment buildings.

Fragments of a passport found at the scene point to nineteen-year-old Zakir Abdulzhaliyev from the village of Tykyi-Mekteb in the Stavropoli krai as the driver. A Nogai (an ethic group found in the North Caucasus) by nationality and a Sunni Muslim, he was wanted for draft dodging and had been hiding out with Nogai diasporas in Dagestan and Chechnya.

Basayev's tactical objectives in terrorizing Chechnya are to kill "infidel occupiers" and their collaborators, eliminate the pro-Moscow Chechen leadership before the October 2003 Chechen presidential election and the December parliamentary elections, and demonstrate to the Chechen people—and the world—that Basayev and Maskhadov are as much in charge of Chechnya as President Putin and Kadyrov.

WHAT'S AHEAD—ARE WOLVES THINKING GLOBALLY TOO?

Terror against Russia since the summer 2002 reorganization has been focused and well planned, organized, and executed. While this testifies to the effectiveness of the summer 2002 reorganization, it also demonstrates Basayev's dominant position in the Majlis ul-Shura, his leadership and organizational skills, and his Che Guevara–like strength and determination to fight Russia to the end. Wolves have built a competent terror organization with good intelligence, counterintelligence, training, technical, logistics, and operational capabilities. Basayev has also built a rich cadre of female suicide terrorists. Most importantly, the intensity of the terror is increasing. Unless Basayev and Maskhadov are killed soon and their financial networks destroyed—and unless Russia seriously deals with its own internal corruption, which is facilitating terrorism—the terror will become even more deadly, maybe chemical, biological, or even nuclear.

As horrible as the terror acts in Chechnya were in the winter of 2002 and spring of 2003, they did not extract the kind of "maximum damage" that Basayev promised after Dubrovka. That requires another sensational act of terrorism in a major Russian city or a strike against a "strategic property" in Russia or assets abroad resulting in significant Russian or foreign civilian casualties, or the assassination of Kadyrov. The Kremlin should expect such an event before the first anniversary of the Dubrovka siege.

A June 2003 discovery of a large cache of explosives in a Moscow suburb may have precluded an early summer attack in that city. And the FSB says that it thwarted a suicide truck bombing in Saint Petersburg during the huge tricentennial celebrations there in early June 2003. Police say the planned attack was linked to the seizure of two more KamAZ trucks filled with explosives during a security dragnet in North Ossetia following the May Znamenskoye bombing.

Despite pro-Moscow Chechen and Russian proclamations that "there is no war, only bandits" left in Chechnya and that "the Chechen war is as good as over—it's rather virtual than actual," it is genuinely difficult to see an end to this war any time soon. In guerrilla action alone, Wolves are killing more federal troops and Chechen police every day than ever before, possibly making the losses since the summer 2002 reorganization greater than in any other recent period of war. The summer 2003 return of a Russian artillery battalion to Chechnya that had been earlier withdrawn shows Moscow's concern for these kinds of casualties.

The war will also surely spread beyond the geography of the North Caucasus and the territory of Russia, presenting a new source of international terrorism. There is already evidence of this. Just a week before the December 2002 Grozny attack, French counterintelligence organs investigating al Qaeda activities and the recruitment of French nationals to fight in Chechnya uncovered a Wolves' terrorist cell in the advanced stages of an operation to attack the Russian embassy in Paris. French counterterrorism Judge Jean-Louis Bruguiere ordered the arrest of nine members of the Paris "Chechen Network." At least three of those arrested—Merouane Benahmed (a French Algerian, a former member of the Algerian Armed Islamic Group, and a bomb-making and electronics expert); Menad Benchellali (a French national who is the cell's chemical expert and whose brother, Mourad Benchellali, is being held by the United States at Guantanamo Bay, Cuba); and Nourredine Merabet (a French Moroccan)—had trained in Afghanistan and fought in Chechnya. They had also recently trained in toxic substances with al Qaeda in the Pankisi Gorge, after which they met with unnamed "Chechen military chiefs" to plan operations against Russian targets in France. "We know that some of the suspects were trained with Chechens in Georgia and Chechnya. The Chechens are experts in chemical warfare," Judge Bruguiere concludes.

Chechen Network members confessed that they intended to carry out terror attacks, including chemical weapons attacks, against Russian targets in France. One cell member admitted that he had practiced bomb building in the Pankisi Gorge with the goal of targeting Russians abroad as well as Jews in Israel. Chemical lists and diagrams for chemical formulas for making explosives and toxic gases, along with electronic components to detonate explosives, a CBW protective suit, unidentified chemicals in hair shampoo bottles, and forged passports were found in the terrorists' hideout.

Those arrested have also been linked to al Qaeda and radical Islamic terrorist cells in Germany, Great Britain, and Spain. Benahmed, Merabet, Benchellali, and a fourth person, Ahmed Belhout, had earlier worked with a sixteen-member al Qaeda cell in Spain to purchase and smuggle military materials into Chechnya. Spanish police broke up the cell in January 2003. Spanish Interior Minister Angel Acebes said that the cell had been supplying Wolves with "the latest generation communications means and other kinds of equipment." Several members of the cell were later implicated in the September 2001 attack on the World Trade Center.

Another al Qaeda trained, funded, and affiliated organization, the Asbat al-Ansar (a.k.a. Usbat al-Ansar) has also helped Wolves. Asbat al-Ansar is based in a refugee camp in Lebanon and is tied to the Palestinian terrorist Munir Maqdah and the Takfir-al-Hijra group. According to the Australian government, when Khattab was alive, al-Ansar sent fighters and resources to Chechnya. In January 2001, two Ansar members launched an RPG attack against the Russian embassy in Beirut, Lebanon, killing a guard and wounding eight other people. One terrorist was killed and the other captured. Several Ansar members later tried to break into the embassy but were stopped by Lebanese security forces.

France has further linked Merouane Benahmed to Rabah Kadre, a thirty-five-year-old Algerian-born senior European al Qaeda figure arrested in Great Britain in January 2003 in connection with toxic ricin production. The French interior minister also suggests a link between traces of ricin found in two small flasks in a Gare de Lyon train station luggage locker and the Chechen Network.

The existence of the Chechen Network indicates that Basayev probably planned a coordinated terror attack abroad to roughly coincide with the December 2002 Grozny government building bombing. More importantly, though, it provides the first evidence that Wolves are thinking about international terror operations and are accordingly organizing with al Qaeda's help.

The Paris Chechen Network also raises fresh questions about the evolving character of the Wolves' relationship with Osama bin Laden and al Qaeda. In 2002, the U.S. government conceded that "there is no question that there is an international terrorist presence in Chechnya that has links to Osama bin Laden." It may be the case that the relationship is considerably more complicated and dynamic than the statement implies—and is still evolving.

As far back as 1996, President Yeltsin accused Dudayev and the Chechen leadership of being part of an international conspiracy to establish an Islamic state in the North Caucasus in order to block Russia's access to the Black and Caspian Seas. Russian newspapers at the time portrayed Chechen field commanders as being tied to renegade, terrorist Islamic states.

On 7 March 1996, President Yeltsin ordered the FSB to get busy and uncover all Chechen international connections. He was on the right track. Nine months later, Dr. Ayman al-Zawahiri—now Osama bin Laden's partner and, according to Israeli intelligence, the "operational brains" behind the 11 September 2001 attack on the United States—accompanied by Chechen guides, crossed the border into Dagestan and headed for Chechnya. The head of the Egyptian Islamic Jihad cell in Azerbaijan and another Islamic militant were with him. Zawahiri, traveling under a Sudanese passport with the name Abdullah Imam Mohammed Amin, was extremely well documented to disguise his true identity. In actuality he was head of the Egyptian Islamic Jihad, on the run, and desperate to establish a new base of operation. From what he had heard from Khattab, Chechnya sounded like the right place for him.

Andrew Higgins and Alan Cullison wrote in their July 2002 *Wall Street Journal* exposé of Zawahiri's trip to Russia (based on files in Zawahiri's computer, which was found in Kabul; court documents; and interviews with Russian investigators) that immediately after he entered Dagestan, Zawahiri and his friends were picked up by the Russian police on a visa violation and put in jail. Zawahiri and company spent the next five months in a Makhachkala jail pending an FSB investigation to verify their identities and trial.

Despite the discrepancies found in Zawahiri's documents and business contacts, his true identity and the identities of his friends were apparently not uncovered. Zawahiri told the judge that he had come to Russia to find out about the price of leather, medicine, and other goods, and that he was ignorant of Russia's visa regime. Mr. Amin's piety—he kept dropping to his knees and praying during court proceedings—along with a good dose of money, may have swayed the judge, who rejected the prosecutor's recommendation of a three-year prison sentence, giving Zawahiri and his friends six months, counting the five months they had already served, instead.

"God blinded them to our identities," Zawahiri wrote in his diary. Zawahiri had had enough of the North Caucasus—it had given him an ulcer. He left to join up with Osama bin Laden instead. Another man who tried to make it to Chechnya was Khalid Sheikh Mohammed, the mastermind of the 11 September 2001 attack on America. He had arranged to meet with Khattab in the spring of 1997, but, being unable to transit Azerbaijan, turned around and went back to Pakistan. Shortly afterward, he too joined Osama bin Laden.

A year later, Osama bin Laden called a June emergency session of the Islamic League. It met in Kandahar, Afghanistan, and was attended by one hundred or so international delegates, including at least one "Chechen." That delegate was surely Khattab, which would explain his failure to participate in the Gudermes Wahhabi uprising that summer.

Global ideological and terrorist action plans were adopted at the Kandahar meeting chaired by Osama bin Laden. The idea of reuniting Chechnya and Dagestan, by force if necessary, and thoughts on how to finance the effort were almost certainly discussed and approved at that meeting. The event coincided with subsequent sketchy information from both Pakistani and Indian sources that Osama bin Laden would soon deploy through the cover of Taliban assistance a special terrorist cell or brigade code-named "al-Dargo" to help stage acts of terrorism in Russia.

A few months later, the Arab language *Al-Hayat* newspaper reported that a Chechen in charge of Ichkeria's foreign ministry department responsible for Afghanistan was negotiating with the Taliban to give Osama bin Laden political asylum in Chechnya. Yaragi Abdullayev, deputy to Chechnya's Foreign Minister Movladi Udugov, made a special trip to

Kabul to further pursue the negotiations. Udugov publicly confirmed that the negotiations had taken place, but President Maskhadov would say only that "it is just conjecture."

As the FSB pursued Yeltin's 1996 order, Khattab's links to Osama bin Laden, al Qaeda, and the Taliban began to surface, ultimately leading the Kremlin to conclude that Khattab was in fact Osama bin Laden's representative in the North Caucasus and that certain Arabs under his command— namely Sheikh Abu Omar, Jordanian Abu Yakub (Khattab's chief of intelligence who was killed in October 2001), Abu Jar (also killed), and senior mujahideen commander Abu al-Waleed were actually prominent al Qaeda personnel assigned to Khattab.

Khattab's ties to Osama bin Laden became more transparent when a videotape found in an al Qaeda safe house in Afghanistan in June 2002 showed Osama bin Laden using Khattab's videos as training aids. The videotape bought by *Newsday* shows Osama bin Laden instructing student terrorists and then flashes to a clip of Khattab calling for the destruction of the Russian government. Segments that follow document the shooting of already dead Russian soldiers as well as suicide bombers preparing for their summer 2000 missions. In February 2002, Philip Remler, the U.S. Charge d'Affairs in Tbilisi, Georgia, flatly stated that "for his part, [Khattab] is connected to Osama bin Laden."

Kidnapper Arbi Barayev used to boast about his closeness to Osama bin Laden. Basayev says that he has yet to meet Osama bin Laden but would like to. Maskhadov claims that he has never met Osama bin Laden either but says that "international terrorist networks, including al-Qaeda, have established themselves in Chechnya." Of course, he might just be trying to scare Russia, but no one would know better than the president of the Chechen Republic of Ichkeria himself if his claim is true.

Judge Jean-Louis Bruguiere concludes from his own independent investigations that Chechnya and the North Caucasus are today being used as a practical training ground for al Qaeda operatives who are getting dispatched to Europe to commit acts of terror. There is logic in this: "Chechnya is closer to Europe than Afghanistan," he says.

Judge Bruguiere is right. The mother of Ahmed al-Ghamdi, one of the hijackers aboard the airliner that crashed into the south tower of the World Trade Center in New York, says that her son had also trained in Afghanistan and fought in Chechnya before getting his World Trade Center assignment.

The family of Khalid Almindhar, another of the 9/11 terrorists whom the CIA described as an "al Qaeda veteran," says that he spent time in Chechnya after training in Afghanistan in 1996. As many as half of the

9/11 hijackers, including Mohamed Atta, either had spent time in Chechnya in the interwar period, fought in the first year or so of the second Chechen war, or had intended to go and fight in Chechnya.

Mounir al-Motassadeq, who was convicted in Germany in February 2003 as an accomplice to the 9/11 hijackers, told the court that al Qaeda's Hamburg cell members and several of the hijackers originally went to Afghanistan in the fall of 1999 for training. Some were supposed to go on to Chechnya after that but received their U.S. assignments instead. They were recruited by Mohamedou Ould Slahi (a.k.a. Abu Musab), al Qaeda's operative in Germany. Zacarias Moussaoui, the "twentieth hijacker," also recruited fighters to go to Chechnya for practical fighting experience.

There is also evidence that Chechen Wolves are integrating into al Qaeda fighting units. Chechens were found in al Qaeda units in Afghanistan in 2001, in Pakistan in 2002, and in Iraq in 2003.

The Pentagon publicly acknowledged that Chechen nationals fought in the defense of Kunduz, Afghanistan. U.S. troops also clashed with them in Operation Anaconda. "There are lots of them and they sure know how to fight," one American officer told *Agence France-Presse*. General Tommy Franks, the commander of U.S. forces in Afghanistan, announced, "The number of nationalities represented in the detainees we have [captured in Afghanistan] is about thirty-five and, to be sure, the Chechen nationality is represented among those nations." Other Chechens captured in Afghanistan by the Northern Alliance forces were immediately turned over to Russia. Those who escaped from Afghanistan are either still with al Qaeda holed up somewhere, hiding out in the Pankisi Gorge, or have been reintegrated back into Basayev's and Maskhadov's forces.

There is more. In June 2002, Pakistani troops assaulting an al Qaeda hideout on the border of Afghanistan killed two Chechen fighters and captured a third—a fifteen-year-old boy. The remaining Chechens fled, but not before killing ten Pakistani troops in a fierce gun battle. Four of those who got away were killed a month later in a gunfight with Pakistani police at a security checkpoint. They were on their way to Peshawar, escorted by an undercover Pakistani military intelligence agent who had represented himself as a member of the Harkat-ul-Ansar terrorist organization, when they were cornered by police and killed.

More Chechen fighters were killed and captured on 15 June 2004 when Pakistani troops stopped their minibus for a document check in the Southern Waziristan province bordering Afghanistan. Four days earlier, Pakistani soldiers had killed thirty-five terrorists, some of whom were Chechens, in a ground and air operation against al Qaeda and Taliban hideouts in the province. Udugov denies that there are any "Chechen units" in Pakistan or Afghanistan.

The presence of al Qaeda in the Pankisi Gorge for nearly a year after fleeing Afghanistan in 2001 also provided new opportunities for Wolves and al Qaeda to work together and further integrate as indicated by the formation of the Paris terrorist cell and even a reported visit by the notorious al Qaeda operative Abu al-Zarqawi to the Pankisi Gorge.

In early February 2003, U.S. Secretary of State Colin Powell told the United Nations Security Council that al-Zarqawi had helped plot terror attacks against targets in Europe and Russia. "Members of Zarqawi's network say their goal was to kill Russians with toxins," Powell told the Security Council. He also established a direct link between al-Zarqawi and members of the Paris Chechen Network, but the French say they have no evidence of this.

In short, the relationship between Wolves and Osama bin Laden is taking on new dimensions that include the potential of joint international operations. The threat they pose to the United States is real and is likely to grow before it diminishes. U.S. State Department spokesman Richard Boucher said in his official announcement designating the three Chechen groups as terrorist organizations that "they have threatened the safety of U.S. citizens and U.S. national security or foreign policy interests." The U.S. embassy's Web site in Moscow is more forthright in its warning that "these groups have been determined to have committed, or to pose a significant risk of committing, acts of terrorism that threaten the security of U.S. nationals or the national security, foreign policy, or economy of the U.S."

The U.S. government worries that Osama bin Laden might be tempted to employ Chechens to attack targets within the United States. In February 2003, the U.S. Customs Service urged law enforcement officers to be on the lookout for six Chechens who might enter the United States through Mexico using fake Georgian passports.

A further dimension is unfolding with the war in Iraq. Either those Chechens who were already in Iraq or a fresh group of mercenaries (or both) joined other Muslim volunteers from Algeria, Tunis, Egypt, and Saudi Arabia in fighting coalition forces in the city of Nasiyria and elsewhere. A half dozen or so were killed in Iraq by coalition forces.

More Chechens are now, in 2004, entering Iraq through Syria. It is unclear how many, but Dr. Alexei Maleshenko of the Carnegie Center in Moscow says, "Dozens, if not hundreds, of Chechens have headed to Iraq to fight the U.S. occupation." Coalition intelligence indicates the number is around three hundred.

If closer logistical, manpower, financial, and operational cooperation with al Qaeda are evolving, there is ideological agreement too. However, much of the Western press still wants to portray "Chechens" as fighting only to oust "foreign occupiers from their homeland," "gain independence from a former imperialist power," and "be left alone." Chechnya is still painted as "something isolated." Two prominent May and June 2003 journal articles concluded that "Chechens have not signed on to the worldwide Jihad vision of al-Qaeda" and they "are not conducting an al-Qaeda style, ideologically motivated Jihad."

It is true that there are purely Chechen separatists fighting in Chechnya, but, in both proclamation and deed, Basayev and Maskhadov are clearly conducting an "al-Qaeda style, ideologically motivated Jihad." Why did Barayev seize Dubrovka and dress his Black Widows in traditional black Islamic robes with veils covering their faces if not to underscore their Islamic identities to the world? And why are Wolves trying so hard to gain worldwide recognition as genuine international Islamic terrorists? Is it only for the money?

One Russian diplomat told me that he believes Movsar Barayev's real mission at Dubrovka was to impress Osama bin Laden. Dubrovka did make a huge impression on the Islamists' commander in chief. He included the Moscow siege in his November 2002 audiotaped list of al Qaeda targets (along with Tunisia, Yemen, Karachi, Kuwait, and Bali, Indonesia) struck since the attack on the World Trade Center and the Pentagon in 2001. Moreover, Osama bin Laden reminded President Putin, "If you were distressed by the killing of your nationals in Moscow, remember ours in Chechnya."

Movladi Udugov long ago signed on to the worldwide jihad vision of al Qaeda. If fact, if it were up to him, Wolves would become al Qaeda's front line fighters today. "We are ready to become the vanguard of Muslim nations and the defenders of Islam worldwide," he proclaimed to the world when Osama bin Laden called on Muslims to "deploy on all fronts" to fight the evil "Crusader Coalition" in early 2003.

Udugov tells Muslims of the world that the United States and Russia are the principal perpetrators of the present worldwide attack on Islam and that Russia is doing America's dirty work in the North Caucasus because the United States cannot personally be the policeman there itself: "Russia is serving the world's policeman—the United States . . . as an instrument to suppress Islam in exchange for economic aid."

Zelimkhan Yandarbiyev signed on too—the United Nations Security Council in June 2003 added his name to its list of people with suspected ties to Osama bin Laden and al Qaeda.

The Azzam organization years ago publicly declared Basayev "Islamically aligned." It's easy to understand why. Today, Basayev tells us that the U.S.-led Crusader Coalition has cleverly divided the world up into "Muslim zones of influence" and is busy systematically eliminating Muslims where they are found.

"America," Basayev adds, "led by Adolf Bush and the most dangerous terrorist organizations on earth [the Pentagon and the CIA] . . . is running around the world with its nightstick for the purpose of establishing a dictatorship and subjugating everybody to its world government." Just look around for yourself, he says: "The fact that the U.S. is consolidating its position in a number of republics of the former Soviet Union is graphic proof of it." And what is Russia doing to stop it? Nothing, because "Russia is secretly dreaming of becoming an American satellite," Basayev says. "Today, America is an aggressor which has gone too far. . . . We are involved in a battle for faith. . . . Only Islam stands in the way of satanic globalization and against the takeover and management of the world's economy and values common to mankind. Only Islam stands in the way of mankind's corruption."

No wonder Shamil Beno, Dudayev's Chechen foreign minister and once Basayev's close friend, says that Basayev has "changed from a Chechen patriot into an Islamic globalist."

If the reader still has doubts where Wolves stand ideologically, this pair of May 2003 Majlis ul-Shura statements speak for themselves: "Muslims of the world must unite and become as one body. . . . We must not consider the situation in Ichkeria as something isolated. Our homeland is part of the [worldwide] Islamic Ummah [nation] . . . and our common mission is to establish the law of Almighty Allah everywhere on Earth."

Furthermore, "If we had just had a fraction of the resources and armaments that the Muslims of Afghanistan, Pakistan and Iraq once had at their disposal, then the Muslims of Ichkeria would have [long ago] conducted a jihad not only against Russia, but against Kafir [infidels] everywhere else in the world."

Maybe the Russian president is right when he insists that he is fighting both Chechen separatists and al Qaeda.

EPILOGUE

BASAYEV'S TERROR "WHIRLWIND"— 5 JULY 2003–5 JUNE 2004

It was a warm and sunny day in Moscow. It was also the Fourth of July 2003, and I was on my way to the airport for a meeting with my publisher the next day. The manuscript was finished.

I tallied the terror body count since 23 October 2002 one last time. At least 164 hostages and terrorists perished at Dubrovka. More hostages later died in hospitals, but we will never know how many. Another 233 people, including twelve suicide terrorists, had died since, not to mention the eleven hundred or so people who lost limbs or were in some other way wounded or suffered in terror acts in those nine months.

I expected an attack in Moscow soon, but I did not imagine that on 5 July Basayev would begin an intensified terror campaign that would leave another 215 dead (including fourteen suicide terrorists) and 530 wounded over the next eleven months, concluding with the assassination of President Akhmat Kadyrov on 9 May 2004. As of this writing (1 June 2004) no fewer than 2,250 people have been killed or wounded by Basayev's organized terror since the siege at Dubrovka began.

BLACK WIDOWS HUNT AT A ROCK CONCERT— 5 JULY 2003

Within hours after I arrived home, I heard the terrible news; two of Basayev's female suicide bombers had blown themselves up at a Moscow rock concert. The target was the annual Krylya (Wings) beer and rock festival at Tushino airfield.

221

The beautiful weather that Saturday, 5 July, had turned out forty thousand young rock fans. The punk rock group King and Clown was in full swing when nineteen-year-old Zulikhan Yelikhadzhiyeva arrived at Tushino. After a long wait in the ticket line, she passed through the ticket verification and alcohol control checkpoints and headed for the line of people waiting at the security checkpoint, the last obstacle between her and the sea of spectators already out on the airfield.

"She had a classic figure . . . but she was dressed a little strange," Alexei, a teenage boy behind her in line, recalls. "Despite the heat, she was wearing a light coat with something a little bulky, maybe books or a cosmetic bag, underneath; I couldn't tell."

Thirty feet from the metal detectors and the bomb-sniffing dog, the girl that had attracted Alexei's attention stopped abruptly. She took out her mobile phone and said something to somebody at the other end. But when she adjusted the weight under her coat, she caught the eye of a vigilant young policeman who proceeded to lead her by the elbow out of the line.

"That's when there was a small firecracker like explosion," witnesses recall. Zulikhan fell.

"What's your name, where did you come from?" the dazed policeman asked the girl on the ground lying in a pool of her own blood. The two pounds of plastic explosives in the suicide belt around her waist had only partially detonated, leaving a gaping hole in her stomach.

"Leave me alone, I've failed. . . . I'll not meet Allah now," the girl sullenly replied. Then she died.

Minutes later, another explosion one hundred times more powerful rang out. A second Black Widow, Zinaida Aliyeva (Marem), twenty-six, standing in the ticket line, had detonated her bomb. She instantly killed eleven others. Seven more people died later in the hospital. The crowd, spellbound by the performance of the rock group Krematorii (Crematorium), had hardly noticed the "loud clap" outside. "All I saw was a cloud of smoke," one spectator recalls. Police let the show go on to avoid mass panic and a human stampede.

Zulikhan and her friend Zanaida had come to Moscow on a flight from Ingushetia in mid-May and rented an apartment together. Their arrival had attracted the attention of the police, but, since a thorough search of their apartment had failed to turn up anything suspicious—and since their passports were in order—the women were released.

Zulikhan's passport found at the scene identified her as a nineteen-year-old unmarried girl from Kurchaloi, Chechnya. She had lived there with her father, a younger sister, younger brother, and a stepbrother, Danilkhan, her same age.

Neighbors say that Zulikhan was a "quiet" and "self-controlled" girl, "well known for her beauty." She enrolled in medical college in 2002. According to neighbors, "She studied. She was a cultured girl, a modern girl." But Zulikhan did the forbidden—she fell in love with her stepbrother, Danilkhan (or "Zhaga" as she intimately called him). Several months before her appearance in Moscow, she ran off with him to Dagestan.

The need to honorably absolve herself of the guilt and shame of her incestuous relationship with her stepbrother so they could be together in paradise and she could escape the wrath of her relatives on earth clearly motivated her to become a shakhida. April 2003 entries from her diary, as well as an undelivered letter to Zhaga found in her pocket at Tushino, show that she saw martyrdom as the only way to get to heaven and be with Zhaga. Contrary to what the media reported, her brother did not force her to become a shakhida.

"My dear Zhaga is leaving this evening," she wrote on 14 April. "I will miss him terribly, but soon he'll come for me. . . . We had such a happy time today, but something within my soul isn't right. I laugh, but inside my heart cries. . . . This night I cried myself to sleep. I need him so much."

"Zarema, Nuseiba, Khadishta and I laughed and joked," Zulikhan wrote on 15 April, "but all the time my heart was aching and wanting Zhaga so much. He doesn't understand how much I love him, how I would give my life for him if I had to. I don't fear death as much as I fear falling into the hands of my relatives."

Her departing letter included the following:

> I have only one request of you; that you forgive me my little Zhaga. Don't think that I don't love you and don't think of you. I don't have anyone besides you in this world and it is for that reason that I became a shakhida on the path of Allah.
>
> Please, I beg you; don't punish anybody [for what I have done]. I am doing this on my own free will—nobody made me do it . . . I don't want to live in this dirty world and go to hell. I am so fearful of this and of dragging you with me.
>
> We are pushing one another into hell and for that reason we must go to paradise together. Makhmad [Zhaga], give my things to somebody. You are everything that I have. And if you like, I will show you there just how much I love you and will love you. Besides Allah and you, I don't need anybody else . . . Nothing else matters to me; not here, not there.

She begged Zhaga to give up the fight with Russia ("Let Allah judge them, not you") and become a shakhid too so "we can be together":

Don't go to the forest [to fight] or anywhere else, just pick up a [suicide] belt and become a shakhid on the path to Allah and we will be together … Don't live on this earth Zhaga. Come quickly to me. I will anxiously wait for you and will never let anybody else have you. Leave everything and everybody behind. They will get what they deserve from Allah; he will judge them, not you. Please, I am on my knees begging you to become a shakhid. I will anxiously wait for you. I love you, love you, and will love you there in the sky.

Zhaga never committed suicide; he was caught in August 2003 and is awaiting trial.

All that is known about Zinaida Aliyeva (Marem), the second Tushino bomber, is that she had lived with her fighter husband in the mountains and had become pregnant but was made to abort her baby on orders from her husband's commander. Then her husband was killed, so she was left with no reason to live. That is the story Zulikhan told Zarema Muzhikhoyeva, the next Black Widow to appear in Moscow.

DEATH STALKS MOSCOW'S MAIN STREET— 9–10 JULY 2003

Four days after Tushino, twenty-three-year-old Zarema Muzhikhoyeva, an Ingush by birth from the village of Assinovskaya, Chechnya, began a long and strange seven-and-a-half-hour terror ordeal up Tverskaya Ulitsa, Moscow's main street.

There are essentially two versions of Zarema's story, both told by her— the first to police right after her capture, the second to *Izvestiya* reporter Vadim Rechkalov a month before her March 2004 trial.

At first, she told police that her mission was to blow up the Push-kinskaya Square McDonald's or the Yelki-Palki restaurant on Tverskaya Ulitsa, whichever had more customers. In the *Izvestiya* version, her target was the smaller Mon Kafe, located at Mayakovskaya Square.

Zarema's ill-fated mission began at the Kremlin's Red Square at 4 p.m. Her curator—Lida (Black Fatima), in the first version and a man, Igor (Ruslan), in the second) gave her explosives, several hundred rubles, and dropped her off near the Church of Vasiliya Blazhenovo with instructions to catch a cab to her target. Carrying her heavy bomb in her big leather shoulder bag, Zarema did as she was told. But in the first story, the taxi driver took her to the small McDonald's beside the Central Telephone and Telegraph office on Tverskaya Ulitsa instead of the Pushkinskaya Square McDonald's at the top of the hill. Not knowing her way around, it took her some time to make her way up Tverskaya. She eventually found Yelki Palki, but the presence of the restaurant's security guard at the door scared her away. She turned around and headed down the steps and through the underground passageway to get to McDonald's on the other side of the street but found security guards in the passageway too, so she turned around and went back up to the street.

For the next four and a half hours, she wandered around not knowing what to do. At 10 p.m., exhausted and scared, Zarema walked into the Mon Kafe restaurant, sat down, opened her bag, and tried to detonate her bomb. But the bomb didn't go off. She went outside, checked the tumbler (on/off switch), went back inside, and tried again, and again. Then she became hysterical and screamed in a mix of Russian and Chechen that she was going to blow up the place.

How she ended up an hour later at the upscale Imbir restaurant at #1 Tverskaya-Yamskaya is unclear. One media report said that Zarema and a Chechen man, Zarub Dadayev, left the Mon Kafe together and went to the Imbir with the intent of finding a more crowded restaurant to blow up. At 11 p.m., Dadayev entered the restaurant. Zarema waited outside, but then the police arrived.

Newspapers reported that Zarema screamed, "I'll blow up this place," as police demanded that she put her bag down. The police then grabbed her, handcuffed her, and put her bag on the sidewalk, but video film from an adjacent bank's security camera shows that she put the bag on the asphalt in front of the Imbir restaurant, then walked over to the bank's guards and said something to them. They or the Mon Kafe guards then detained her, and the police showed up only to put the handcuffs on her and take her away.

For the next two hours, the FSB tried unsuccessfully to destroy the bomb using a robotic hydro-cannon. Thinking that it must be a dud, a young FSB explosives expert decided to get a closer look. The bomb blew up in his face, killing him.

Zarema told Rechkalov that she had made up nearly everything in her first statement to police, including the existence of Lida (Black Fatima), because she thought the court-appointed attorney that had visited her in jail right after her arrest was really someone sent by Igor. Zarema claims that she took Lida's name from the shakhida who blew herself up in Mozdok on 4 June 2003, the scar on Lida's lip from Igor, and other parts of Lida's physical description from women she saw on Tverskaya Ulitsa. She made it all up because she wanted Igor to believe that she really did try to detonate the bomb. She only later realized that her attorney was not someone sent by Igor when she heard the details of Lida's description broadcast over her prison cell radio.

In the *Izvestiya* version, Zarema says that she never entered the Mon Kafe but sat at a table outside the restaurant's entrance as she had been instructed to do. She didn't order. When a waiter approached her, she stood up and walked away. Then she went back to her table. She tried to make herself look suspicious so she would get caught. Once, when a man from another table approached, she got up and walked to the other side of the street and stood between two cars. There she opened a pocket of her bag and fooled with the tumbler—"to kill time, so Igor's people following her wouldn't get suspicious." She again returned to her table.

Zarema finally got the attention of two guards standing inside the restaurant's doorway by making faces and sticking her tongue out at them. When they approached her, she stood up and backed off. "Do you have a passport?" one of them asked. "No!" They took another step forward and asked: "Are you Russian?" They got a second "No!" "What do you have in your bag?" they asked. "Explosives!" she answered, "a suicide belt." "What? You're lying!" they retorted. "So I opened the bag, took a step forward and showed them," she says. "They told me to get out of there, so I walked away."

Zarema had flown in from Nazran, Ingushetia, using her own passport on 3 July. In the first story, Lida picked her up at Vnukovo Airport and whisked her away to a safe house in the village of Tolstopaltsyevo, sixty-six miles outside Moscow. In the *Izvestiya* story, she took a cab to the Rus café near the Paveletskaya metro station where Ruslan (who now called himself Igor) was waiting for her, and from there they went in his car to Tolstopaltsyevo. However, in her court trial, the taxi driver said that he took her straight to Tolstopaltsyevo from the airport.

She stayed in the house at Tolstopaltsyevo with Igor (Ruslan) and Andrei (real name Arbi Khabrailov, thirty-four), "our bodyguard and explosives expert." The owner of the house testified in court that he had rented it to one Igor Saayev, whose real name was Ruslan Saayev, thirty-three. He was later killed in Chechnya in a gunfight.

The day after Zarema's arrival in Moscow, Igor brought Zulikhan and Marem to stay with them. Igor came home the evening of the Tushino bombing and asked if Zarema had seen the news on TV. "They showed me the mountain of bodies at Tushino," she said. "I saw for the first time what it would look like. If I told you [Rechkalov] that I felt sorry for them, you wouldn't believe me. . . . Frankly speaking, I felt sorry for Zulikhan more than the others because I had seen her alive that morning. And if you really want the truth, I felt more sorry for myself."

Zarema went through the ritual videotaping the night before her mission so everybody back home could see that she was a hero. Igor gave her the customary black dress, scarf, a veil, and a piece of paper with a message in big letters written on it that she had to read in front of the video camera. As the videotape rolled, she read from the paper held by Igor: "My day has come. Tomorrow I will go against the unbelievers in the name of Allah, in the name of myself and you, and in the name of peace."

Igor promised to give her grandparents a copy of the tape because she wanted them to know that she was "a good girl after all, and that I would not bother them anymore."

She got her bomb instructions the next morning after prayers. They were technical and tedious. Andrei told her that she would not wear the shakhid belt around her waist, but carry it in a shoulder bag. Then he explained how he had attached the four detonators to the bomb to ensure that the Tushino problem (failure of Zulikhan's bomb to fully detonate) would not happen again; how he had made technical modifications to ensure maximum destruction; how the wires were attached; and how to use the on and off tumbler (switch) to detonate the bomb. Finally, "Andrei told me that I should stand up, face toward the café, and rest the bag on my breast before switching the tumbler to 'on,' so the force of the explosion would reach the people inside."

When the instruction was over, Zarema dressed up to look like a modern Moscow girl—in new blue jeans, T-shirt, shirt, sneakers, a baseball cap, and dark sunglasses. "I looked in the mirror and liked the way I looked. I had never dressed this way. For a moment I was happy," she recalls before she and Igor left for Moscow.

Zarema is charged with terrorism, murder, criminal conspiracy, and unlawful possession of explosives. Her attorney says that she intentionally tried to get caught and did not try to detonate the explosives and therefore is not guilty of terrorism. The *Izvestiya* story conveniently builds that defense.

To further back up her story, Zarema says that she was sent to Mozdok a month earlier to blow up a military bus there but couldn't do that either. "I understood then that I could never do such a thing." She made up a story about the bus not arriving on time as an excuse for not carrying out the bombing.

Zarema also claims that she would have run away from Tolstopaltsyevo if she had had the chance, but Igor constantly reminded her that his people were watching the house. She was afraid they would kill her, a death that would not land her in heaven. So she decided to get caught and hide in prison instead.

Moreover, Zarema helped the MVD and FSB find explosives in Moscow, Ingushetia, and Chechnya and provided information leading to the arrest of thirteen of Basayev's people. Acting on Zarema's information, police raided the single-story house and garage in Tolstopaltsyevo, where they found a half dozen suicide belts buried in the backyard.

But in court, the prosecution stuck to Zarema's original story. The government's chief investigator testified in court that Zarema had told her that she had come to Moscow specifically to carry out a terror act and that she planned to blow up the Pushkinskaya Square McDonald's. However, if the court testimony by bomb experts is true, she may well have changed her mind. They say that the detonators on her bomb were attached to two separate tumblers, so that if one did not work the other one would. "She could have detonated the bomb if she really wanted to," they concluded.

Whether Zarema had changed her mind or not, the jury found her guilty on all counts. Hearing the verdict, she stood up and shouted, "When I get out of jail in twenty or twenty-five years, I'm going to come back and blow you all up. . . . You made a terrorist out of me and I will come back and finish what I didn't do on Tverskaya." But the judge's lighter sentence of twenty years in a general woman's prison instead of the customary "strict regime" may have made her change her mind. "Do you understand the sentence," the judge asked. "No problem, your honor," she said, smiling.

In reading the sentence, Judge Peter Studner linked Zarema's act of terrorism with the fact that she had joined a Wahhabi jamaat in Chechnya in December 2002 and, six months later, become a member of a group organizing terror acts in Grozny. He said that she had been carrying at least sixteen pounds of explosives and had twice tried to detonate the bomb on Tverskaya Ulitsa.

Zarema claims that money, not religious conviction, had motivated her. She recounted in the *Izvestiya* article how her mother had abandoned her when she was ten months old and her father died when she was seven. Her husband, a businessman twenty years her senior, was killed in a business dispute when she was pregnant, so in good Chechen tradition her in-laws took her little girl and gave it to the family of her dead husband's brother. Zarema lived with her grandmother because her own home had been destroyed by war.

Zarema says that she was desperate to get her daughter back. She had relatives in Moscow she could stay with, so she concocted a plan to steal her grandmother's jewelry valued at $800 to finance a new life. She took the jewelry, which was hidden at her aunt's house, and sold it at an Ingush market for $600, then went for her daughter on the pretext of a visit. Her mistake was leaving a note telling her plans to her grandmother, who summoned relatives to intercept her and the little girl at the airport.

After the huge family scandal that Zarema had created, her aunt told her that it would be better if she were dead. So she thought, "What a great idea." Zarema figured out a way to die with dignity and, at the same time, repay her $800 debt. She went to Raisa Ganiyeva for help. Zarema had heard that a martyr's family would receive $1,000. By killing herself, Zarema would be able to pay off her debt and have a little bit left over to help her daughter. It all seemed so logical.

BOMBS, BOMBS, AND MORE BOMBS—
17–24 JULY 2003

Basayev's terror whirlwind touched down again on 17 July when a powerful bomb packed into a seventy-five-millimeter artillery shell along with nails, nuts, and other shrapnel killed a pregnant woman, a five-year-old girl, and two police officers outside the Khasavyurt district police station. The bomb had been in the cargo container of an abandoned motor scooter at the police station. Thirty-five others were hospitalized.

Three days later, police found a white Russian Zhiguli passenger car with two hundred pounds of explosives parked on a street close to the rebuilt Chechen government building in Grozny that Basayev had blown up in December. The car was waiting for its suicide driver.

On 24 July, at 10 p.m., a police dragnet netted three male suicide bombers in Nazran, Ingushetia. When the BMW was stopped, one terrorist opened fire with a Kalashnikov and was killed; the second blew himself up with a suicide belt that failed to fully detonate; and the third escaped in the midst of the confusion.

Three days later, twenty-six-year-old Iman Khachukayeva approached a base in Totsin-Yurt, Chechnya, housing the special security unit of Kadyrov's son and detonated her bomb, killing herself and a local resident. A military review was underway as the woman tried to enter the compound.

SUICIDE INFERNO AT MOZDOK'S MILITARY HOSPITAL—
1 AUGUST 2003

A week later, on 1 August, fifty Russian soldiers, doctors, and nurses perished when a KamAZ truck rammed full speed into the 58th Army's military hospital in Mozdok, North Ossetia. The truck, driven by a male suicide bomber with a female accomplice controlling the detonator, was able to completely destroy the four-story block building, in which all military personnel wounded in Chechnya were cared for. The structure was defenseless because the hospital's security commandant had failed to erect concrete security barriers.

The FSB says the hospital explosion as well as the Tushino and Tverskaya Ulitsa bombings had been organized by Zaurkhan Shogenov from Kabardino-Balkaria, his brother Temirkhan, and their gang. Temirkhan, who provided the communications equipment for the operations, was arrested in late August, while Zaurkhan and other gang members were later killed in a nasty gunfight with police. Basayev, who has personally claimed credit for the Moscow as well as the Mozdok bombings, paid Shogenov a considerable sum of money to carry them out.

Police also arrested Magomed Kodzayev, the Wahhabi leader of Ingushetia and Kabardino-Balkaria, as well as some corrupt police officers of the Kabardino-Balkaria Interior Ministry implicated in the attack.

Maskhadov denied in an October *Novaya Gazeta* interview that he was in any way responsible for the hospital bombing. "I couldn't do that, in principle. . . . I condemn targeting innocent civilians. . . . It was Basayev," Maskhadov said. "He has acted independently ever since I removed him as Chairman of the Military Committee of the State Defense Committee following the Moscow theater siege."

But who would believe Maskhadov, especially after he told *Le Monde* that same month that "Basayev has no links with international terrorism . . . no contacts either with al-Qaeda or with Bin Laden. . . . Basayev has his methods, but he has nothing to do with international terrorism." Repudiating his own earlier statement about al Qaeda having established itself in Chechnya, Maskhadov now claimed that "Chechen fighters have always distanced themselves from al-Qaeda. . . . We don't even know Osama bin Laden."

TERROR PREVENTED AND NAMED—8 AUGUST 2003

A week after the Mozdok bombing, Moscow police seized a blue Zhiguli automobile with two men and a woman inside. Police found suicide belts and a map of the capital with potential targets marked on it, including the Moscow Aerospace Institute and the Kurchatov Institute. Police say the group was plotting to steal a city fire truck to ram into one of the marked targets.

That same week, U.S. Secretary of State Colin Powell publicly designated Basayev a terrorist with links to al Qaeda, someone who "has committed, or poses a significant risk of committing, acts of terror against U.S. interests." This was the first U.S. government acknowledgment that Basayev has links to al Qaeda. On 13 August, the United Nations 1267 Sanctions Committee also included Basayev on its consolidated list of international terrorists with links to al Qaeda.

These actions angered Basayev, who retaliated by declaring the United States a terror target, saying that Powell's announcement amounts to America "accepting part of the responsibility for the atrocities in Chechnya."

BUS STOP AND TRAIN TERROR IN SOUTHERN RUSSIA— 25 AUGUST, 3 SEPTEMBER, AND 1–5 DECEMBER 2003

During the Monday morning rush hour on 25 August, preset timing devices detonated three small bombs on top of bus stop shelters in

Krasnodar, Russia. The bombs had been put there with the intent of killing riders who usually would have been standing under the shelters. But the bright, sunny weather, which compelled people to stand on the street and soak up sunshine that day, saved lives. No one was killed.

Krasnodar's bus stops were targeted a second time on 1 December. Three more rooftop bombs were detonated at seven-minute intervals at separate bus stops during the morning rush hour, this time killing three people and wounding seventeen.

On 3 September, Wolves targeted university students traveling on a commuter train in southern Russia. Two remotely detonated bombs on the railroad tracks blew up cars of the electric commuter train near the city of Kislovodsk. The bombs killed six people, wounded thirty others, and left a large hole in the floor and a twisted mass of steel in one car while derailing two other cars.

Like the bus stop bombs, the train was attacked again on 5 December. Only this time, four Chechen suicide bombers (a man and three women), each armed with the equivalent of several pounds of explosives, blew up the early morning train carrying students and other commuters as it departed from the Yessentuki train station. The huge explosion ripped the train carriage in half, killing forty-two people and hospitalizing one hundred others. The remains of one bomber, a man, were found with hand grenades still taped to his leg. Two of the bombers jumped from the train just before the explosion. A third woman survived the blast but later died in the hospital.

Ibragim Israpilov, a relative of the deceased Khunkar-Pasha Israpilov who died in the early 2000 exodus from Grozny, has been arrested and charged with organizing the Yessentuki train attack.

A JOINT SUICIDE OPERATION IN MAGAS— 15 SEPTEMBER 2003

Nine days later, two more members of Basayev's suicide battalion attempted to crash their GAZ-53 truck (lighter than the KamAZ) into the newly constructed three-story FSB concrete building in Magas, Ingushetia. But their six-hundred-pound bomb blew up sixteen feet short of its target. Nevertheless, the explosion killed three people and sent the building's new roof flying, broke windows, knocked down doors, and destroyed the interior. It also put a huge hole in the ground and left a mess of tangled cars in the parking lot. A man and a woman, both sitting in cars parked near the building, were killed instantly. A third person died at the hospital. Another twenty-eight people were hospitalized.

Ingush-born Magomed Yevloyev, alias Amir Assadula, the self-described "Ingush chief of staff" of Basayev's Riyadus-Salikhin Islamic

Batallion, told kavkazcenter.com that the attack in Magas was a joint operation with the "Stavropol staff" of the Islamic Brigade and that the operation had been carried out by a fighter of Nogai nationality and his wife.

October, the month of Ramadan, was relatively quiet, although four
days before the October Chechen presidential election, the mayor of Shali
and his son were assassinated. This was the fourth pro-Moscow Chechen
mayor in as many months to be murdered. But there were no suicide
bombings on election day. Kadyrov was elected the new president of
Chechnya by a huge percent of the vote, but Wolves vowed to continue the
war and the terror anyway, "just as we did after Zavgayev was elected
Chechen president in 1995."

A BLACK WIDOW HUNTS NEAR THE KREMLIN—
9 DECEMBER 2003

On Tuesday, 9 December, just before 11 a.m., one of Basayev's Black
Widows struck across the street from the Kremlin and just down the block
from the Russian State Duma.

"Where is your Duma?" she asked a businessman coming out of the
main entrance of the plush National Hotel located at the intersection of
Makhovya and Tverskaya streets. Before he could answer, the woman's
bomb went off.

The force of the explosion all but evaporated the bomber's body. "I
saw these bits of flesh, these fatty chunks of flesh scattered everywhere. It
was just ***king awful," a British traveler told *The Moscow Times* newspaper. All that was left was her head, close-up photos of which were published in *Kommersant Daily* the next day.

A second woman, originally thought to be an accomplice, died too, as
did the businessman and three other passersby. The fifty-five-year-old
businessman's body was found face up, in front of an expensive Mercedes
parked at the hotel's entrance. A uniformed parking lot attendant and a
woman in a black dress fell further from the car. A sixth person died on the
way to the hospital. Fifteen others were wounded and hospitalized. One
witness saw three young girls "trying desperately to get up on their knees,
but who kept falling back because their legs wouldn't support them. Soot
covered their faces and the head of the third one was very bloody."

A single female bomber carried out the attack. Fifteen minutes before
the explosion, two women, one later positively identified as the bomber,
had asked a man near the Lenin Library metro stop how to find the
Russian State Duma. The unidentified bomber was in her midthirties.
Explosives had been hidden in a black shoulder bag like the one carried by

Zarema. Bomb components were identical to those found at Tushino and Tverskaya.

The bomber's handler, described as an older woman, short in stature, is thought to be the same Black Fatima that figured in the Tushino and Tverskaya bombings. A new police sketch of her is nearly identical to the one taken from a witness at Tushino.

The bombing came only days after national elections to the State Duma, which was the likely target. For some reason, the terrorist detonated her bomb early. The bombing might also have been intended to mark the ninth anniversary of the start of the 1994–1996 war with Russia. But kavkazcenter.com and Maskhadov's Press Office of Ichkeria's Foreign Ministry said neither was the case. Both initially alleged the bombing was "organized and directed by Russian secret services and military intelligence for propaganda purposes," just as "the FSB was responsible for the Yessentuki train bombing" days earlier. At the end of the month, though, Basayev acknowledged that "[both bombings] were pre-planned combat operations . . . carried out by our brigade's fighters."

BEHEADING, HOSTAGE TAKING, AND DEATH OF THE ANGEL—15–31 DECEMBER 2003

Barely a week after the Moscow suicide bombings, on 15 December, a heavily armed band of forty Chechen, Dagestani, and Arab fighters led by Ruslan Gelayev conducted a bold and bloody raid into the rugged, snow-covered Tsutinsky district of Dagestan.

Some of Gelayev's men arrived at the isolated mountain village of Shaura, located about nine miles from the border with Georgia, late in the day on 15 December. One version of what happened next says that a local inhabitant drove to the neighboring village of Mokok to alert the Russian border guard post there, which hastily dispatched a unit of eight men and its commander to Shaura, but they were caught in an ambush. Another version says that Wolves went to Mokok themselves and opened fire on the post in order to draw guards into the waiting ambush. All border guards died in the ambush. Wolves gutted those wounded and beheaded the unit's commander, Captain Ragim Khailikov, before seizing their weapons—along with the captain's head—and returning to Shaura, where they celebrated.

Wolves departed early the next morning, taking four civilian hostages with them. Russian forces later killed eight from the pack. But despite claims that the remainder were surrounded, that night Wolves seized a second village, Goloty, three miles to the north of Shaura. They released two hostages but took four more after some residents refused to quarter them in their homes overnight. The next morning, Gelayev left the village and the hostages behind.

Two thousand Russian federal troops, local hunters, volunteers, and helicopter units blockaded roads and hunted Wolves from the air. More were killed. Then, just before the new year, GRU spetnaz troops spotted what was left of Gelayev's band holed up in a cave. The dawn helicopter and ground forces assault killed more Wolves and captured five. But Gelayev and three fighters got away. Gelayev's reprieve was only temporary. He was wounded in the hand in an exchange of gunfire with border guards at the end of February 2004 while trying to cross into Georgia, where his wife and son live. Using his grandfather's traditional Chechen "kinzhal" (knife), which he always carried with him, Gelayev sawed through his wrist to cut off his hand but died from the loss of blood. The other three made it to the Georgian border but were captured by Georgian border guards and promptly handed over to Russia.

Interrogation of those captured revealed that most were unemployed men recruited by Gelayev in August 2003 and paid $500 to $3,000 to go on the mission.

TUNNEL TERROR IN MOSCOW—6 FEBRUARY 2004

The scene could have been straight out of a horror movie: ripped chunks of wet, human flesh everywhere; pieces of arms and legs strewn about; even whole bodies beside the rails and in the carriage itself, the epicenter of the terrible blast. The tunnel air smelled of burnt flesh, rubber, plastic, and wiring—and a dark, gritty, fog-like black cloud choked the still living who were painted with red blood, their own and others'.

But this was no imaginary horror; it was the real handiwork of another Basayev-dispatched suicide bomber or bombers, this time on a green-line subway train headed into the center of Moscow during morning rush hour (8:32 a.m.) on 6 February 2004.

"It looks like people in [the second car of the train] have been put through a meat grinder," a policeman told me.

"Glass flew everywhere. My face and hands were all cut up," recalls Lena, a survivor in the first car.

Anna Sergeyevna, at the far end of the third car, remembers reading a book when she heard something like a "hard clap," then "broken glass flew past my face. I thought half my face had been torn off, and then I felt a rush of hot air. Glass was bouncing off the walls of the tunnel and back into the train. You could smell burning bodies and wire."

Denis, in the first car, remembers people screaming, smelling burning rubber, and seeing fire in the second car. "Then a black fog engulfed us."

"I thought [the smoke] must be gas. I removed my cap and put it over my mouth so I could breathe," Aleksei recalls.

Irina, a student, described the floor of the tunnel as being "covered in blood, strewn meat, pieces of arms and legs, and passengers' belongings everywhere. At first we tried to step over or around them, but it was impossible. Then we found a whole body."

Forty passengers are officially dead, but like Dubrovka, we will never know how many really died. "May God grant us less than one hundred dead," one doctor said at the scene.

Nobody remembers seeing anybody alive in the second car: "All were motionless there." But five people in the blast car did miraculously survive. Vladimir Molotkov, forty-nine, was one of them. He had been at the far end of the car, furthest from the explosion.

Elena Prevo and Valeriya Dontsova lived too. "My face was cut up and glass fragments had penetrated my entire body," Elena said. Valeriya and her husband had been on their way to work. "When I came to, I heard someone calling 'Lera, I love you.' But it wasn't my husband's voice. I couldn't find him. I saw bones and meat and I thought I must be dead," Valeriya recalled. Her husband survived too.

This time, a male of "Caucasian appearance" is the prime suspect. All day long television screens flashed a police sketch of a dark-skinned man, age thirty to thirty-five, with a clean-shaven full face, wearing a black coat and a cap with artificial fur. Two other men accompanied him, one of whom bought a metro ticket and sarcastically remarked to the cashier, "You are going to get a holiday" (meaning that trouble was coming). In fact, the police sketch was of the man who made the nasty comment to the cashier, but the comment was made right after the bombing, not before. Later on, police announced that a metro camera had caught a younger man and a woman with two large suitcases boarding the second car. Sketches of the three are pasted to the passenger side, rear door, and windows of Moscow's police cars.

This was Basayev's fifth terror production in Moscow since Dubrovka. Only this one was flawless, with just the right mix of everything: at least five (maybe even eleven) pounds of explosives (nitrate) laced with a flammable liquid (trinitrotoluene) carried onto the train in a suitcase or suitcases; a competent suicide bomber or bombers who held the explosives to ensure maximum destruction; a crowded Moscow subway during morning rush hour; a train carriage with lots of glass (windows); a tunnel blast site nearly equidistant between two subway stops (Avtozovodskaya and Paveletskaya); and, most importantly, a functioning detonator.

The bomb acted like a stick of dynamite inside a sealed barrel. The blast pressure wave had nowhere to go; it could only bounce back off the walls of the train car and the tunnel and increase, giving passengers in the car little chance of survival. If they hadn't been killed by flying glass, metal, plastic, and wood paneling, most would have died from internal hemor-rhaging. The blast was so powerful that the walls and ceiling of the nor-mally rectangular-shaped car, ten feet wide by sixty-five feet long, were pushed up and out. Even the vertical bars that support the overhead hand rails were bent outward in the middle.

Was the metro bombing what Wolves' spokesman Amir Ramzan really had in mind when he told Russian freelance "journalist" Andrei Smirnov in a 29 November 2003 interview, "We shall definitely repeat [in 2004] the *Nord-Ost* events, but this time it will be something of a technological disaster."

"A SMALL BUT IMPORTANT VICTORY": THE ASSASSINATION OF PRESIDENT KADYROV— 9 MAY 2004

Despite the success of the Moscow operation, the three months following the subway attack gave the impression that the strength of Basayev's "terror whirlwind" was beginning to weaken.

"The terrorist is now engaged in hooliganism," a Russian newspaper journalist wrote about Basayev's early spring attacks on electrical trans-mission towers outside Moscow and on natural gas pipelines in Russia and Dagestan. Some of Basayev's terrorists were also getting sloppy. Twenty-one-year-old Zara Murtazaliyeva, who was recruiting Chechen teenage girls living in Moscow for suicide missions, foolishly got caught with explosives in her purse. That same month, suicide car bombers tried to assassinate Chechen MVD Deputy Minister Sultan Satuyev and, a month later, Ingush President Murat Zyazikov, but they managed only to blow themselves up. And Abu al-Waleed was either killed or left Chechnya in April.

There were signs of weakening on Maskhadov's side too. In March, Magomed Khambiyev and Boris Aidamirov, the former head of Ichkeria's "Special Department," surrendered to President Kadyrov. In April, Maskhadov's chief of security and Sharani Turlayev, Maskhadov's person-al bodyguard, laid down their arms too. Eighteen more fighters were killed. And just before President Putin's second presidential term inauguration, Ramzan Kadyrov announced that Maskhadov would surely be caught in a week or two.

Yet despite these developments—or because of them—Basayev vocal-ized qualitatively new threats against Russia in the spring. In March, he told the Kremlin that he would not only blow up natural gas pipelines, but poison, start fires, bomb orthodox churches, maybe use chemical and toxic weapons ("we reserve the right," he said), and even attack Russia abroad in 2004.

In April, Basayev added Kadyrov's head to his laundry list, boldly announcing, "We will throw [President] Kadyrov's head at Maskhadov's feet this summer."

Kadyrov's administration dismissed Basayev's threat to assassinate the Chechen president as little more than the ravings of a lunatic. "We have our Raduyev too, you know," they are fond of saying. Painting Basayev as just another Raduyev is fashionable because it is one way of publicly diminishing his credibility.

But Basayev is no Raduyev and to prove it, he delivered Kadyrov's head—figuratively speaking—ahead of schedule. On 9 May, a powerful bomb at Grozny's Dinamo sports stadium killed the president of Chechnya. The 10:30 a.m. bomb blast during opening ceremonies marking the annual World War II Victory Day celebrations over Nazi Germany ruptured Kadyrov's internal organs and left his head and body torn and ripped from the flying chunks of concrete, brick, and steel.

"We apologize to the President of the Chechen Republic of Ichkeria Aslan Maskhadov for being unable to literally throw Kadyrov's head at his feet as we had promised a month ago," Basayev smugly conceded.

The bomb killed others too; the list of the dead and wounded reading like a Chechnya's "Who's Who." The dead included Khusein Isayev, head of Chechnya's State Council; Adam Baisultanov, chief of State Council security; Eli Isayev, Chechnya's finance minister; Adlan Khasanov, a Reuters photographer and television cameraman who was filming the event; and two of Kadyrov's bodyguards. An eight-year-old girl died as well. Chechnya's emergency center reported twenty-four dead, but the official government count is only seven.

Among the wounded were Chechen economics minister Abdul Magomadov; presidential press secretary Abdulbek Vakhayev; Alum Alkhanov, Chechnya's MVD chief; General Valery Baranov, commandant of federal forces in the North Caucasus, who lost his leg; Grigoriy Fomenko, the Russian military commandant of Chechnya; and Chechen film star Tamara Dadashyeva, who had just finished singing "My Chechnya." Sixty others were hospitalized or treated at the scene. The families of some simply carried them off without medical treatment.

The bomb had been neatly packed inside a 152-millimeter artillery shell and embedded in the new concrete structure of the stadium's VIP section, which had been under reconstruction since a 2003 bomb blast. Work had been completed only on 7 May.

That wasn't the only bomb in the stadium that day. In fact, the complex was infested. A second device was found buried in the seating section below the blast area. A third bomb—a 1.5-liter bottle filled with plastic explosives—was left by a spectator in the bleachers. And another bomb was found in the gym.

How did Basayev do it, or did he do it? How did he know that Kadyrov would be at the stadium that day? Did he have inside help?

We know that an explosion had been planned for 9 May because a freshly installed detonator wire was found at the blast scene. But Kadyrov was not supposed to be there; his visit was unplanned and came as a complete surprise to everybody, even to his ministers. Some thought that he would be in Moscow until the following day, while others said that he was supposed to review a military parade at Grozny's Severny airport. Kadyrov's chief of security later explained that the president decided to go to the stadium at the last minute "so people would know that he wasn't afraid." The bombing was probably scheduled just in case Kadyrov did show up, but, if he didn't come, the bomb wouldn't be wasted on whoever would be present in the VIP section that day.

Regardless of what is turned up in the post-blast investigation, it is unlikely that the Chechen government will ever concede that Basayev killed Kadyrov. It is too embarrassing. And Russia is saying only that its law enforcement organs are pursuing all leads, including the probability that it was an "inside job." The Russian deputy general procurator for the southern okrug concludes, "Security at the stadium made it impossible for any ordinary person to enter the grounds that day and do what was done." He is blaming Kadyrov's son's private security force—the Kadyrovsky spetnaz, which provided stadium security—for involvement in the attack.

I am convinced that Basayev not only planned and organized the bombing but had inside help from the stadium's construction crew and the Kadyrovsky spetnaz. Building the bomb into the stadium's structure and installing a detonation wire just hours before the celebration required the kind of planning, organization, coordination, and inside help that Basayev is good at. And isn't it odd that the Kadyrovsky swept the stadium the night before and the morning of 9 May but did not find the wire leading to a seat in the spectator section? A thorough visual search would have turned up the wire, but both metal detectors and bomb sniffing dogs found nothing. And how did the terrorist know not to use a radio-controlled detonation device unless he simply guessed that electronic jamming would be in effect at the stadium that day?

Inside help shouldn't surprise anyone because Basayev loyalists and other Wolves are surely buried deep inside Chechnya's security apparatus. Many people I talk to believe this, and the fact that former fighters who have given themselves up in return for amnesty are recruited into the ranks of the Kadyrovsky adds credibility to that suspicion. The Russian military intensely distrusts the Kadyrovsky, and the Kremlin must surely worry that some day the Kadyrovsky could become a serious liability, the likelihood of which is greater now than ever before.

Basayev is claiming credit for Kadyrov's assassination. "[The bombing] will go down in annals of military sabotage. It was executed with meticulous detail," he told a post-op leadership meeting of the Riyadus-Salikhin Reconnaissance and Sabotage Battalion.

"The verdict of the Shariah Court has been carried out against the national traitors and apostates Kafir-ov [Kadyrov] and Isayev," Basayev wrote in an e-mailed message to Udugov for posting on the Kavkaz Center Web site on 17 May. "By the mercy of Allah, the people of Chechnya celebrated two holidays on 9 May, one over Fascism and a small, but important victory over Russianism."

This "small, but important victory" is indeed significant. Basayev can finally be satisfied that he has extracted the kind of "maximum damage" that he promised after Dubrovka.

This bomb has practically turned the political clock back four years. Since his appointment as Chechnya's interim leader in 2000 and later as president, Akhmat Kadyrov had managed to reestablish local political control, earn the skeptical support of the majority of Chechens, and bring back some semblance of order, calm, and stability to Chechnya. He killed many field commanders and got dozens of fighters to surrender; dismantled some of those despised checkpoints; rebuilt a few of Grozny's buildings; began paying pensions; got pubic transport in the city running again; and opened some schools and hospitals. Although he used cruel methods and manipulated his election to the presidency in October 2003, Kadyrov did manage to create a sense of coming peace and stability, giving ordinary Chechens hope for a better future.

But Basayev's bomb has derailed that momentum, dashing the hopes of people and leaving a political power vacuum that cannot be filled anytime soon. Thirty-year-old Sergei Abramov—ex-banker, financial whiz kid, and Kadyrov's first deputy prime minister—will serve as the acting president of Chechnya until a new presidential election can be held on 29 August 2004. And tough guy Ramzan Kadyrov, twenty-seven, now elevated to the position of first deputy prime minister, will run the government. But with all due respect to the boys, Chechnya remains leaderless.

Basayev's bomb also blew a hole in President Putin's "Chechenization" policy. Sergei Markov, a Russian analyst with the Institute of Policy Research, perfectly described its impact when he wrote, "The death of President Akhmat Kadyrov of Chechnya has struck a mighty blow to Moscow's Chechen Policy in so far as the key link, on which it was staked, has been knocked out; the motor which played a very important role in moving Chechnya away from war and chaos towards peace has been destroyed."

Wolves will now desperately try to exploit the opportunities created by Kadyrov's death and the crisis in Russia's Chechen policy. They are guaranteed a fresh influx of foreign funding, and recruitment of fighters in Chechnya and from surrounding republics will be easier now. A new campaign of attacks against "hypocrites, national traitors, and invaders" in Chechnya has already begun. There will be renewed bloodshed on all sides. Ramzan Kadyrov is promising blood revenge to get even with those who killed his father; more blood feuds will erupt as clans compete in the struggle for power; and Wolves will endeavor to kill Sergei Abramov, Ramzan Kadyrov, and whoever declares his candidacy for the August Chechen presidential election.

"The situation is worsening drastically," Interior Minister Rashid Nurgaliyev told the Russian State Duma on 17 May. And Chechen Aslanbek Aslakhanov, President Putin's Chechnya advisor, seriously doubts that the present Chechen government can keep everything under control until the August presidential election.

To make matters worse, Basayev has announced that he has got some brand new "spetzoperations" in mind for Russia. The amir of death is promising "a series of special operations which will deliver a severe blow to the enemy, both militarily and politically." He is pledging that the blows will be "very painful for the Putin regime and will take Russia by surprise."

Whatever surprise Basayev will pull out of his bag of dirty tricks, it will surely be new, imaginative, and spectacular, and will probably take place this summer before the August Chechen presidential election.

Neither should anyone be surprised if Wolves open a "second front" of military-type operations in one of Chechnya's neighboring republics. Basayev, Akhmadov, al-Waleed, and others have long warned that such operations will come in 2004. Ingushetia, in particular, is often mentioned.

For months now, Russian and Ingush security forces have been conducting harsh cleansing operations in Ingushetia to route out Wolves— Chechens, Ingush, and foreign mercenaries—hiding out there. Basayev's Ingush Chief of Staff Magomed Yevloyev has warned that unless the "disappearances and murders" are stopped, those in the republic responsible for cooperating with Russia will be obliged to pay the price. "They will be severely punished," and "Ingushetia could become a second Chechnya," Shura spokesmen warn.

How are Basayev's latest threats being officially treated?

"Basayev and Maskhadov are always claiming they are going to do something but hardly ever do it," Russian military authorities in the North Caucasus say in response.

I also found those who had earlier dismissed Basayev's threat to behead Kadyrov still in a state of denial, dismissing his newest threats as "mere propaganda, not worth paying attention to."

One of them told me, "He is just slinging banana peels."

I worry that this will be an especially bad summer because of those slippery banana peels. I also worry that Russia may be losing its war on terrorism.

24 AUGUST 2004 POSTSCRIPT

Wolves have taken to the skies. The al Qaeda–like seizure and downing of two Russian domestic airliners by Black Widows on 24 August 2004 is a grave development that the United States and the international community must not sweep under the rug as an "isolated incident" unique to the conflict of the North Caucasus. With forged visas (not long ago, you could buy one at Sheremetovo airport), the suicide bombers could just as easily have boarded one of the weekly Moscow-to-New York, Washington, D.C., London, or Paris flights. The terror monster that has grown up out of Chechnya must no longer be ignored by the rest of the world.

CHRONOLOGY OF TERROR

ASSASSINATIONS, BOMBINGS, HOSTAGE TAKING, HIJACKINGS, AND KIDNAPPINGS—A PARTIAL LIST

1991

9 November

Shamil Basayev hijacks a TU-154 Russian airliner departing from Mineralnye Vody, Russia, to Istanbul, Turkey, with 178 passengers aboard. Turkish authorities classify the hijacking as a political protest against Russia and allow the plane to fly on to Grozny, Chechnya, where the passengers are released.

1992

July

On their way to Abkhazia, Basayev and his men hijack a Russian bus in Pyatigorsk, Russia, when police attempt to detain their automobile caravan. Hostages are taken, but the incident is resolved peacefully in the Karachaevo-Cherkessia Republic.

27 December

Three men hijack a bus with two policemen and twenty construction workers in Lermontovsk, Stavropol territory, Russia. The terrorists demand a plane to fly to Turkey and threaten to blow up the bus. After Turkey denies them landing rights, they demand safe passage back to Chechnya.

1993

23 December

Four armed men burst into a school in the Rostov region and seize teachers and twelve students who are taken on a stolen bus to a nearby military airfield. The terrorists receive a cash payment of $10 million ransom and escape to Chechnya in the helicopter provided to them but are caught four days later.

1994

26 May

Four terrorists seize an excursion bus full of schoolchildren, parents, and teachers near the village of Kinzhal in the Stavropol region of Russia. They demand narcotics, a helicopter, $10 million in cash, and weapons. They free all but four women hostages and fly to Chechnya the next day with the cash and hostages. Three terrorists are immediately arrested in Chechnya, and the fourth escapes with part of the cash.

28 July

Three terrorists seize a bus with forty passengers on a scheduled run between Stavropol, Russia, and Mozdok, North Ossetia. They demand two helicopters, a plane to Makhachkala, Dagestan, arms, and $5.8 million. Russian antiterror forces free the hostages on 29 July.

28 July

Also on 28 July, four terrorists seize a scheduled bus with passengers in the Pyatigorsk region of Russia and demand $15 million. The bus is driven to the airport in Mineralnye Vody where hostages are transferred to a helicopter. When antiterror forces storm the helicopter, one terrorist detonates a grenade, killing four passengers and wounding nineteen.

1 August

Chechens Magomed Bitsyev, Saidbek Tepsuyev, Temir-Ali Mazhaycv, Akhmed Makhmayev, and Alavdi Vakhidov seize a bus with thirty passengers in Vladikavkaz, North Ossetia. They are paid $10 million in ransom and flown by helicopter to Chechnya. They are caught and imprisoned in 1996.

Unknown Date

Six people are killed when a bomb explodes in the Moscow-to-Baku train passing through Dagestan.

1995

March

The head of the Russian border-guard unit and the commander of the border-guard post are assassinated in the Botlikh region of Dagestan.

31 March

American disaster aide worker Fred Cuny, along with his interpreter, Galina Oleinika, and two Russian doctors, Sergei Makarov and Andrei Seryed, is seized by an armed gang outside Stary-Atchkoi, Chechnya, on the way to a meeting with Aslan Maskhadov. They are murdered, with evidence pointing to Chechen counterintelligence chief Rizvan Elbiyev as the assassin.

14 June

Shamil Basayev and his "intelligence-diversion battalion" shoot up the town of Budennovsk, Russia, and take sixteen hundred town residents hostage in the city's hospital. Sixty townspeople and police are killed, 143 more civilians die, and 415 are wounded at the hospital. Forty-three terrorists and Russian troops are also killed.

24 June
A bomb on the railroad tracks at the Dagestani-Chechen border derails eight passenger cars of the Makhachkala-Astrakhan train. No one is killed.

1 July
Two terrorists hijack a Domodedovo Airlines Il-62 plane flying from Yakutsk, Russia, to Moscow with 184 passengers aboard. They demand 1.5 million rubles ($330). When the plane lands for refueling in Norilsk, police arrest the hijackers as they leave the aircraft to collect their money.

14 October
A masked terrorist seizes an Intourist bus with twenty-five South Korean tourists, a Russian driver, and a tour guide aboard. He demands $10 million, arms, and an airplane. Alfa antiterror forces storm the bus and kill the terrorist.

November
Moscow's appointed leader of Chechnya, Chechen Doku Zavgayev, and several bodyguards are wounded by a bombing assassination attempt in Grozny.

23 November
Basayev delivers a large canister of cesium-137 radioactive waste to Moscow's busy Izmailovsky Park to demonstrate that he is capable of detonating a "dirty bomb" in the capital. He threatens to turn Moscow into a radioactive "eternal desert." His is the first-ever act of nuclear terrorism.

December
A bomb explodes outside the Russian administrative building in Grozny, killing eleven and wounding sixty.

14 December
Thirty-six construction workers from the Stavropol region of Russia are kidnapped in the Chechen village of Achkhoi-Martan. Some are freed nine months later after ransom is paid; others become slaves.

Unknown Date
Russian Nizhegorodskaya oblast resident Vadim Tsiputan is kidnapped and spends the next five years as a slave to Chechen warlords. He is bought and sold several times and is finally rescued by Russian forces in Dagestan in 2000.

1996

January
Warlord Arbi Barayev kidnaps twenty-nine Russian engineers from the TETs-2 heating plant in Kirov, Chechnya.

9 January
Chechen warlord Salman Raduyev takes two thousand people hostage in a Kizlyar, Dagestan, hospital siege replicating Budennovsk. Seventy-eight people are killed. An agreement is reached for the release of hostages except for voluntary hostages who are supposed to accompany Raduyev in buses back to Chechnya.

10 January
Raduyev and his hostages become trapped in the village of Pervomaiskoye, where he takes two dozen policemen hostage but then escapes to Chechnya, taking sixty-four hostages with him (including five women, three children, and seventeen policemen). Fifteen hostages are killed and seventy-four are wounded in the fighting with Russian federal forces at Pervomaiskoye. Sixty-five hostages are found alive in Pervomaiskoye.

23 January
Muhammed Tokcan, a Turk of Chechen origin and a Basayev associate, along with several other Turkish nationals and three Chechens hijack the Avrasiya sea ferry with two hundred passengers aboard. The hijackers surrender to Turkish authorities after Raduyev escapes from Pervomaiskoye. Basayev says he had helped Tokcan plan the hijacking of a ship.

29 January
Russian Orthodox Priests, Fathers Anatoly Chistousov and Philip Zhigulin, are kidnapped on their way to Grozny after negotiating the release of Boris Sorokin, a Russian soldier, in Urus-Martan, Chechnya. Father Chistousov is shot to death on 14 February 1996. Father Zhigulin is released 160 days later. He writes,

> For the first time, I saw the sun after four months. . . . We lived in the basements of destroyed buildings. . . . People were held captive in a burrow, which was very narrow, and people couldn't stand or move. Later on, as federal troops were advancing, we were moved to the mountains and placed into blindages, where up to 100–130 people lived. This lasted for 3.5 months. The blindages were completely flooded with rain. The hostages were sitting there at a temperature of zero; the Chechens took our clothes away. It is just a miracle that the other people and I survived under those awful conditions.

17 March
A bomb is found and disarmed on a scheduled bus run from Moscow to Krylatskoye.

27 April
Two employees of the Medecins Sans Frontieres (Doctors Without Borders) organization are kidnapped outside Grozny. A ransom of $200,000 is demanded and paid for their release on 26 May 1996.

11 June
A bomb explodes in a Moscow subway car between the Tulskaya and Nagatinskaya metro stops. Four people are killed and twelve wounded.

28 June
A bomb left in a bus in Nalchik, capital of the Kabardino-Balkaria Republic, kills eight passengers and wounds twenty.

1 July
A bomb is disarmed in the Prokhladny railroad station in the Karbardino-Balkaria Republic.

12 July
A bomb explodes in a Moscow trolleybus near the Prospect Mira metro subway station, wounding twenty-eight people. A second bomb in a Moscow trolleybus kills several others.

19 July
A bomb left in a shopping bag at the railroad station in Voronezh, Russia, fails to explode after its detonator goes off at 6 a.m. A man and two women leave the device and flee by car. Salman Raduyev claims credit.

25–27 July
A bomb blows up an empty railroad car on the Astrakhan-Volgograd train in Volgograd. A day later, a bomb is disarmed at the Astrakhan train station. And on 27 July, a bomb is found on the railroad tracks near Smolensk, Russia.

28 July
In Grozny, kidnappers take Frenchman Michael Penrose, twenty-four, and Brit Frederic Malardeau, thirty-five, captive. Both are employees of the Action Against Hunger humanitarian organization. They are freed on 22 August by Russian soldiers closing in on the hideout of those holding the hostages.

2 August
A bomb is found and disarmed in a car of the Volgograd-Astrakhan train in Astrakhan, Russia.

15 August
A bomb is disarmed in the Central Shopping Center in Pyatigorsk, Russia.

16 September
A lone terrorist seizes a bus in Makhachkala with twenty-seven hostages and demands a helicopter and $100,000. Dagestani Duma Deputy Gadzhi Makhachyev persuades the terrorist to release the hostages in exchange for personally driving him back to Chechnya. The terrorist receives sixty million rubles and returns to Chechnya.

28 September

Sandro Pocaterra, forty-one, and doctors Guiseppe Valenti, sixty-two, and Augusto Lombardo, thirty-six, volunteers with the Italian humanitarian organization InterSos, are taken captive after leaving Nazran for Grozny to deliver medical supplies. The Italian foreign ministry says that no ransom demands were made and their release on 29 November 1996 was secured through "contacts made at the highest government levels and numerous interventions with Moscow authorities . . . and contacts with influential figures in Chechnya by InterSos workers."

October

Arbi Barayev kidnaps a wealthy Chechen resident of Goiti Demelkhanov, Chechnya. He receives $60,000 cash and an expensive foreign car as ransom.

October

Two doctors of the International Committee of the Red Cross hospital in Novye-Atagi, Chechnya, are kidnapped, while three Slovakian construction workers are seized in Ingushetia and taken back to Chechnya for ransom.

October

A person calling himself "The Mole" leaves a bomb made with a coffee can and one pound of explosives at the Baltiisky train station in St. Petersburg. A note inside the can demands that the city pay him $100,000 and close a city gas station or more bombs will appear on trains.

6 October

Lieutenant General Anatoly Romanov, the MVD peace negotiator in Chechnya, is left in a coma after a bomb attack in Grozny in an attempt to assassinate him. He later dies.

8 October

In Khasavyurt, Dagestan, a bomb destroys an MVD Zil-130 vehicle, killing one person and wounding four.

17 October

Armed with a knife, a Nigerian national who boards Aeroflot flight SU-417 bound for Lagos, Nigeria, hijacks the TU-154 aircraft with 180 passengers aboard after a stopover in Valetta, Malta. Two Austrian police officers on board the plane notice a disturbance in the cockpit and subdue the hijacker using pepper spray. The hijacker is handed over to Nigerian authorities when the plane lands in Lagos. No one is hurt.

November

Three Chechen men kidnap Vitaly Kozmenko, seventy-three, in Grozny. He is released in late 1998 in exchange for his wife's legal services (she is a lawyer) in a high-profile political case in Dagestan. This same month, Arbi Barayev kidnaps several Russian troops for ransom.

10 November
A bomb blast linked to the Russian mafia kills fourteen and wounds several dozen at a Moscow graveside memorial service for Mikhail Likhodei, the leader of an Afghan war group who was assassinated in 1994.

16 November
An eighty-two-unit apartment complex housing officers and families of the Caucasus border guards detachment is blown up in Kaspiisk, Dagestan, killing sixty-eight people.

December
Raduyev's men seize a United Nations official and his interpreter but soon release them.

6 December
A man bursts into the cockpit of a Krasnoyarsk Aviation Company YAK-40 aircraft during a flight from Krasnoyarsk, Russia, and shouts, "Let's fly to Holland; there narcotics are sold freely." The man attacks the pilot and a fight ensues in which the hijacker is overpowered and turned over to police when the plane lands.

14 December
Raduyev takes six Dagestani policemen and twenty-one Russian Penza OMON police troops hostage on the Chechen-Dagestani border, returning to Chechnya with the OMON police hostages. All are ultimately released at the insistence of the Chechen government.

17 December
Fernanda Calado (an International Committee of the Red Cross Spanish nurse), Ingeborg Foss and Gunnhild Myklebust (both Norwegian Red Cross nurses), Nancy Malloy (a medical administrator with the Canadian Red Cross), Sheryl Thayer (a New Zealand Red Cross nurse), and Hans Elkerbout (a construction technician from the Netherlands Red Cross) are brutally executed in their sleep at the newly opened Novye-Atagi International Committee of the Red Cross hospital. A seventh, Christophe Hensch, is shot in the shoulder and left for dead. The Black Arab, Khattab, is strongly suspected.

19 December
A bomb explodes in a subway car at the Lenin Square metro stop in St. Petersburg, Russia. No one is hurt.

25 December
Masked gunmen execute six middle-aged Russians in their central Grozny apartments.

26 December
Just after midnight, a bomb under the seat in a practically empty subway train traveling between the Vyborgskaya and Ploshchad Muzhestva metro stations in St. Petersburg wounds one passenger.

1997

19 January

Roman Perevezentsyev and Vladislav Tibelius, two Russian ORT television journalists, are kidnapped. They are released on 18 February after a negotiated settlement.

2 February

Robert Hill, the technical director of a Swedish company, is kidnapped in Ingushetia and taken to Chechnya for ransom.

23 February

Italian photojournalist Mauro Galligani with the Italian weekly *Panorama* magazine is kidnapped in Grozny. His kidnappers demand $1 million in ransom. He is released on 12 April without payment of ransom for unknown reasons.

Spring

Six villagers from Zmeiskaya, North Ossetia–Alaniya, are kidnapped and moved to Chechnya. Friends and relatives collect and pay $400,000 in ransom, resulting in their release on 7 July.

4 March

Nikolai Zagnoiko, an ITAR-TASS correspondent, and three employees of Radio Rossiya are kidnapped in Grozny. They are released in June for an undetermined sum of cash.

14 April

Chechen Zaindi Tibiyev seizes a bus with thirty passengers at the Makhachkala airport. He demands a helicopter and $100,000. Hostages are released through negotiation, and Tibiyev is captured alive.

21 April

An attempt is made to blow up a statue in Nalchik, capital of the Karbardino-Balkaria Republic.

23–28 April

A land-mine bomb placed in the railway station in Armavir, Russia, kills three and wounds nine. Five days later, two of Salman Raduyev's female terrorists, Aset Dadashyeva and Fatima Taimaskhanova, plant a bomb in the Pyatigorsk railway station waiting room, killing two people and wounding thirty. Raduyev also claims credit for a third bombing in Bira, Russia.

10 May

Russian NTV television reporter Yelena Masyuk and her crew, Ilya Mordyukov and Dmitry Olchyev, are kidnapped in Samashki, Chechnya. NTV pays several million dollars for the release of Masyuk and the others on 17 August 1997.

Summer
Arbi Barayev takes six Ingush police captive to exchange for six of his own men captured while attempting a kidnapping in Ingushetia. One is killed.

9 June
Austrian Ponter Zaltsman, kidnapped earlier, is released from captivity following payment of a ransom.

11 June
Barayev's gang kidnaps Ilyas Bogatyryev and Vladislav Chernayev, a Russian television journalist and his cameraman.

3 July
Four French employees of Medicins Sans Frontieres are kidnapped in Nazran, Ingushetia. A ransom of $1 million is demanded for them. On 20 October, one of them, Andre Christopher, manages to escape.

3 July
British humanitarian workers Camilla Carr, forty, and Jon James, thirty-eight, employees of a small UK-based NGO, the Centre for Peacemaking and Community Development, are kidnapped in Chechnya. Their release on 20 September 1998 is brokered by Salman Raduyev for several million dollars ransom.

8 July
A remote-controlled land mine blows up a bus in Dagestan transporting Russian border guard troops, killing eleven.

9 July
Dushan Kobach, a Slovakian construction worker, is kidnapped in Nazran, Ingushetia.

2 August
Four French aid workers, Andi Chevalier, Pascal Porcheron, Laurent Molle, and Regis Greves-Viallon of the EquiLibre humanitarian organization, are kidnapped in Dagestan. A ransom of $3 million is demanded. They are released on 17 November 1997 for "a considerable sum of money."

3 August
Klaus Shmuk, the German director of the pharmaceutical firm Vectfarm, and Stanimir Petrovich, a Slovak and director of the pharmaceutical firm Albanaeksportimport, are kidnapped at the Sleptsovskaya airport in Ingushetia. They were on their way to a meeting later in the day with President Maskhadov. Their abductors demand $3.5 million in ransom.

3 August
A former hostage and a political leader in North Ossetia states at a Moscow press conference that he and two North Ossetian officials and their bodyguards were taken captive by twenty armed men as they were on their way to a meeting with Chechen officials. The kidnappers demanded $5 million in ransom but reduced it to $1 million after eight months.

He was finally released for $50,000.

26–28 August
The director of MAGAS, a Russian construction company, is abducted from his home in Ingushetia. Two days later, Ingush police shoot at and arrest two kidnappers who seize a Russian Orthodox priest and are trying to put him in their car. At about the same time, the dean of the social sciences faculty of the University of Grozny is kidnapped.

September
Latvian businessman Viktorac Gryovich and Turkish businessman Isa Andi are kidnapped in Chechnya. The latter is released on 21 October 1998.

7–11 September
Two officials of the North Ossetian MVD are kidnapped in the Prigorodny district of North Ossetia. Four days later, the head of the Federal Security Service (FSB) office in Ingushetia and his assistant are kidnapped.

23 October
Hungarian nationals Dunaisky Gabor and Olach Ishtvan, both with the Churches of Joint Action, are kidnapped in Grozny. They are released on 25 July 1998.

4 November
Swedish citizen Peter Zollinger is kidnapped while working on an airport construction project in Nazran, Ingushetia. The sum of $1 million ransom is demanded. He is released on 21 June 1998 after a compromise is reached on the amount of the ransom.

20 November
Two Ukrainian citizens who had come to Chechnya to bury their mother are seized for ransom.

December
Yugoslavian Milan Evtich, director of a brick factory, is kidnapped in the village of Nesterovskaya, Ingushetia, and transported to Chechnya for ransom.

10 December
A Rossiya Airlines IL-62 with 142 passengers and thirteen crew flying from Magadan, Russia, to Moscow is hijacked. The hijacker, armed with a fake explosive device, demands $10 million, safe passage to Switzerland, and a meeting with Swiss and Russian officials when the plane lands in Moscow. He allows forty-eight passengers to deplane at Sheremetovo airport and is seized when he comes out of the plane to talk with officials.

16 December
Two terrorists seize a scheduled bus with fourteen passengers in Omsk, Russia. They demand two million rubles ransom and a meeting with the oblast's governor, who persuades them to give up without resistance.

17 December
Five Polish citizens are kidnapped while trying to deliver a shipment of food aid to Chechnya

on behalf of the National Federation of Anarchists in Poland. The kidnappers demand $3 million ransom. All five are freed on 9 February 1998 in a Russian spetnaz operation.

21–22 December
One hundred and fifteen Chechen, Ingush, Central Asian, and Arab fighters commanded by Khattab cross the Chechen border and attack the Russian Army's 136th Motorized Rifle Brigade in Buinaksk, Dagestan. Russia says the surprise attack resulted in three dead and sixteen wounded.

Unknown Date
Viskhan Israilov and two accomplices kidnap Chechen banker Vakha Magomadov and demand $1 million ransom. He is rescued by Chechen spetnaz, and Israilov and his accomplices are apprehended.

1998

8 January
Swiss Pentecostal missionaries Daniel and Paulina Brulin are kidnapped in Makhachkala and taken to Chechnya for ransom. A sum of $100,000 is demanded. They are released in June 1998.

9 January
Turkish businessman Akhmed Shetyurk is kidnapped in Achkhoi-Martan, Chechnya. His kidnappers demand $500,000.

21 January
Three Turkish citizens are kidnapped in Nalchik, capital of the Karbardino-Balkaria Republic, and transported to Chechnya for ransom. Kidnappers demand $1 million for their release.

29 January
Vincent Cochetel, the UNHCR office head, is kidnapped in Vladikavkaz, North Ossetia. He is freed in December 1998 for $5 million ransom.

Spring
Jewish businessman Savi Azaryev is kidnapped in the city of Volgograd, Russia. His brothers pay his ransom after receiving video footage of his fingers being cut off.

Spring
Twenty-two-year-old Kazakh businessman Alisher Orazaliyev is kidnapped and held in a basement in Urus-Martan along with Vladimir Yatsin (kidnapped on 20 July 1999). Orazaliyev witnesses Yatsin's execution in early 2000. He is freed by Russian forces.

19 March
Ilya Lysakov, the deputy head of the Rostov administration, is kidnapped and taken to Chechnya. He is released in June 1999.

27 March
Pyotr Markov, priest of the St. Nicholas church, is kidnapped in the village of Assinovskaya, Chechnya, and released in May for an unknown ransom.

April
Forty-year-old Oleg Yemelyantsyev, an Israeli citizen born in Russia, is kidnapped in southern Russia while trying to sell his apartment. A ransom of $200,000 is demanded. He is freed by Russian troops.

16 April
A military convoy in Dagestan approaching the Chechen border is ambushed, resulting in the death of a Russian Army general, two colonels, and three soldiers.

27 April
Konstantin Rysev, Josef Korotzhen, and Konstantin Pridorogin, employees of the Latvian construction firm Latviya Tilti, are kidnapped in Yandari, Ingushetia. One is beheaded. A videotape of the execution is sent to the remaining families to secure a ransom for their release.

1 May
Russian presidential envoy Valentin Vlasov is kidnapped in Chechnya. Chechen officials say that $7 million is demanded for his release. Three million American dollars are paid for his release on 13 November.

Summer
My American colleague is kidnapped and taken to a garage outside of the city of Volgograd, Russia. He escapes on the first night of his capture. Magomed Chaguchiyev, a Moscow mathematics professor, is also kidnapped. He is released after his family pays his ransom.

8 June
Terrorists seize a scheduled bus from Nazran to Nalchik with forty passengers in the city of Beslan, North Ossetia. Hostages are released through negotiations.

23 July
Nine out of thirty members of an Ingush musical theater group, which had come to Urus-Martan to negotiate the release of two kidnapped victims, are themselves taken captive.

23 July
An assassination attempt is made on President Aslan Maskhadov, resulting in the death of two bodyguards. He receives minor injuries.

25 July
Father Zakhary, an Russian Orthodox priest; the acting church-warden of the Grozny parish, Yakov Ryashin; and a member of the St. Archangel Michael Church in Grozny are kidnapped.

August
Barayev makes a second assassination attempt on President Maskhadov.

October
Mishra Raghunatkh, twenty-two, an Indian student studying medicine in Dagestan, is kidnapped while attending a student party near Kizlyar, Dagestan. His kidnappers demand $1 million ransom first from his parents and then from the Indian embassy. He becomes Arbi Barayev's slave when the ransom isn't paid and is rescued only in May 2000, when Russian forces trap the group of Barayev's men holding Mishra.

October
A mine that is attached to a container of cesium-137 is left on the railroad tracks outside Argun, Chechnya.

3 October
Akmal Saidov, head of the social and economic department of the Russian government's representative office in Chechnya, is kidnapped and assassinated after attending a speech by President Maskhadov. His body is found on 3 October on the Chechen-Ingush border with a note attached that is signed "The Wolves of Islam."

3 October
British Granger Telecom workers Darren Hickey, twenty-seven, Rudolf Petschi, forty-two, Stanley Shaw, fifty-eight, and Peter Kennedy, forty-six, are taken from their beds at 4 a.m. by twenty armed men. Their severed heads are found in a bag alongside the road on 8 December, while their bodies are discovered in a forest outside Grozny on 26 December.

25 October
Shadid Bargishyev, head of the newly created Administration for Combating the Abduction of People in Chechnya, is killed by a remote-controlled car bomb after he announces a government operation to free the Granger Telecom workers Darren Hickey, Rudolf Petschi, Stanley Shaw, and Peter Kennedy. Barayev is likely responsible.

11 November
Missionary and university instructor Herbert Gregg is kidnapped in Dagestan after visiting a local orphanage. He is tortured and one of his fingers is cut off during captivity. The sum of $1 million ransom is demanded. Russian and Ingush Interior Ministry troops rescue Gregg on 29 June 1999.

10 December
Mansur Tagirov, Chechnya's prosecutor general, is kidnapped while investigating the Granger Telecom murders. Barayev is likely responsible.

Unknown Date
The body of Russian soldier Yevgenny Rodionov is sold back to his mother. He was executed in captivity because he refused to remove a Christian cross from the chain around his neck.

Unknown Date

Valentina Yokhina, a Russian mother from Perm who had come to Chechnya in search of her missing son, is herself kidnapped. Another Russian mother, Antonina Borshchova from Rostov-on-Don, is also kidnapped while looking for her missing son in Chechnya.

1999

January

Mikhail Kurnosov, thirty-six, the son of a prominent Russian nuclear researcher, is kidnapped from a ski resort in the North Caucasus and transported back to Chechnya for ransom. He is beaten to death in March 2000.

January

Anton Marianov, a journalist with the Russian newspaper *Natcheku*, is kidnapped in Chechnya. He is released in early June 1999.

January and April

Twelve Russian soldiers are kidnapped. They are released in June 1999 following a negotiated settlement.

23 February

Allan Zharabov participates in the kidnapping in Grozny of Anatoly Mitrofinov, President Aslan Maskhadov's Russian advisor on ethnic (Russian) relations. Mitrofinov is later found murdered. Zharabov states after his arrest in 2004 that Shamil Basayev ordered the kidnapping because he was afraid of the influence that Mitrofanov, who was Russian, had over Maskhadov.

5 March

Gunmen in the back of the Askhab Airlines Tupolev TU-134, in which Major General Gennady Shpigun, a Russian MVD envoy to Chechnya, is returning to Moscow, stop the aircraft on the runway in Grozny and remove General Shpigun from the plane. His kidnappers demand $15 million ransom. He is found dead two years later.

19 March

The main market in Vladikavkaz, North Ossetia, is bombed, killing sixty-seven people and wounding more than one hundred others.

21 March

A radio-controlled land mine hidden in a sewer drain close to President Maskhadov's house detonates in another attempt to assassinate the Chechen president. The twenty-two-pound bomb leaves a crater sixteen feet wide and ten feet deep, killing one person and wounding four of Maskhadov's bodyguards.

28 March

ITAR-TASS journalist Said Isayev is kidnapped from his residence in Grozny. He is released in June. The circumstances surrounding his release are unclear.

5 May
New Zealander Geraldo-Cruz Ribero, an employee of the ICRC regional office in Nalchik, is abducted on his way to work. Russian and Ingush Interior Ministry forces rescue him in late July. Three Chechens and a resident of Karbardino-Balkaria are charged in the kidnapping.

12–14 May
Russian Naval Captain Andrei Ostranits is kidnapped in Makhachkala, Dagestan, and taken to Chechnya. His kidnappers want $30,000 ransom for his return.

17 May
Bombs explode in the basements of three residential buildings where military personnel live in the Sputnik district in Vladikavkaz, North Ossetia. The explosions kill five and wound fifteen.

18 June
Chechen fighters attack Russian border posts in Dagestan. Seven border guards are killed and fifteen wounded.

19 June
Ruslan Isayev, chairman of the Chechen Red Cross and Red Crescent Society in Chechnya, is kidnapped.

27–29 June
For three days in a row, major hostage taking incidents take place in Dagestan and Ingushetia. Chechen fighters also ambush three Russian Army officers and their military driver on their way to Vladikavkaz.

20 July
ITAR-TASS photojournalist Vladimir Yatsin, fifty-one, is kidnapped in Nazran, Ingushetia. A ransom of $2 million is demanded from his family. Yatsin is executed in February 2000 because he is physically unable to keep up with his captors as they exit Urus-Martan.

9 August
Polish professors Zofia Fisher-Malanowska, sixty-five, and Ewa Marchwinska-Wyrwal, fifty-five, both with the International Center of Ecology at the Polish Academy of Sciences, and two male Dagestani scientists are kidnapped in Dagestan. A demand of $2 million ransom is made. The second Chechen war starts before the kidnappers can collect the money, but the professors are found alive by Russian forces.

23 August
Twelve-year-old Adi Sharon is kidnapped outside his home in Moscow, Russia, and transported to Chechnya. Kidnappers demand $8 million ransom. Adi is rescued by the FSB in June 2000.

31 August
The underground Manezhny Mall next to the Kremlin in Moscow is bombed, killing one person and wounding forty-one others.

4 September
A powerful car bomb destroys two sections of a five-story apartment building in Buinaksk, Dagestan, housing families of the 136th Military Brigade, killing sixty-four people and wounding 174.

8 September
A nine-story apartment building at #19 Guryanova Ulitsa, Moscow, is bombed, killing ninety-four and wounding two hundred.

13 September
A basement bomb in an eight-story apartment building at #6 Kashirskoye Shosse, Moscow, completely destroys the building, killing 124 and wounding more than 150.

14 September
A bomb is found and disarmed in an apartment building on Borisovskie Prudy, Moscow.

16 September
A truck bomb blows the facade off a nine-story apartment building at #35 Octyabrskoye Shosse, in Volgodonsk, Russia, killing eighteen and hospitalizing sixty-nine others.

1 October
French freelance photographer Brice Fleutiaux, thirty-two, is kidnapped in Grozny. At the end of the month, the FSB announces that it has a videotape on which Brice states, "I am in a cellar with no light, electricity, or window. My captors turn up at any time of the day or night and beat me with their weapons. I have been ill for a week. The conditions are unbearable. . . . Do something quickly." Some sources say a $1.5 million ransom demand is made, but Russia says Chechens wanted to trade him for an imprisoned Chechen field commander. Brice became his captors' slave, cook, and photographer. He is rescued by Russia in June 2000. Suffering from the ordeal and the breakup of his marriage, Brice takes his own life in 2001.

3 October
Russian journalist Dmitri Balbourov with the newspaper *Moskovskiye Novosti* is kidnapped in Nazran.

15 October
ITAR-TASS journalist Said Isayev is kidnapped again, only this time he escapes after a week in captivity.

Unknown Date
A twelve-year-old Russian girl is kidnapped and held in an underground dugout for months before her rescue by the FSB in 2000.

Unknown Date
Twenty-year-old Kiril Perchenko, a student and son of a Moscow art dealer, is kidnapped in Moscow by a freelance kidnapper, transported to Chechnya in the back of a lorry, and sold to the Akhmadov family. He witnesses the execution of other kidnap victims. Perchenko escapes in February 2000.

2000

January
A man kills himself with a suicide bomb outside the Russian embassy in Beirut, Lebanon. One person is killed besides the bomber. Also, in January, two members of the Asbat al-Ansar organization launch an RPG attack on the Russian embassy in Lebanon, killing one and wounding six. Later, members of Asbat al-Ansar attempt to break into the Russian embassy.

13 May
A radio-controlled land mine blows up in an attempt to assassinate Ramzan Kadyrov, son of Mufti Akhmat Kadyrov, as his car passes by. Kadyrov receives a concussion and wounds but survives.

7 June
Khava Barayev and Luiza Magomadova drive a truck bomb into the police commandant's office in Alkhan-Yurt, Chechnya. Wolves claim twenty-five policemen are killed, but Russia says only two besides the bombers die and five are wounded.

11 June
A man and a woman blow themselves up in a car at a Russian checkpoint in Grozny. Besides the bombers, two are killed and another person is wounded.

12 June
A former Russian soldier who had converted to Wahhabism detonates his car bomb at a Russian checkpoint in the Chernorechnye district of Grozny, killing two besides himself.

28 June
A bomb is left on a passenger bus in Nalchik, Karbardino-Balkaria, killing six and wounding forty.

July
Two bombs are found and defused near the Chechen government administrative building in Grozny, Chechnya.

2 July
A bomb explodes in a bathhouse in Dagestan frequented by the Russian military. Three are wounded.

2–3 July

A series of coordinated suicide bombings in Gudermes, Urus-Martan, Argun, Novogroznensky, and Naibyora, Chechnya, kill at least fifty people, mainly Russian spetnaz policemen, and wound 125. Ramzan Akhmadov, commander of the operation, called the attacks "planned actions to carry out terrorist attacks."

9 July

A second market bombing in Vladikavkaz, this time with a bomb left under a car, kills nine and wounds eighteen. That same day, a bomb left in a shop in Rostov-on-Don, Russia, kills four people.

August

The Ostankino television tower in Moscow is set on fire. Four people are killed. Basayev says he paid a tower employee $25,000 to set the fire.

August

A Chechen plot to assassinate President Putin during a Commonwealth of Independent States summit in Yalta is foiled by Ukrainian security services. Both Chechen and Arab accomplices are implicated in the plot.

August

Basayev claims that the sinking of the *Kursk* nuclear submarine was a deliberate act of sabotage by a suicide saboteur aboard the submarine during the testing of a new torpedo. One hundred and eighteen crew members and others are killed.

2 August

A suicide car bomber kills the deputy head of the Russian administration in Urus-Martan, Chechnya. Other suicide car bombings that month in Khankala, Argun, and elsewhere kill at least thirty and wound fifty.

8 August

A bomb left in a bag on the floor of a crowded underground pedestrian passageway at Moscow's Pushkinskaya Square during the evening rush hour kills thirteen and wounds 118. The next day, an eleven-pound bomb left at Moscow's Kazanskaya train station is found and disarmed.

September

Chechens take three senior Russian officers hostage in the Chernorechnye district of Chechnya. Days later, two Chechen men are shot near Grozny's bus station in an attempt to abduct two more Russian soldiers. That same month, an attempt is made to abduct Russian soldiers in the Vedeno region, resulting in the death of a Russian police sergeant.

12 September

A truck bomb in the Oktyabrsky market in Grozny kills a woman and her daughter.

21 September

Three North Ossetian men from Vladikavkaz burst into a hotel in Sochi, Russia, and take five guests hostage. Claiming to be Chechen sympathizers, they demand a ransom of $30 million, a meeting with President Vladimir Putin, as well as the release of all Chechen prisoners held by Russia. Their demands are later reduced to a cash payment of $3 million. One hostage escapes and two more are released, while the terrorists are persuaded to surrender on 22 September.

6 October

Three bombs—one in the Kazachem market in Nevinomyssk, Russia, one at the Pyatigorsk railway station, and one at the Pyatigorsk city administrative building—kill nine people and wound sixty. A Chechen and a former Pyatigorsk policeman are charged with the Pyatigorsk bombings.

9–12 October

A bomb left in a hotel in Budennovsk is found and disarmed. Three days later, a car bomb explodes outside a Grozny police station, killing at least ten people.

November

The market in Vladikavkaz, North Ossetia, is bombed for the third time since 1999, killing five and wounding forty. That same month, the pro-Moscow Chechen administrative head of Mesker-Yurt, Chechnya, is assassinated.

November

A second Chechen plot to assassinate President Putin during an official visit to Azerbaijan is uncovered by Azerbaijani security services. The would-be assassin, an ethnic Kurd and Iraqi citizen, Kianan Rostam, is assisted by Arab accomplices and is said to have been hired by Arbi Barayev. Rostam is convicted in court and sentenced to prison.

12 November

A lone Chechen hijacks a Vnukovo Airlines TU-154 with forty-eight passengers and ten crew members as it departs from Makhachkala, Dagestan, for Moscow. The hijacker, claiming he has explosives strapped to his body, forces the plane to refuel in Baku, Azerbaijan, and then fly to Israel. The hijacker, who appears to have been a mentally disturbed person, is talked out of the plane. Israel Radio announces that the hijacking is linked to events in Chechnya.

7–9 December

Two car bombs at the main outdoor market in Pyatigorsk kill seven and wound forty-four. Two days later, two more car bombs kill nineteen people in Alkhan-Yurt.

16 December

Sixteen-year-old Mareta Dudayeva attempts to drive a truck into a Leninsky district police station in Grozny. She is wounded by police gunfire and is unable to detonate her bomb. That same day, a little-known suicide bombing in Alkhan-Kala, Chechnya, kills sixteen and wounds twenty.

2001

Yearlong
Eighteen district town administrators, five religious leaders, plus 240 pro-Moscow Chechen police officers, civil servants, and informants are assassinated in Chechnya.

January
A bomb intended to disrupt the regional governor's election is disarmed at a polling station in Volgograd, Russia, just before voters arrive. That same month, a small bomb explodes in a Moscow apartment building elevator shaft. No one is killed or wounded.

9 January
Medecins Sans Frontieres' Kenneth Gluck is kidnapped in Starye-Atagi, Chechnya. He is held for twenty-five days and then released with a note from Basayev saying the kidnapping had been a mistake.

5 February
A bomb under a bench explodes in Moscow's Belorusskaya metro station, wounding ten people. That same day, an artillery shell car bomb is found and defused in a residential neighborhood in Kizlyar, Dagestan.

8 February
A bomb in the courthouse in Shali, Chechnya, partially destroys the building, but no one is killed. That same month, a bomb is found and disarmed on railroad tracks in Gudermes, Chechnya, and two Chechens are caught with explosives in a market in Moscow.

March
Supyan Arsayev, brother of the former Chechen minister of Shariah security, and his two teenage sons hijack a Vnukovo Airlines plane with 172 passengers aboard as it departs Istanbul, Turkey, for Moscow. The aircraft is flown to Medina, Saudi Arabia, where it is stormed by Saudi special forces. One Russian stewardess, one passenger, and one hijacker are killed.

March
The Vladikavkaz market is bombed for the fourth time in two years, killing four and wounding four. Also in March, three bombs—one in a market, another at a police station, and a third in a car—kill twenty-one people and wound 150 in the Stavropol region and in the Karachaevo-Cherkessia republic.

April
A bomb explodes inside the Vedensky, Chechnya, district government administrative building.

June
A Chechen village mayor is executed. Barayev's men carry out several retaliatory murders of pro-Moscow Chechen officials, each time leaving a note behind reading "For Barayev." Terrorists also carry out a series of bomb attacks in Grozny, Gudermes, and Argun in which several Russian officers and senior pro-Moscow Chechens are killed.

July
A resident of Alkhan-Kala is executed for treason.

31 July
Chechen Sultan-Said Idiyev, armed with a Kalashnikov and a grenade bomb around his neck, seizes a bus traveling from Nevinomyssk to Stavropol, Russia, with thirty-seven passengers. In Mineralnye Vody, Idiyev demands the release of those Chechens imprisoned for the 1 August 1994 bus hijacking in Vladikavkaz. He demands six Kalashnikovs, two grenade-throwers, and a box of ammunition. He shoots one hostage in the knee and throws him out of the bus but is himself killed by a Russian sniper's bullet fourteen hours later.

September
Kidnappers take a wealthy Russian businessman and his assistant captive and hold them in an oil refinery in the Selsky district of Grozny. In July 2002, the businessman is rescued by police, but his employee is never found.

September
A car bomb in Argun, intended for the pro-Moscow Chechen head of the local administration, destroys the local administration building and wounds one person.

3 September
A bomb in the men's toilet rips through the government administrative building in Grozny with the pro-Moscow Chechen leadership being the intended target. There are no casualties.

9 November
Wolves pay Ruslan Chakhkiyev and Movsar Temirbiyev $1,000 to put a bomb in the Falloi market in Vladikavkaz.

10 November
The Vladikavkaz market is bombed again, killing six and wounding sixty.

29 November
Sixteen-year-old Aizan Gazuyeva uses grenades hidden under her dress to kill Russian General Geidar Gadzhiyev in Urus-Martan after he refuses to tell her the fate of her detained husband. The bomber and three others are killed.

2002

Yearlong
Pro-Moscow Chechen police officers and members of their families are regularly assassinated. In one case, the son of a police officer is tied to a concrete post and blown to bits.

February

Fifteen-year-old Zarema Inarkayeva tries to deliver a bomb to a Grozny police station, but it fails to detonate. She says she had been kidnapped and told that her family would be killed if she didn't do the job.

18 April

A bomb blast kills sixteen pro-Moscow Chechen OMON police. The blast comes a few hours before Putin makes his annual television state of the nation address in which he states that the war in Chechnya is over.

22 April

Ruslan Chakhkiyev and Movsar Temirbiyev carry out a second bombing in the center of Vladikavkaz. An unknown number of people are killed.

28 April

A bomb hidden in a pipe barrier used to block the entrance to the Vladikavkaz market in North Ossetia kills eight and wounds thirty-seven.

9 May

A MON 90 mine hidden under a parked bus explodes as the World War II Victory Day parade passes by in Kizlyar, Dagestan, killing forty-five and wounding one hundred. The bombing is carried out in retaliation for the assassination of Amir Khattab.

June

Three Chechen officials are kidnapped in the Nozhai-Yurtkovsky district of Chechnya. Arbi Barayev's Special Purposes Islamic Regiment also executes a village mayor and, a month later, a resident of Alkan-Kala for treason.

July

Russian humanitarian aide director Nina Davidovicha with Druzba, a Russian NGO doing work in Chechnya for UNICEF, is kidnapped. She is released in December 2002.

August

An Igla surface-to-air missile takes down a giant MI-26 transport helicopter in Khankala, Chechnya, killing 127 policemen, FSB, military personnel, and children. Chechens Aslakhanov, Dzhantemirov, and Saidullayev are charged with the terror act, tried, and sentenced in May 2004.

12 August

Medecins Sans Frontieres' Arjan Erkel, thirty-two, is kidnapped by three gunmen in Dagestan. He is released without ransom on 11 April 2004 through the efforts of the Dutch government and the Russian Veterans of Foreign Intelligence organization, which had been hired by Medecins Sans Frontieres in 2003.

19 October
A car bomb on the street beside the Yugo-Zapadnaya McDonald's in Moscow kills one and wounds eight. The bombing is part of a planned series of explosions leading up to the seizure of the Dubrovka theater by Chechen terrorists.

23 October
At least forty-one Chechen terrorists belonging to Basayev's Riyadus-Salikhin Reconnaissance and Sabotage Battalion of Shakhids seize the Dubrovka theater center in Moscow with 761 theatergoers and staff inside. At least 129 hostages die, and more than three hundred are hospitalized. Most of the terrorists die in the Russian storm of the theater.

13 November
Aleksander Panov and Musa Satushyev are kidnapped by the Yamadayev brothers, a family that specializes in kidnappings, from a Red Cross convoy of three vehicles stopped between Radujnoye and Kerla-Yurt on the way to the Karbardino-Balkaria Republic. According to the pro-Moscow Chechen government, they are freed in a special rescue operation in two weeks without ransom being paid.

December
French intelligence discovers a "Chechen Network" in Paris, France, preparing chemical and other terror attacks against the Russian embassy and other targets.

December
Moscow police catch two Chechen men with explosives, ball bearings, and other material in the outdoor market near the Yugo-Zapadnaya metro stop in Moscow.

27 December
Chechen Gelani Tumriyev, his fifteen-year-old daughter, and his son drive powerful truck and car bombs into the Chechen government administration building in Grozny, completely destroying the complex. Eighty-three people are killed and 150 are wounded. Basayev claims he pushed the remote-control buttons detonating the bombs.

2003

March
Six Chechen police officers are kidnapped in Yalkhoi-Mokhk, Chechnya.

April
A bomb in a Grozny garbage pile destroys a construction minibus, killing an unknown number of people, while another bomb attached to the bottom of a manhole cover in Grozny kills eight.

April
A bomb inside a couch kills Dzhabrail Yamadayev, the commandant of a special pro-Moscow Chechen military group in the Gudermes district of Chechnya.

April
The bodies of two more police officers are found in Nozhai-Yurt, and Wolves kidnap Alkhazur Musalatov, vice president of the Chechen Academy of Sciences.

April
Three pro-Moscow Chechen officials are kidnapped while on a hunting trip and assassinated. Their bodies are found in the village of Michurin, Chechnya. Wolves also kidnap Alkhazur Musalatov, vice president of the Chechen Academy of Sciences.

Mid-April
A minibus traveling on the road from Khankala airbase is split in half by a remote-controlled land mine, killing fifteen. A second explosion kills two rescue workers. One is wounded.

9 May
An unsuccessful attempt to disarm a bomb found in Grozny's Dinamo football stadium just before the annual World War II Victory Day parade kills one Murmansk OMON policeman and wounds two others.

12 May
Two men and female suicide bomber Zarina Alikhhanova drive their truck bomb into the Nadterechny, Chechnya, district government building, killing sixty and wounding up to one hundred.

13 May
Two or three female suicide bombers attempt to kill Akhmat Kadyrov during a religious ceremony in Iliskhan-Yurt, Chechnya. Twenty-six people are killed and one hundred wounded. Kadyrov escapes unharmed.

4 June
A female suicide bomber, Lidiya (Lida) Khaldykhoroyeva, attempts to board a military bus near the Prokhladny Russian air forces base in Mozdok, North Ossetia. She detonates her bomb, killing eighteen, when the bus driver refuses to let her board.

13 June
A traffic police building under construction in Gudermes, Chechnya, is bombed, destroying the building, but no one is killed. The same day Sirazhdin Zamayev, the pro-Moscow Chechen principal of a high school in Basayev's home district, is murdered on school grounds.

Mid-June
A man and a woman attempt to drive a KamAZ truck with two metric tons of explosives into the MVD building in Grozny, but barriers and police gunfire stop the truck. Six are killed besides the bombers and thirty-six are wounded.

24 June
Pregnant suicide bomber Luiza Asmayeba, twenty-two, on her way to a Grozny target dies along with two male fighters in a shootout with police. Before her death, she tells police she wanted to cleanse herself after being raped by Chechen fighters.

5 July
Nineteen-year-old Zulikhan Yelikhadzhiyeva and twenty-six-year-old Zinaida Aliyeva blow themselves up at the annual Wings rock and beer festival at Tushino airfield, Moscow. Fourteen people are killed and sixty wounded.

9–10 July
Twenty-three-year-old Zarema Muzhikhoyeva attempts to blow up a restaurant on Moscow's main street, but her bomb refuses to detonate until an FSB sapper attempts to disarm it. He is killed.

17 July
A powerful bomb packed into an artillery shell left in a motor scooter outside a Krasavyurt, Dagestan, police station explodes, killing five people and wounding thirty-five.

24 July
A police dragnet nabs three male suicide bombers in Nazran, Ingushetia. Two bombers are killed and a third escapes.

27 July
Twenty-six-year-old Iman Khachukayeva blows herself up outside the base housing Ramzan Kadyrov's Kadyrovsky Spetznaz special Chechen security unit in Totsin-Yurt, Chechnya. The bomber and a local resident are killed.

1 August
A suicide truck bomber crashes into the Russian military hospital in Mozdok, North Ossetia, killing fifty and wounding eighty-two.

8 August
Moscow police catch two men and a Chechen woman in a car with suicide belts and a marked-up map with potential targets. Police say they were going to steal a fire truck and crash it into one of the targets.

22 August
Nine Russian soldiers die and two are injured by a remote-controlled car bomb that explodes near their column of military vehicles.

25 August
Three small bombs on the roofs of bus stop shelters in Krasnodar, Russia, detonate but fail to kill anyone. Dagestani Wolves use a car bomb to assassinate Magomedsalikh Gusayev, a Dagestani government minister, on his way to the office. He had long been on Basayev's hit list for his role in opposing the establishment of an Islamic state in Dagestan in 1999 and had survived several assassination attempts.

3 September

A powerful bomb on the railroad tracks outside Kislovodsk, Russia, blows up several train cars, killing six passengers and wounding fifty-four.

15 September

A man and wife suicide team attempt to blow up the new FSB building in Magas, Ingushetia, but fail to get close enough. Three people in the parking lot are killed and twenty-eight wounded.

1 December

Krasnodar's bus stops are targeted a second time. This time three people are killed and seventeen wounded.

5 December

Four Chechen suicide bombers (a man and three women) blow up an early morning train carrying students and other commuters as it departs from the Yessentuki train station, killing forty-two and wounding one hundred others.

9 December

An unidentified lone Black Widow blows herself up outside the National Hotel in Moscow, killing six and wounding fifteen. Her likely target is the Russian State Duma.

15 December

A large group of Chechen fighters led by Ruslan Gelayev enters Dagestan, kills nine Russian border guards, beheads their commander, and takes eight hostages in the villages of Shaura and Mokok. The hostages are later freed.

2004

6 February

One or two suicide terrorists bomb the green-line subway train near the Paveletskaya metro stop in Moscow, killing at least forty passengers and wounding a hundred.

18 February

Wolves bomb two natural gas lines in Ramenskoye, south of Moscow. Six days later, Basayev claims responsibility.

5 March

Moscow police arrest twenty-one-year-old Zara Murtazaliyeva, a Chechen woman from the village of Naurskaya, Chechnya, with a small amount of plastic explosives as she walks along Vernadsky Prospect.

11 March

A suicide car bomber attempts to assassinate MVD Deputy Minister Sultan Satuyev as he leaves work, but terrorists detonates their bomb too early. Other terrorists open fire on his car, but he is not hurt.

15 March
Wolves blow up three electrical transmission towers in the Leninsky district outside Moscow. A Chechen flag is left at the scene. Basayev claims responsibility.

2 April
Wolves bomb two gas pipelines in Dagestan just south of the town of Manaskent. No one is hurt in this unpopulated area.

6 April
A suicide car bomber attempts to assassinate Ingush President Murat Zyazikov on the way to his office in Magas from his home in Nazran. The bomber's car overtakes the president's armored limousine and then crashes into the passenger's side of the president's car. He is unhurt, but six other people are wounded.

3–4 May
Just before and after midnight, two attempts are made to kill Suliman Yamadayev with a remote-controlled land mine as Yamadayev returns home to Gudermes in his car. No one is killed.

9 May
At 10:30 a.m., a bomb hidden in the concrete structure of the VIP section of the Dinamo stadium in Grozny kills President Akhmat Kadyrov and at least six other people during World War II Victory Day celebrations. Fifty-four others are wounded, including members of the Chechen government and General Valery Baranov, commander of Russian forces in the region, whose leg is amputated.

22 May
A radio-controlled mine planted in the road close to the settlement of Katyr-Yurt in the Urus-Martanovsky region blows up an MVD convoy, destroying a police UAZ vehicle and an armored MVD transport and killing three policemen and eight soldiers. Five more are wounded.

25 May
At 2 p.m., a radio-control-detonated 152-millimeter shell bomb buried in the road kills OMON Captain Vladimir Zayev and his driver, Pavel Galutskikh, and wounds two others when it blows up their KamAZ truck. The attack takes place a few miles outside Grozny.

29 May
At 7:27 a.m., two bombs on railroad tracks derail the Moscow-to-Vladikavkaz passenger train near the Yelkhot station. Nine cars are derailed, but because of the slow speed of the train, no one is killed. The bombs go off under the fourth and last cars.

INDEX

Abdulazimov, Dzhabril, 206
Abdulkarimov, Abdulkhalim, 167
Abdullayev, Yaragi, 89, 215
Abdulsheikhov, Arslanbek
Alimpashayevich, 192
Abdulzhaliyev, Zakir, 211
Abdurakhmanov, Kazim, 167
Abdurazakov, Murad, 167
Abitayev, Apti, 74
Abkhaz Battalion, 14–15, 17–18, 75
Abkhazia, 14–17, 27, 242
Abramov, Sergei, 239–40
Acebes, Angel, 213
Achkhoi-Martan, Chechnya, 205,
244, 252; fighting in, 177
Action Against Hunger, 246
Adbus-Salam, Abdul Khalim ibn.
See Khalim, Abu
Adilsultanov, Muslim Salmanovich,
192
Administration for Combating the
Abduction of People in
Chechnya, 74
Adukov, Abdurakhman, 78
Aeroflot airlines hijacking, 247
Afghan Alumni, 35–36, 90, 167
Afghanistan, 4, 24, 35–36, 46, 79,
84, 112–15, 132, 136, 140, 148,
155, 164, 167, 199, 213–18;
Basayev's training in, 16;
Chechens fighting in, 217; sup-
port in second Chechen war,
113–14, 154
Agapov, Boris, 139
Agence France Presse, 217
Agishbatoi, Chechnya, fighting in,
177
Aidamirov, Boris, 236
Akhmadov, Abu, 75
Akhmadov, Ramzan, 75–76, 108,
110, 116–17; release of Kenneth
Gluck, 120; suicide operations,
124, 259
Akhmadov, Rizvan, 75; Movsar
Barayev murders, 182
Akhmadov, Ruslan, 75–76, 147
Akhmadov, Uvais, 75, 79
Akhmatkhanov, Khamlkhazhi
Akhmarovich, 192
Akhmetov, Akhmed
Mumadiyevich, 192
Alauri, Ibragim, 164, 165, 166
al-Badr terrorist organization, 141
Albanaeksportimport pharmaceu-
tical company, kidnapped
employees, 250
Al-Baraka bank, 147
Al-Baraka Investment and
Development Company, 147
Alfa antiterror unit, 189, 244

Algeria, 218; foreign fighters in
Chechnya, 154
Algerian Armed Islamic Group,
213
Al-Haramein Islamist Foundation,
135, 142–43
Al-Hayat Arab-language newspaper
(London), 89, 154, 215
Alikhhanova, Zarina, 208, 265
Al-Irshad journal (Pakistan), 113,
141
Aliyev, Adolla, 98
Aliyev, Ali Maksudovich, 192
Al-Jazeera television, 181, 191
Al-Jihad-Fisisubililah Special
Islamic Regiment. See Special
Purposes Islamic Regiment
Alkhan-Kala, Chechnya, 68, 110,
111, 127, 163, 261, 262
Alkhanov, Alum, 237
Alkhan-Yurt, Chechnya, suicide
bombing in, 122, 258, 260
Alkhazurov, Aslanbek, 159
Alkhazurov, Hizir, 200
Alkhazurov, Idris Makhmudovich,
192
All National Congress of the
Chechen People, 95
Allah's warriors, 2
Alleroi, Chechnya: fighting in, 177;
Khattab training camp in, 39
Almindhar, Khalid, 216
Al-Rashid charity organization,
141, 150
Al-Sharq Al-Awsat Arab-language
newspaper (London), 136, 166
Al-Watan Al-Arabi Arab-language
weekly magazine, 105, 154–55
Alyamkin, Igor, 183
Amir Muawia training camp,
Afghanistan, 16
Amur, Russia, 197
Ankara, Turkey, 13
ANS television (Azerbaijan), 134
Ansalta, Dagestan, 100
Ansari, Abu Waleed al-. See Waleed,
Abu al-
Arab Revolutionary Council, 199
Arbatov, Alexei, 137
Argumenty i Fakty newspaper
(Russia), 23, 26, 30
Argun, Chechnya, 171; bombings
in, 33, 123–24, 127, 262, 259;
counterfeit dollars in, 137; dirty
bomb found in (1998), 198,
254; fighting in, 117
Armavir, Russia, railroad station
bombing (1997), 57, 83, 249
Arnaout, Enaam, 150
Arsanov, Vakha, 43–44, 57, 68, 87,

97; on embezzlement, 137, 139;
opposition to Maskhadov,
94–95
Arsayev, Aslambek, 120
Arsayev, Supyan, 120–21, 261
Asbat al-Ansar terrorist organiza-
tion, 213, 258
Askhab airlines, 255
Aslakhanov, Aslanbek, 187; on
embezzlement, 138, 240
Assadula, Amir. See Yevloyev,
Magomed
assassinations, 126–28, 232, 236,
253, 255, 259, 262–65, 267–68;
plots against President Putin,
118, 126
Assembly of Caucasus Mountain
Peoples, 10
Assinovskaya, Chechnya, 183, 224
Astrakhan, Russia, 53, 246
Atgeriyev, Turpal-Ali, 94, 159–61
Atmikily, Chechnya, 110
Atta, Mohammed, 217
Aushev, Ruslan, 72; on Berezovsky-
Basayev relationship, 139; on
Berezovsky-Raduyev relation-
ship, 63
Avar, Saudi Arabia, 33
Aviso fraud scheme, 135
Avrasia sea ferry hijacking (1996),
53, 146, 245
Aydin, Ramazan, 146
Azerbaijan, 19, 35, 36, 75, 106, 126,
142, 144, 146–48, 151, 164,
182, 214; Basayev in, 13; capture
of Ruslan Akhmadov, 147;
Chechen drug trafficking in,
147; Khattab's post office box
in, 147; Muslim organizations
in, 147; as a traditional supply
route to Chechnya, 147
Azerkhanov, Ruslan, 162–63
Azzam, Abdullah, 35
azzam.com, xi, 33, 152
Azzam Publications, 33, 102–103,
152

Bachi-Yurt, Chechnya, 164, 171
Badi-Yurt, Chechnya, 209
Baiev, Khassan, 54, 111
Baikhatov, Arsen Nazhmudinovich,
192
Baikhatov, Rashid Savatdiyevich,
192
Baisultanov, Adam, 237
Bakar, Abu: as common name, 184;
as training camp instructor, 39.
See also Elmurzayev, Ruslan
Abu-Khasanovich
Bakhvalov, Sergei, 177–78

Baku-Novorossiisk pipeline, 136
Bakuyev, Baudi, 183
Bakuyev, Doud, 183
Bamut, Chechnya, 26, 40; fighting in, 177; nuclear warheads in, 14
Baranov, Valery, 164, 237
Barayev, Arbi Aloudinovich, 4, 5, 40, 61, 67–79, 104, 120, 122–23, 136, 139, 182–83, 209–10, 229, 244, 250; alleged ties to Russian security organs, 162; appearance on Kremlin's death list, 156; assassination of head of Maskhadov's anti-kidnapping unit, 74; on Budennovsk raid, 68; Camilla Carr and Jon James kidnapping (1997), 64; death, 163; family, 182; feud with Gelayev, 109; and Granger Telecom kidnapping, 68, 79; in Gudermes uprising (1998), 41–42; in invasion of Dagestan (1999), 99; plot to assassinate Putin, 126, 260; in Special Purposes Islamic Regiment, 41; ties to bin Laden, 78, 216; war record, 115–17
Barayev, Buharu, 163
Barayev, Movsar Bukharovich, 4, 22, 143, 163, 180–90, 193, 203, 206, 219
Bargishyev, Shadid, 74
Barsukov, Mikhail, 51
Basayev, Akhmed, 59
Basayev, Khamid, 97, 117
Basayev, Shamil, 4–5, 7–31, 43, 52–53, 58–59, 61, 65, 74, 79, 82, 84, 91, 92, 96, 101, 108, 116–18, 128, 132–35, 142, 151, 156–57, 168–69, 179, 189, 198–200, 204–206, 211, 216, 237, 255, 266; ANS television address (2000), 116–17, 134, 143, 152, 163; and atrocities in Abkhazia, 15; background, 8, 11, 16, 20; bee-sting guerilla tactics, 115, 117; call for liberation of Dagestan, 91; character, 8, 28; chemical weapons training (1994), 16, 199; command of Chechen Eastern Front (1999), 172; Dagestan invasion (1999), 2, 92–93, 98–102, 104; defense of Boris Yeltsin, 9; on democracy, 28; in Dubrovka siege, 178–91; education, 8; effectiveness in government office, 31, 92–93; execution of Russian pilots, 22; first act of nuclear terrorism (1995), 25, 244; first Moscow suicide mission, 20–24; and foreign fighters, 19; health, 7, 27, 31, 111, 115–16, 164, 197; heroes of, 3, 11; hijackings, 3, 7, 13–14, 146, 242; hostage taking,

20–24, 51–52, 243; justification of terrorism, 104; and Kursk nuclear submarine sinking, 125; as Moscow businessman, 8; opposition to Maskhadov's presidency, 94–97; political vision for North Caucasus, 12; presidential campaign, 12, 28–30; reconciliation with Maskhadov (2002), 170–72; and reorganization of Chechen armed forces (2002), 173–74, 197; second suicide battalion, 123–24; on sending fighters to Palestine, 112; terror claims, 25, 191, 205, 233, 239; threats against Russia, 7, 25, 199; threats against the United States, 204, 220, 230
Basayev, Shervani, 22, 38, 95, 99,106
Basayeva, Zinaida, 20
Batchayev, Timur, 105
Bazhiyev, Nurdi, 72
beheadings, 15, 127, 181, 252; Akhmadov brothers' methods, 77; of border guards captain, Dagestan (2003), 233; of nine OMON policemen, 33–34; of Peter Kennedy, Rudolf Petschi, Stanley Shaw, and Darren Hickey (1998), 43, 77–78; of Russian soldiers, 26, 32–33, 37; Beirut, Lebanon, 122
Belarus, 151, 152
Belhout, Ahmed, 213
Beloruskaya, Moscow, subway station bombing, 120
Benahmed, Merouane, 213, 214
Benchellali, Menad, 213
Benchellali, Mourad, 213
Benevolence International Foundation (BIF), 147, 150–51
Benin, Masood al-, 99–100, 102
Beno, Shamil, 220
Benoi, Chechnya, 45
Berezovsky, Boris, 47, 61, 64, 83, 118; accusations against FSB (1999), 106, 139; business ties with Basayev, 139; FSB investigation of, 140; government fraud charges against, 140; and kidnapping and people-for-sale business, 63; negotiations for the release of Carr and James, 73
Beslan, North Ossetia, 253
Beyazit Mosque, Turkey, 145
Bimurzayev, Magomed-Emin Saidanovich, 193
bin Laden, Osama, 3–5, 16, 33, 35, 40, 114, 117, 150, 164, 214–16, 218, 219; alleged purchase of Granger Telcom workers' heads, 67, 78–79, 154; alleged visits to

Chechnya, 155; asylum offer, 80, 89; and Basayev, 216; clash-of-civilizations strategy, 79; dispatch of fighters to Chechnya, 154; financial support to Wolves, 153–54; meeting with Islamists in Afghanistan (1998), 91, 215; ties to Barayev, 78, 216; ties to Khattab, 215–16; training camps, 114
Bira, Russia, bombing in, 57
Bitsyev, Magomed, 243
Black Fatima (Lida, Lyuba), 224, 233
Black Sea, 11, 15, 214
Black Widows, 186–89, 201, 208–209, 221, 224, 232, 241, 267. *See also* female terrorists
Bobryshev, Dmitry, 77
Bodansky, Yoseff, 155, 199
Bogatyryev, Ilyas, 72, 250
bombings: apartment building, 2–3, 65, 104–107, 118, 134, 149, 157, 177, 248, 256–57; bus stop, 231; subway station, 53, 119–20, 185, 226, 235, 245–46, 258–59, 261, 267
bombs: bus, 246, 258; car and motorscooter, 120, 185–86, 236, 246–47, 257–60, 262, 264, 266–68; dirty, 198–99, 244, 254; fuel air explosives (vacuum bombs), 101; railway, 53, 57, 83 119–20, 160, 231, 243–44, 246–49, 260, 268; suicide belts, 186, 222, 227, 229, 266; truck, 103, 106, 122–24, 198, 205, 208, 211, 257, 259–61, 264–66;
Booker, Sandy, 180–81
Borisov, Arnold, 125
Bosnia, 16, 35–36, 167
Botlikhsky district, Dagestan, 243; Chechen invasion (1999), 98, 100, 101
British Broadcasting Corporation (BBC), 78, 187
Bruguiere, Jean-Louis, 213, 216
Brulin, Daniel and Paulina, 252
Budanov, Yuri, 33–34, 123
Budennovsk, Russia: hospital siege (1995), 20–24, 50–51, 180, 210, 243; hotel bomb, 119, 260
Buinaksk, Dagestan, 92, 167; Khattab's attack on 136th Motorized Rifle Brigade (1997), 45, 63, 252; military apartment buildings bombing (1999), 65, 103, 106, 134
Bulgarian Academy of Sciences School of Management, 48
Bush, George W., 141, 220

Calado, Fernanda, 248
Carr, Camilla, 64, 68, 73, 78, 95, 250

Caspian Sea, 11, 214
Caucasian Common Market, 64
Caucasus Islamic Institute, 40, 99
Caucasus Wars, 209
Center for Social and Political Parties and Movements, 96
Center of Voluntary Labor Associations, 48
Central Asia, 8, 16, 45, 150
Central Asia-Caucasus Institute, 140
Central Bank (Russia), 135
Central Front for the Liberation of the Caucasus and Dagestan, 46
Central Intelligence Agency (CIA), 106, 220
Central Sector of the Eastern Front, 207
Centre for Peacemaking and Community Development, 73, 250
cesium-137, 25, 198, 244, 254
Chabanmakhi, Dagestan, 93
Chachayev, Lom-Ali, 13
Chaguchiyev, Magomed, 78
Chakhiyev, Ruslan, 121, 262–63
Chechen Academy of Sciences, 207
Chechen-Aul, Chechnya, fighting, 117
Chechen deportations (1944), 1, 8, 88
Chechen government administrative building bombing (2002), 205, 264
Chechen independence, 5, 83, 84, 109
Chechen Information Center, 130
Chechen-Ingush Autonomous Soviet Socialist Republic, 8
Chechen-Ingush Supreme Soviet, 10
Chechen Islamic Order (1997), 86
Chechen mafia, 9, 20, 22, 135–37, 142, 147
Chechen national character, 8
Chechen National Security Service, 41
Chechen Network (Paris terrorist cell), 206, 213, 214, 218, 264
Chechen parliament, 60, 63: on Basayev's effectiveness in office, 93; and Maskhadov, 95; suspension of, 96
Chechen Presidential Guards, 13
Chechen Press Agency, 133, 174
Chechen Republic of Ichkeria, 5, 37, 97, 172, 174, 205, 237; embassy in Afghanistan, 114
Chechen Revolution, 10–11, 81
Chechen State Defense Committee (2000), 113
Chechenetz analytical think tank, 82
chechnya.genstab.ru, xi
Chechnya Relief Campaign (Saudi Arabia), 142

Chelyabinskaya Oblast, Russia, 158
Cheptsk Mechanical Plant, 139
Chernyayev, Vladislav, 72
Chernobyl nuclear power plant, Ukraine, 201
Chernomirdin, Viktor, 23
Chernorechnye district, Grozny, 259
Chilayev, Islam, 162–63
children: as fighters, 217; terror victims, 3, 67, 69–70, 104–105, 136, 180–81, 187–88, 258; as terrorists, 3, 123–25, 182–83, 201, 205, 210–11, 261–63, 264
China, 140
Chiri-Yurt, Chechnya, 139; fighting in, 117
Chistlishche (Russian film), 19
Chistousov, Anatoly, 245
Chitigov, Rizvan, 200
Christopher, Andre, 250
Church of Vasiliya Blazhenovo, 224
Churches of Joint Action, 251
Churchill, Winston, 28
cleansing operations (Russian), 203
CNN Italia, 146
Cochetel, Vincent, 64, 252
Collins, Aukai, 37
Commanders Council, 61–62, 94–97
Committee for Cooperation with Chechnya (Turkey), 145
Committee on Judges and Fatwas, 44
Commonwealth of Independent States (CIS), 126
Confederation of Caucasus Mountain Peoples (1991), 12, 14
Congress of Chechen-Dagestani Nations, 97
Congress of Peoples Deputies of the RSFSR, 13
Congress of the Muslims of the Caucasus, 42
Congress of the Peoples of Chechnya and Dagestan, 91–94, 99–100, 103; organization, 80, 87
Congress of War Veterans, 61
constitutional referendum (Chechnya, 2003), 207
Cooperation with the People of Chechnya (Turkey), 145
corruption, xii, 5–6, 21–22, 65–66, 71, 76, 102, 134, 137–38, 183, 208; counterfeiting, 137; embezzlement, 137–39, 145–46, 150; facilitates terrorism, 6, 138, 212
Council of Europe, 70
Council of the Russian Federation, 179
Cullison, Alan, 214
Cuny, Fred, 119, 243

Dadashyeva, Aset, 57, 160, 249
Dadashyeva, Tamara, 237
Dadayev, Zarub, 225
Dagdizel Defense Plant, 125
Dagestan, 2, 4–5, 11–12, 28, 46, 48, 62, 76, 78, 80, 85–87, 91, 94, 98, 100, 105–106, 108, 111, 118, 129, 136, 141–42, 149, 153–54, 157, 159–60, 179, 206, 214–15, 233, 243, 247, 250, 253, 254, 256, 259–60, 266; bombings in, 114, 121,167, 248, 263; invasion of (1999), 2, 91–104; Khattab in, 45–46, 86, 91–94, 97–102, 252; Wahhabi influence and activity in, 44–45, 93, 97
Dagestanskya Pravda newspaper (Dagestan), 159
Dailah Al-Baraka Group, 147
Daoud, Abu, 154
Daoud, Mohamed, 164
Darr, Abu, 143
decapitation. *See* beheadings
Dekkushev, Adam, 105, 106
De Waal, Thomas, 176
Die Deutsche Welle radio (Germany), 98
Dinamo sports stadium (Grozny): 2003 bombing, 208, 265; 2004 bombing, 237
disinformation, xi, 80
Domodedovo Airlines, 244
Donsova, Valeriya, 234
drug trade. *See* narcotics trafficking
Dubrovka theater siege, 2–4, 22, 128, 142–43, 153, 178–96, 203, 212, 264; and bin Laden, 219; Black Widows in, 182–86, 188–89, 192–96; as a family affair, 182; hostage rescue operation, 188–91; Maskhadov on, 191; official list of dead terrorists, 192–96; resulting change in Chechen strategy, 197; resulting change in Russian national security posture and military doctrine, 202–204
Ducze Islamic fighters' training camp (Turkey), 146
Dudayev, Dzhokhar, 13, 17–26, 47–49, 54–55, 68, 95, 114, 122, 135, 142, 144, 159–60, 214; arming Chechnya, 14; awarding Raduyev for hostage taking, 52; and Boris Yeltsin, 9; and Budennovsk raid, 20; and Chechen Revolution, 9–10; death, 26; declaration of Chechen independence, 2, 13; election to presidency (1991), 12; financial support from Libya, 145; plan to hijack a Russian nuclear submarine, 125, 15; political opposition to, 17; rumors of return from the

dead, 54; on unification of
Chechnya and Dagestan, 11–12
Dudayev, Ibragim, 127
Dudayev, Lecha, 111
Dudayeva, Alla, 20
Duisi, Georgia, 130, 143
Dundayeva, Raisa, 24
Dyshne-Vedeno, Chechnya, 8;
fighting in, 175
Dzhabrailov, Salgir Isayevich, 193
Dzhafarov, Vakha, 57, 59
Dzhantemirov, Doka, 175
Dzhumayev, Abu-Bakar, 119
Dzokhar's Way terrorist organiza-
tion, 57

East Germany, 145
Eastern Front, Chechnya, 109
Echo Moskvy radio (Russia), 89
Ediyev, Sultan Said, 121
Egypt, 218; foreign fighters in
Chechnya, 154
Egyptian Islamic Jihad, 214
Elbiyev, Rizvan, 243
Eldarkhanov, Taifura, 98
Eldarov, Abdul Kadyr, 125
El Mundo newspaper (Spain), 154
Elmurzayev, Ruslan Abu
Khasanovich, 191–93; in
Dubrovka theater siege, 179–81,
184–85, 190
Emergency Situations Ministry
(Russia), 77
Energetik sanatorium, 136
EquiLibre (France), 73, 250
Erbakan, Necmettin, 145, 146
Erkel, Arjan, 120
Estrada theater, Moscow, 179
Ethiopia, 26
Executory Process Department of
the Ministry of Shariah Security
(Chechnya), 41, 74

Fairbanks, Charles H., 140
Fariza, Atfayva, 121
Fath, Ipak, 144
Fatih Mosque, Turkey, 145
Federal Bureau of Investigation
(FBI), 150, 151
Federal Justice Ministry (Turkey),
146
Federal Republic of Germany, 151
Federalnoye Slyzhba Bezopasnosti
(FSB), xi, 52, 68, 111, 117–18,
121, 124, 139, 144, 149, 159,
165, 170, 175, 180, 200, 208,
216, 225, 229, 232, 251, 266–67;
agents taken hostage, 68; alleged
infiltration of Dubrovka terror-
ist group, 189–90; capture of
Raduyev (2000), 157–58; and
Moscow apartment building
bombings (1999), 106; operation to eliminate Arbi Barayev,
163; plot to assassinate Khattab,

163–64; rivalry with GRU, 162;
suicide bombing in Magas,
Ingushetia, 231; on war in
Chechnya, 156, 203
female terrorists, 212;
Abdurzakova, Zulai, 209;
Alikhhanova, Zarina, 208, 265;
Aliyeva, Sekilat Uvaisovna, 183,
192; Aliyeva, Zinaida (Marem),
222, 224, 226, 266; Asmayeba,
Luiza, 210, 265; Bairakova,
Zareta Dolkhayevna, 184, 192;
Bakuyeva, Aishat (Luiza), 183;
Barayeva, Khava,122, 210, 258;
Bicultanova, Marina
Nebiyullayevna, 193; Bitsiyeva,
Zura Pezvanovna, 182,193;
Bityeva, Zaira Bashirovna, 193;
Dadashyeva, Aset, 57, 160, 249;
Dudayeva, Mareta, 124;
Dugayeva, Madina Movsarovna,
193; Dundayeva, Raisa, 24;
Elmurzayeva, Seda
Seitkhamzatovna, 193;
Ganiyeva, Fatima
Sulumbekovna, 182, 194;
Ganiyeva, Khadchat (Milano)
Sulumbekovna, 182, 194;
Gazuyeva, Aizan, 124–25, 210,
262; Inarkayeva, Zarema, 125;
211; Khachukayeva, Iman, 229,
266; Khadzhiyeva, Aiman
Vaguetovna, 184, 194;
Khadzhiyeva, Koku Vaguetovna,
184, 194; Khadzhiyeva,
Maryam, 184; Khaldykhoroy-
eva, Lidya (Lida), 209, 225, 265;
Khusenova, Liana Musayevna,
195; Kurbanova, Aiman
Khasanovna, 183; Kurbanova,
Raiman Khasanovna, 183, 195;
Magomadova, Luiza (Kheda),
122, 258; Meferkhanova, Yakha
Khamidovna, 178, 184, 195;
motivation, 209–11, 223, 228;
Mugayeva, Malika Daudovna,
195; Murtazaliyeva, Zara, 236;
Musalayeva, Larisa, 209;
Mutayeva, Malizha Daudovna,
192; Muzhikhayeva, Zarema,
183, 224–28, 233, 266; Shakova,
Fatimat Mukhamedovna, 195;
Taimashkanova, Fatima, 57,
160, 249; training, 201;
Tumriyeva, 205; unidentified
suicide bombers, 185, 211, 230,
232, 267; Vataliyevna, Yassira,
178–79; Yelikhadzhiyeva,
Zulikhan, 222–24, 226, 266;
Yupayeva, Zaira Bashirovna ,
196
fentanyl, 189–91
Fetesova, Larisa, 50
Financial Committee of the Majlis
ul-Shura, 173

financing, 17, 139, 173–74; for
Budennovsk siege, 134; to destabilize Dagestan, 92; for
Dubrovka theater siege, 178;
foreign sources, 133–35,
140–46, 149–55, 164, 171, 197,
204; and narcotics trafficking,
136; for rebuilding Chechnya,
83, 137–38; sources of, 134; of
terror and fighters, 5, 134–55;
174, 219
First World Congress of Vinakh
Diaspora, 81, 85
Fisher-Malanowska, Zofia, 76, 256
Fleutiaux, Brice, 257
Fomenko, Grigoriy, 237
foreign fighters in Chechnya, 20,
32, 35–37, 93, 113, 135, 154,
212; Aqueedah, Abu Bakr, 19,46;
Assadula, Amir (British), 99;
Aydin, Ramazan (Turkish), 146;
Bakar, Abu, 39, 184; Benahmed,
Merovane (Algerian), 213–14;
Benchellali, Menad (French),
213; Benin, Masood al-
(French), 99–100, 102; Collins,
Aukai (American), 37; Darr,
Abu (Saudi Arabian), 143;
Djaffa, Xavier (French), 99; FSB
list, 135; Ghamdi, Ahmed al-,
216; Ghamibi, Yakub al-, 19;
Hidayatullah, (Pakistani), 113,
141; Jafar, Abu Abdullah
(Pakistani), 99; Jar, Abu 216;
Kandagary, Abu Said al-
(Afghan), 154; Khattab (Saudi
Arabian), *See* Khattab; 140;
Khakhim, Abu, 99; Madani,
Hakim al-, 19, 102; Merabet,
Nourredine (French Moroccan),
213; al-Moutana, 206; Musab,
Sheikh Abu (Algerian), 99;
Mustafa (Turkish), 146; Rostam,
Kianan (Iraqi), 126; Saif, Abu
Omar Muhammad al-, 44, 46,
106, 149, 153, 191, 216; from
Saudi Arabia, 44; al-Tabuki, 102;
Tokcan, Muhammed (Turkish),
53, 245; from Turkey, 146;
Waleed, Abu al-, 19, 46, 127,
167, 191, 206, 210, 216, 236;
Yakub, Abu (Jordanian), 114,
216
Foreign Ministry of the Russian
Federation, 151
Foss, Ingeborg, 248
Foundation Regarding Chechnya,
143
Franchetti, Mark, 186
France, 16; and Chechen cell in
Paris, 206, 212–14, 264
Franks, Tommy, 217
Frantsuzov, Taukan. *See*
Gochiyayev, Achimez
fraud, 135, 138

Free Caucasus radio station, 81
Freedom Square, Grozny, 62
Fund of the Muslim Brotherhood, 40, 125, 149, 206

Gabor, Dunaisky, 251
Gadafi, Muhammar, 145
Gadzhiyev, Geidar, 125, 262
Gagra, Abkhazia, 14–15
Gagry Front, Abkhazia, 14
Gaisumov, Hussein, 159
Gakayev, Magomed Khussein, 119
Galashki, Ingushetia, 148; fighting in, 176
Gall, Carlotta, 51
Galutskikh, Pavel, 268
Gamsakhurdia, Zviad, 58
Ganiyev, Rustam, 183
Ganiyeva, Raisa, 28, 182–83
Gantemirov, Beslan, 10, 17–18
Gare de Lyon train station, France, 214
Gasanov, Nizami Isa-ogly, 194
gas, homemade, 135, 136
gazeta.ru, xi
Gazhiyev, Mahmed, 125
Gazuyev, Zelimkhan, 124
Geifman, Alla, 70
Geifman, Grigory, 70
Gekhi, Chechnya, fighting in, 117
Gelayev, Ruslan, 19, 44, 126, 233; appearance on the Kremlin's death list, 156; and Arbi Barayev, 109–10, 162; attack against Russian border guard post, Dagestan (2004), 149, 233, 267; death, 234; fighting in Abkhazia, 14–15; fighting in Galashki, Ingushetia (2002), 148; and Maskhadov, 95, 109; in Pankisi Gorge, 148; return to Chechnya (2002), 176; withdrawal from Grozny (1999), 111
Gelayev Spetsnaz, 15–16, 19
Geliskhanov, Sultan, 68
General Dudayev's Caucasian Liberation Army, 55, 62, 109, 120
Georgia, 11, 14–15, 58–59, 86, 114, 130, 148, 170, 176, 234; extradition of Chechen fighters, 149; as transit route to Chechnya, 143, 204, 216
Gerayev, Mahmut, 159
German BND intelligence service, 54
German-Caucasian Society, 151
Germany, 54, 199, 213
Ghamdi, Ahmed al-, 216
Ghamibi, Abdel Aziz al-. *See* Waleed, Abu al-
Gishmurkayeva, Aset Vakhidovna, 194
Gluck, Kenneth, 119–20, 26
Gochiyayev, Achimez, 105–106, 118

Goettemoeller, Rose, 202
Gorbachev, Mikhail, 9
Gordali clan (teip), 47
Gosatomnadzor, 201
Grachev, Pavel, 26
Granger Telecom, 67, 74, 77, 254
Great Britain, 213
Great Chechnya, 2, 40, 80, 85–87. *See also* imamate
Grey Wolf terrorist organization (Turkey), 14
Grozny, 13, 16, 18, 25–27, 31, 55, 60, 70, 93, 119, 121, 124, 136, 139, 154, 171–72, 175, 183, 186, 206–208, 210–11, 242, 244–45, 248, 251, 254, 258–63, 264; bombardment of (1994), 19; Chechen atrocities in, 19; Chechen defense of (1999) 110–11; Chechen government administration building bombing in (2002), 204–205; Chechen withdrawal from (1999), 111; Dudayev's opposition attacks in, 17–18; fighting in (1999–2000), 116–17
"Grozny Offensive" (1996), 7, 27–28, 37
GRU. *See* Main Intelligence Directorate of the Russian General Staff
Gryzlov, Boris, 147
Guantanamo Bay, 213
Gubaryeva, Sasha, 180
Gubaryeva, Svetlana, 180–81
Gudauta, Abkhazia, 16
Gudermes Center of Voluntary Labor Associations, 48
Gudermes, Chechnya, 101, 171, 206–207; bombings in, 33, 120, 123, 125, 259, 262, 265, 268; fighting in (1999–2000), 109, 117, 175; Russian withdrawal (1995), 49; Wahhabi uprising in, 41–42, 74, 93
Gudermessky district, Chechnya, 48–49, 211
guerilla warfare, 113, 115–22, 175, 197
Guevara, Che, influence on Basayev, 3, 11, 212
Gulag Archipelago, 1, 8
Gurov, Alexandr, 157
Gusayev, Magomedsalikh, 266

Halim, Abdul. *See* Khalim, Abdul
Halo Trust, 151
Hamas, 112, 149
Harkat-ul-Ansar terrorist organization (Pakistan), 16, 217
Harvard University, 51
helicopters, 23, 49–50, 52, 69, 101–102, 115, 117, 136, 147, 171, 234, 242–43, 246, 249, 264; shootdown of Mi-26, 175

Hensch, Christophe, 248
Hezbollah, 40
Hickey, Darren, 67, 77, 254
Higgins, Andrew, 214
hijackings, 3, 7, 13–14, 53, 69, 120–21, 146, 242–46, 251, 260–62
Ho Chi Minh Trail, 148
holy war, 2, 46, 48, 90, 99, 122–23, 128, 134, 153, 169, hospitals, hostage taking in, 7, 20–24, 50–51
hostage taking, 20–24, 51–52, 55, 69, 233, 242–45, 259–60, 264

Ichkeria newspaper (Chechnya), 131
Idrisov, Hazmat, 137
Ignatovskaya, Oksana, 181
Iliskhan-Yurt, Chechnya, 208
Ilyasov, Stanislav, 127
Imam Shami, 11–12, 85–86
imamate: description, 2; establishment of, 97–103; Majlis ul-Shura (2002) on, 173; in North Caucasus, 4, 62, 80, 85–87, 91, 149, 214, 266. *See also* Great Chechnya
Imayev, Usman, 145
Imbir restaurant (Moscow), 225
Inarkayeva, Zarema, 125
Indian embassy in Dagestan, 254
infocentre.ru, xi
Information Committee of the Majlis ul-Shura, 173
information wars, 80, 128–33
Ingushetia, 11, 45, 72, 119, 136, 148, 176, 222, 227, 240, 241, 247, 249–51, 256
Institute of Land Tenure Engineers (Moscow), 8, 11
Institute of Policy Research, 240
intelligence exchange, between the United States and Russia, 98
intelnet.org, 40
International Battalion. *See* Peacekeeping Brigade of the Congress of Peoples of Chechnya and Dagestan
International Brigade. *See* Peacekeeping Brigade of the Congress of Peoples of Chechnya and Dagestan
International Committee of the Red Cross (ICRC): kidnapped employees, 247, 256; murder of employees (1996), 3, 38–39, 248
International Friendship Square (Grozny), 70
International Organization of the Capitals of Islamic States, 84
International Policy Institute for Counterterrorism (Israel), 35
Inter-Service Intelligence (Pakistan), 16, 140

InterSos, 147
Iran, 136, 139
Iraq, 199, 218
Isayev, Eli, 237, 239
Isayev, Khusein, 237
Isayev, Said, 256–57
Islamic Army of Dagestan, 100,
    104; *See also* Islamic Liberation
    Army of Dagestan
IslamicAwakening.com, 152
Islamic constitution (Chechnya),
    61
Islamic International Brigade, 99,
    203–204. *See also* Peacekeeping
    Brigade of the Congress of
    Peoples of Chechnya and
    Dagestan
Islamic Jihad organization, 149
Islamic League, 91, 215
Islamic Liberation Army of
    Dagestan, 105. *See also* Islamic
    Army of Dagestan
Islamic Manifesto, 65
Islamic Movement of Uzbekistan
    (IMU), 39
Islamic Nations movement, 4, 80,
    82, 85–87
Islamic Observation Center
    (London), 144
Islamic Peacekeeping Army. *See*
    Peacekeeping Brigade of the
    Congress of Peoples of
    Chechnya and Dagestan
Islamic Peacekeeping Brigade. *See*
    Peacekeeping Brigade of the
    Congress of Peoples of
    Chechnya and Dagestan
Islamic Peacekeeping International
    Brigade. *See* Peacekeeping
    Brigade of the Congress of
    Peoples of Chechnya and
    Dagestan
Islamic Regiment (1995), 24, 36
Islamic Regiment of Special
    Meaning. *See* Special Purposes
    Islamic Regiment
Islamic Relief Organization (IRO),
    150
Islamic Salvation Fund (Pakistan),
    153
Islamic Shura of Dagestan (1999),
    100
Islamic Special Purposes Regiment.
    See Special Purposes Islamic
    Regiment
Islamic state. *See* Great Chechnya,
    imamate
Islamic University of Grozny, 183
Ismailov, Aslambek, 110, 111
Israel, 213
Israilov, Khanpasha, 206
Israilov, Viskhan, 252
Israpilov, Khunkar-Pasha, 40, 43,
    97, 231; death, 111; deposed, 79;
    fighting alongside Ruslan

Akhmadov (1999), 110; on kid-
    napping, 72–73; in Kizlyar raid,
    50; opposition to Maskhadov's
    presidency, 44, 60, 94–95; sup-
    port for Basayev (1999), 101
Israpilov, Ibragim, 231
Istanbul, Turkey, 9, 145
ITAR-TASS news service (Russia),
    61, 72, 77, 164, 200, 249, 255
Ivanov, Sergei, 141, 153, 172, 197,
    202–203, 204
Ivanovo, Russia, 137
Izmailov, Vyacheslav, 105
Izmailovsky Park, Moscow, 25
Izvestia newspaper (Russia), 24,
    183, 224, 226–27, 225, 227–28

Jafar, Abu Abdullah, 19, 99, 140,
    141
Jalalabad, Pakistan, 34
jamaat, 105, 228
James, Jon, 64, 68, 73, 78, 95, 250
Janes Intelligence Digest, 152
Jar, Abu, 216
Jerusalem, 99
jihad. *See* holy war
Joint Saudi Committee for the
    Relief of Kosovo and Chechnya,
    142
Jordan, 121, 141, 143, 144
Judd, Frank, 132

Kabardino-Balkaria Republic, 70,
    136, 229–30, 246, 249, 252, 256,
    258, 264
Kabul, Afghanistan, 35, 89, 214
Kadre, Rabah, 214
Kadyrov, Akhmat, 208, 212, 221,
    240; accomplishments, 239;
    assassination of (2004), 236–37,
    265; assassination attempts
    against, 127, 207–208; on
    Chechen government adminis-
    trative building bombing
    (2002), 205; election to
    Chechen presidency (2003),
    232; as Mufti of Chechnya, 88;
    on Wahhabis, 41
Kadyrov, Ramzan, 238, 239, 240,
    258
Kadyrovsky spetsnaz, 238, 266
kafir (infidels), 101, 103
kafir-1, 127
Kafkasya Yardimlasma Dernegi aid
    organization (Turkey), 145
Kalinin Nuclear Power Plant,
    201–202
Kalinovskaya, Chechnya, 117
KamAZ trucks, 20, 200, 204, 208,
    212, 229, 231, 265
kamikaze airliner attacks, 80
Kandahar, Afghanistan, 89, 91, 121,
    153, 215
Karachaevo-Cherkessia Republic,
    11, 14, 105, 120, 136, 184, 242

Karachi, Pakitan, 141
Karamakhi, Dagestan, 94, 97, 104;
    fighting in (1999), 104;
    Khattab's family ties in, 44, 104;
    liberated Islamic territory decla-
    ration, 93; Russian bombard-
    ment and surrender of (1999),
    104; Wahhabis control of, 44, 92
Karavayeva, Yulia, 65
Kaspiisk, Dagestan, 125: military
    apartment building bombing
    (1996), 248; Victory Day bomb-
    ing (2002), 114, 121, 167, 263
Kasyanov, Mikhail, 202
Katayev, Ayub, 119
Katyr-Yurt, Chechnya, 268
kavkazcenter.com, 125, 128, 130,
    153, 232–33
Kavkaz-Center News Agency, 132,
    180
kavkaz.org, xi, 113, 132, 167, 187;
    attempts to close down, 130;
    financing, 142; in Internet wars,
    132; popularity and Russian
    hacking of, 129–30; Udugov
    establishes, 128
Kavkaz television, 79, 85, 88, 98,
    128, 132
Kavkaz training center, 57, 65
Kazakhstan, 75, 139, 155, 177
Kazantsyev, Viktor, 188–89, 205
Kazi-Kumakh Lak movement
    (Dagestan), 86
Kenkhi, Chechnya, 101
Kennedy, Peter, 67, 77, 254
Khabrailov, Abi, 226
Khachilayev, Magomed, 63, 86–87,
    91, 93–94
Khachilayev, Nadirshakh, 63, 91,
    104
Khakhamada, Irina, 187
Khalif newspaper (Chechnya), 97
Khalikov, Ragim, 233
Khalilov, Rappani, 167
Khalim, Abdul, 173–74
Khalimov, Islam, 41, 85
Khambiyev, Magomed, 38, 46, 98,
    102, 236
Khamzatov, Turpal Kamiyevich,
    194
Khankala air base, Chechnya, 207,
    259
Khankala, Chechnya, 19, 26, 203,
    264
Kharayev, Apti, 75
Khasanov, Adlan, 237
Khasanov, Musa, 131
Khasavyurt, Dagestan, 23, 28, 184;
    bombings in, 229, 247, 266
Khasavyurt peace agreement
    (1996), 28, 82, 85
Khaskhanov, Aslambek, 185
Khattab, xi, 4, 5, 32–46, 60, 62, 65,
    68, 74, 128, 142, 144, 156, 160,
    181, 206, 214–15; adoption by

Basayev family, 90; and apartment building bombings (1999), 105–106; arrival in Chechnya (1995), 4, 19, 35; assassination attempt against, 45; attack against Russian military garrison at Buinaksk, Dagestan (1997), 45, 252; beheadings by, 26, 32–34; Chechen military awards, 37; command of foreign fighters, 24–25; command of Peacekeeping Brigade of the Congress of Peoples of Chechnya and Dagestan, 91; Dagestan invasion (1999), 45, 86, 98–104; death, 121, 151, 163–66, 174; family, 33, 166; fighting in Afghanistan, 34–35, 164; financial channels, 90–91, 144, 151, 152–53, 155; and Gudermes uprising (1998), 42; and ICRC murders (1996), 38; on imamate, 2 , 91; influence on Basayev, 90; Internet and video sales, 33–34; justification of terrorism (1998), 103; and Little Wahhabi Republic, 86; marriages, 44; on Maskhadov, 133; in Nagorno-Karabakh conflict, 36; personality cult, 34–35; plan to assassinate Kadyrov, 127; relationship with Basayev, 90; on Russian sale of arms, 102; in second Chechen war, 112–13, 115–17; support of Wahhabis in Dagestan, 45; threats against Russia, 103, 105; ties to bin Laden, 91, 153, 216; and Training Center of the Armed Forces of Chechnya, 38–40, 57; in Yaryshmardy attack (1996), 24
Khultygov, Lecha, 41, 59, 92
Khunov, Fuad Shakhambiyevich, 194
Khusainov, Rascha Saidaminovich, 194
Khusainov, Rasul Saidaminovich, 194
kidnappings, 3–4, 62–63, 67–73, 75–79, 139, 178, 207–208, Basayev on, 67; and Berezovsky, 62; contracts for, 69; Jewish victims, 70; statistics in Chechnya, 71, 77; victims, 21, 50, 64, 67, 70–72, 76, 77–78, 95, 119, 243, 246–58, 263–65, 267
King Fahd, 142
Kirov, Chechnya, 244
Kislovodsk, Russia, 105, 266
Kisriev, Enver, 51
Kizlyar, Dagestan, 22, 71, 120, 160, 254; hostage taking in, 21, 49, 160–61, 180, 245

Klebnikov, Paul, 64, 83
Kobach, Dushan, 250
Kodzayev, Magomed, 230
Kommersant Daily newpaper (Russia), xi, 157, 174, 232
Kommitent Gosudarstvenny Besopastnosti (KGB), 10, 106
Komsomol (Young Communist League), 48
Komsomolskoye, Chechnya, 101, 109, 176,
Komsomolskoye Plemya newspaper (Chechnya), 80
Komsomolskaya Pravda newspaper (Russia), 28, 53
Koran, 26, 33, 74, 96
Korigov, Daud, 72
Kosovo, 35
Kotelnikov, Anatoly, 199
Krasnodar, Russia, 231, 266–67
Krasnoyarsk Aviation Company, 248
Krasnoyarsk, Russia, 177
Krasnoyarsk State University (Russia), 177–78
Krasnoye Znamya newspaper, 81
Krym-Gerei, Sergei, 199
Krymshamkhalov, Yusuf, 105, 149
Kulary, Chechnya, 163
Kulikov, Anatoly, 25, 51, 80
Kunduz, Afghanistan, 217
Kungayeva, Elza (Kheda), 33–34, 123
Kurchaloevsky district, Chechnya, 117, 177, 201
Kurchaloi, Chechnya, 177, 222
Kurchatov Institute, Russia, 179, 230
Kursk nuclear submarine, 125–26, 178, 259
Kuwait, 219; foreign fighters in Chechnya, 154
Kuwait Society for the Revival of the Islamic Heritage, 147

Laipanov, Mukhita. See Gochiyayev, Achimez
Lake Kazenoi-am, Chechnya, 115
Land Tenure Engineers Institute, Moscow, 8
Lashkar-e-Tayyiba organization (Pakistan), 140
Lebanon, 122; foreign fighters in Chechnya, 154
Lebed, Alekhandr, 27–28, 154
Lefortovo Prison, Russia, 159, 161
LeMonde newspaper (France), 146
Lenta.ru, 132
Lermontov, Mikhail, 130
Liberation newspaper (France), 102
Libya, 145
Lichtman, Laura, 70
Lieven, Anatol, 15
Lidove Noviny, 7, 99, 104
Likhodei, Mikhail, 248

List.ru, 13
Little Wahhabi Republic, Dagestan, 44–45, 86, 97
Loginov, Yevgenny, 23
Luzhkov, Yuri, 64
Lysakov, Ilya, 252

Machevsky, Alexandr, 188
Mafusayev, Ise, 24
Magadan, Russia, 251
Magadansk region, Russia, 137
Magas, Ingushetia, FSB building bombing (2003), 231, 267–68
Magerlamov, Oleg Alaidarovich, 195
Magiayev, Ruslan, 105
Magomadov, Abdul, 237
Magomedov, Akhmed, 39, 90
Magomedov, Bagautdin, 41, 98
Magomedov, Yunus, 162
Main Intelligence Directorate of the General Staff (GRU), 14, 105–106, 163, 181, 234; alleged infiltration of Dubrovka terrorist group, 189–90; Basayev raid on (1991), 10; rivalry with FSB, 162; training Basayev (1992), 14
Majlis ul-Shura (2002–present), 176; and Basayev, 173, 191, 212; collective decision making in, 173; committees, 173; establishment, 153, 172–73; on imamate in North Caucasus, 173; and Maskhadov, 173; payments to families of martyrs, 210, 228; planning session, 177; statement of Islamic globalism, 220; strategic plan of operation (2002), 174
Makhachkala, Dagestan, 63, 129, 182, 243, 246, 249, 256, 260; Raduyev's trail in, 159–61
Makhachyev, Hadj, 86
Makhmayev, Akhmed, 243
Malashenko, Alexei, 218
Malashenko, Igor, 72
Malloy, Nancy, 248
Mamayev, Artur, Shamil, and Zaur, 167
Manezhny Mall, Moscow, bombing, 103, 257
Manifesto of the Jamaat of Dagestan to the Moslem World (1997), 46
Maqda, Munir, 213
Marchwinska-Wyrwal, Ewa, 76, 256
Markaz-i-Dawar training camp, Pakistan, 16
Markov, Pyotr, 253
Markov, Sergei, 240
Marsho television, 59
Maskhadov, Aslan, 5, 14, 22, 44, 52, 58, 62–65, 68, 79, 82, 87, 92–98, 109, 129–30, 139, 142, 157, 161,

175, 177, 187, 191, 205, 209, 241, 250, 254–55; announcement of full Shariah rule in Chechnya, 88, 96; appointment of Basayev to office (1997), 30; assassination attempts against, 74, 253–55; ban on Wahhabism (1998), 42; on Basayev, 7, 62, 90, 92; 98, 109; and bin Laden, 216, 230; defense of Grozny (1994, 1999), 18–19, 111; denial of involvement in, airliner hijacking (2001), 121; —, Budennovsk raid (1995), 20; —, Chechen government administrative building bombing (2002), 205; —, Dubrovka siege, 191; —, Mozdok hospital bombing (2003), 230; —, Znamenskoye truck bombing, 209; deportation of Khattab (1998), 42; disbanding Special Purpose Islamic regiment, 74; dismissal of Udugov from National Security Council, 129; election to Chechen presidency (1997), 5, 29–30; embezzlement accusations against, 138; and financing, 139, 144–45, 151, 153, 164, 174; ideology shift, 172; in Internet wars, 131–33; on invasion of Dagestan, 102; and kidnappings, 61, 64, 71–72, 79, 142; meeting with Prime Minister Primakov, 60, 88, 90, 92; opposition to, 56, 59–60, 62, 88–89, 94–97,142; organization of the Supreme Military Council, 169; power (2002–2004), 173–74; on Raduyev, 47; reaction to Granger Telecom beheadings, 79; reconciliation with Basayev and Udugov (2002), 171; removal of Udugov from office, 88, 100; and reorganization of Chechen armed forces (2002), 171–74; request that fighters return from Pankisi Gorge, 170; on second Chechen war, 108–109; travels to the United States (1997), 84, 147; on Udugov, 67, 129, 132–33; vision for Chechnya, 90; on the Wahhabi threat and anti-Wahhabi campaign, 41–42; on Yandabiyev, 133

Maskhadov-Udugov Internet wars, 131–33

Masyuk, Yelena, 67, 71–72, 249

Mayakovskaya Square, Moscow, 224

Mazhayeva, Temir-Ali, 243

McDonald's restaurants, Russia: Moscow Pushkinskaya Square restaurant targeted (2001,

2003), 186, 224, 228; Moscow Yugo-Zapadnaya restaurant car bombing (2002), 185, 264

Medicins Sans Frontieres (Doctors Without Borders), 119–20, 245, 250, 261, 263

Medina, Saudi Arabia, 121,

Mehk Khel, 96, 97

Merabet, Nouredine, 213

Meshcheryakova, Lena, 69–70

Meskerty, Chechnya, fighting in, 177

Mesker-Yurt, Chechnya, 127

Mezhidov, Abdul Malik: as Chief of the Executory Department of Sharia Security, Chechnya, 41; in Dagestan invasion, 99; death, 111; demotion, 42; in Gudermes uprising (1998), 74; and Shpigun's kidnappings, 61

Mezhiyev, Akyad, 185

Mezhiyev, Alikhan, 178, 185

Michurina, Chechnya, 207

Microlink Data, 130

mid.ru, xi

Military Command Council (Chechnya), 112

Military Committee of Majlis ul-Shura, 173

military doctrine, strategy, and tactics, 197, 202–204

military industrial mafia, 129

Mineralnye Vody, Russia: airliner hijacking (1991), 13, 121, 242: bombings in, 120

Ministry of Shariah Security (Chechnya), 43, 75

Mironov, Vyacheslav, 19

Mitrofanov, Anatoly, 255

Mohammed, Khalid Sheikh, 215

Mokok, Dagestan, 233

Molle, Laurent, 250

Mon Kafe, 224–25

Mordyukov, Ilya, 249

Morocco, foreign fighters in Chechnya, 154

Moroz, Nina, 50

Moscow, Russia, 76, 103, 134, 137, 162, 212, 236, 244; apartment building bombings in (1999), 3, 65, 105–106, 120, 134; bus, trolley, and subway train/station bombings in, 118–19, 234–36, 245–46, 262; Dubrovka theater siege, 2, 170, 179–91, 264; McDonald's restaurants targeted in, 185–86, 224, 228, 264; nuclear terrorism in, 3, 24–25, 198–99, 100–101, 244, 254; Ostankino television tower fire, 119, 259; other terrorism in, 244–45, 248, 251, 257, 267; Pushkin Square passageway bombing, 118, 259; suicide bomber attacks in, 221–24,

221–28, 230, 232–36, 241, 264, 266–67

Moscow State University (Russia), 8, 81

The Moscow Times newpaper, 232

Moskovskaya Pravda, 9

Moskovskiye Novosti newspaper (Russia), 162, 257

Moskovsky Dvorets Molodyozhi Theater (Moscow), 179

Moskovsky Komsomolets newspaper, 48

Motassadeq, Mounir al-, 217

Moussad (Israeli intelligence), xi

Moussaoui, Zacarias, 217

Mozdok, North Ossetia: bus hijacking in, 243; suicide bomber attack (2003), 209, 225, 227, 265; 58th Army military hospital truck bombing (2003), 229–30, 266

Muhammud, Jad Jayev, 125

Mujahideen Military Command Council, 113

Mujahideen United Armed Forces of Dagestan, 99

Mukhanitz, Vladimir, 119

Muklebust, Gunnhild, 248

Murdalov, Aslan, 185

Murtazaliyeva, Zara, 236, 267

Murtazayev, Badrudi, 75–76

Musalatov, Alkhazur, 208

Musayev, Ibragim Adlanovich, 195

Musalayeva, Larisa, 209

Muslim Brotherhood. See Fund of the Muslim Brotherhood

Muslims of Russia organization, 142

Mutalibov, Askhab, 24

Mutayeva, Malizha Daydovna, 195

Nadterechny district, Chechnya, 177, 206; suicide truck bombing (2003), 208

Nagatinskaya subway station, Moscow, 53

Nagorno-Karabakh conflict, 13, 36

narcotics trafficking, 69–70, 76, 136–37, 243

Nasir, Javed, 16

Nation of Islam, 85

National Bank of Ichkeria, 31, 92, 145

National Center for Strategic Research and Political Technologies, 128

National Congress of the Chechen People, 10, 81

National Federation of Anarchists (Poland), 251

National Guards, 10, 13, 18, 73, 74: Wahhabi attacks on (1998), 41–42

National Hotel, Moscow, 232; suicide bombing at, 267

National Security Council
(Chechnya), 129
NATO, 201
Naurskaya, Chechnya, 267
Nazran, Ingushetia, 72, 77, 119,
225, 229, 250, 256, 268
Nemtsov, Boris, 83, 187
Nesterovskaya, Ingushetia, 251
Nevada, 152
Nevinomyssk, Russia: bus hijacking
in, 121; market bombing in,
119, 260
The New York Times, 51
Newsday magazine, 124, 216
Newsline journal (Pakistan), 16
Nezavisimaya Gazeta newspaper
(Russia), 16, 88, 94, 131, 157,
159
Nivat, Anne, 102
Nizami-i Alem Acaklari organiza-
tion (Turkey), 146
Nord Ost, 2, 180–81
North Caucasus, 5, 6, 9, 11, 40, 50,
79, 86, 107, 151, 211, 214–16
North Ossetia, 11, 60, 118, 209,
212, 225–27, 229–30, 243,
249–51 263, 265–66
Northern Alliance, 217
Novalaksky district, Dagestan,
fighting in (1999), 103
Novaya Gazeta newspaper (Russia),
174, 190, 230
Novogroznensky, Chechnya, 50,
109, 156; suicide bombing in,
259
Novoroznezhsky nuclear power
plant, Russia, 202
Novye-Atagi, Chechnya, 38, 247
Nozhai-Yurt, Chechnya, fighting
in, 116, 208, 265
NTV television, 25, 71, 105, 181,
186
nuclear terrorism, 3, 14, 212; and
dirty bombs, 24–25, 198–99;
smuggling of materials, 139,
177–78, 198; theft and sale of
materials, 137, 139,154, 177–78,
198–99; threats by Basayev, 25;
threats by Dudayev, 125; threats
by Raduyev, 158
Nurgaliyev, Rashid, 240

Obolensk, Russia, 200
Obshchaya Gazeta newspaper
(Russia), 25
oil, 83, 86, 110, 135; theft in
Chechnya, 135–36
Oktyabrsky market, Grozny, bomb-
ing, 119
Olchyev, Dmitry, 249
Oleinika, Galina, 243
Omar, Abu: appeals for aid, 149,
153; in Dubrovka planning,
191; as emissary of the Muslim
Brotherhood, 149; instructions

for Moscow apartment building
bomber, 106; marriage, 44; as al
Qaeda representative, 216; in
raid on Russian military garri-
son, Dagestan (1997), 46
Omarov, Magomed, 160
OMON police, 63, 103, 114, 263,
265; troops kidnapping, 55, 248;
execution of, 33
Omsk, Russia, 251
Onishchenko, Gennedy, 200
Operation Anaconda, 217
Operation "Jihad," 21, 191, 175
Operation "Whirlwind," 208
Operation "Wolf Hunt," 111–12,
156
Orazaliyev, Alisher, 77, 250, 252
Order of Nations Honor, 37
Orel-Avia airline company, 22
Organization for Security and
Cooperation in Europe (OSCE),
28, 30
Oridi, Hairi al-, 112
Orientir newspaper (Chechnya), 81
ORT television, 72, 249
Orthodox Christian blocade, 86
Organization for Security and
Cooperation in Europe (OSCE),
84
osmium-187, 139, 177
Ostankino television tower fire
(2000), 119, 259
Ostranits, Andrei, 256
Ozdayeva, Fatima, 176

Pakistan, xii, 16–17, 34–36, 59, 136,
140–41, 143, 164, 217
Palestine, 112, 197
Palestinian Liberation
Organization (PLO), 112
Panj Border Guards Unit Outpost
#12, Russia, 36
Pankisi Gorge, 110, 130, 148–49,
204; flow of fighters to
Chechnya from, 148, 170,
175–76; as haven for Chechen
and foreign fighters, 148; al
Qaeda in, 148; Saudi support in,
143; terrorists killed and cap-
tured in, 149; terrorist training
in, 148–49, 200, 213
Panorama magazine (Italy), 249
Panov, Alexander, 264
Parliamentary Assembly of the
Council of Europe, 132
Party of Freedom (Chechnya), 97
Patarkatshvili, Badri, 139, 140
Peacekeeping Batallion. *See*
Peacekeeping Brigade of the
Congress of Peoples of
Chechnya and Dagestan
Peacekeeping Brigade of the
Congress of Peoples of
Chechnya and Dagestan, 87,
203–204; Dagestan invasion,

99–104; leadership of, 91, 93;
military exercises, 93
Perchenko, Kiril, 76, 258
Pervomaiskoye, Dagestan, 51–52,
159–60, 245
Petschi, Rudolf, 67, 77, 254
Pinigun, Vasily, 76
Pobedinskoye, Chechnya, 109
Politkovskaya, Anna, 174, 187–88
Powell, Colin, 218, 230
Pozdyakov, Anatoly, 117
Presidential Berets, 48
Presidential Palace, 18
Presnensk transfer prison, 161
Prevo, Elena, 235
Prima News Agency, 169
Primakov, Yevgeny, 60, 88, 90, 92
Profile magazine (Russia), 102
Prokhladny air forces base, North
Ossetia, 209
Provisional Council of United
Opposition, 17
Pushkinskaya Square, Moscow, 118,
119, 259
Putin, Vladimir, 106, 116, 126, 167,
184, 188, 203, 240, 260; on
apartment building bombings
(1999), 107; on bin Laden's visit
to Chechnya (1999), 155; decla-
ration of war in Chechnya, 128;
on fighting in Chechnya, 220;
and new national seucirty con-
cept (2002), 202; on Raduyev, 4,
47; refusal to negotiate with
Maskhadov, 165
Pyatigorsk, Russia: bus hijacking
in, 242–43; 246; bombings in,
57, 83, 119, 160, 260
Pyskov paratrooper division, 6th
Company, 115

al Qaeda, 3, 5, 35, 78–79, 90,
153–54, 164,199–200, 212–14,
219, 230; Chechens fight
among, 217; in Chechnya, 216;
in Pankisi Gorge, 148, 200, 218;
Khattab's fighters in, 164; North
Caucasus jihad support, 213,
218
Qatar, 130, 134, 141, 143, 202
qoqaz.net, 100, 102

Radio Free Europe/Radio Liberty,
131
Radio Ichkeria, 131
Radio Rossiya, 72
radium-226, 25
radon nuclear waste disposal site,
Chechnya, 25, 198
Raduyev, Dzokhar, 161
Raduyev, Salman Salmanovich,
4–5, 12, 31, 46–66, 58, 68, 71,
73, 92–94, 101, 108, 157, 161,
210; armies, 48, 55, 62–63, 237,
246, 250: assassination attempts

against, 49, 53, 55; capture, 117, 156–59; character, 47; court trials, 159–61; criminal activities, 47, 57, 137, 139; family, 48, 161, 254; hostage taking, 21, 50–52, 55, 245, 248; Islamic manifesto, 65–66; in kidnapping and people-for-sale business, 63–64; Kizlyar, Dagestan raid, 21, 50–52; mental health, 54–55, 57–58, 60, 159; on 1997 presidential election, 55; opposition to Maskhadov, 57–62; on permanent war with Russia, 55; plan to attack Russian nuclear facilities and strategic installations, 117, 158; prediction of terror attack on Russian cities (1999), 66; and Pyatigorsk railroad station bombing, 57, 160; relationship with Berezovsky, 63–64; Russian soldier execution, 49; war record, 49, 109

Raduyeva, Lida, 48, 161
Rajbaddinov, Jaruel, 97
Ramazanov, Sirazhdin, 100
rambler.ru, 130
Rechkalov, Vadim (*Izvestiya* reporter), 183, 226
Red Square, Moscow, 24
Refah Party (Turkey), 145
Remler, Philip, 216
Reorganization of the Chechen armed forces (2002), 171–75, 212. See also Majlis ul-Shura
Republic of Tartastan, 82
RIA Novosti news service (Russia), 26
ricin, 200
Riyadus-Salikhin Reconnaissance and Sabotage Battalion of Shakhids, 204, 264; appearance on U.S. terrorist list, 203; creation, 178; 191
Rodionov, Yevgenny, 76, 254
Rokhota, Dagestan, 100
Romanov, Anatoly, 24, 247
Romanova, Olga, 180
Romashchenko, Anna, 50
Rosenergatom, 201
Roshal, Leonid, 187
Rostam, Kianan, 126, 260
Rostov Institute of the National Economy, 48
Rostov-on-Don, Russia, 76; bombing in, 118, 255
Rostovskaya nuclear power plant, Russia, 202
Rozek, Edward, xii
RTR television (Russian), 164
Russian Army, 4, 18, 32, 38, 45, 2, 102, 108–10, 112, 135, 167, 171, 12, 199, 202–203, 252, 256
Russian embassy, Lebanon, suicide bombing, 122, 258

Russian embassy, France, terror threat against, 149, 206, 212–13
Russian Federation, 105
Russian Federation Council, as terror target, 179
Russian Federation State Duma, 157, 232, 240; car bombing (2001), 186; as terror target, 179
Russian Information Center Web site, 130
Russian Ministry of Interior, 227
Russian parliament, 179
Russian pilots, 20, 22
Russian Security Council, 30, 57, 80
Russian Soviet Federated Socialist Republics (RSFSR), 9, 12
Russian Supreme Court, 161
Russian Veterans of Foreign Intelligence, 263
Rutskoi, Alexander, 10
Ryazan, Russia, 137
Rybkin, Ivan, 80, 82, 172

Saakasvili, Mikhail, 149
Saayev, Ruslan (Igor), 226–27
Saidov, Akhmal, 2, 77, 254
Saif, Abu Omar (Umar) Muhammad Al Qaseemi al-. *See* Omar, Abu
Salamov, Movsar. *See* Barayev, Movsar
Salamov, Salam, 128
Salikhov, Alisultan, 103
Samashki, Chechnya, 72, 177, 249
San Remo International University, 48
Saralyev, Ilyas, 119, 260
Saratov, Russia 76,
Sarayev, Oleg, 201
sarin nerve gas, 199
Satuyev, Said-Ali, 13
Satuyev, Sultan, 236, 267
Saudi Arabia, 33, 98, 121, 165; financial and material support, 44, 141–44, 154; hijacking of Russian aircraft to, 261; Maskhadov on, 62
Saudi Press Agency, 142
Saxton, Jim, xii
Scott, Roderick John, 176
Sergeyevna, Anna, 234
Serzhen-Yurt, Chechnya: 38, 101, 117
Severny airport, Chechnya, 61
Shalazhi, Chechnya, 110
Shali, Chechnya, 165, 171; bombing in, 120, 261; fighting in, 117, 177
Shamanov, Vladimir, 109, 112, 156
Shariah courts, 88. *See also* Supreme Shariah court
Shariah law, 33–34, 41–42, 88, 96; criminal punishments, 33; declaration in Chabanmakhi,

Kadar, and Karamakhi, Dagestan, 93; declaration in Chechnya, 41
Sharo-Argun, Chechnya, 110; fighting in, 115
Sharon, Adi, 67, 256
Shatoi, Chechnya, 19, 40, 77, 100, 110
Shaura, Dagestan, 233
Shaw, Stanley, 67, 77, 254
Sheremetovo Airport, Moscow, 241
Shermetova, Sanobar, 162–63, 184
Shevardnadze, Eduard, 176, 204; and Abkhazia rebellion (1992), 14; assassination attempt against (1998), 39–40, 58–59
Shevardnadze Trail. *See* Pankisi Gorge
Sheyman, Victor, 152
Shidayev, Magomed Abuyazidovich, 195
Shkolninkova, Maria, 186
Shodroda, Dagestan, occupation (1999), 100
Shogenov, Temirkhan, 229
Shogenov, Zaurkhan, 229
Shpigun, Gennady Nikolayevich, 61, 63, 255
Shura of the Muslims of Ichkeria and Dagestan, 114
Sixth Battalion "Borz," 48
Slahi, Mohamedou Ould, 217
slave trade, 71, 136
Sleptsovskaya airport, Ingushetia, 250
Slovo journal (Russia), 65
Smolensk, Russia, railroad car bomb (1994), 53
snipers, 50, 53, 110, 159, 165, 206
Sobraliyev, Khanpash, 185
Sochi, Russia, 83, 260
Society for Social Reforms (Kuwait), 149, 150
Sodbusinessbank (Russia), 135
Soldiers of Freedom movement, 57
Solikamsk, Russia, 161
Solzhenitsyn, Alexandr, 1, 8
Somalia, 26
Soslambekov, Yusuf, 14
Southern Waziristan provice, Pakistan, 217
Special Purposes Islamic Regiment, 4, 72–73, 127, 182; appearance on U.S. terrorist list, 68, 203; disbanding, 42, 74; in Gudermes Wahhabi uprising (1998), 41–42; organization, 68, 73
St. Petersburg, Russia, 118, 212; Metro subway system attacks, 248
Starkova, Tamara, 188
Starye-Atagi, Chechnya, 40, 42–43, 88, 119, 261; fighting in, 117
Stary-Atchkoi, Chechnya, 243

State Committee for Fuel and
    Energy (Chechnya), 95
State Research Center for Applied
    Microbiology, 200
State Security Court (Turkey), 145
Stavropol region, Russia, 69, 118,
    120, 136, 242–43
Stepashin, Sergei, 61, 94
storman.e, 130
Studner, Peter, 228
Sudan, 26
Sufi Naqshbandi and Qadiri
    Islamic orders, 42, 62, 90
Sukhumi, Abkhazia, 12, 15
Suleimenov, Movsar. *See* Barayev,
    Movsar.
Sunday Times newspaper
    (London), 78, 186
Supreme Council of Islamic
    Jamaats, 75, 104
Supreme Shariah Court, 9, 42, 60,
    96
Suvorov-Yurt, Chechnya, 48
Suweilem, Samir bin Salekh al-. *See*
    Khattab
Svoboda Radio, 23
Syria, 218
Tablighi Jamaat terrorist organiza-
    tion (Pakistan), 16, 24, 36
tactics, 110. *See also* guerilla war-
    fare
Tagayev, Magomed, 100, 102
Tagirov, Lecha Gapurovich, 195
Tagirov, Mansur, 75, 254
Taimaskhanova, Fatima, 57, 160
Tajikistan, 35–36, 46
Takayev, Atli, 210
Takfir al-Hijra, 213
Takhigov, Nazhmudin, 38
Taliban, 4, 62, 129, 136, 143,
    216–17; fighters dispatched to
    Chechnya (2000), 154; political
    asylum offers to Maskhadov
    (1999), 108; recognition of
    Chechen independence, 114,
    154; second Chechen war sup-
    port, 114, 154
Tando, Dagestan, 100
Tangi-Chu, Chechnya, 34
tanks, 17, 19, 37, 45, 134, 171
Tashkent, Uzbekistan, 39
Tatayev, Usman Alaudinovich, 178,
    196
Teatralnaya Square, Grozny, 17, 59
telephone intercepts, 115, 126,
    143–44, 154, 200
Temirbiyev, Movsar, 121, 262–63
Tepsuyev, Saidbek, 243
Terek River, 50
Tereshenko, Roman, 76
Terkibayev, Khanpash Nurdyevich,
    190
terrorist targets: electrical tansmis-
    sion towers, 237, 268; natural
    gas pipelines, 237, 267; nuclear

power plants, 158, 201–202
Thayer, Sheryl, 248
thorium, 25
Tibiyev, Zaindi, 249
Timoshev, Movladi
    Sandarbeyevich. *See* Udugov,
    Movladi
Timuryeva, 205
Tokcan, Muhammed, 53, 245
Tolstopaltsyevo, Russia, 226–27
Tolstoy-Yurt, Chechnya, 18
Topol, Eduard, 180
torture techniques, 3, 15, 32, 67, 70,
    76–78, 254, 257
Training Center of the Armed
    Forces of the Chechen Republic
    of Ichkeria, 39–57, 105, 155,
    206; bombing, 101; graduates in
    Dagestan invasion, 99; out-
    lawed, 97; specialities and train-
    ing regime, 39
training, military, in Afghanistan,
    114
Transitions Online Web site, 128
Treaty of Mutual Military
    Assistance (1999), 46
Treaty on Peace and Mutual
    Relations between the Russian
    Federation and the Chechen
    Republic of Ichkeria (1997), 83
Troops of the Confederation of
    Caucasus Peoples (1991), 12
Troshev, Gennady, 18
Trust Credit bank, 135
Tsiputan, Vadim, 70
Tsumadinsky district, Dagestan,
    fighting in (1999), 101
Tsuntyinsky district, Dagestan,
    233–34
Tumriyev, Gelani, 205, 264
Turkey, 13, 49, 136, 144–47, 242; as
    haven for Chechen fighters, 146;
    channel for financial support to
    Chechnya, 145; as gateway to
    Chechnya, 143; foreign fighters
    in Chechnya, 145–46,154;
    recruitment and training of
    fighters in, 146
Tushino Airfield, Moscow, suicide
    bombings (2003), 221
*Twelve Methods of Self Sacrifice for
    Fighting and Killing*, 40

Udugov, Movladi, 44, 56, 58–59,
    67, 79–89, 93, 117, 122, 140,
    146, 206, 218, 239; announce-
    ment of attack against targets
    inside Russia (2000), 118, 124;
    on Basayev, 99; on Budennovsk
    as heroic act, 23; on Chechen
    and Dagestani rise against
    Russia, 86; in Dagestan invasion
    (1999), 80, 85–88, 100, 103, 129;
    during Dubrovka theater siege,
    187; as ideologist and propa-

gandist, 4, 80, 85–87, 128–33;
    negotiation for bin Laden's
    political asylum, 80, 215–16; as
    negotiator and foreign minister,
    82–85; opposition to
    Maskhadov, 4, 96–98; presiden-
    tial campaign (1997), 82, 142;
    relationship with Berezovsky,
    140; threat of kamikaze airliner
    attacks against Kremlin (1996),
    80; on Wolves as al Qaeda's
    front line fighters, 219; work
    habits, 80, 82
Ukrainian Academy of Military
    Science, 28
Umarov, Dokka, 173
Umarov, Isa, 85
Union of Political Strength-Islamic
    Order, 81
Union of Soviet Socialist Republics
    (USSR), 1, 220
United Arab Emirates, 143, 151;
    foreign fighters in Chechnya,
    154
United Dagestan-Chechen Jamaats,
    97
United Forces of the Dagestani
    Mujahideen, 100
United Nations, 3, 28, 84, 230, 248
United States, 3, 16, 129, 134, 149,
    155, 191, 198, 203, 218, 230;
    Basayev's threats against, 204,
    220; on bin Laden's links to
    Chechen terrorists, 153, 214;
    Customs Service, 218; embassy
    in Russia, 218; intelligence shar-
    ing with Russia, 150; State
    Department, 68, 99, 141;
    Taskforce on Terrorism and
    Unconventional Warfare, 155;
    Treasury Department, 203, 204
Ur-Rahman, Abd, 41, 74
Urus-Martan, Chechnya, 17, 43, 54,
    61, 68, 71, 75–76, 79 88, 99, 101,
    105, 112, 124, 162, 185, 245,
    252, 259; fighting in, 116–17;
    suicide bombing in, 123–24,
    259; as Wahhabi stronghold
    (1998), 40
Usbat al-Ansar. *See* Asbat al-Ansar
Ustinov, Vladimir, 160

Vachagayev, Mairbek, 98, 146, 175,
    201
Vakhayev, Abdulbek, 237
Vakhidov, Alavdi, 243
Vakidov, Umar, 137
Vasiani Russian military base,
    Georgia, 114
Vectfarm pharmaceuticals, kid-
    napped employees, 250
Vedeno, Chechnya, 86, 92, 101;
    fighting in, 115–17
Vedensky district, Chechnya:
    bombings in, 127, 261; fighting

in, 117, 164
Vershbow, Alexander, 151
Versiya, 98
video recordings, xi, 3, 76, 100, 117, 225; as means of extracting ransom, 73, 252; as means of funding, 34,144, 153; Khattab's videos, 24, 26, 33–34, 40, 216; of Dagestan invasion, 99–100, 102; of Dubrovka siege, 144, 153, 180–81; of Kaspiisk Victory Day attack (2002), 168; of Khattab's burial, 166; of minibus bombing (2003), 207; of Mi-26 helicopter downing (2002), 175; of OMON police beheadings, 33–34; of Dubrovka planning session, 191; of suicide ceremonies, 123, 226; of suicide missions, 123; of ransom victim's execution, 252
Vishnevsky, Yuri, 201
Vladikavkaz, North Ossetia, 243, 252, 262; bombings in, 256, 259, 263
Vladikavkaz, North Ossetia, market bombings, 118–19, 121, 167, 255, 260–63
Vlasov, Valentine, 64, 67, 74, 253
Vnukovo Airlines hijacking, 120, 260
Vnukovo Airport, Moscow, 13, 121
Volgodonsk, Russia, bombing of apartment building in (1999), 65, 106
Volgograd, Russia, 70, 119, 246, 252, 261; colleague kidnapped from, 73
Volnykin, Igor, 198
Voronezh, Russia, 206; railway station bombs, 53, 246
Vympel antiterror unit, 189

Wahhab, Abd al-, 33
Wahhabi bloc of opposition, 88
Wahhabi Fighting Squards of the Islamic Jamaat of Dagestan, 62
Wahhabis, 12, 86, 88, 141, 163–64, 207, 228; anti-Wahhabi rally, 62–63; and Arbi Barayev, 68; and Chechen youth, 68; community and activities in Dagestan, 4, 44–45, 62, 92–94, 97; community in Chechnya, 4, 40–43, 68, 75, 85; dangers of, 60, 92; and Gudermes uprising (1998), 41–42, 74–93; influence in Chechen government, 40; and Khattab, 86, 97; laws and punishments of, 33; military alliance pact with Raduyev, 62; outlawed, 41–43, 62

Waleed, Abu al-, 127, 167, 191, 240; as advisor to Basayev, 167; appointment as Commander of the Chechen Eastern Front (2002), 173; arrival in Chechnya (1995), 19; disappearance of, 236; on female suicide bombers, 210; in Grozny suicide bombing (2002), 206; as member of al Qaeda, 216; as member of the Muslim Brotherhood, 167; in raid on Russian military garrison, Dagestan (1997), 46; relationship with Basayev, 206; ties to Karmakhi, Dagestan, 44
Wall Street Journal, exposé of Ayman al-Zawahiri's trip to Chechnya, 214
Warriors of Allah, 209
weapons: air-to-surface missiles, 14, 170, 175–76; anthrax, 200; AT-3 Fagot wire-guided missile, 37; biological, 163, 199–200, 212–13; chemical, 3, 17, 110, 199–200, 212–13, 237; explosives, 105, 167, 186, 204–05, 208, 212, 222, 226–28, 231, 235–37; GRAD missiles, 109; Hound Russian mortar, 37; log saw, 77; mines, 52, 115, 121, 167, 207, 263–65, 268; missiles, 198; ricin, 200; RPG-7 rocket-propelled grenade launcher, 18, 37, 110, 115; sleeping gas, 78, 189–91; surface-to-air missiles, 116, 170, 175–76, 197; Wolves' acquisition of, 6, 13–14, 66, 102, 114–15, 143, 145, 150, 152, 171, 197
Wolves of Islam, 2, 77, 254
Wolves Without Borders, 58

Yakub, Abu, 19, 114, 216
Yakutsk, Russia, 244
Yalkhoi-Mokhk, Chechnya, 207, 264
Yamadayev, Dzhabrail, 207, 264
Yamadayev, Suliman, 41, 207, 267
Yamkovoy, Nikolai, 168
Yandarbiyev, Zelimkhan, 18, 26–29, 41, 68, 97, 132–33, 144, 202; appearance on UN list of terrorists, 219; assassination of, 202; conversations with Barayev at Dubrovka, 187; embezzlement by, 137; financial aid search, 153; opposition to Maskhadov (1997–1999), 57, 74, 132
Yaryshmardy, Chechnya: Khattab attacks Russian military unit in (1995), 24

Yassin, Ahmad, 112
Yassira, Vataliyeva, 178–79
Yastrzhembsky, Sergei, 140
Yatsin, Vladimir, 77, 252, 256
Yavlinsky, Grigory, 187
Yekaterinburg, Russia,, 199
Yelikhadzhiyev, Danilkhan, 222–24
Yelikhadzhiyeva, Zulikhan, 222–24, 226, 266
Yelkhot train station: bombs derail train at, 268
Yelki-Palki restaurant, Moscow, 224
Yeltsin, Boris, 13–14, 26, 28, 37, 67, 104: on war with Chechnya (1996), 3, 25; declaration of state of emergency in Chechnya (1991), 13; and Dudayev's arrest, 13; and investigation Chechen international connection, 214; and White House barricades (1991), 9
Yemelyantsyev, Oleg, 70, 77, 253
Yemen, 219; foreign fighters in Chechnya, 154
Yermolovskaya, Chechnya, 40; fighting in, 115
Yessentuki train station attack, 231, 267
Yevloyev, Magomed, 231–32, 240
Yokhina, Valentina, 76, 255

Zainudinov, Isa, 103
Zakayev, Akhmed, 138, 161, 174, 189; on Chechnya, 205; on attacks againt Russian nuclear power plants, 201
Zarqawi, Mussab al-, 218
Zavgayev, Akhmed, 207–208
Zavgayev, Doku: accusation against Udugov, 81; assassination attempt against, 24; presidential campaign (1995); 49, 232; in pro-Moscow Chechen administration, 49; resignation, 10, 207
Zavorokov, Gennady, 25
Zawahiri, Ayman al-, 214–15
Zharabov, Allan, 255
Zhigulin, Philip, 245
Zhironovsky, Vladimir, 22
Zhitch, Nikolai, 98
Ziberkhali, Dagestan, occupation, 100
Znamenskoye, Chechnya, truck bombing in (2003), 208, 212
Zorka childrens camp, 136
Zuziyev, Hamzat, 120
Zyazikov, Murat, 236, 267

ABOUT THE AUTHOR

Paul J. Murphy, Ph.D., is a former U. S. senior counterterrorism official who lived, worked, and traveled extensively in Russia and Central Asia between 1994 and 2004. He studied in the former Soviet Union; has taught politics and business at universities in the United States, Australia, and Russia; and has appeared as a commentator on American, Australian, and Russian television and radio programs. As a U.S. congressional advisor on Russia in 2002, he dealt with issues related to counterterrorism cooperation between the United States and Russia. This is his fifth book.